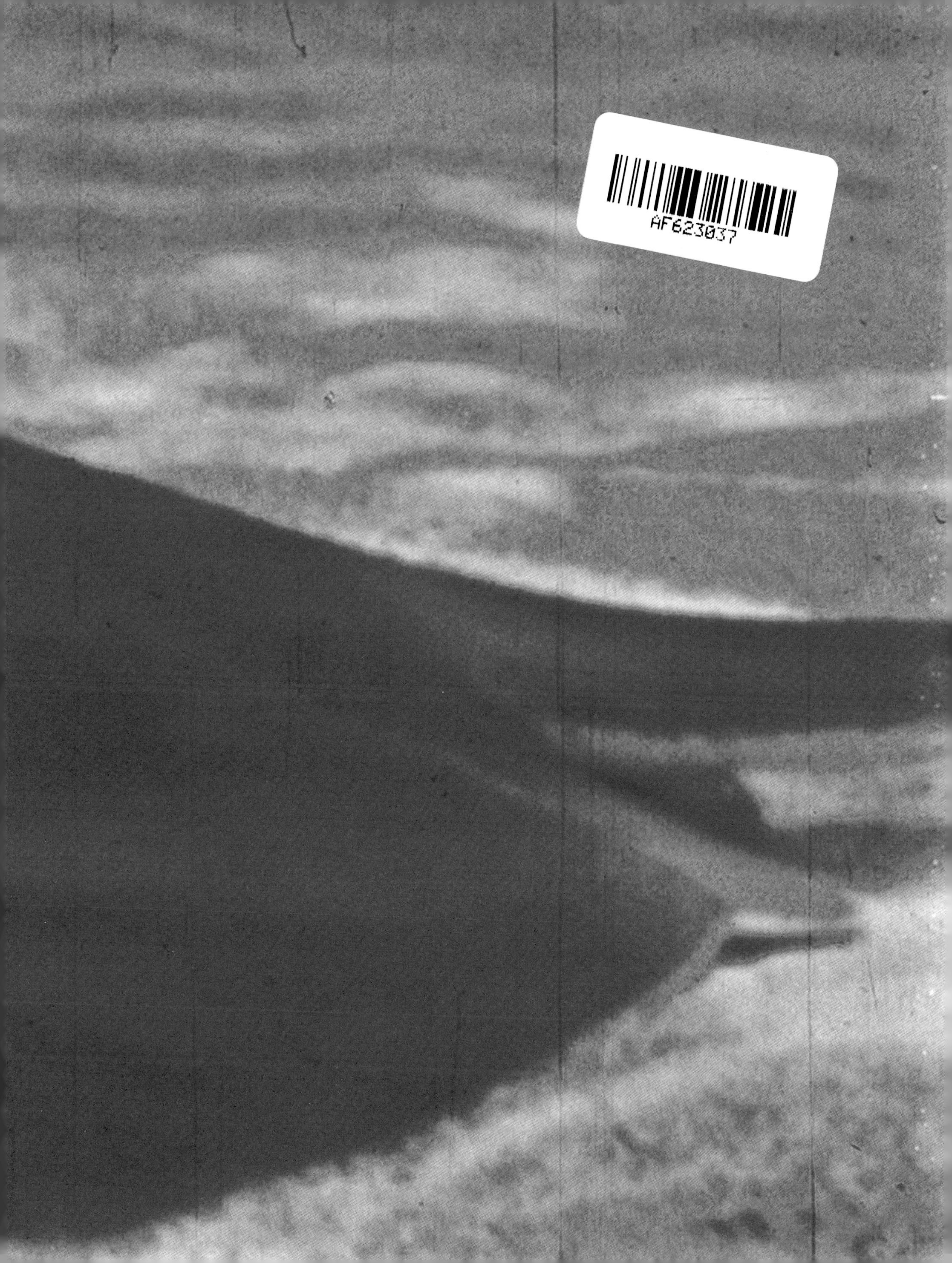

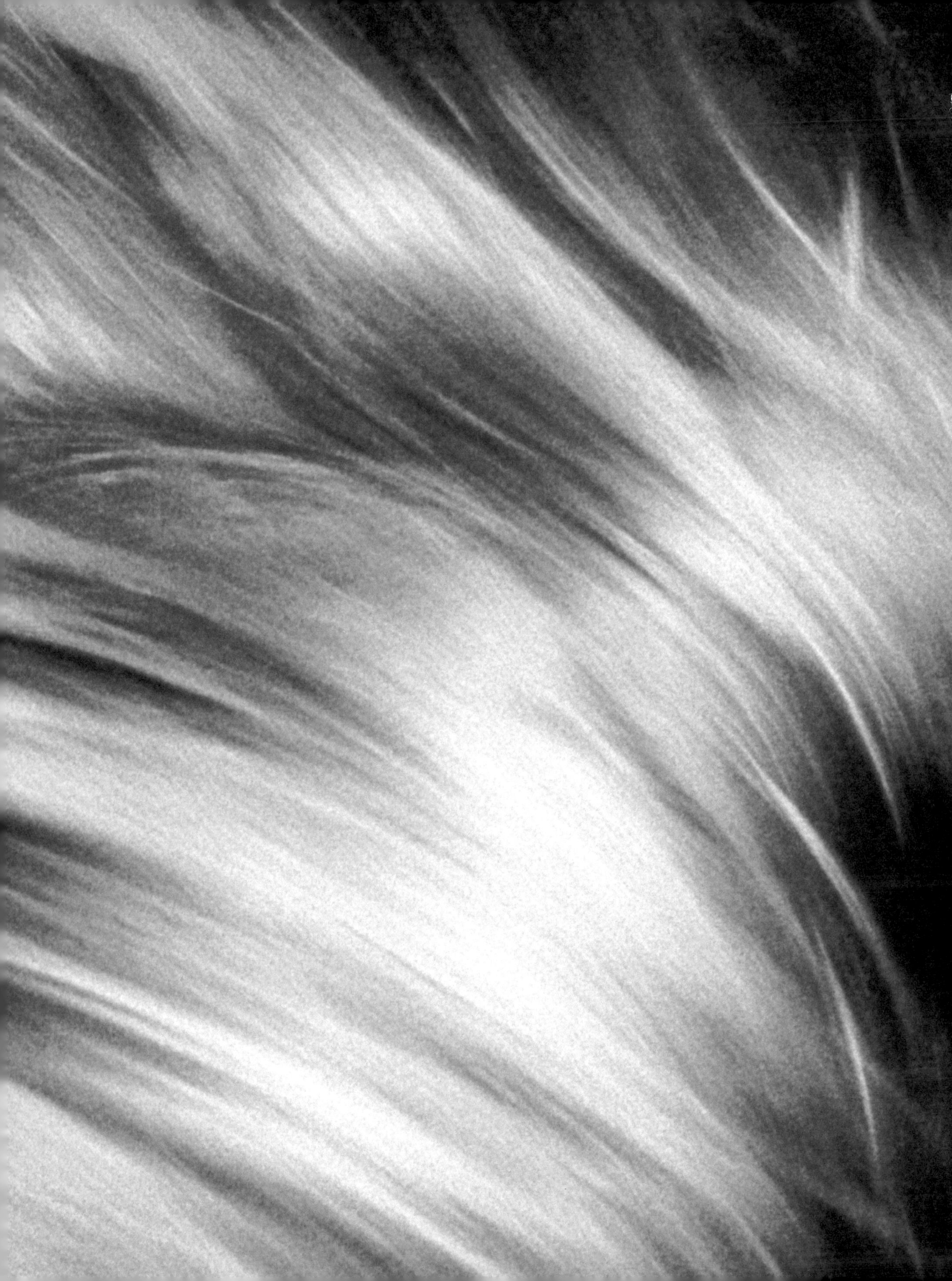

Leslie Thornton

Edited by
Natalie Bell, Dan Kidner, and Milan Ther

Leslie Thornton

Sternberg Press

Kunstverein Nürnberg – Albrecht Dürer Gesellschaft

Contents

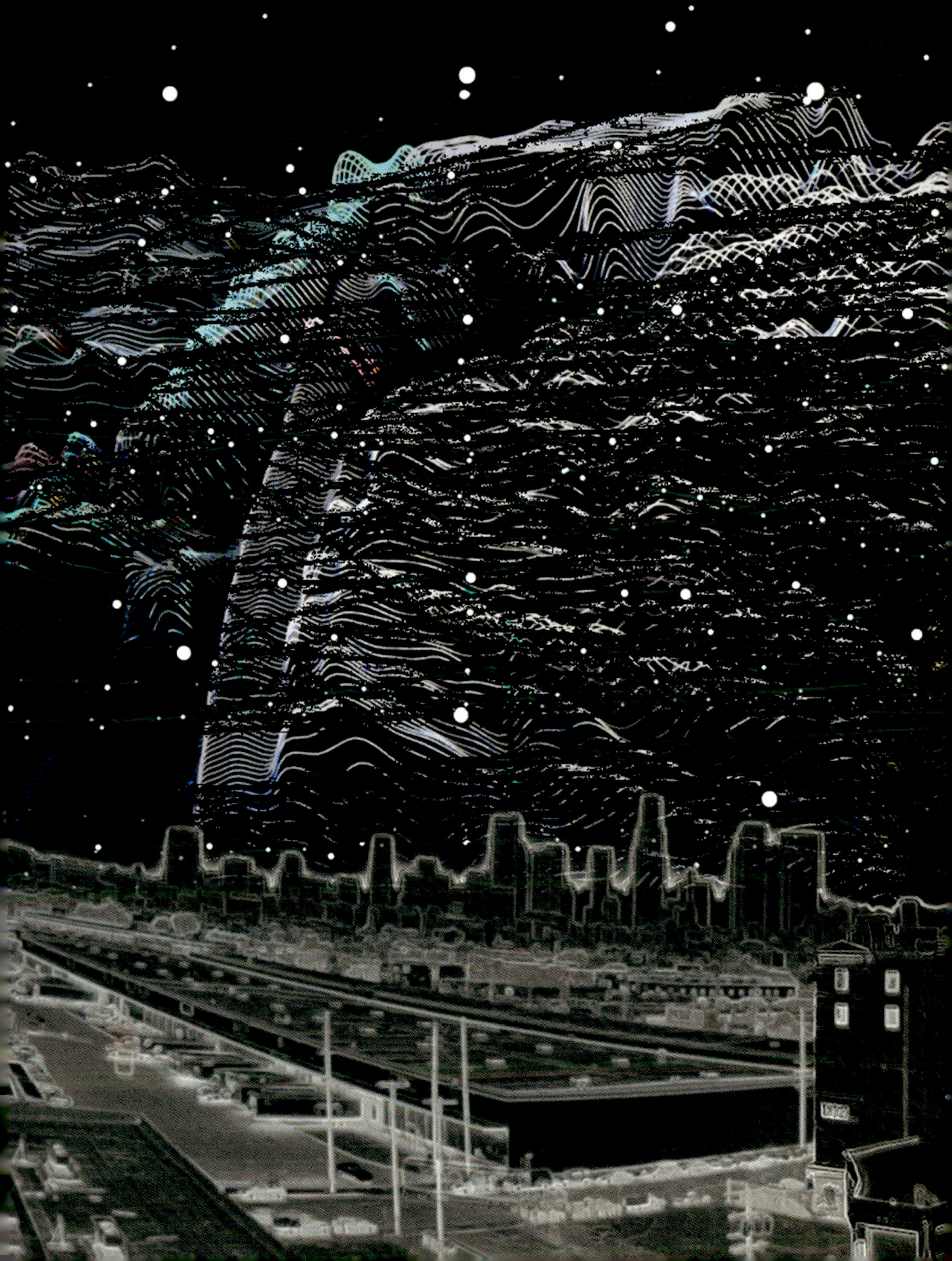

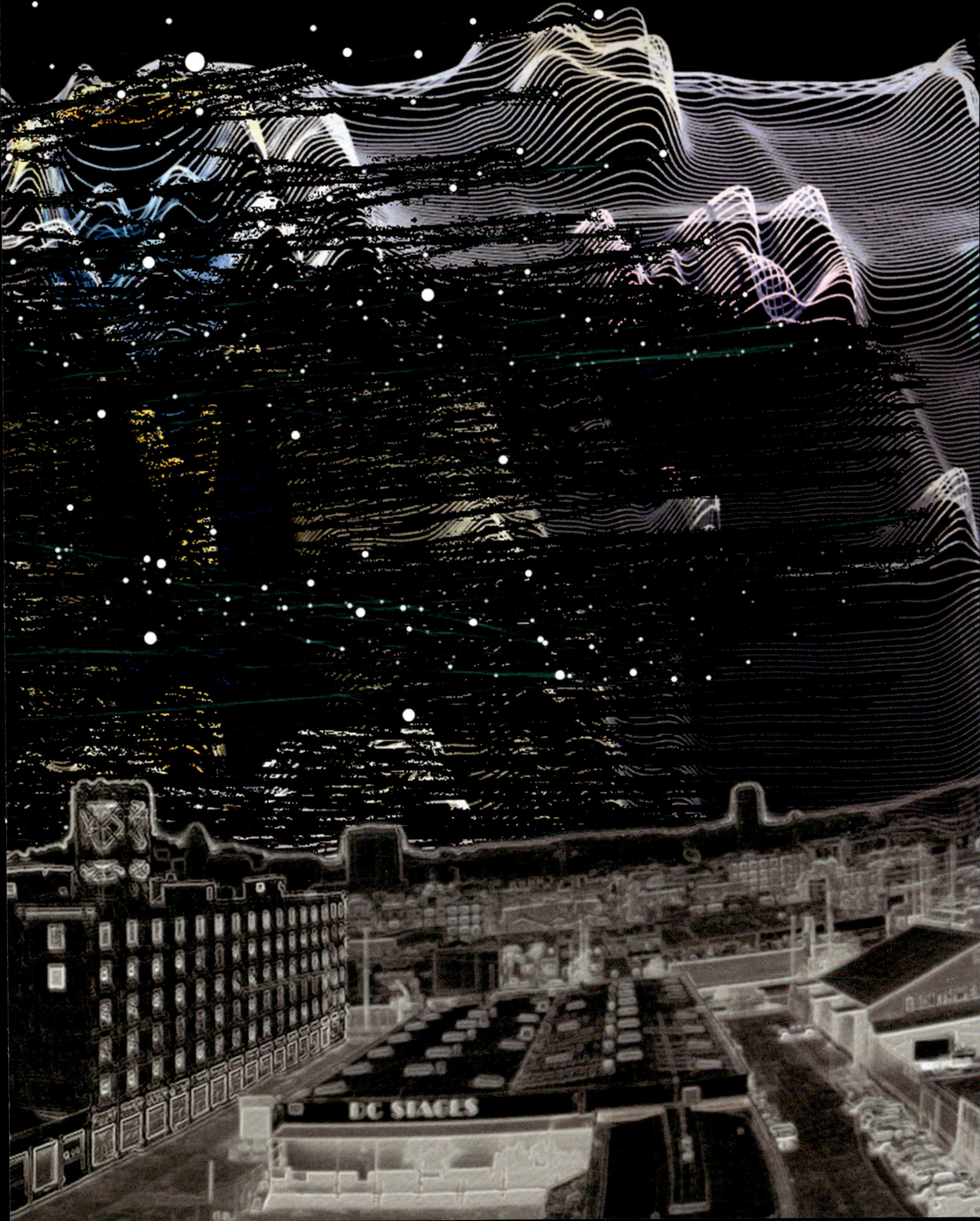
DC STAGES

Directors' Foreword

Leslie Thornton's work defies easy categorization. In a career spanning over four decades, she has produced a pioneering body of works in film, video, and media, and over the last ten years, her impact in the art world has become increasingly acknowledged. Thornton's iconoclastic take on the moving image exposes the limits of language and vision while centering the ways these remain fundamental to historical narratives, cultural assumptions, and scientific discourse. Where her works have drawn on the strategies of documentary, they have also actively refused narrative and objectivity—as evidenced in her yearslong cycles—and often resisted closure, producing a decidedly eccentric and unique history. This volume marks her first scholarly monograph, and it is our honor to publish it on the occasion of "Begin Again, Again," her 2021 exhibition at MIT's List Visual Arts Center, curated by Natalie Bell, and "GROUND," her 2020 show at Kunstverein Nürnberg, curated by Milan Ther and Ann-Kathrin Eickhoff. Both exhibitions marked her first major solo presentations in US and European institutions, respectively.

Within this book's pages, Bell's introduction offers an overview of the contents, which begin with perceptive essays by Erika Balsom and Dan Kidner that serve to contextualize Thornton's aesthetic practice and filmic language. Nine film-specific texts by curators, scholars, and artists—including Rosalyn Deutsche, Su Friedrich, Chrissie Iles, Dan Kidner, Chris Kraus, Mason Leaver-Yap, James Richards, Milan Ther, and Thomas Zummer—offer deep insight into key works of Thornton's, nearly all of which were on view in either "GROUND" or "Begin Again, Again." A conversation between Thornton and Ther, realized on the occasion of her exhibition at Kunstverein Nürnberg, brings the artist's own reflections on her work and process into focus. We are also delighted to have the elegant graphic design of Shan James and James Goggin of Practise, the insightful color and image expertise of Sebastiaan Hanekroot of Colour and Books, and the keen eyes of Sam Korman and Sarah Stephenson, who have edited and copyedited throughout. The book's distribution around the world would not be possible without Sternberg Press, and we thank their team, particularly Ames Gerould and Tatjana Günthner, for their partnership in valuing this endeavor.

Exhibitions such as the two that this monograph accompanies can only result from the combined efforts of incredibly dedicated teams at each institution and the involvement of unwavering supporters. As always, our gratitude goes to the List Center's enthusiastic supporters; through their generosity, the List's audiences can investigate the artist's significant oeuvre and pioneering vision. The List Center exhibition was made possible with the support of Fotene and Tom Coté, Audrey and James Foster, Idee German Schoenheimer, Joyce Linde, Cynthia and John Reed, and Sara-Ann and Robert Sanders. This exhibition was also supported by generous donors of the 2020 McDermott Award Gala, hosted by the Council for the Arts at MIT. Thornton's presentation at Kunstverein Nürnberg was made possible by the zumikon Kulturstiftung, with kind support by Rodeo, London/Piraeus, Neutex, Hornberger Raumausstattung, and The Block. The making of the film *Ground* would not have been possible without Arts at CERN, Centre d'Art Contemporain Genève, the Biennale d'Image en Mouvement 2018, and the Caltech-Huntington Program in Visual Culture. The operating support of Kunstverein Nürnberg comes from its members, the Kulturreferat der Stadt Nürnberg, Bayerisches Staatsministerium, Bezirk Mittelfranken, and Beko Grundig Deutschland GmbH.

Finally, we are immensely grateful to Leslie Thornton for bringing her work firstly to Nuremberg and then once again to Cambridge, nearly forty years after she produced some of her early pieces as a student at MIT. It is a deep honor to have mounted these exhibitions and be able to spend time with her prescient, perceptive work.

Paul Ha
Director, MIT List Visual Arts Center

Milan Ther
Director and Curator, Kunstverein Nürnberg

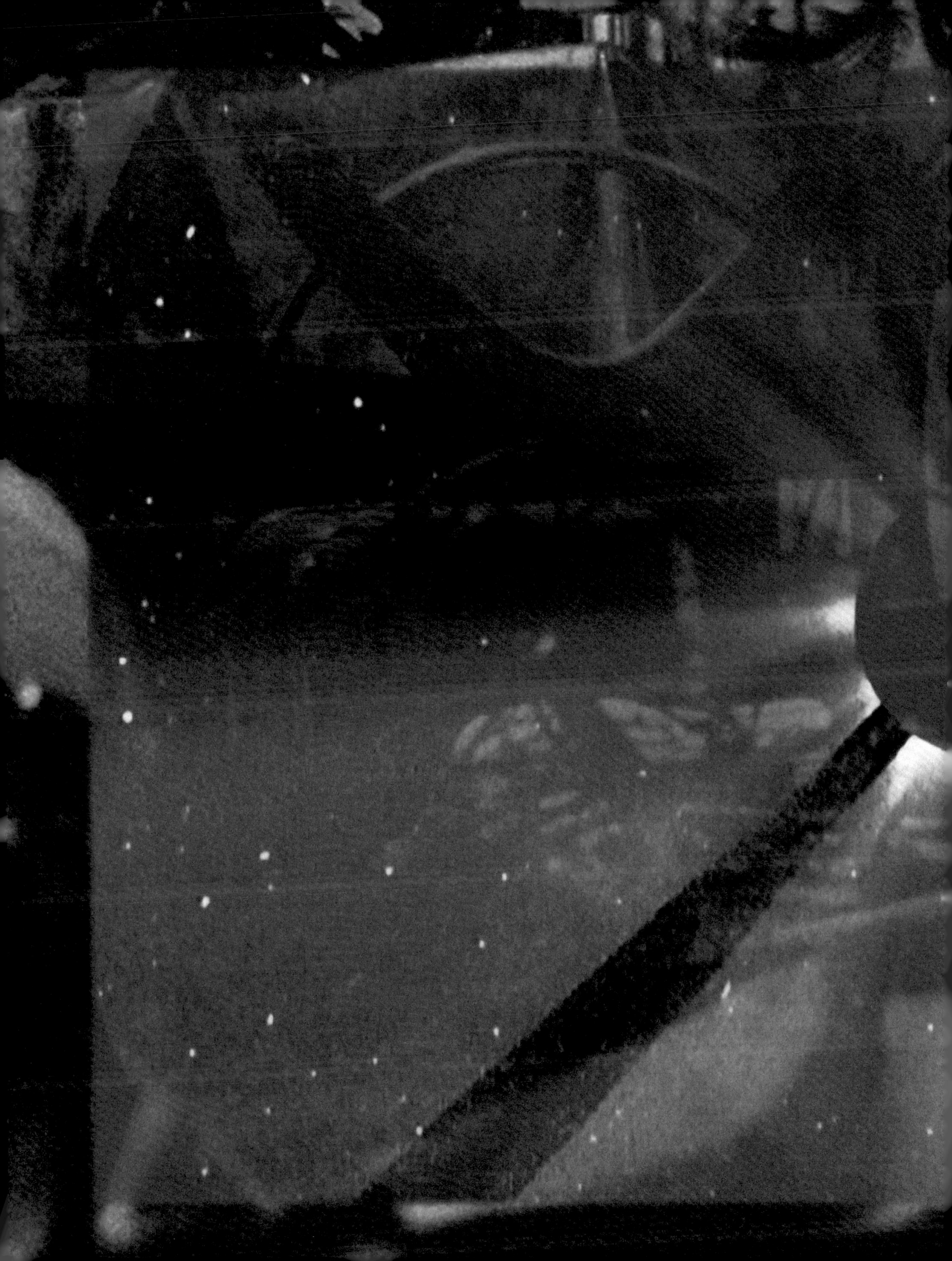

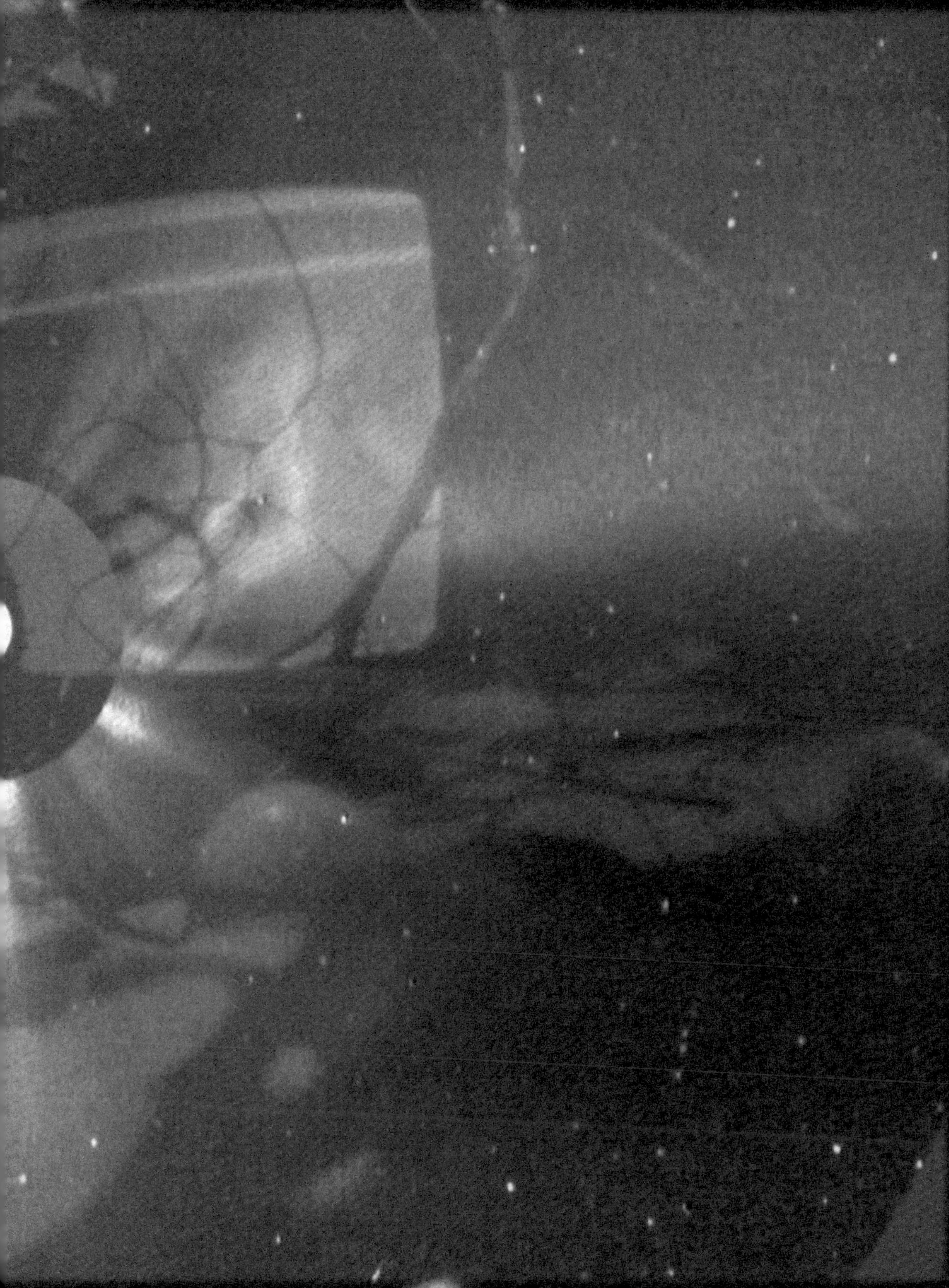

Introduction

Natalie Bell

In a career spanning over four decades, artist and filmmaker Leslie Thornton has stretched the boundaries of film, video, and installation. Her iconoclastic works exploit the faults and fissures inherent to time-based media and recording technologies and revel in the saturation of images and information that technology yields. They also probe the liminal space between thought and language and embody the fraught processes of looking and learning. Most importantly, her works underscore a concern about how technology has the capacity to exceed human control and understanding, a thread that begins with the development of the atomic bomb and continues to more recent explorations of artificial intelligence.

Thornton has been hailed as a contemporary of artists and filmmakers such as Chris Marker, Trinh T. Minh-ha, Ericka Beckman, and Harun Farocki, and like many of her peers with an unbounded commitment to the moving image, she has worked across and between the relatively siloed spaces of the art world and the film world. While her works have drawn on the strategies of documentary and experimental film, they have also actively refused narrative and—as evidenced in her yearslong cycles, like *Peggy and Fred in Hell* (1983–2015)—often resisted closure, presenting a certain hermeneutic challenge for critics and art historians alike. Within the scope of this book, we have focused on works that engage these features: radical open-endedness, disavowal of authorial or stylistic consistency, deliberate estrangement of language, and strategies of excess and overload that assume haptic and psychic dimensions.

Kicking off this collection of essays, Erika Balsom draws a through line across the selection of Thornton's moving image works that anchor this publication, arguing how the artist's films and videos offer a different take on "a feminist exploration of selfhood."[1] The "deaths of man" referenced in Balsom's title can be found in Thornton's concern with disembodied speech and ventriloquism, which "vanquishes the stylistic consistency that

1 Erika Balsom, "The Deaths of Man," in this publication, 41.

often serves as an authorial signature" and "[shatters] patriarchal notions of authority and mastery to reimagine subjectivity."[2] The artist's formal maneuvers of montage and the productive estrangement of sound and image are certainly part of an effort to consider how the self is defined and embodied, and how the making of the self is fundamentally a process: "A concatenation of otherness [...] that remains open to derailment, to unmaking and remaking, at every turn."[3] Demonstrating the inherent instability of the self (and the excess of culture that informs it) is another way of insisting on the impossibility of authority, consistency, or mastery of knowledge. Just as Thornton refuses easy signifiers and instead shepherds her viewers into the "thickness of sensory experience," Balsom argues, she also seems to suggest that clarity is not necessarily a virtue in itself but "a demand that belongs to a pernicious regime of instrumentality."[4] Citing the figurative death of humankind invoked by Michel Foucault in the final sentences of *The Order of Things*, Balsom also reveals how in Thornton's work (particularly *Peggy and Fred in Hell*), a relation between an epistemological and existential death of mankind comes into view, and how in later works, "distinctions between nuclear research and nuclear disaster, technological advancement and technologized annihilation, become muddled."[5]

Dan Kidner picks up on the thread of destruction in his essay, "Unhappy Times on a Warming Planet." Considering the place of "catastrophic thinking" in Thornton's porous filmic practice, he argues for the way her works "[act] catastrophically [as] she purposefully blows apart a work, wills its destruction, opens it up to contagion by other works, courts misunderstanding, sends viewers down blind alleys, and resists growth and linearity as organizing principles."[6] Considering the work of Amitav Ghosh as well as Isabelle Stengers, Kidner notes that a refusal of narrative form is also a way of generating low-level anxiety in the viewer, which mirrors what it means to live at the margin of impending disaster. Kidner also observes, unflinchingly, how anthropogenic climate change and economic liberalism have shaped our global status quo into one in which we are living with viruses, wildfires, extreme weather, and, as his title captures, an increasingly warming planet. Rather than embracing affirmative politics that builds on thinly veiled euphemisms of resistance and resiliency, Kidner shows us how Thornton's works "take root in destroyed, exploited landscapes" so that we pay closer attention and "better understand the present and future ruins that we may have to call home."[7]

In her conversation with Milan Ther, Thornton speaks of her recent work *Ground* (2020) as an "apocalyptic precipice," inadvertently

2 Balsom, 43.

3 Balsom, 45.

4 Balsom, 43.

5 Balsom, 47.

6 Dan Kidner, "Unhappy Times on a Warming Planet," in this publication, 57.

7 Kidner, 59.

8 Leslie Thornton, "No Romance: Milan Ther and Leslie Thornton in Conversation," in this publication, 73.

9 Chrissie Iles, "Where Does the 'I' End," in this publication, 79.

10 Iles, 80.

11 Chris Kraus, "Intimate Cruelty," in this publication, 93.

articulating the mood of a pre-pandemic moment. Moving through subjects that span her practice (such as science, language, and knowledge formation), the artist recalls the thirty-two-year process of making *Peggy and Fred in Hell* and discusses how language and voice operate with respect to consciousness, visibility, and comprehension. Speaking firsthand of her process and her own experiences with the ruins of the past—particularly her family's engagement with atomic history—Thornton emphatically denies indulging in any drama around these events: "I use myself as an instrument," she insists, "There is no romance in this."[8]

The book's subsequent essays (nine in total) each take a focused look at a particular work or pair of artworks, spanning from Thornton's first moving image pieces to her most recent. The selection offers a distinctive survey of nearly four decades of her practice while highlighting the works included in her List Center and Kunstverein Nürnberg exhibitions.

In her essay on *X-TRACTS* (1975), Chrissie Iles analyzes Thornton's use of countdown and structural editing techniques in a film composed of her own fragmented, scrambled, and reassembled voice and image. Early in the film, Iles notes, Thornton rolls away from the camera, and in this simple but provocative gesture, "[opens] up a literal and associative space in which her body shifts from object into subject, transitioning from materiality into representation."[9] The rupture characterizing the editing of the work also speaks to an openness—and as Iles explains, "each fissure points to the gap and the fragment as a radical, generative space through which new futures can be built."[10] Taking up *All Right You Guys* (1976), Chris Kraus follows scenes that jump between two women, Eleanor and Liz, reading the work as "a kind of anti-documentary documentary."[11] If it is indeed a documentary of sorts, it is one that "examines the nature of persona, presentation, and identity," and, as Kraus puts it, "experiments, dangerously, with how close one might come to a subject while maintaining a critical eye."[12]

Su Friedrich tackles *Jennifer, Where Are You?* (1981), diving into the film's central juxtaposition: the presence of a young girl (the film's unnamed subject) and a demand that is both the work's title and a bellowing call that recurs every thirty seconds. The anxiety that burrows into this film is inscrutable, and Friedrich isn't wrong to note that many have professed not to understand the film, given that, as they claim, "nothing happens."[13] In that nothingness, Friedrich tells us, "muteness prevails."[14] *Jennifer*, seen through Friedrich's eyes, is more than just "a question(ing)

12 Kraus, 93.

13 Su Friedrich, "Jennifer No Name," in this publication, 106.

14 Friedrich, 107.

of authority and authorship."[15] It also calls the viewer back to their childhood and makes them part of this child's "first stubborn avowal of self" and "her struggle against the chaos of authority and fear."[16]

In contrast to the muteness of the child in *Jennifer* are the "ill-disciplined voices" of Thornton's protagonists in *Peggy and Fred in Hell*. In his essay on Thornton's epic cycle, Kidner gives behind-the-scenes insight into their performances for the camera and the "circulating logic" of the thirty-year-long work. As he explains, the piece participates in "a complex network of themes, questions, and discourses that now seem prescient: ecological catastrophe, nuclear annihilation, forced migration, language formation, gender identity, and the use of AI technologies to surveil and harvest information."[17] Central to Kidner's analysis is the general "porosity, instability, and resistance to meaning [...] constitutive of Thornton's method."[18] Just as the children appear alone in an incoherent world, *Peggy and Fred* casts viewers adrift in a realm of "simultaneous movement and stasis," charting a space between the human and technology that also animates countless other works by the artist.[19]

Writing of *Strange Space* (1993) and *The Last Time I Saw Ron* (1995), artist James Richards (a recent collaborator of Thornton's) muses on how these works can be both "about technology" and "*of* technology" while still "rooted in [...] the physicality and mortality of being human."[20] Both feature Thornton's friend and collaborator Ron Vawter (then in treatment for AIDS), and their dense emotional poetics is met with forensic distance in a layering of voice, sound, and image characteristic of the artist's work. Distinguishing these pieces, however, is their capacity to serve up metaphysical intimacy and a tactile sense of technological mediation.

Rosalyn Deutsche's text, "Love and Death," probes both emotional ties and simultaneity within *Let Me Count the Ways* (2004–ongoing), a touching work that delves into Thornton's father's role in both preparing and delivering the atom bomb. Linking Thornton's piece to Sylvia Plath's poem "Daddy" (which engages her father's Nazism), Deutsche describes how the work "juxtaposes the intimate domestic sphere with a historical atrocity."[21] Forging connections to thinkers such as Paul Virilio and Akira Mizuta Lippit, Deutsche also reminds us of weighty relationships between photography and war (the atom bomb is itself a light weapon) as well as the value of "symbols that bear witness to the avisuality," or "the unrepresentability of the catastrophe."[22]

Thornton's focus on nuclear disaster continues through stories of "kin and consequences," writes Mason Leaver-Yap in their essay on

15 Friedrich, 107.

16 Friedrich, 106.

17 Dan Kidner, "Oh, the Storm," in this publication, 143.

18 Kidner, 144.

19 Kidner, 143.

20 James Richards, "Life Force," in this publication, 126.

21 Rosalyn Deutsche, "Love and Death," in this publication, 165.

22 Deutsche, 166.

23 Mason Leaver-Yap, "The Shock of Comprehension," in this publication, 183.

24 Leaver-Yap, 183.

25 Leaver-Yap, 183.

Cut from Liquid to Snake (2018), which also attends to the "porosity between the technologies of annihilation and description" that animates her practice.[23] This work in particular, as Leaver-Yap observes, associates atomic history and modes of witnessing in a way that "brings home the horror of the atomic bomb [...] embodying the difficulty of comprehension."[24] A key facet of this piece is Thornton's use of a stereoscopic, binocular-like technique that serves up "both an image of a void and its technological abstraction," again offering one of the artist's strategies for depicting the ineffability of atomic devastation without resorting to clichéd symbols or images.[25]

In Thornton's recent *Ground* (2020), ineffability is transposed into a kind of ambient, existential anxiety. Ther traces the contours of this "palpitating, formless" work that, through wavelength-like distortions, takes us into an abstracted landscape with the hovering figure of a scientist narrating various research and scientific processes.[26] In Ther's reading, the film also seems to ask, "What leads humans to create spaces they cannot enter?"[27] What is it that possesses us to let technology exceed us?

In the book's final text, Thomas Zummer offers a personal look at Thornton's most recent work, *HEMLOCK Handmade* (2021), which marks the start of a new cycle entitled *HEMLOCK.* As Thornton's longtime partner, Zummer possesses an unusual intimacy with Thornton's practice and way of looking, and he was witness to the transformative pandemic season the two experienced in rural New England's remaining hemlock forests. Tracing a dialectic between immersion (a stepping in and losing oneself) and withdrawal (*ekstasis*, or abstraction), Zummer underscores important nodes in Thornton's way of working while shedding light on the phenomenological and epistemological dynamics in this emerging body of work.

Across all these texts, we can find critical insights into Thornton's absorbing work, with each essay luring us to another. We are also able to decipher the broader themes—porosity, instability, and a perpetual making and unmaking—that render us, as viewers and readers, part of the open-endedness of the artist's films. While by no means an exhaustive survey of a heterodox practice, this book offers a focused—and, we hope, foundational—take on her subjects and strategies and establishes Thornton's importance as one of the most original moving-image makers of the postwar generation.

26 Milan Ther, "Out of This World," in this publication, 195.

27 Ther, 195.

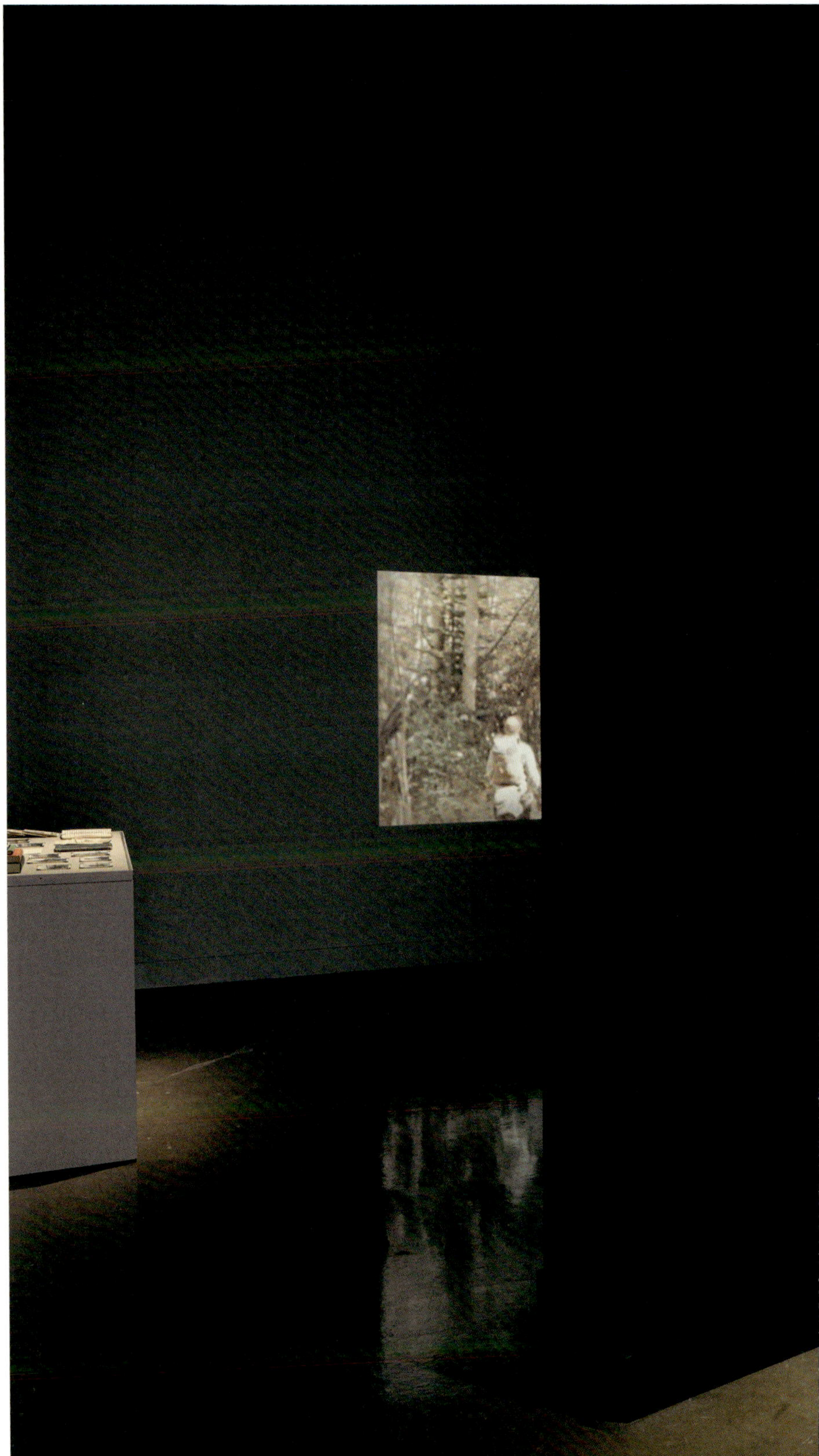

Exhibition view: "Leslie Thornton: Begin Again, Again," MIT List Visual Arts Center, 2021

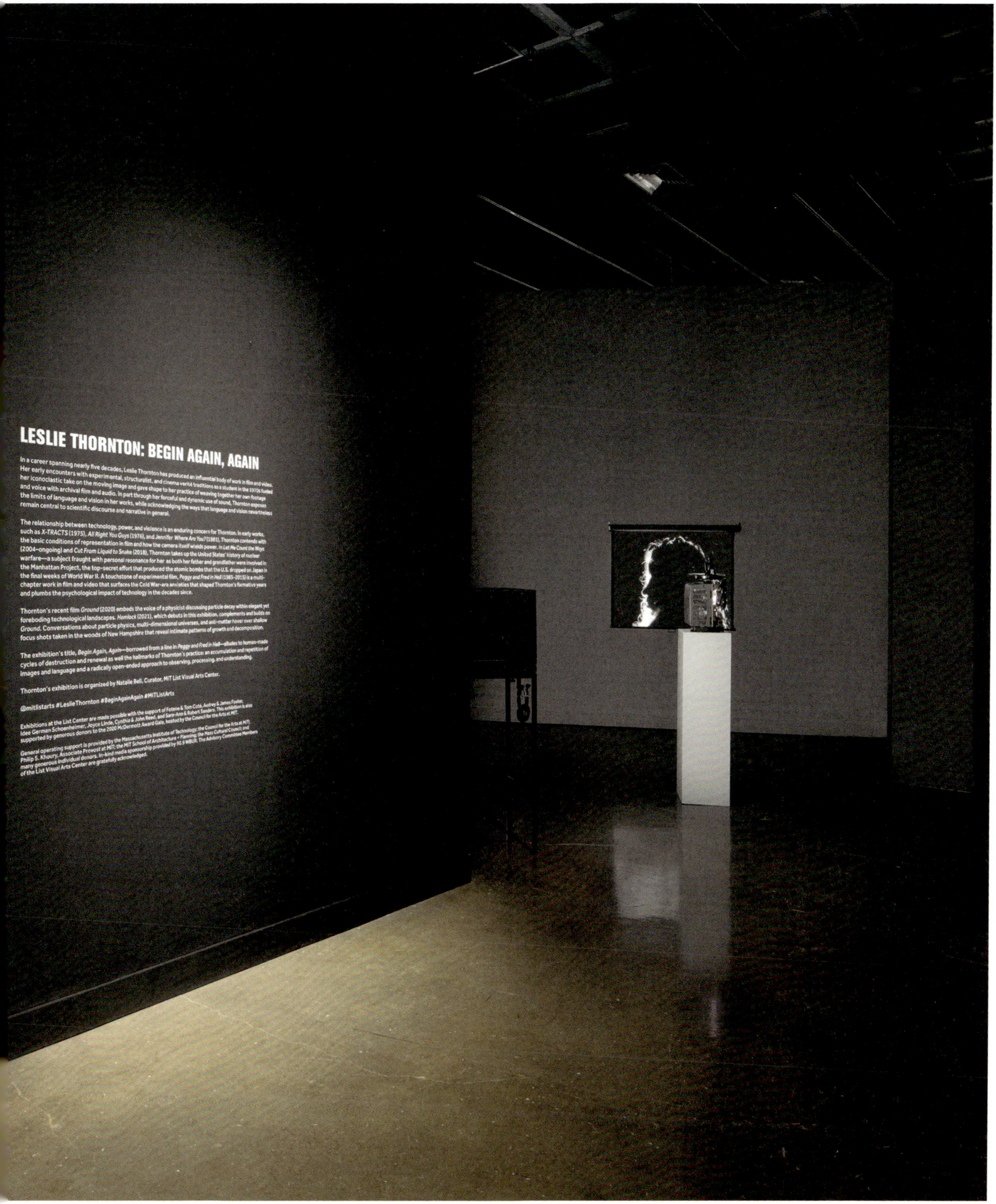
LESLIE THORNTON: BEGIN AGAIN, AGAIN
In a career spanning nearly five decades, Leslie Thornton has produced an influential body of work in film and video. Her early encounters with experimental, structuralist, and cinema verité traditions as a student in the 1970s fueled her iconoclastic take on the moving image and gave shape to her practice of weaving together her own footage and voice with archival film and audio. In part through her forceful and dynamic use of sound, Thornton exposes the limits of language and vision in her works, while acknowledging the ways that language and vision nevertheless remain central to scientific discourse and narrative in general.
The relationship between technology, power, and violence is an enduring concern for Thornton. In early works, such as X-TRACTS (1975), All Right You Guys (1976), and Jennifer Where Are You? (1981), Thornton contends with the basic conditions of representation in film and how the camera itself wields power. In Let Me Count the Ways (2004–ongoing) and Cut From Liquid to Snake (2018), Thornton takes up the United States' history of nuclear warfare—a subject fraught with personal resonance for her as both her father and grandfather were involved in the Manhattan Project, the top-secret effort that produced the atomic bombs that the U.S. dropped on Japan in the final weeks of World War II. A touchstone of experimental film, Peggy and Fred in Hell (1983–2015) is a multi-chapter work in film and video that surfaces the Cold War-era anxieties that shaped Thornton's formative years and plumbs the psychological impact of technology in the decades since.
Thornton's recent film Ground (2020) embeds the voice of a physicist discussing particle decay within elegant yet foreboding technological landscapes. Hemlock (2021), which debuts in this exhibition, complements and builds on Ground. Conversations about particle physics, multi-dimensional universes, and anti-matter hover over shallow focus shots taken in the woods of New Hampshire that reveal intimate patterns of growth and decomposition.
The exhibition's title, Begin Again, Again—borrowed from a line in Peggy and Fred in Hell—alludes to human-made cycles of destruction and renewal as well the hallmarks of Thornton's practice: an accumulation and repetition of images and language and a radically open-ended approach to observing, processing, and understanding.
Thornton's exhibition is organized by Natalie Bell, Curator, MIT List Visual Arts Center.
@mitlistarts #LeslieThornton #BeginAgainAgain #MITListArts
Exhibitions at the List Center are made possible with the support of Fotene & Tom Coté, Audrey & James Foster, Idee German Schoenheimer, Joyce Linde, Cynthia & John Reed, and Sara-Ann & Robert Sanders. This exhibition is also supported by generous donors to the 2020 McDermott Award Gala, hosted by the Council for the Arts at MIT.
General operating support is provided by the Massachusetts Institute of Technology; the Council for the Arts at MIT; Philip S. Khoury, Associate Provost at MIT; the MIT School of Architecture + Planning; the Mass Cultural Council; and many generous individual donors. In-kind media sponsorship provided by 90.9 WBUR. The Advisory Committee Members of the List Visual Arts Center are gratefully acknowledged.

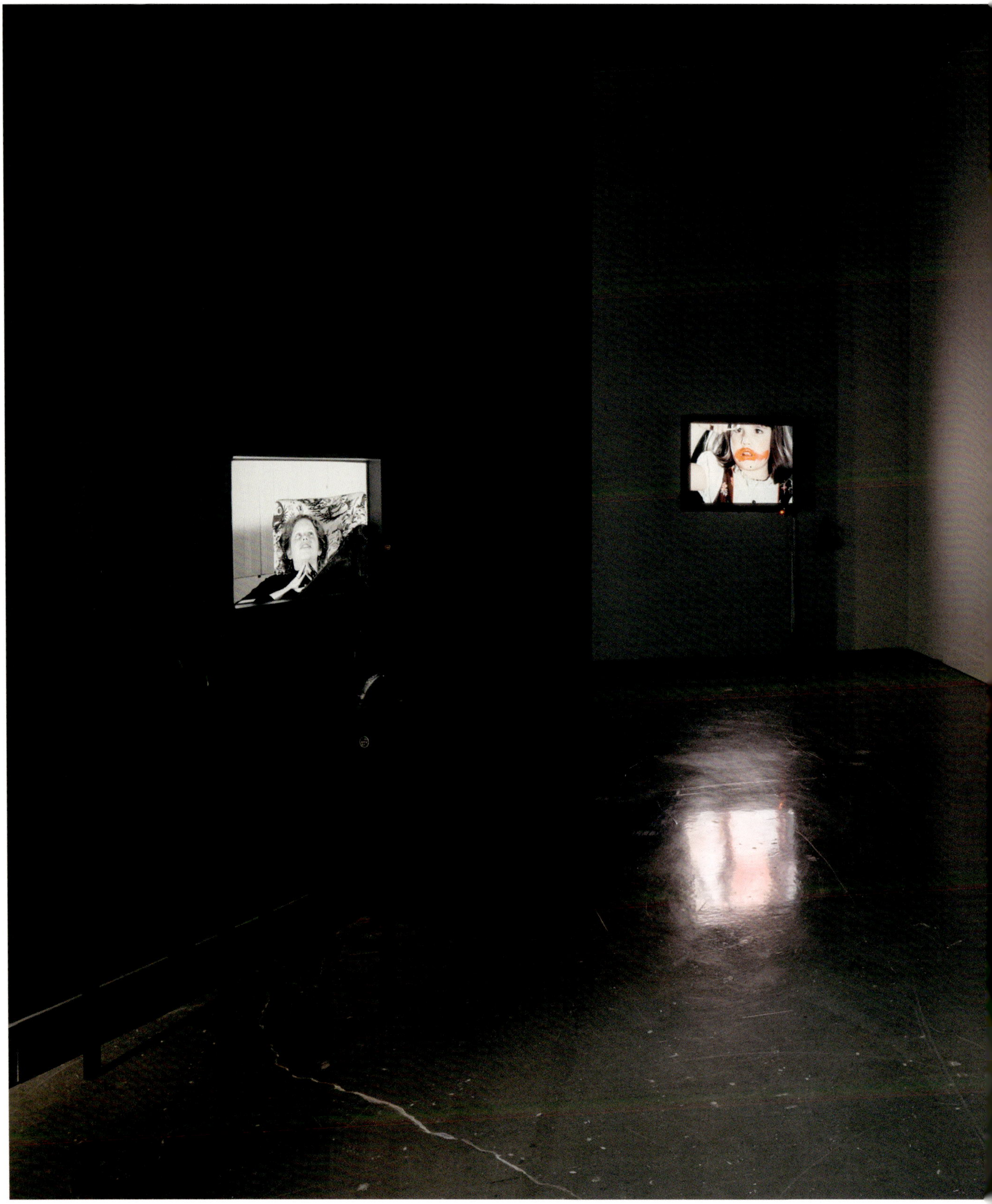

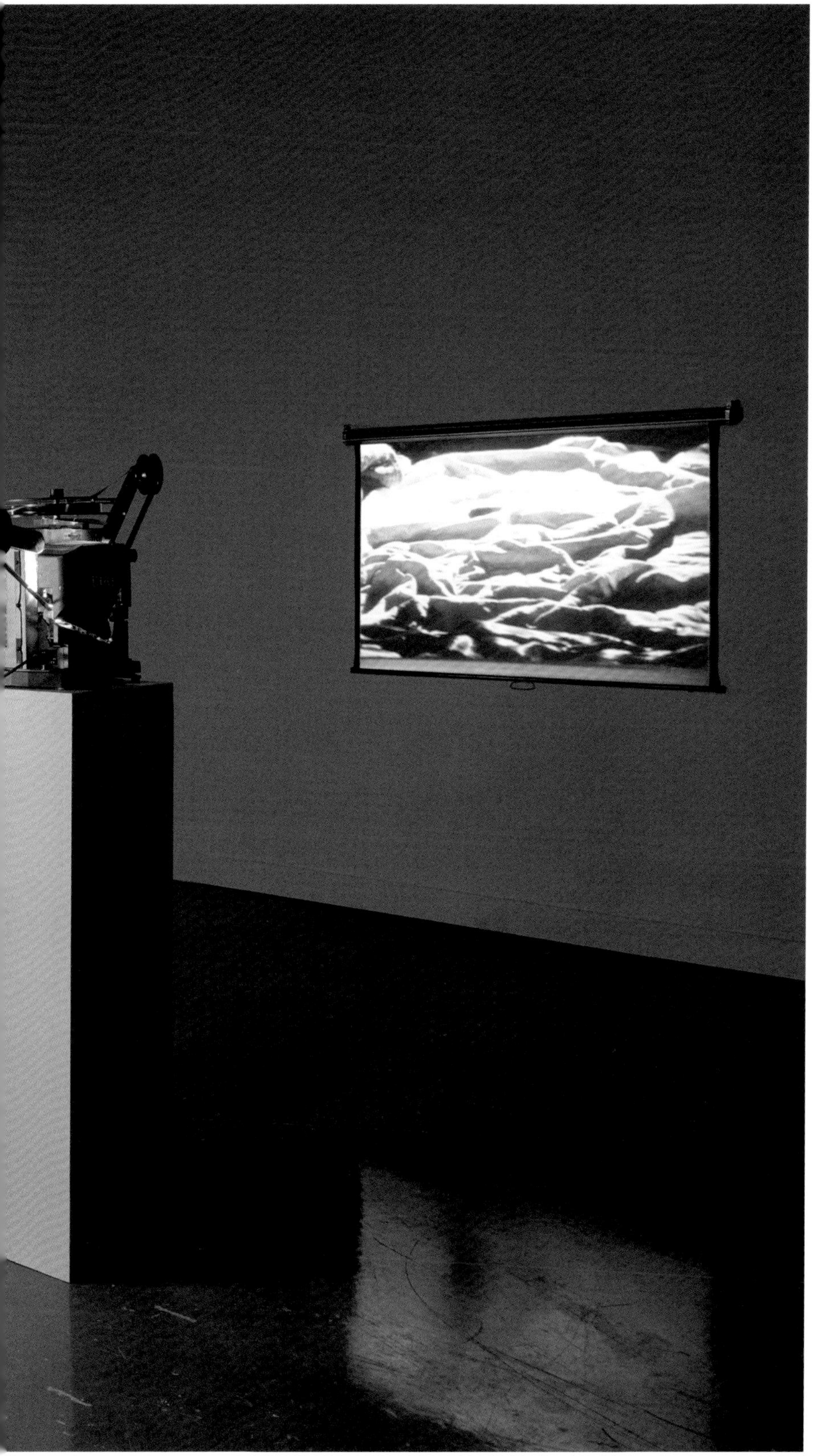

L–R: *All Right You Guys*, 1976, *Jennifer, Where Are You?*, 1981, and *X-TRACTS*, 1975. Exhibition view: "Leslie Thornton: Begin Again, Again," MIT List Visual Arts Center, 2021

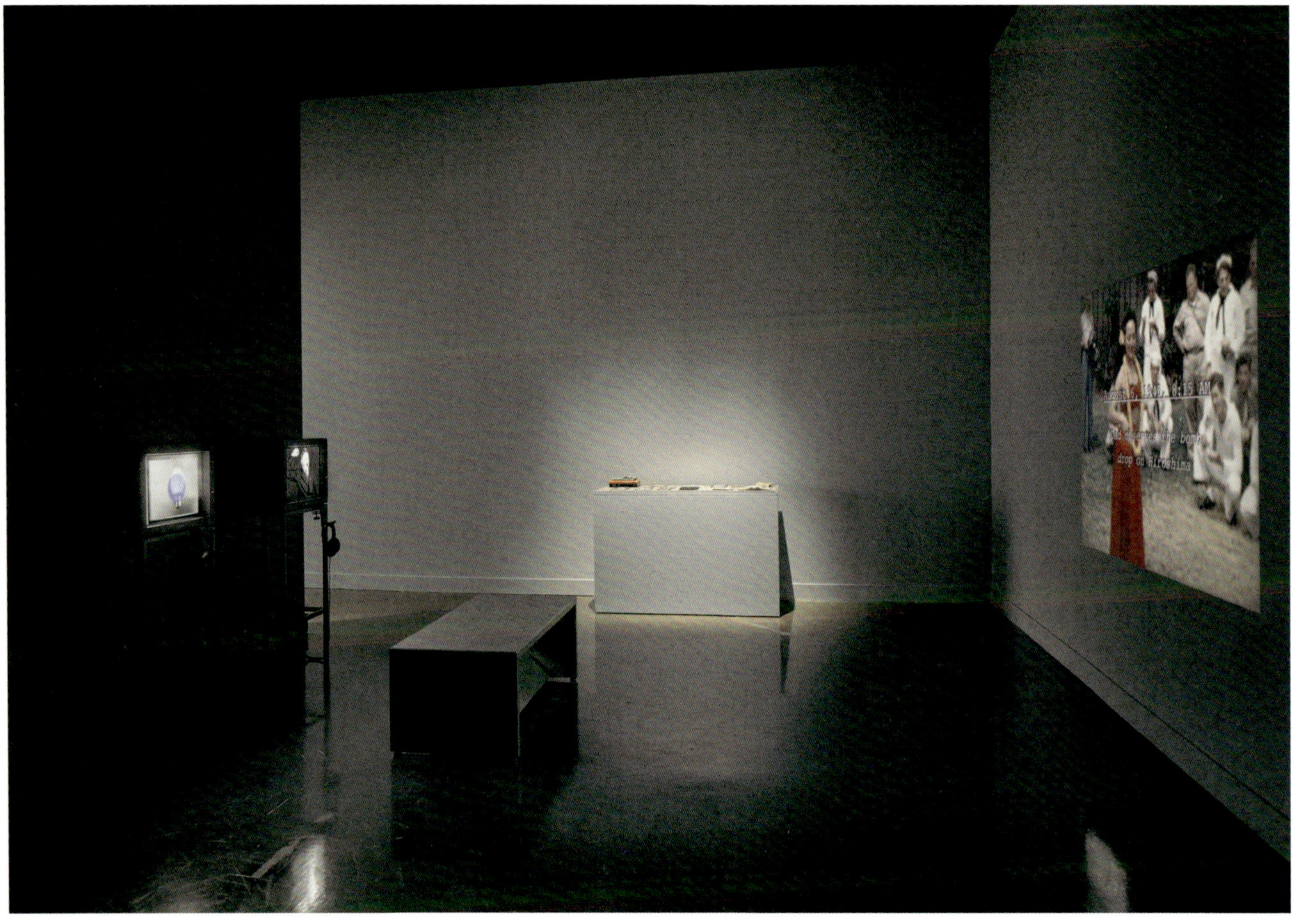

Installation view: *Let Me Count the Ways*, 2004–ongoing. Exhibition view: "Leslie Thornton: Begin Again, Again," MIT List Visual Arts Center, 2021

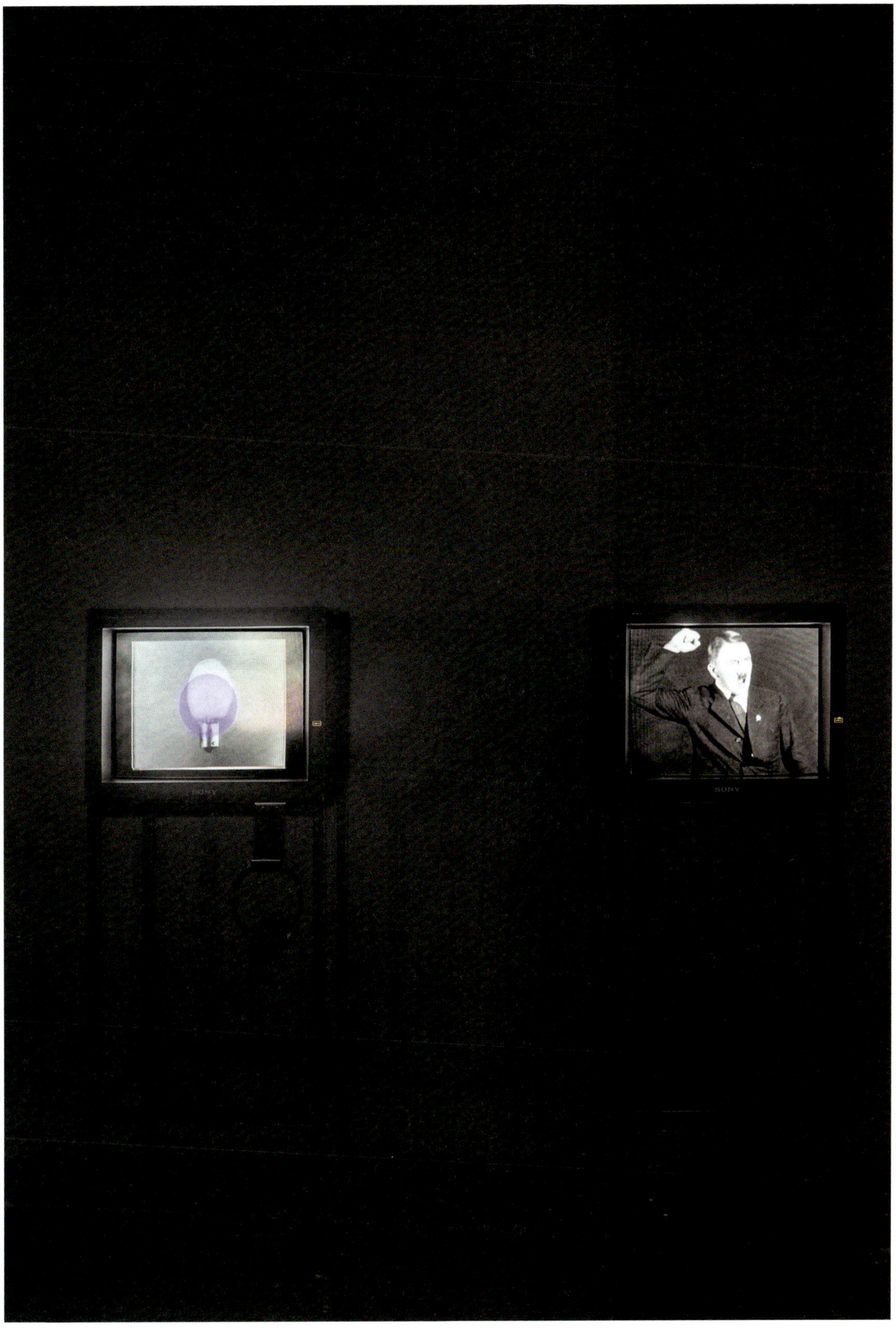

Installation view: *Peggy and Fred in Hell*, 1983–2015. Exhibition view: "Leslie Thornton: Begin Again, Again," MIT List Visual Arts Center, 2021

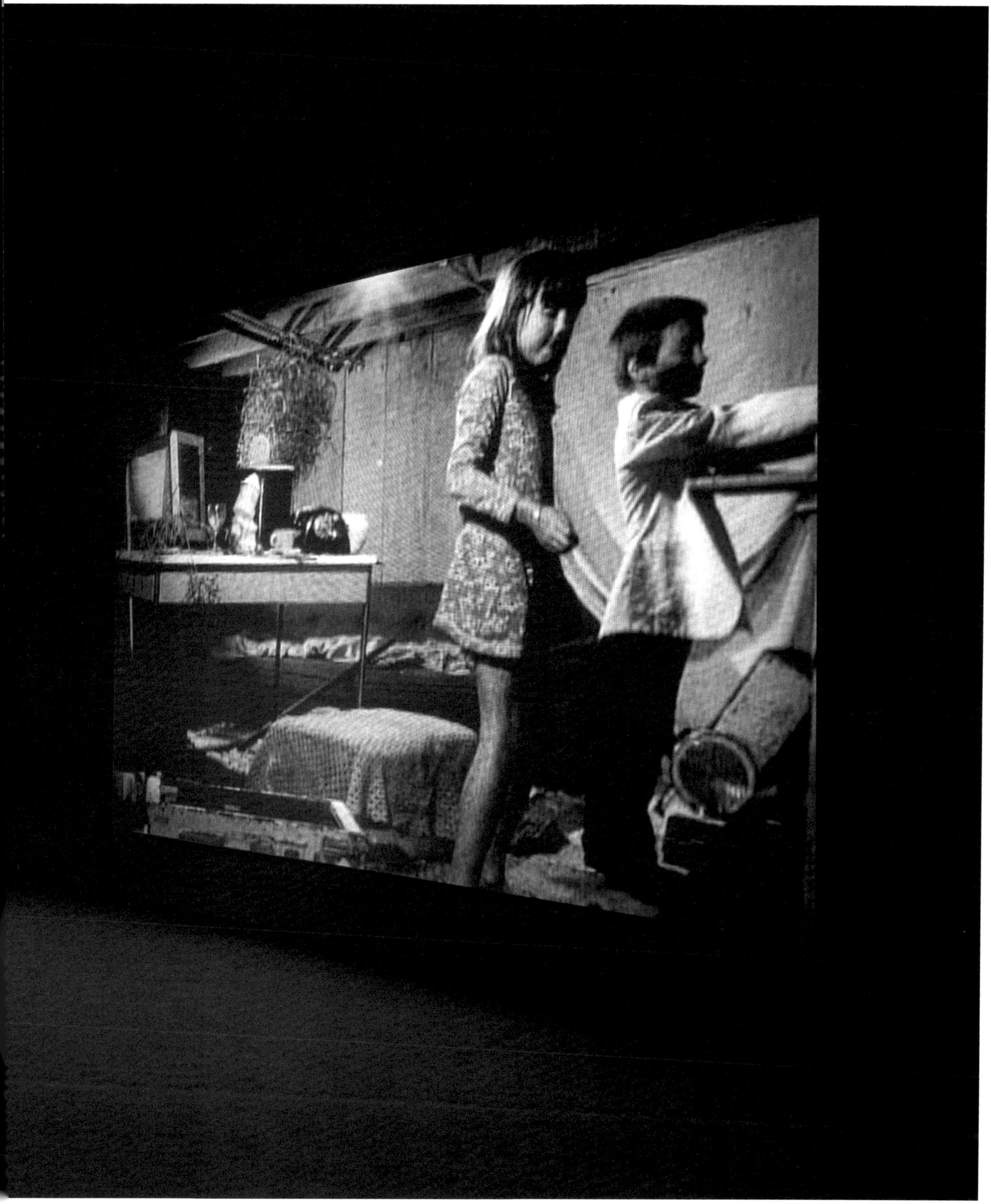

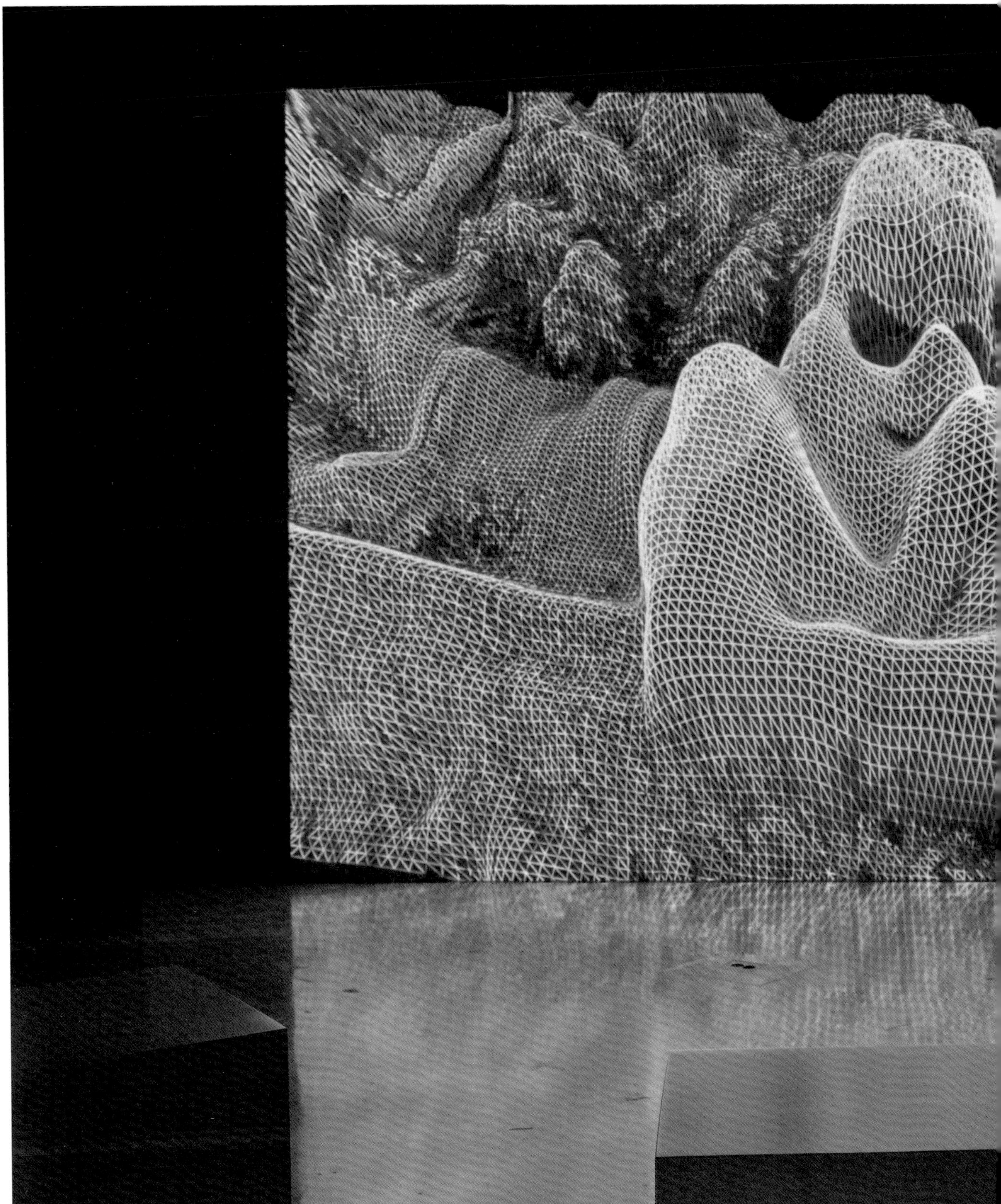

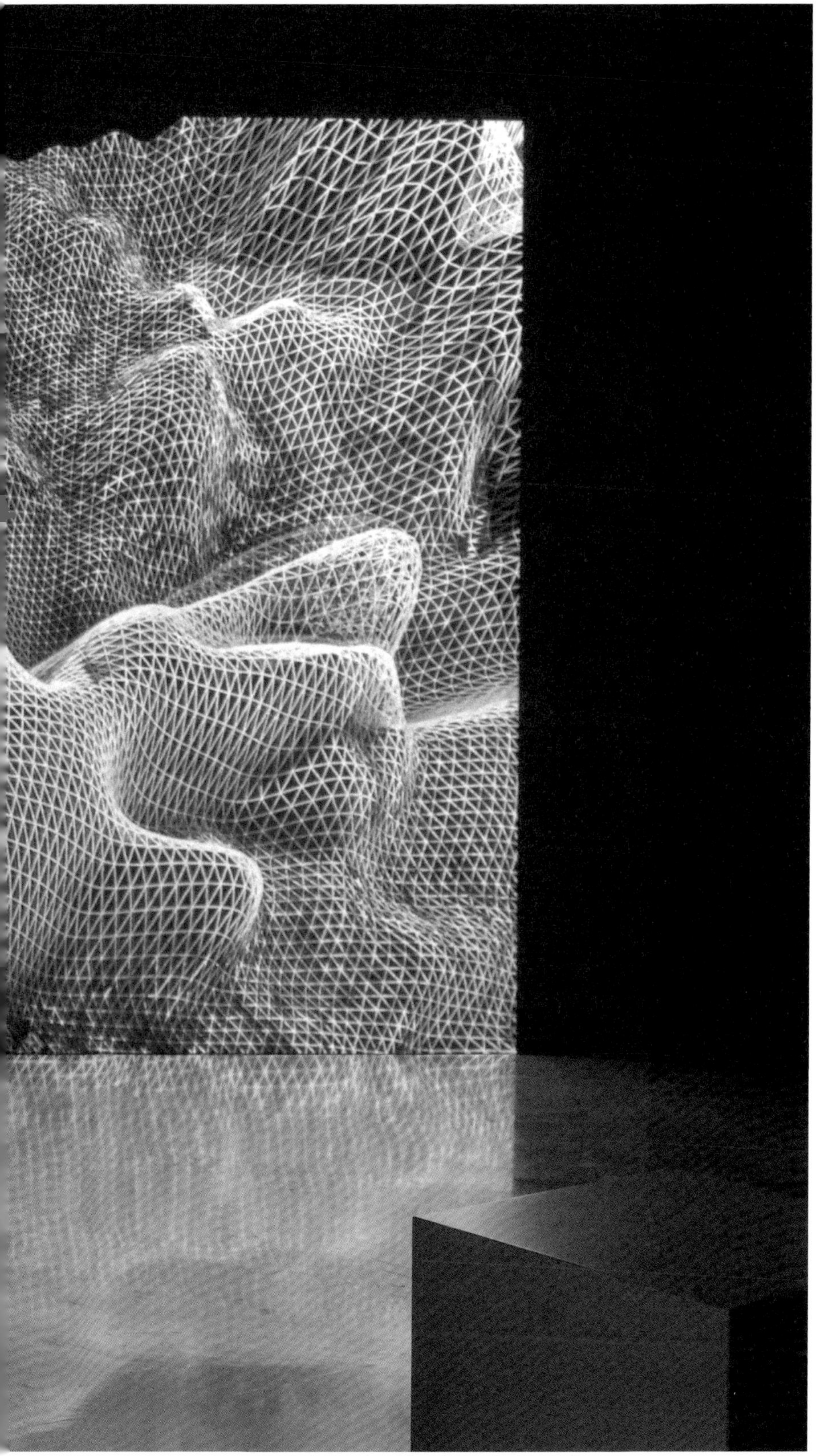

Ground, 2020. Exhibition view: "Leslie Thornton: Begin Again, Again," MIT List Visual Arts Center, 2021

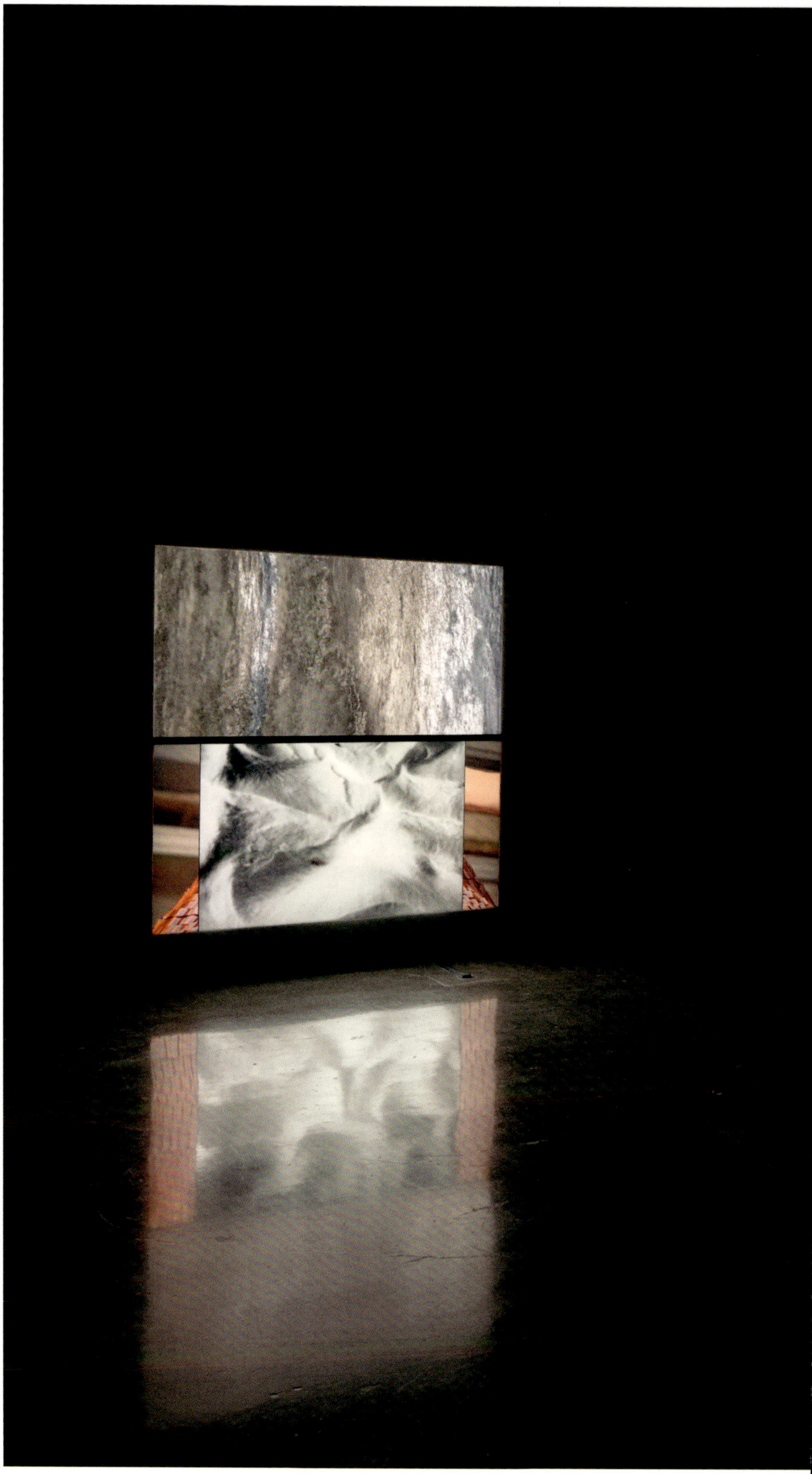

L–R: *HEMLOCK Handmade*, 2021, and *Cut from Liquid to Snake*, 2018. Exhibition view: "Leslie Thornton: Begin Again, Again," MIT List Visual Arts Center, 2021

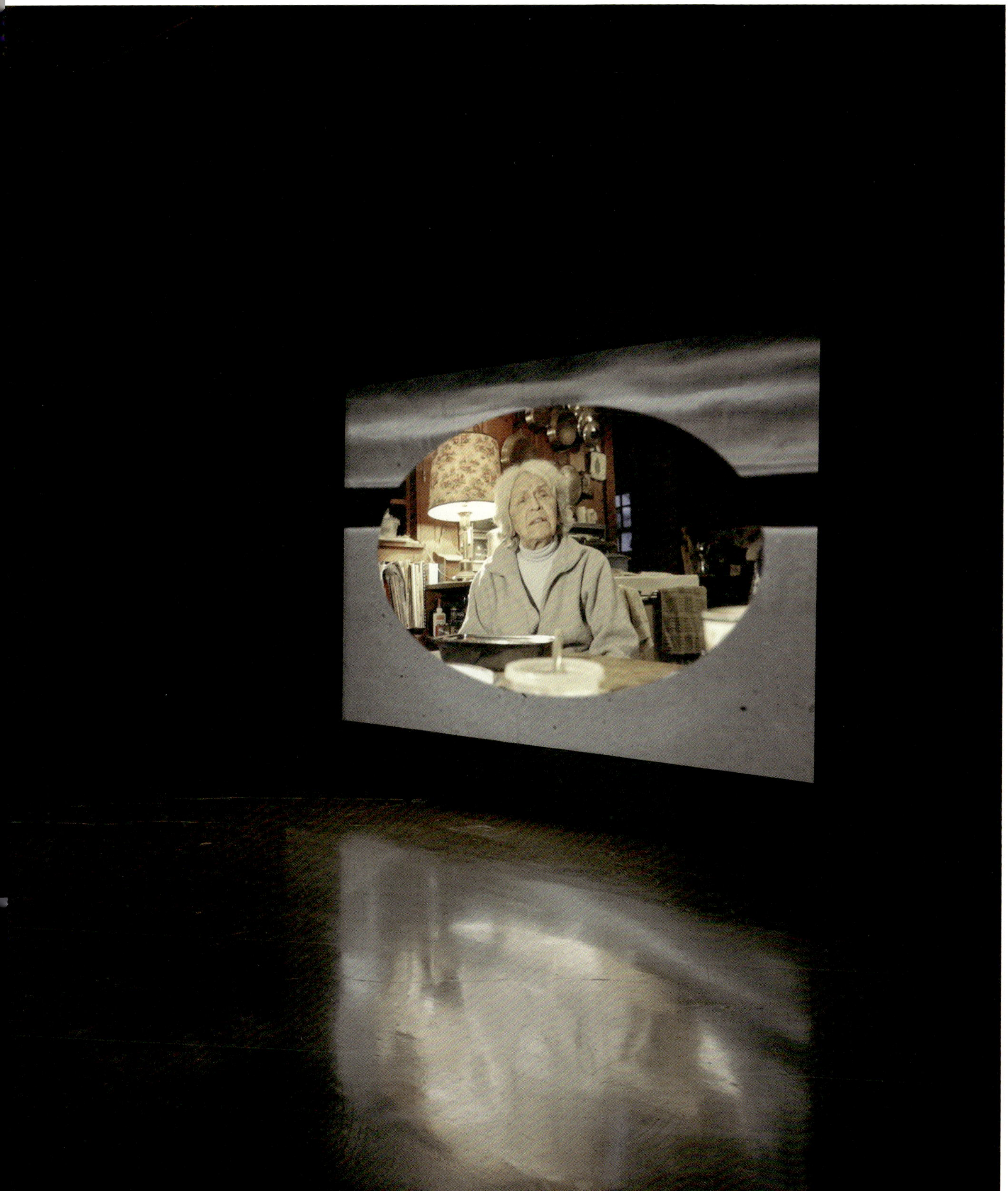

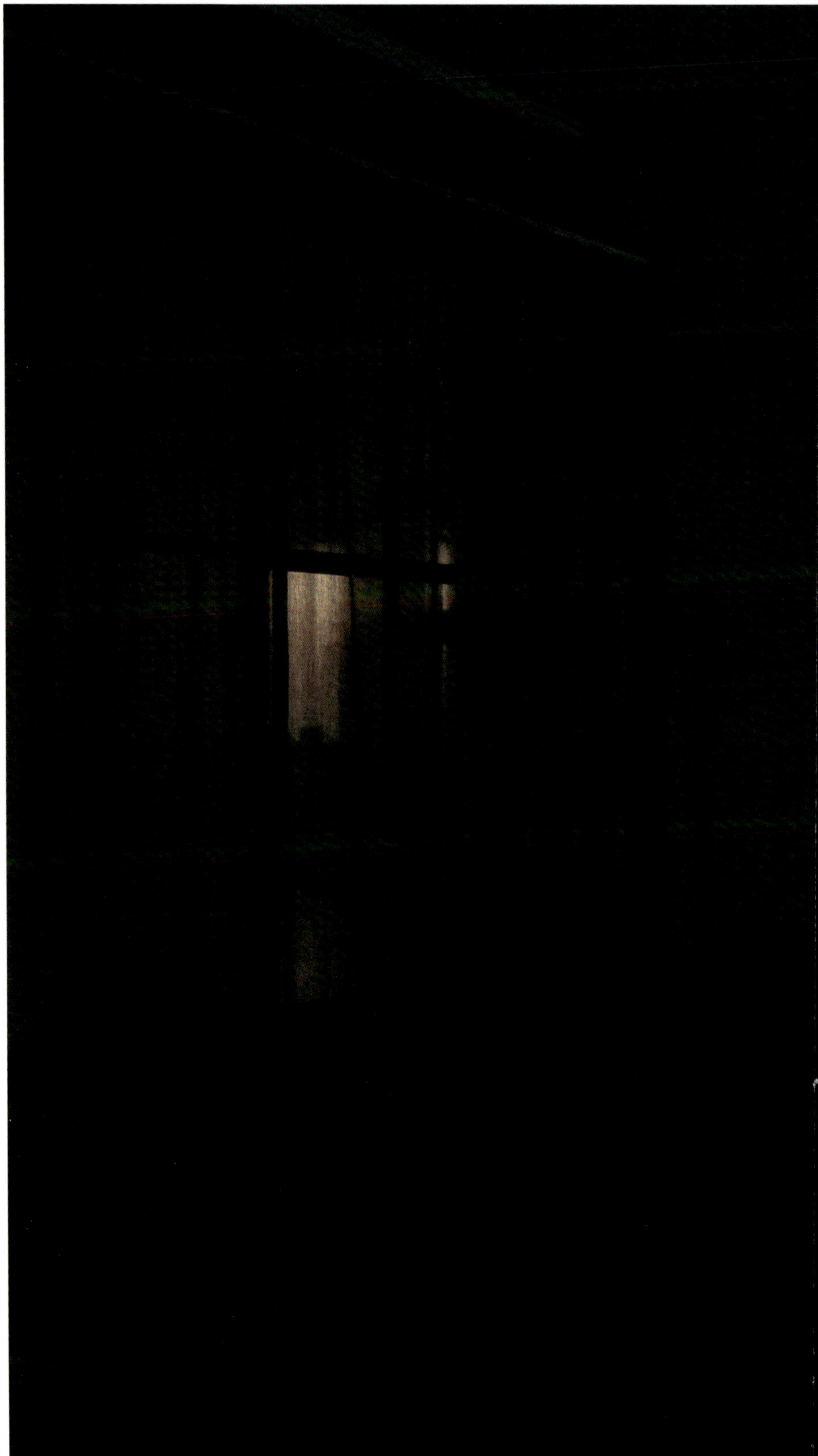

Ground, 2020. Exhibition view:
"Leslie Thornton: GROUND,"
Kunstverein Nürnberg, 2020

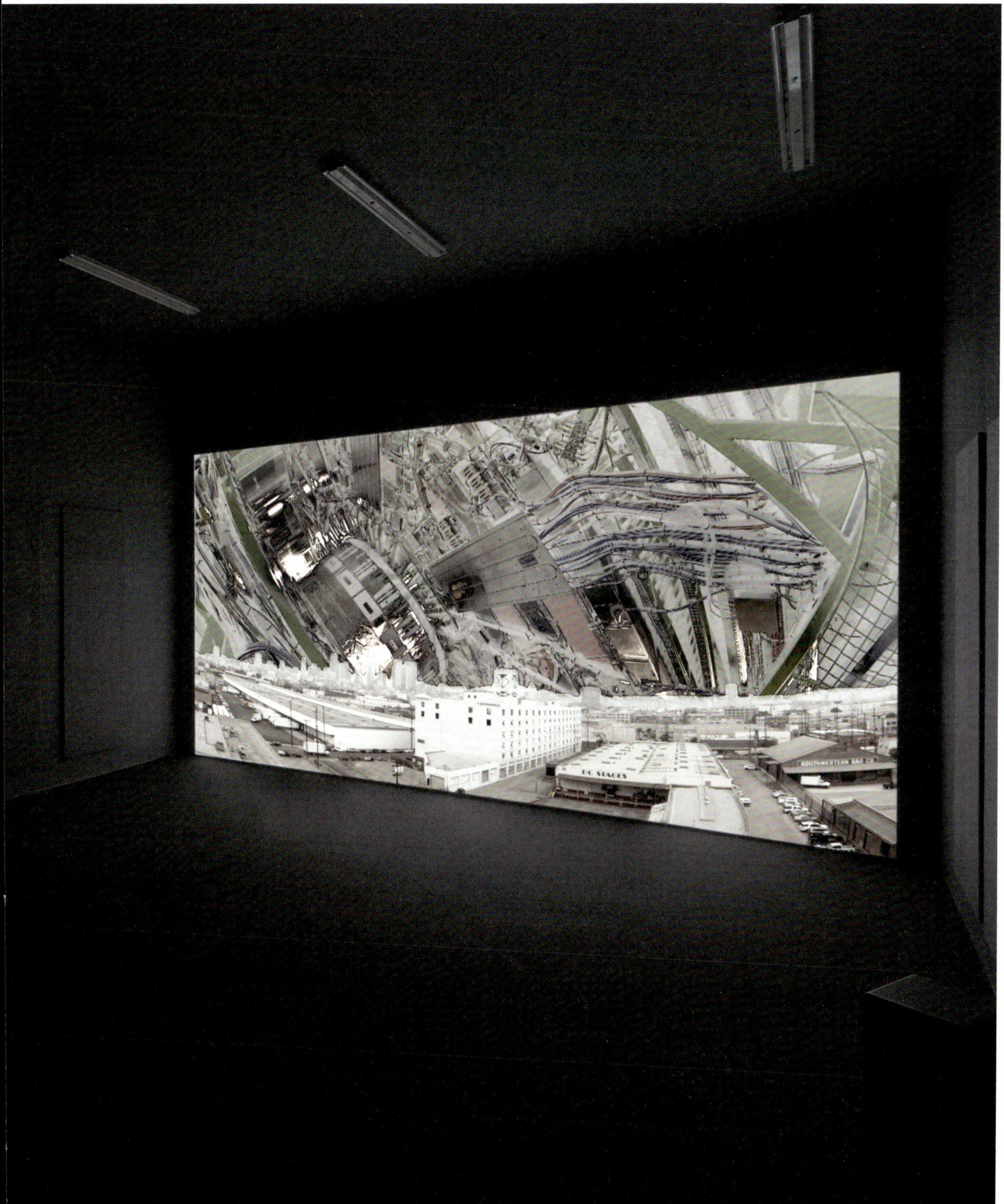

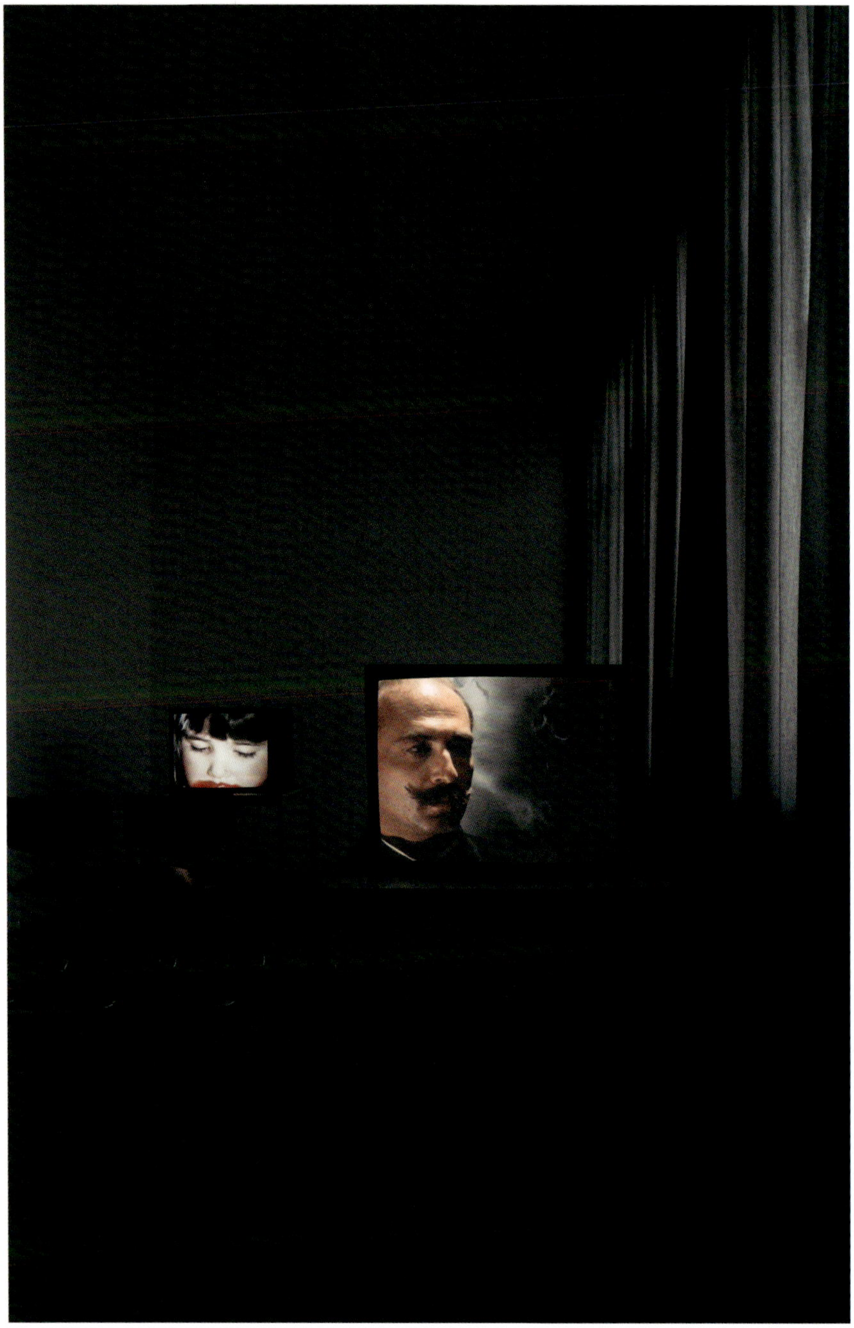

L–R: *Jennifer, Where Are You?*, 1981,
and *The Last Time I Saw Ron*, 1995.
Exhibition view: "Leslie Thornton:
GROUND," Kunstverein Nürnberg, 2020

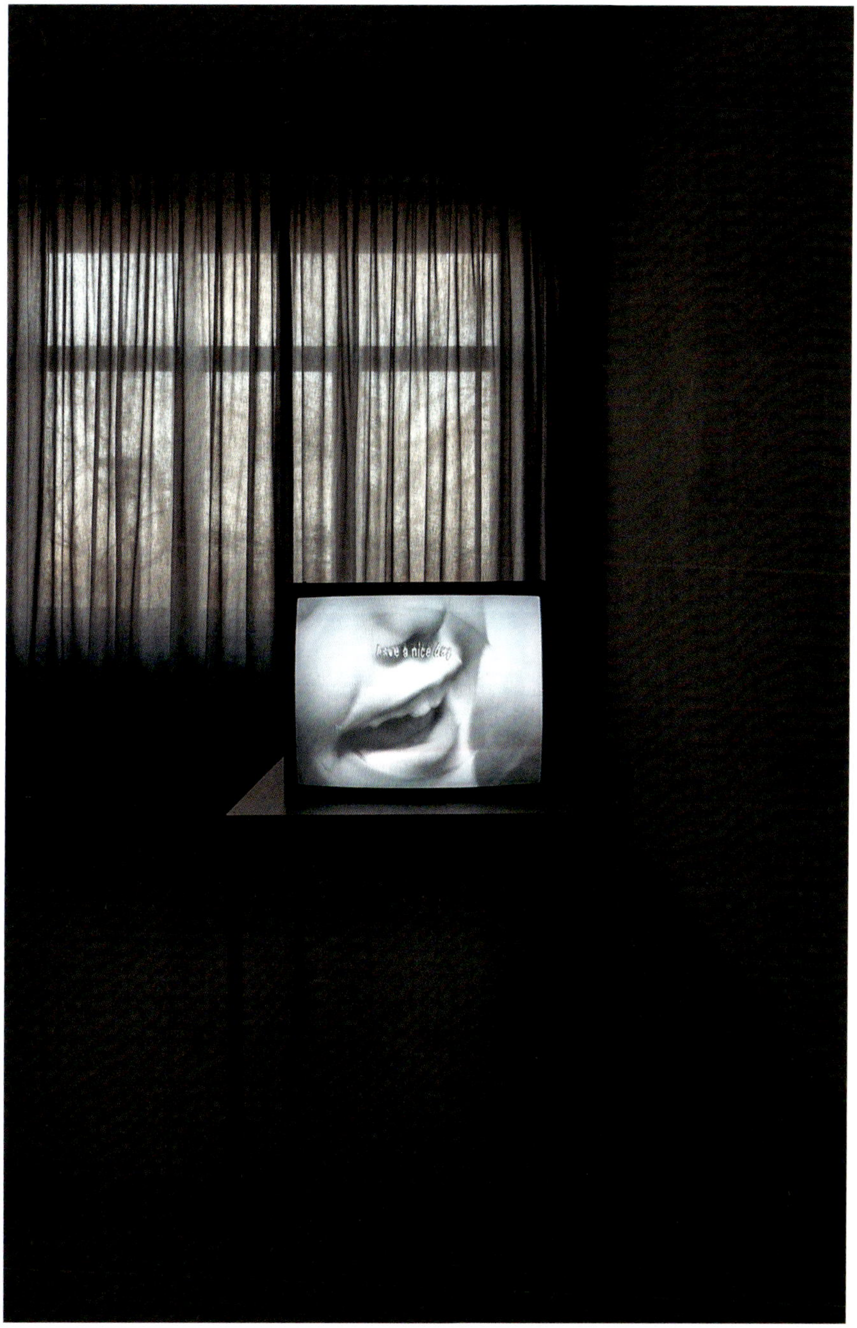

Peggy and Fred in Hell, 1983–2015.
Exhibition view: "Leslie Thornton:
GROUND," Kunstverein Nürnberg, 2020

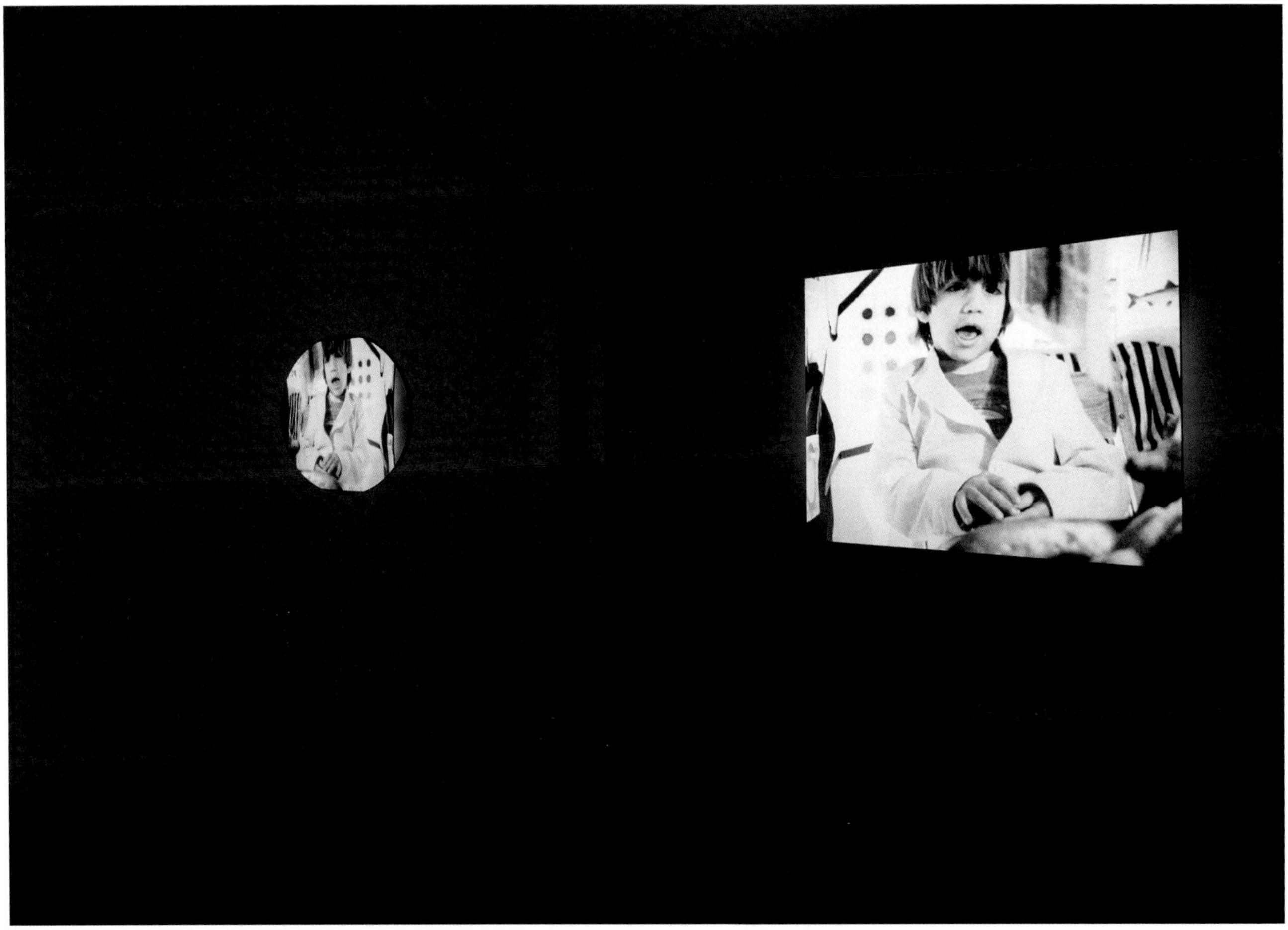

Installation view: *Peggy and Fred in Hell: Folding*, 1983–2015. Exhibition view: "The Inoperative Community," Raven Row, London, 2015

Peggy and Fred in Hell: Folding, 1983–2015 (detail). Exhibition view: "The Inoperative Community," Raven Row, London, 2015

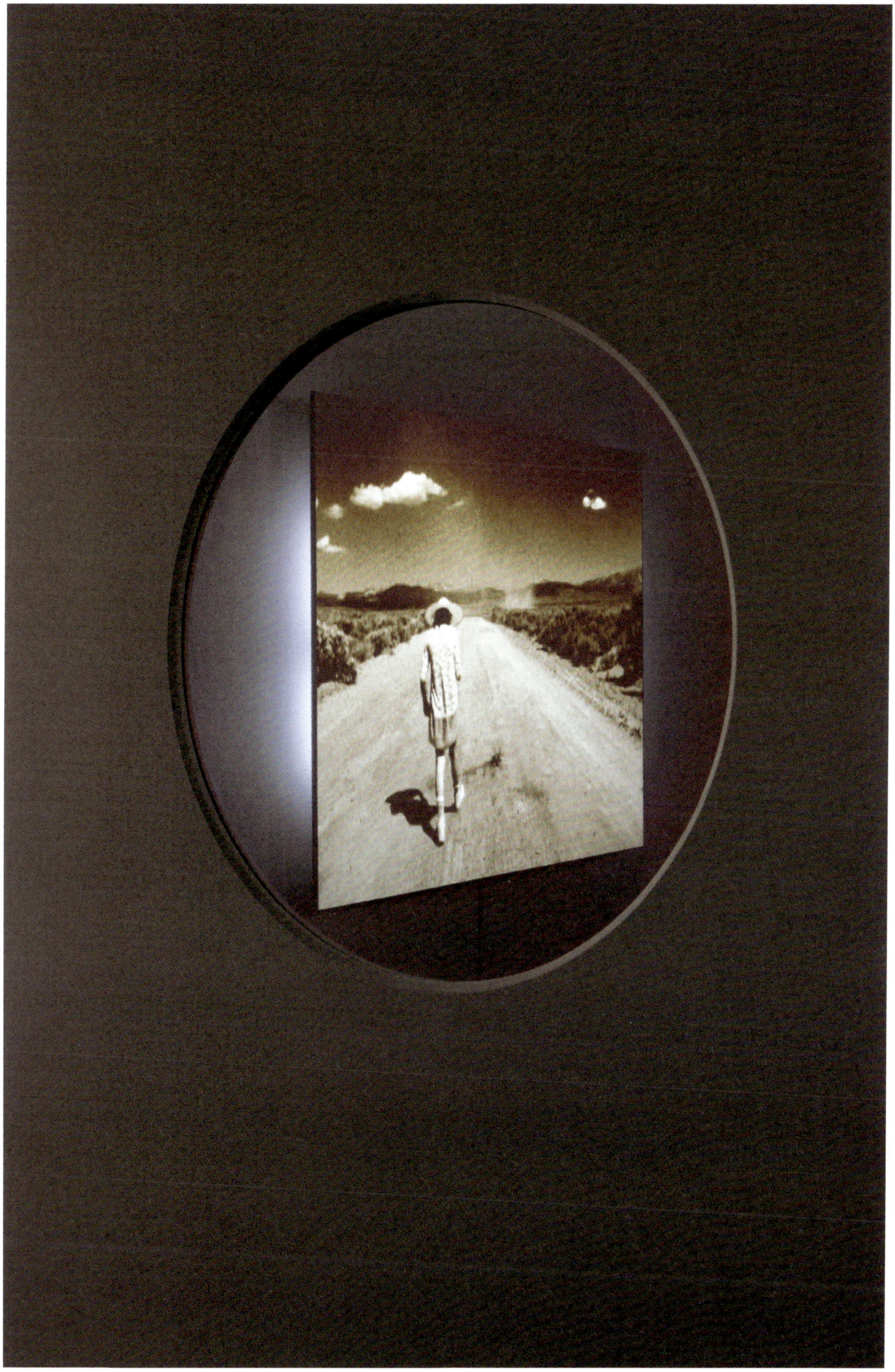

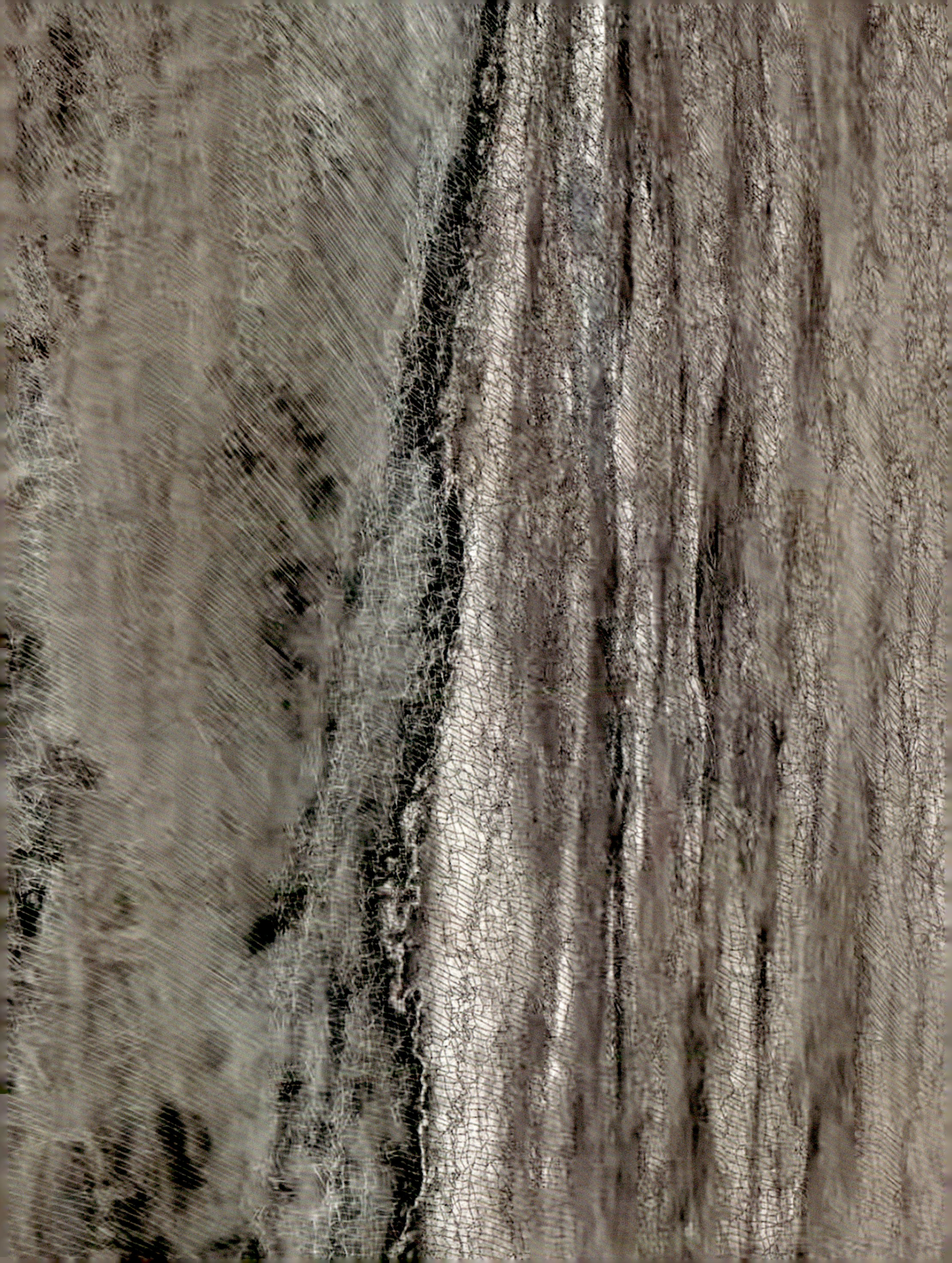

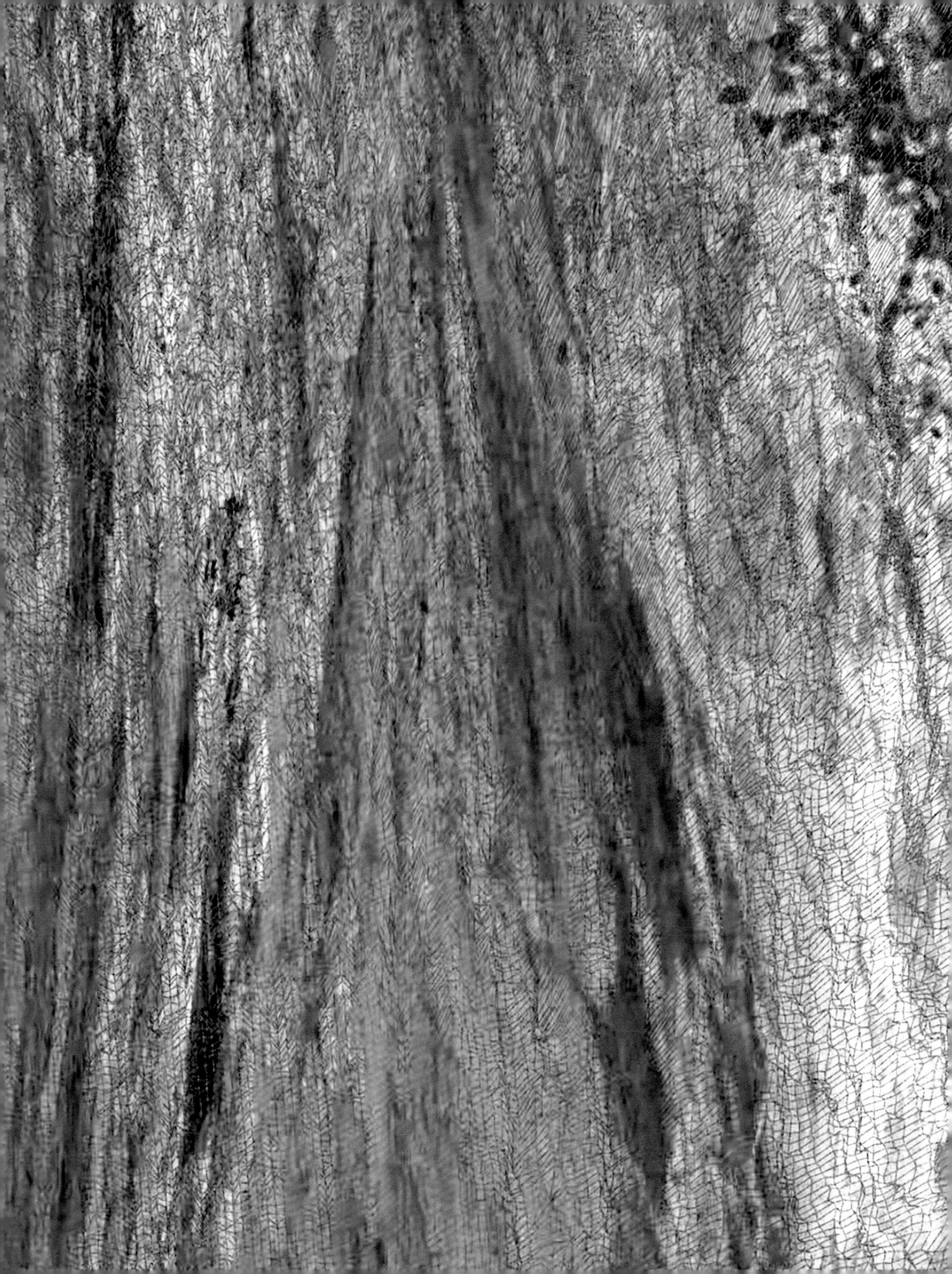

The Deaths of Man

> True, it is strange to inhabit the earth no longer,
> to use no longer customs scarcely acquired,
> not to interpret roses, and other things
> that promise so much, in terms of a human future;
> to be no longer all that one used to be
> in endlessly anxious hands, and to lay aside
> even one's proper name like a broken toy.
>
> —Rainer Maria Rilke, *Duino Elegies*, as quoted in *Strange Space* (1993)

Oh, the storm! It blows in from paradise.[1] The ship is going down, and a call goes out to abandon the vessel: *women and children first*. For the Boy Scouts, it is the motto of the sea. This credo at once elevates and diminishes those it speaks of, sharpening the blade of values that prevail on firm ground, not just in moments of unexpected cataclysm, but in more mundane ways as well. Women and children have long been Others of the master's discourse, objects to be shuffled about according to patriarchal will rather than subjects in their own right, spoken of and spoken for more than they are permitted to speak. Although they are in some respects treasured—put first—they are simultaneously denied full participation in the category of the human. Perceived as irrational and inscrutable, as incapable of transcending their beastly corporeality, they are part of the enigmatic ground against which man produces himself as knowing master.

What is to be done? One possibility is to pursue a feminist effort of inclusion, to seek access to the privileged position of sovereign subject, to install woman as a new master. But if the game is rotten, destructive of lives and worlds, what's the point in trying to play? Leslie Thornton takes

1 "Oh, the storm!" is the closing exclamation of Leslie Thornton's *Peggy and Fred in Hell* (1983–2015), uttered by an artificial intelligence peering down at a destroyed earth. In his discussion of Paul Klee's 1920 *Angelus Novus* in "Theses on the Philosophy of History," Walter Benjamin uses a meteorological metaphor to puncture a belief in progress: "Where we perceive a chain of events, [the angel of history] sees one single catastrophe which keeps piling wreckage upon wreckage and hurls it in front of his feet. The angel would like to stay, awaken the dead, and make whole what has been smashed. But a storm is blowing in from Paradise; it has got caught in his wings with such violence that the angel can no longer close them. [...] This storm is what we call progress." See Walter Benjamin, "Theses on the Philosophy of History," in *Illuminations*, ed. Hannah Arendt, trans. Harry Zohn (New York: Schocken, 1969), 257–58.

a different path, shattering patriarchal notions of authority and mastery to reimagine subjectivity for a time when "man" no longer occupies the center of the world. The women and children who animate her early works exist outside the bounds of chivalrous protection. They come first, not in that they are a priority for rescue, but because they sense the coming storm, the time when all proper names will be put aside.

Thornton's first 16mm film, *X-TRACTS* (1975), made in collaboration with Desmond Horsfield, begins with a man counting to six over black leader, his delivery marking out an even beat. When he finishes the count, he starts over, this time with close-ups of a female body filling the screen: a tuft of pubic hair, the curve of a waist, a foot. In these opening seconds, the film stages a condensed drama of normative sexual difference. His counting connects him to the realms of rationality and calculation; her mute, bare flesh—parceled into part-objects, face withheld—is given over to the camera for consumption. The film seems to reproduce a dominant logic, whereby he is language and mind, while she is image and body. But suddenly, Thornton's voice intrudes on the soundtrack, jutting in with fragments of speech carved so small that initially no meaning surfaces, upsetting the cleavages the film so swiftly established at the start. The man is cut off before he finishes the word "six," never to be heard from again.

In the remaining eight minutes, the metric order promised by the introductory counting unravels, as does the gendered binary it inscribed. Glimpses of life cascade forth in brief monochrome bursts, occasionally punctuated by spells of blackness. The inert stillness of the initial nudes gives way to lively movement. Horsfield's Bolex camera pans and whirls; within the frame, Thornton circulates through her environs, now and then returning the gaze of the machine. In this patchwork portrait, the comforts and energies of quotidian existence—walking in the woods, applying lipstick, showering—appear as so many shards that have splintered from a larger continuum of activity, their internal plenitude standing in tension with the unwavering regularity of the montage.

On the soundtrack, Thornton pours out palaver that skirts the threshold of sense. The audio, too, has been subject to extensive editing, such that full words, partial phrases, and orphaned phonemes jostle together in glossolalic tumult. Rationally articulated speech—for Aristotle, the difference between man and beast—breaks into a jumble of sounds.[2]

Only occasionally does a snatch of meaning congeal: the sentence, "Of necessity, I become an instrument," stands out as a rare moment of syntactical coherence, one that speaks to a notion of the self as means rather than origin. The musicality of the voice is released from its subordination to signification, in a manner Trinh T. Minh-ha would later describe as characteristic of women's writing: "Going beyond the convention Presence-God-Author and feeling the urgency of a decentralizing movement, they take up speech not to identify it with themselves or to possess it, but to deliver it from its enslavement to mastery. The consequences of such a position disrupt our slightest actions, for they challenge an entire tradition based on the worship of illusory centers."[3]

What specific tradition was it that Thornton was challenging? *X-TRACTS* was made when the artist was twenty-four, shortly after she obtained a bachelor's degree in fine arts at SUNY Buffalo, a university known for its strong commitment to experimental film and media art. *X-TRACTS*, in part, reckons with the lessons and limits of two of her teachers at the school, each of them prominent representatives of a distinctly male-dominated avant-garde: Stan Brakhage and Paul Sharits. With Brakhage, a Romantic lyricist, Thornton shares an interest in personal experience and somatic camerawork; with Sharits, a structuralist, the use of a gridded score to determine the editing of sound and image.

In early works like *X-TRACTS* and *All Right You Guys* (1976; also made in collaboration with Horsfield), Thornton combines elements of each of these filmmakers, deploying them against one another to invent a form that departs from both. Her imposition of a rule-based structure puts pressure on notions of realist immediacy and subjective expressivity, and yet, the textured reality of her life and the spontaneity of the camera's encounter with it shine through the grid in a manner altogether at odds with the pared-down system of a work such as Sharits's *T,O,U,C,H,I,N,G* (1969)—a flicker film that uses a precise patterning of boldly colored frames to foreground the materiality of the medium and engender a mesmerizing perceptual experience.

Thornton's formal negotiations are inextricable from a feminist exploration of selfhood, one that seeks to dismantle a subject predicated on a mind/body split and deep interiority. To generate the soundtrack for *X-TRACTS*, she began by reading aloud her adolescent diaries. She cannibalizes this private, stereotypically feminine mode of writing, so often held to be an unhampered transmission of innermost feeling, mangling it beyond recognition. The indifferent and impersonal incisions of

2 As Anne Carson has written, "The formal definition of human nature preferred by patriarchal culture is one based on the articulation of sound. As Aristotle says, any animal can make noises to register pleasure or pain. But what differentiates man from beast, civilization from the wilderness, is the use of rationally articulated speech: *logos*." Anne Carson, "The Gender of Sound," in *Glass, Irony and God* (New York: New Directions, 1992), 128.

3 Trinh T. Minh-ha, "*L'Innécriture*: Un-writing/Inmost Writing," in *When the Moon Waxes Red* (New York: Routledge, 1991), 136.

the editing process aggressively deny any continuity of speech, refusing the latter's habitual associations with spontaneity and self-presence. Thornton breaks the synchronization of sound and image upon which naturalistic representation relies, untethering the female voice from embodiment. Yet, she goes beyond simply installing woman as a new "voice of god," omnipotent and authoritative, to decidedly refuse the fantasy of communicative transparency altogether. Through the montage procedures Thornton inflicts upon the recording of her reading, the grain of the voice—impersonal and voluptuous, what Roland Barthes calls "the body in the voice as it sings"—comes to prevail over the signified.[4] Speech escapes its fleshy home, but only to insist on its materiality all the more.

As Anne Carson observes, "Putting a door on the female mouth has been an important project of patriarchal culture from antiquity to the present day. Its chief tactic is an ideological association of female sound with monstrosity, disorder and death."[5] At the outset of her career, Thornton unlocked this door: not to refuse such associations, not to insist that woman is as fit to be master as man, but to inaugurate a challenge to the gendered fictions of the speaking subject.

In 1990, Thornton described her practice as "a kind of 'minor literature,'" invoking a concept Gilles Deleuze and Félix Guattari formulated in relation to the work of Franz Kafka.[6] To be minor, they write, is "to hate all languages of masters." It means embracing "the deterritorialization of language, the connection of the individual to a political immediacy, and the collective assemblage of enunciation," with the last explained as a situation in which "there are no possibilities for an individuated enunciation that would belong to this or that 'master' and that could be separated from a collective enunciation."[7]

In 1989, as some critics mourned the end of a heroic avant-garde,[8] Tom Gunning borrowed from Deleuze and Guattari to champion the "minor cinema" of a new generation of artists, including Peggy Ahwesh and Nina Fonoroff, who, like Thornton, reject the Romantic ego and "assert no vision of conquest, make no claims to hegemony."[9] In the ruins of the prior avant-garde's insistence on authority, originality, and medium specificity, Thornton forged one of the decade's most vital practices, turning to repurposed images, hybrid formats, and juvenile protagonists to transpose experimental film into a minor key.

As Thornton's practice developed, the attachment to systematic construction glimpsed in her early films gave way to a looser and more intuitive manipulation of materials of diverse provenance. This orientation distanced her from two especially salient tendencies of experimental film of the 1970s: the reductionism of structural film and the high discursivity of the "New Talkies."[10] Her promiscuous repurposing of existing images and sounds vanquishes the stylistic consistency that often serves as an authorial signature. Image textures clash and signifiers pile up, unmoored from their original contexts. And unlike the feminist filmmakers who embraced theoretical language, Thornton remained suspicious of logocentrism, instead modeling how speculative thinking can occur through the thickness of sensory experience.

A work such as *Adynata* (1983), for instance, approaches the intersecting spectacles of femininity and Orientalism through nondidactic, sometimes opaque, assemblages of image and sound, which recall the lesson of the rhetorical device that lends the film its title. Adynaton—adynata in the plural—is a form of extreme hyperbole that stages a literal impossibility, as exemplified in the expression "When pigs fly!" By sacrificing plausibility to the effort of communication (pigs will never fly, after all), adynaton avows that language has a limited ability to capture thought and experience.

In *Adynata*, an array of Orientalist signifiers—gardens, music, clothing—accumulate as so many sensations that link to one another in associative ways. Here, as throughout Thornton's oeuvre, there is no predetermined meaning to be decoded through the act of viewing. Rather, the spectator slips and stumbles along the signifying chain, feeling her way through a dense thicket of provocations in a time unbeholden to efficiency. Clarity, these films suggest, is not always a virtue; on the contrary, it is a demand that belongs to a pernicious regime of instrumentality.

4 Roland Barthes, "The Grain of the Voice," in *Image Music Text*, ed. and trans. Stephen Heath (London: Fontana Press, 1977), 188.

5 Carson, "The Gender of Sound," 121.

6 Leslie Thornton, quoted in Laleen Jayamanne, Leslie Thornton, and Trinh T. Minh-ha, "If upon Leaving What We Have to Say We Speak: A Conversation Piece," in *Discourses: Conversations in Postmodern Art and Culture*, ed. Karen Fiss, Russell Ferguson, William Olander, and Marcia Tucker (New York: New Museum and MIT Press, 1990), 50.

7 Gilles Deleuze and Félix Guattari, "What Is a Minor Literature?," in *Out There: Marginalization and Contemporary Cultures*, ed. Russell Ferguson, Martha Gever, Trinh T. Minh-ha, and Cornel West, trans. Dana Polan (New York: New Museum and MIT Press, 1990), 67 and 60–61.

8 A notable text in this regard is Fred Camper's "The End of the Avant-Garde," in which the author holds that "the works of the newer generation of filmmakers for the most part lack the authentic power of the original, and often still-active masters." The recourse here to notions of authenticity, originality, and mastery is symptomatic. See Fred Camper, "The End of the Avant-Garde," *Millennium Film Journal* 16/17/18 (Fall/Winter 1986–87): 109.

9 Despite its appositeness to his argument, Gunning does not discuss Thornton's work but notes early on that "there is a great deal of new work that I have not seen (most importantly, everyone tells me, the work of Leslie Thornton)." See Tom Gunning, "Towards a Minor Cinema: Fonoroff, Herwitz, Ahwesh, Lapore, Klahr, and Solomon," *Motion Picture* 3, nos. 1–2 (Winter 1989–90): 2.

10 Annette Michelson summarizes the "New Talkies," sometimes also called "New Narrative," as "essentially the independent productions which have been not only affected by theory but which act as channels for an articulation involved with the theoretical." Exemplary films include Yvonne Rainer's *A Film about a Woman Who…* (1974) and Laura Mulvey and Peter Wollen's *Riddles of the Sphinx* (1977). See Giuliana Bruno, "Women in Avant-Garde Film: An Interview with Annette Michelson," *Millennium Film Journal* 16/17/18 (Fall/Winter 1986–87): 146.

As part of her challenge to this regime, Thornton turns to children. The protagonists of *Peggy and Fred in Hell* (1983–2015) are youngsters who live in rubble, alone with television and each other. Thornton created and reworked this superlative film cycle over decades and across technological formats, pilfering the audiovisual archive, combining found images and sounds with her newly shot footage. She moves with and against the currents that flow through the sea of signs to imagine a world after this world's end, one colder than the Cold War. Thornton never specifies what disaster has left her characters alone in this wasteland—such explanatory gestures are against the spirit of her practice—but the dystopian picture that takes shape suggests a time and place in which the promise of better living through technology has proved incontrovertibly false, leaving poison and ruination in its wake.

In line with this rejection of any belief in an ameliorative teleology, the brother and sister never grow up, in spite of the many episodes of *Peggy and Fred*. Instead, they grow sideways in a postapocalyptic environment, appearing now older, now younger, but never in a sequence that conforms to biological maturation.[11] Linear progress—cause and effect—has collapsed. The not-quite-narrative form of the cycle throws the fundamental assumptions of storytelling into crisis, including all the notions of *Bildung* that tend to accompany adolescent protagonists, be it moral growth, self-realization, or the inevitable assumption of one's proper place in the world of adults.

Following an opening sequence that immediately establishes a concern with vocal embodiment and sexual difference, Peggy and Fred make their first appearances in a cluttered domestic interior, singing words that are not their own, pop songs with lyrics drenched in experiences of love and death they are too young to know. These feral orphans have taken up residence in the realm of the minor, abandoning the fiction of originality. Is it a coincidence that key metaphors for copying make recourse to animality—to ape, to parrot—as if to only repeat were to be less than human? Peggy and Fred pay no mind to such conventions: the siblings are mimetic beings, brilliant dummies animated by a ventriloquist called culture.

They play and improvise, drifting in and out of costumes and situations borrowed from a twentieth-century world that has collapsed. They stretch and deform their speech like Play-Doh, babbling on, creating the new from the old. When Peggy desultorily sings Michael Jackson's "Billie Jean," it is as if she is remembering the song phonetically, toying with repeated sounds, blithely unconcerned with the meaning of the lyrics. Like the trappings of suburban family life that occasionally appear or the scientific drag of the lab coat that Fred often wears, the rendition of the song is emphatically second-hand, a purposefully poor derivation of an original gone missing.

Superficially, the siblings' volubility appears opposed to the silence of the taciturn girl, who may or may not be called Jennifer in *Jennifer, Where Are You?* (1981). She refrains from making a peep as the titular question echoes intermittently amidst other noises on the soundtrack, the disembodied paternal voice reduced to a looped recording drained of vitality. He asks and asks, but she never answers. All the while, she rehearses the affectations of womanhood, gazing into a handheld mirror, that paradigmatic site of subjective (mis)recognition, as she applies red lipstick. Her childish attempt quickly goes awry, however, as she colors outside the lines, smearing the make-up such that her mouth resembles a clown's rictus.

Ignoring the voice that seeks to fix her in place, she mocks what she is meant to become, brazenly if unwittingly exposing normative femininity as a cosmetic masquerade. Images of a house and adults appear inverted along the horizontal axis, emblems of reproductive futurity literally upended. By the film's end, the girl's once-pleasant countenance has soured into sullenness. Glowering, she refuses to blow out the match held in front of her from offscreen, watching it burn, a witness to the luxury of useless expenditure.

The children of these works are threshold beings, curious and inchoate and unruly, strangers to the demand that time, tantamount to money, should be well spent. As Thornton puts it, "Children are not quite us and not quite other. They are our others. They are becoming us. Or they are becoming other. They are at a dangerous point."[12] In her rendering, they make visible how the self, every self, is inseparable from what is outside it: the vast world of readymade language, the immense storehouse of culture. Peggy, Fred, and Jennifer are kin. Molded by external exigencies, they are subjects-in-the-making who never quite take up the place the world of masters assigns to them. They are offspring without parents, inheritors not of private property but of a vast impersonal murmur. They point to how what we call the self is a concatenation of otherness, a process of iteration that remains open to derailment, to unmaking and remaking, at every turn. Whether through the reproduction of existing cultural artifacts (images, songs, scenarios) or the alienated affectations

11 Kathryn Bond Stockton has proposed the notion of "growing sideways" as a queer alternative to forms of growing up predicated on a forward motion "from innocence to the adult position of protecting it." For Stockton, "the child from the standpoint of 'normal' adults is always queer," marked by its strangeness and otherness relative to the norm. See Kathryn Bond Stockton, *The Queer Child, or Growing Sideways in the Twentieth Century* (Durham, NC: Duke University Press, 2009), 7 and 12.

12 Thornton, quoted in Jayamanne, Thornton, and Trinh, "If upon Leaving What We Have to Say We Speak," 54.

of normative adulthood, these films insist that copying lies at the heart of what is often held to be most singular, namely, an individual's subjectivity. In Thornton's words, "Maybe the 'Self' is not that interesting. I don't think it is, but what flows through it can be."[13]

How is the master doing today, when the storm blows still harder? His house is in disarray, turned upside down by new winds, new floods. The planet is warming, and the fictions he held as truths are finally crumbling. On the final page of *The Order of Things*, Michel Foucault imagines that a time will come when "man would be erased, like a face drawn in sand at the edge of the sea."[14] The brackish water surges forth, an inhuman animus before which the embattled sovereign stands little chance. His end is nothing to mourn; let the apes and parrots take over. Foucault trafficked in metaphor, speculating about a transformation of subjectivity—surely, he did not have in mind a time when the shoreline would figure as a place where humanity's vulnerability to environmental crisis is powerfully felt, where the threat of species extinction shows itself with force. These are two very different deaths of man: one epistemological, the other existential.

Yet, through Thornton's work, and in *Peggy and Fred* most powerfully, a relation between them comes into view. At the conclusion of the cycle, in a final episode entitled *The Fold*, Thornton reveals something she had mentioned publicly as early as 1989, but had never made explicit in the work: the children are being observed by an artificial intelligence network.[15] They are just two little objects among objects in a petrified world beyond their control, watched over by a nonhuman entity who speaks in a doubled, high-pitched voice that, despite its emphatically technologized distortions, recalls the filmmaker's.

These children are alone on earth, alone in hell, playing with guns and speaking often of finitude. When the title of a 1987 episode announces that they are in "Kansas," it is no place like home. Throughout, Thornton draws extensively on images of deserts, desolate factories, space travel, and weather systems, pairing them with a collage of disparate sounds to create multilayered evocations of man-made disaster. Everything seems dead or dying. Peggy comes across a flock of ducks, fallen from the sky to rot as burned corpses; a bird that an intertitle names Pete the Penguin appears lost as he waddles through what looks like suburbia, far from his native habitat. Is he the last of his kind to survive in the inferno of Peggy and Fred's world? Or did this species vanish long ago, now existing only as a specter to be glimpsed on an ancient piece of scratched film? The latter seems more likely: Thornton emphasizes the archival materiality of the penguin footage, manipulating it in multiple ways that underline its status as artifact, including reversing its motion, magnifying the damage on the filmstrip, and refilming a projection of it in a seemingly empty space, accompanied by bits of a soundtrack snatched from a stilted narrative film. This animal is embalmed in the image-bank.

Littered with references to science and the military and saturated with unsentimental concern for the fate of creaturely life on a damaged planet, *Peggy and Fred* establishes an iconographic repertoire Thornton continues to explore into the present. Recent videos, such as *Crossing* (2016; made in collaboration with James Richards) and *Cut from Liquid to Snake* (2018), feature bubbling black oil, captive and dead animals, medical imaging, and disembodied voices that tumble in and out of comprehension. Distinctions between nuclear research and nuclear disaster, technological advancement and technologized annihilation, become muddled. Employing emphatically synthetic forms of image processing that definitively break with the photographic paradigm, Thornton crafts a vision of reality in which wild nature has vanished, mass death is ever possible, and algorithmic computation has outstripped the representational capacities of humans.

The women and children protagonists that anchored her earlier works are present no longer, but their lessons concerning the violent reign of "man" persist. Thornton's recent videos manifest an awareness that the nightmare of a world made uninhabitable by the demands of the squall called progress is a notion no longer confined to the fancies of science fiction. Faced with this emergency, these works hint at how to disrupt the workings of the anthropological machine and remake subjectivity otherwise—to leave behind the arrogant invulnerability of the Self, dispense with pretensions of mastery, and topple hierarchies in the interest of survival.

So much existential anxiety is anticipatory, preoccupied with an extinction event to come. Thornton's extraordinary body of work suggests that we need not look ahead: we already live in ruins. Some of these inspire lamentation; others give reason to be glad. Is an inhuman future the only one still possible? Oh, the storm!

13 Thornton, quoted in Jayamanne, Thornton, and Trinh, "If upon Leaving What We Have to Say We Speak," 54.

14 Michel Foucault, *The Order of Things: An Archaeology of the Human Sciences* (London: Routledge), 422.

15 In her text "We Ground Things, Now, on a Moving Earth," Thornton writes of Peggy and Fred, "And they also watch television. Television is part of the Artificial Intelligence network. AI keeps Television on all of the time and so do Peggy and Fred." See Leslie Thornton, "We Ground Things, Now, on a Moving Earth," *Motion Picture* 3, nos. 1–2 (1989): 13.

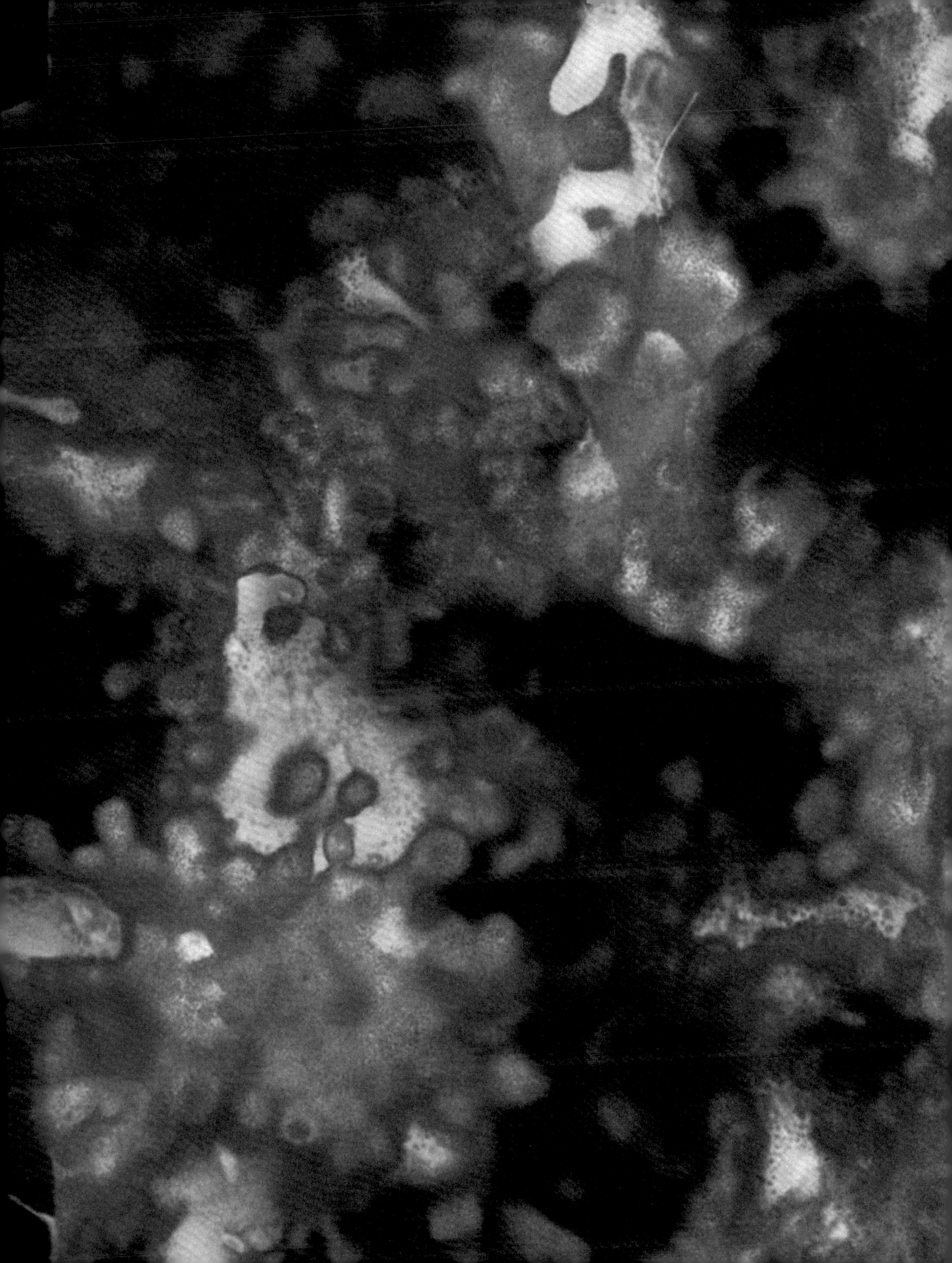

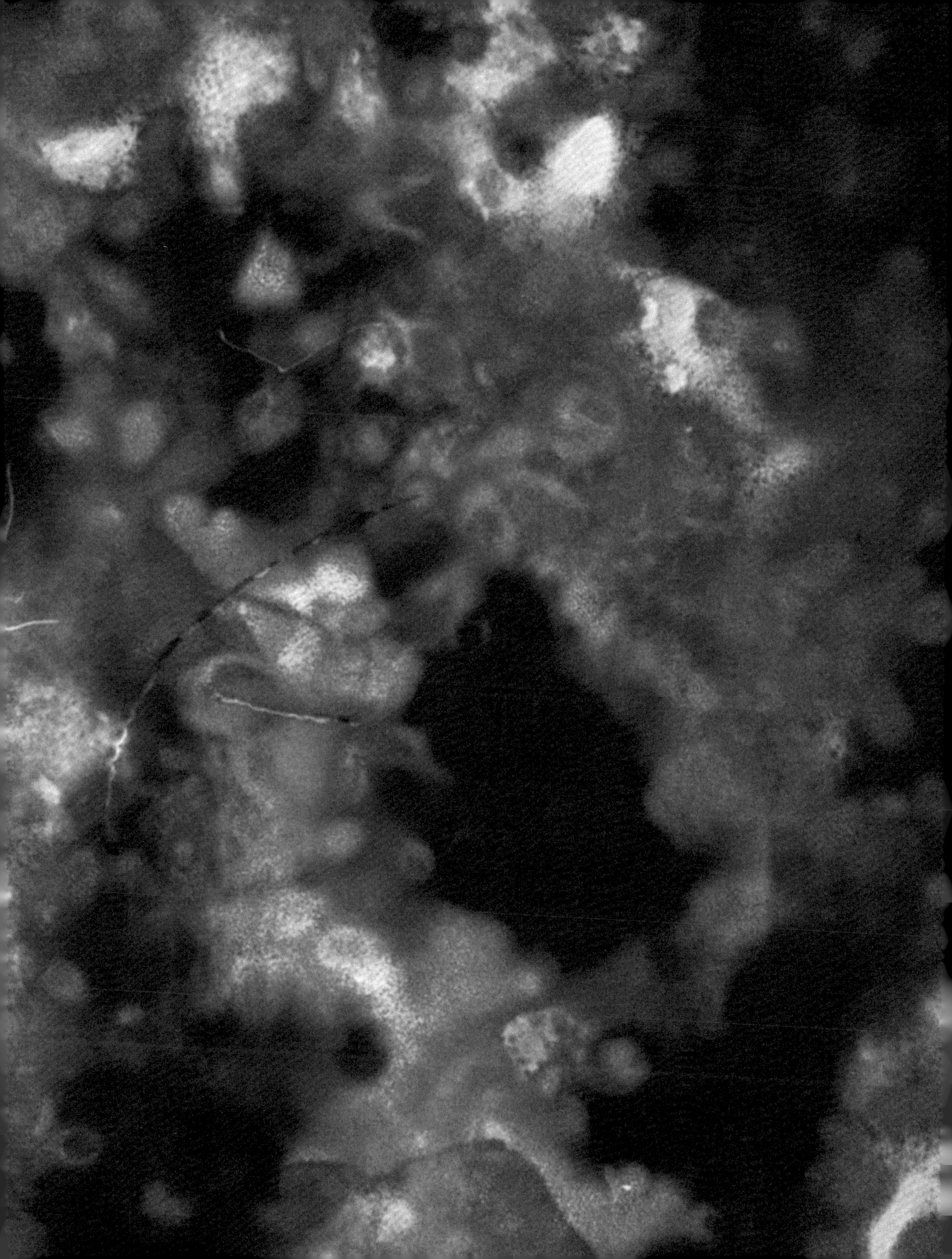

Unhappy Times on a Warming Planet

Dan Kidner

> I say, Bring the simple wine
> that makes me loose and free.
> You say, There is a hurricane
> coming!
> And I say, Let's have some wine
> then, and sit here like old statues
> and watch.
>
> —Jalāl ad-Dīn Muhammad Rūmī, *Unseen Rain: Quatrains of Rumi*[1]

For over forty years, Leslie Thornton has both meditated upon and courted catastrophe in her work. As theme, as form, and as organizing principle, the "dark disaster that brings the light"[2] has served Thornton's practice. Catastrophe's most literal meaning, a downward turn, comes from its ancient Greek roots: κατά (kata), meaning "down," and στροφή (strophē), meaning "turning." In the mid-sixteenth century, the Latin *catastropha* came to mean the dénouement of a tragic drama. The *Oxford English Dictionary* today cites "an event causing great and usually sudden damage or suffering; a disaster." The shifts in definition mirror processes in Thornton's works, which often both narrate and instantiate a movement from lived experience to fiction and back again, or from well-structured plot or scenario to formlessness or fragmentation. Any scaffold that she builds to hold narrative meaning or documentary content is inevitably toppled by an assault on signification, threatening a complete untethering of her images from any metaphorical usefulness or indexical relationship to reality.

Culturally, catastrophic thinking or imagining the worst is a venerable tradition to which Thornton's practice is acutely attuned and

1 Epigraph from Leslie Thornton's *The Last Time I Saw Ron* (1995).

2 Maurice Blanchot, *The Writing of Disaster*, trans. Ann Smock (Lincoln: University of Nebraska Press, 1980), 7.

aligned—from the science-fiction dystopias of Octavia E. Butler, Joanna Russ, and J. G. Ballard, through the critical theory of Theodor W. Adorno and Walter Benjamin, to the more recent theorizing of political scientists, philosophers, and anthropologists as varied as Isabelle Stengers, Anna Lowenhaupt Tsing, Jean-Luc Nancy, Maurice Blanchot, and Slavoj Žižek.[3] To think climate catastrophe means to consider the many and various entanglements between nature and society in order to understand how we've arrived at this precipice. Most of the above thinkers do this through a direct engagement with Marx and historical materialism.

More recently, theorists with a more ambivalent relationship to Marxist theory—those aligned to various forms of new materialism or posthumanism[4]—have mobilized a more affirmative politics. In contrast to this latter orientation, Thornton tends toward the historical *while* maintaining a fascination with and deep interest in scientific practice and research. However, Thornton's practice is not illustrative of any theory, nor doctrinaire. We could perhaps see her as a close relative of Benjamin's destructive character, "whose deepest emotion is an insuperable mistrust of the course of things and a readiness at all times to recognize that everything can go wrong."[5] Her works embrace negativity and incomprehensibility, formally embodying catastrophe—"the destructive character has no interest in being understood [and] tolerates misunderstanding."[6] We might also think of Benjamin's Angelus Novus, famously blown from paradise and propelled into the future while focused on the "one single catastrophe which keeps piling wreckage upon wreckage."[7]

Ostensibly, catastrophe, as theme or setting, looms large in many of Thornton's works. The child protagonists in her epic film and video cycle *Peggy and Fred in Hell* (1983–2015) are adrift in a postapocalyptic world, sifting through the technological detritus of the twentieth century. The exact nature of the apocalypse that has taken place is never specified, although both nuclear and climate catastrophes are hinted at.[8] In *Strange Space* (1993) and *The Last Time I Saw Ron* (1995), both tributes to her friend the actor Ron Vawter, the AIDS epidemic provides the catastrophic backdrop. *Let Me Count the Ways* (2004–ongoing) focuses on the devastation wrought by the bombs dropped on Nagasaki and Hiroshima on August 6 and 9, 1945, and the scientists who were part of the collective effort to design and detonate them (among whom were Thornton's own father and grandfather). A more recent video, *Cut from Liquid to Snake* (2018), connects the atomic bomb to the acceleration of disaster capitalism in Trump's America (another catastrophe). And in the *Binocular*

Menagerie series (2010–14), animals are subjected to kaleidoscopic obliteration, bringing to mind both the ongoing sixth mass extinction and the threat of zoonotic spillover (believed to be the mechanism by which both HIV and Covid-19 jumped the species barrier and spread to humans).[9]

The environmental disasters that occur weekly, if not daily, on our rapidly warming planet—aided and abetted and then profited off of by rampant disaster capitalism—don't always make the headlines, especially if they occur in the Global South. But for many in the richer North, a kind of ambient knowledge of them produces a low-level anxiety that threatens to spill over into panic. Thornton's works, especially those made since the turn of the century, trace this fault-line, formally as well as thematically. The Indian writer Amitav Ghosh has suggested that much literary fiction, and contemporary art and culture more generally, is enthralled to a kind of "great derangement," a blind spot where the climate crisis is concerned. Ghosh maintains that for cultural forms, like literary fiction, anchored to realism and modernism, catastrophism is "un-modern" and hence unthinkable.[10] However, the corrective to this might not necessarily simply be, as Ghosh proposes, that writers and artists imagine a way out of this cul-de-sac by conceptualizing "non-linear change" (i.e., catastrophes) in their work.[11] But rather that artists dare to panic; to inhabit or embody catastrophe, as such, by coupling this panic to a form committed to disturbing narrative.

Thornton's formal strategies, as much as the thematic content of her work, alert us to the chronic emergency that faces us all. Across the many episodes of *Peggy and Fred in Hell*, produced over some thirty years, the artist combines found footage with her own—much of which, seen on its own, might scan as cinema verité. Into this mix, she

3 See Isabelle Stengers, *In Catastrophic Times: Resisting the Coming Barbarism*, trans. Andrew Goffey (London: Open Humanities Press, 2015); Anna Lowenhaupt Tsing, *The Mushroom at the End of the World: On the Possibility of Life in Capitalist Ruins* (Princeton, NJ: Economics Books, Princeton University Press, 2015); Jean-Luc Nancy, *After Fukushima: The Equivalence of Catastrophes* (New York: Fordham University Press, 2015); Blanchot, *The Writing of Disaster*; and Slavoj Žižek, *Living in the End Times* (London: Verso Books, 2010).

4 For salient critiques of new materialism, see Benjamin Noys, *The Persistence of the Negative: A Critique of Contemporary Continental Theory* (Edinburgh: Edinburgh University Press, 2010), and, for a critique of new materialism from the perspective of the climate crisis, in particular the writing of Bruno Latour, see Andreas Malm, *The Progress of this Storm: Nature and Society in a Warming World* (London: Verso, 2018).

5 Walter Benjamin, *Selected Writings, Volume 2: Part 2, 1931–1934* (Cambridge, MA: Harvard University Press, 2005), 542.

6 Benjamin, 542.

7 Walter Benjamin, "On the Concept of History," in *Selected Writings, Volume 4* (Cambridge, MA: Harvard University Press, 2005), 389–400.

8 In the works that make up the *Peggy and Fred in Hell* cycle, it appears that the child protagonists are seeking to create a life in a world ruined by the chimera of continuous economic growth. Through mimicry and scavenging, they are pioneering new ways of thinking and acting. Their parasitic existence, much like a mushroom or fungus, is monitored by an entity also parasitic upon a world that lies in ruins.

9 At the time of writing (November 2020), the world is in the middle of a global health crisis due to the spread of Covid-19, the disease caused by a new coronavirus, SARS-CoV-2. Like other coronaviruses, such as Sars and Mers, SARS-CoV-2 is a virus that jumped the species barrier.

10 Amitav Ghosh, *The Great Derangement: Climate Change and the Unthinkable* (Chicago: University of Chicago Press, 2016), 22.

11 Ghosh, 160.

incorporates clunky visual effects, committing to neither realism nor avant-gardism. Through the course of the project, linearity, indexicality, and causality are abandoned, destabilizing any sense that either an argument is being advanced or an interpretation of what is happening is even possible. This can create anxiety in the viewer, and even panic. Connections can be made between scenes, but these often seem accidental. In *Peggy and Fred in Hell: Folding* (1983–2015), a single-screen work that marked the culmination of this epic, signature cycle, Thornton created a piece that was both the enterprise's summation and its unraveling as a narrative proposition. Once *Peggy and Fred in Hell* neared completion, it became a kind of porous archive that informed and fed other works. A project that began in—and, in large part, was addressed toward—the information explosion, ends when we have drowned in data and false information is weaponized (by the right) as a bulwark against increasingly feeble attempts (from the center) to avert climate collapse.

Paradise Crushed (2003), a late episode in the cycle, begins with text scrolling across the screen, taken from a book on Zuni creation myths, and concludes with footage from a military source of two bombs being exploded. Thornton has inscribed the names "peggy" and "fred" next to each of the bombs, which reinforces the idea that the film's protagonists are ciphers rather than characters or "real" people. Thornton had also long since ceased filming the children—the footage she continued to edit and manipulate through the course of the project was shot between 1983 and 1990. On the soundtrack, we can just about discern a recording of a male voice introducing an interview conducted by a Sergeant Fujitani of a witness to the atomic bomb dropped on Hiroshima. The witness, Miss Palchikoff, offers harrowing testimony about the victims' fingernails: "I think if you pulled them, they just came off."[12] This section of the recording surfaces again in *Cut from Liquid to Snake*, made fifteen years later. A longer excerpt from the interview also features in *Let Me Count the Ways*, where Palchikoff's statements become increasingly contradictory and racist—she claims (falsely) that "not a single white person was injured in any way," and, more disturbingly, that the Japanese consider white people "a kind of God."

The use of the same material across different works to different effects reinforces the idea of porosity as a characteristic of Thornton's practice and also enables viewers to think about being historical subjects.[13] In her essay on *Let Me Count the Ways* in this volume, Rosalyn Deutsche notes that the aerial shots of New York City shown directly after this section and taken before September 11, 2001, reveal in the distance "a tiny World

Trade Center, the very buildings [...] whose fates challenge such a triumphalist discourse. With this shot, Thornton links the terror bombing of Hiroshima to the terrorist attacks on the Twin Towers."[14] For Deutsche, Thornton counters a kind of straightforward, antiwar, "heroic masculinism" with a more feminist attempt to render history as "subjective experience," which "simultaneously casts the artist and viewer as subjects in history."[15]

As we crept into the third decade of this new millennium, while fires raged across southeast Australia (causing one of the worst wildlife disasters in modern history), a virus that jumped the species boundary in China started to spread across the world. These catastrophes, if not directly caused by anthropogenic climate change, then exacerbated by it, are part of our everyday existence and no longer the preserve of science-fiction dystopias. Learning to live with and in the ruins of catastrophes—an endless parade of downturns—requires new skills and ways of thinking, quite possibly something other than the affirmative politics of the new materialists and posthumanists.[16] Thornton's work might present us with a way to think about our catastrophic present by submitting to rather than resisting catastrophic thinking.

Since 2016, the year after the completion of *Peggy and Fred in Hell*, the liberal center that, at the very least, offered some technocratic stability to society in the Global North has come under immense strain. The year 2016 could be seen as the point when liberalism, as an apolitical concept, finally imploded; when the idea that, no matter what political party was in power, certain institutions would endure because the rule of law and the constitution would be upheld crumbled to dust. This is also the year that the American Petroleum Institute finally removed from its website the claim that the human contribution to climate change was "uncertain," and journalists reported the highest monthly temperatures ever recorded on earth.[17]

Among the ruins of liberal democracy then, and in the shadow of corporate America's late and expedient acceptance of anthropogenic climate change, Thornton makes the film *Cut from Liquid to Snake*, which opens

12 Mrs. Kaleria Palchikoff Drago was interviewed years later, in 1994, for the project "Sound Portraits." She recalled that her parents—Russian anticommunists—moved to Japan in 1921 when she was three months old. Her father, Sergei Palchikoff, taught music at the American mission school in Hiroshima. They were living in Ushita, in the suburbs of Hiroshima, when the bomb exploded over the city. She was twenty-three years old when the United States Strategic Bombing Survey started conducting interviews on the streets of Hiroshima in the bomb's aftermath. Hers was the only English-language eyewitness account. See "Kaleria Palchikoff Drago, Witness to the Atom Bomb," Story Corps, https://storycorps.org/stories/kaleria-palchikoff-drago-witness-to-the-atom-bomb/.

13 This Foucauldian idea of the historical subject contrasts from and might even run counter to Deutsche's idea of a "subject in history," but a full exploration of the differences is beyond the scope of this essay.

14 Rosalyn Deutsche, "Love and Death," in this volume, 166–67.

15 Deutsche, 165.

16 Andreas Malm and others have begun to think about alternatives to the affirmative politics of new materialism through a critique of the new materialisms of Braidotti, Latour, et al., and propose a kind of restorative eco-Marxism. See Malm's *The Progress of this Storm*, *Fossil Capital: The Rise of Steam Power and the Roots of Global Warming* (New York: Verso, 2016) and *How to Blow up a Pipeline* (New York: Penguin, 2021), and the Salvage Collective's "The Tragedy of the Worker: Towards the Proletarocene," Salvage, January 31, 2020, https://salvage.zone/editorials/the-tragedy-of-the-worker-towards-the-proletarocene/.

17 Malm, *The Progress of this Storm, Fossil Capital*, 224.

with an overhead shot of (female) soldier ants captured in Los Alamos. On the audio track, we can hear a telephone conversation the artist had with a close friend on the morning that Donald Trump was elected president in 2016. We only hear Thornton's side of the conversation, and only in fits and starts. The gaps between her words have been removed to heighten the sense of alarm and anxiety. Trump's name is also removed because the expression here is of broader anxieties, rather than just a liberal sensitivity toward the trashing of political norms that typified Trump's ascendency and election victory.

Since the financial crash of 2008, and even before, the slow death (or mutation) of the neoliberal project collided with the rise of platform capitalism and network culture and provided cover for catastrophe without end. In 2016, the liberal howl of anguish at the chaos wrought by lurches toward right-wing nationalism on both sides of the Atlantic drew attention away from what was happening behind the scenes—a total transformation of the business of politics and the politics of business. *Cut from Liquid to Snake* connects that moment to past horrors. After the opening sequence, there is an interview with Thornton's aunt, who discusses familial links to the Manhattan Project, and in the final section, over an image of the La Brea Tar Pits in Los Angeles, we again hear the voice that ricochets through many of Thornton's works since 2000: Palchikoff's eyewitness account of the bombing of Hiroshima. This sequence also utilizes a formal device that Thornton has used before, first in the *Binocular Menagerie* series of works. An image is repeated across two apertures that appear side by side; on the left, we see the image *as it is*, and on the right, it is subjected to a kaleidoscopic digital effect, which renders it into visual shards and splinters. The artist has talked of wanting to create an "exotic environment of 'almost nature' [...] in which there is co-habitation of animal, machine, architecture and man."[18]

This uneasy cohabitation in Thornton's work is rendered dystopian because "almost nature" is not nature. In the face of climate breakdown and the collapse of the liberal center, a sense of powerlessness can produce a debilitating melancholy. In *Cut from Liquid to Snake*, Thornton both takes the *longue durée* and submits to panic. She catastrophizes the climate crisis but avoids submitting to or fostering lassitude—not by demanding that we (as individuals) change our behavior or revolt or protest, but simply that we (collectively) come together to bear witness. She asks that we pay attention to patterns of speech, changes in tone, shifts in atmosphere. She asks that, rather than search for the whole within the fragment or seek comfort within narrative continuity, we accept meaninglessness and face the horrors of the twenty-four-hour news cycle—not look away despondently with disgust. Thornton not only thinks catastrophically, but she also acts catastrophically—she purposefully blows apart a work, wills its destruction, opens it up to contagion by other works, courts misunderstanding, sends viewers down blind alleys, and resists growth and linearity as organizing principles.

In her 2009 book *In Catastrophic Times: Resisting the Coming Barbarism*, Isabelle Stengers writes of the importance of learning the art (rather than the science) of paying attention. Stengers questions the very foundations of Western rationality, which insists on development and growth. The fact that we know that "we are destroying to the point of scarcity resources constituted over the course of millions of years of terrestrial history"[19] yet still look away is a conundrum pondered by writers, philosophers, journalists, and political scientists for decades now. Stengers writes that "growth is a matter of what presides over everything else, including—we are ordered to think—the possibility of compensating for all the damage that is its price."[20] In this, she distinguishes the figure of the entrepreneur from Marx's capitalist. The entrepreneur insists on the freedom to gamble on the future, to "transform everything into an opportunity."[21] The entrepreneur has two enablers: the "State" and "Science"—Stengers gives Science a capital letter to distinguish it from "scientific practices."

In many of her works, Thornton traces this confrontation between scientific practices and Science back to its twentieth-century apotheosis—the construction and detonation of atom bombs over Hiroshima and Nagasaki. Both Thornton's father and grandfather worked on the Manhattan Project, initially unbeknownst to each other, and both apparently ignorant, at least to begin with, of the project's ultimate goal. Their earnest practice, rational at the level of means, was irrational at the level of political ends. In *Peggy and Fred in Hell*, these details are not encountered head-on, but in another open-ended constellation of fragmentary films, *Let Me Count the Ways*, the artist is more explicit. *Let Me Count the Ways* is a very different project to *Peggy and Fred*, though it shares some of the formal strategies of the earlier, and overlapping, project: the use of found footage, the disjunction between sound and image, and the abrupt switching between personal and scientific registers and between digitally manipulated found footage and verité footage shot by the artist herself. Although ostensibly autobiographical—in that it contains "found"

18 Leslie Thornton, "Binocular Menagerie," Electronic Arts Intermix, https://www.eai.org/titles/binocular-menagerie/ordering-fees.

19 Stengers, *In Catastrophic Times*, 61.

20 Stengers, 61.

21 Stengers, 65.

footage from her own family archive—Thornton's focus, as always, is on the apocalyptic and wide-ranging effects of an increasingly technologized media and military.

Divided into five episodes, normally shown sequentially as one work, *Let Me Count the Ways* begins with a countdown on the audio track ("Minus ten, nine, eight, seven, six, ...") and an interview between an investigator for the United States Strategic Bombing Survey and a Japanese survivor of Hiroshima, described in the records as a "woman of average intelligence." On the image track, we see US soldiers at Los Alamos and the Pacific island of Tinian shot on Super 16mm film—the footage, now kept in the Los Alamos National Laboratory Archive, was supplied by Gunnar Thornton, the artist's father, who features in these home movies. He is picked out on screen with the inscription "Dad," added by Thornton. This inscription of the autobiographical, argues Deutsche, inserts "subjectivity into the representation of the past and [undermines] our status as objective viewers."[22] This confluence of individual and collective histories merges the sociological and the psychoanalytical, "between the formation of subjectivity and the broader society."[23] By eschewing a more directly personal or diaristic register, Thornton creates a psychic space in which the viewer is unable to dissociate the personal from the sociopolitical. In *Minus 9*, she again recycles the Palchikoff interview. This time, it plays out over an image of a blue disk, which suggests, for Deutsche, that, "despite the vicissitudes of memory, the vision of America's action in Hiroshima persists; like an afterimage, its consequences are inescapable."[24]

The *Minus 8* episode of *Let Me Count the Ways* marries images of plants slowly unfurling, cribbed from the Department of Educational Talking Pictures, with extracts from John Hersey's *Hiroshima* (1946). Hersey's words describe the return of flora and fauna that colonize the city's ruins: "Weeds already hid the ashes, and wildflowers were in bloom among the city's bones. The bomb had not only left the underground organs of plants intact; it had stimulated them." Other writers have made the possibly apocryphal claim that the first flora to grow in the ashes after the Hiroshima atom bomb was a matsutake mushroom. Whether true or not, the image provides Tsing, in her book *The Mushroom at the End of the World*, with a powerful metaphor for growth after the end of growth. For Tsing, harnessing the atom and unleashing its dreadful power was both the culmination of the dream to control nature and the unraveling of that dream.

Western governments in the twentieth century promised stability through constant development and growth, but unfettered capitalism brought precarity and environmental destruction on a massive scale. "On the one hand," Tsing writes, "no place in the world is untouched by that global political economy built from the postwar development apparatus. On the other, even as the promises of development still beckon, we seem to have lost the means."[25] In our own moment, emerging from a global pandemic with environmental collapse at our doorstep and precarity the norm, Thornton's works, like Tsing's matsutake, take root in destroyed, exploited landscapes among collapsing systems and provide us with the opportunity to explore and better understand the present and future ruins that we may have to call home. Like her protagonists in *Peggy and Fred in Hell*, Thornton is forever sifting through her own fragmentary archive, trying to make sense of the past in order to construct a path through the present. Or, as with Benjamin's destructive character, she reduces what exists to rubble, "not for the sake of the rubble, but for that of the way leading through it."[26]

22 Deutsche, "Love and Death," 164.

23 Rosalyn Deutsche, "Leslie Thornton," in *Hiroshima after Iraq: Three Studies in Art and War* (New York: Columbia University Press, 2010), 39.

24 Deutsche, 48.

25 Tsing, "Prologue," in *The Mushroom at the End of the World*, 3.

26 Benjamin, *Selected Writings*, 542.

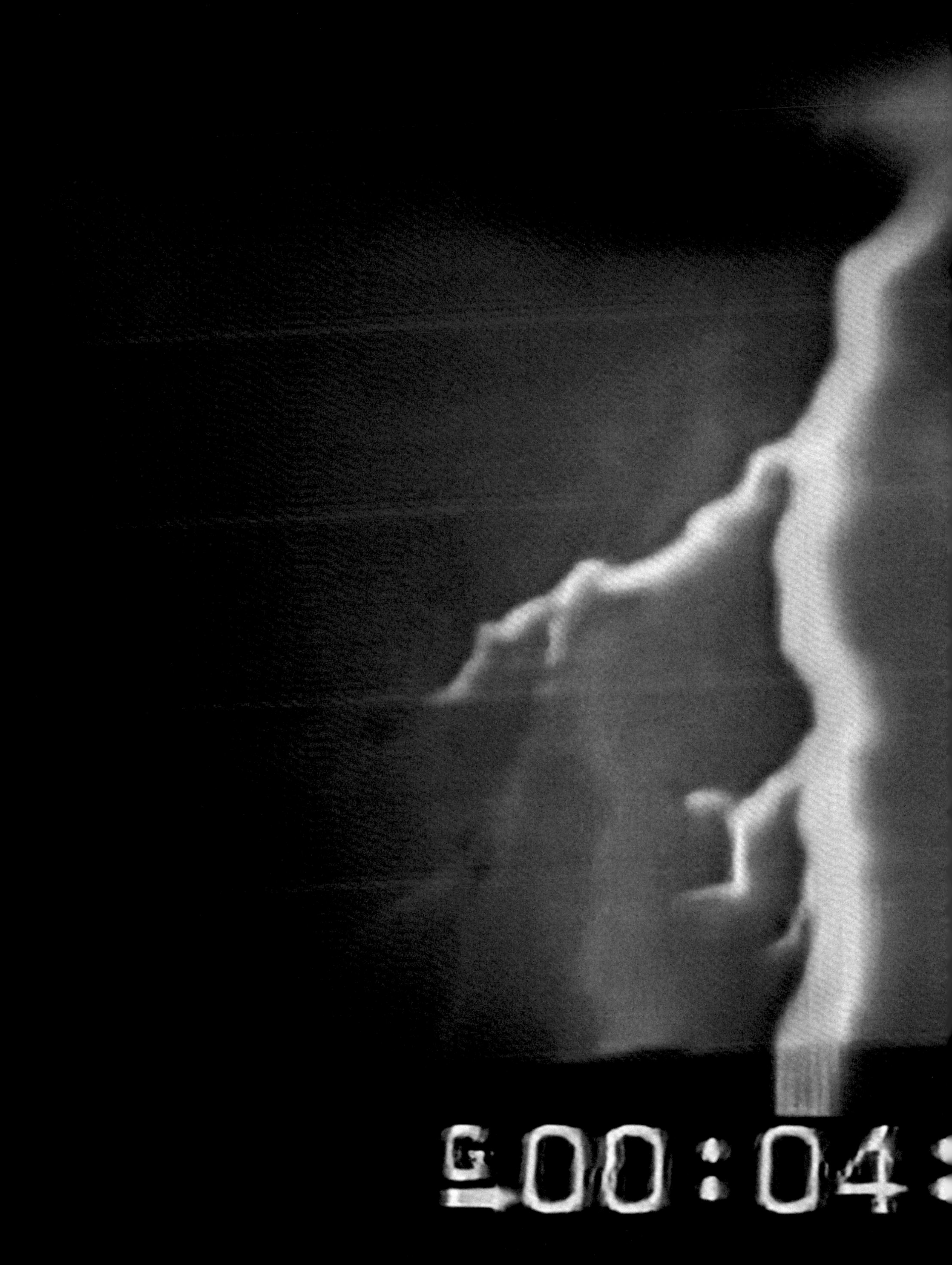
G00:04

40:04

No Romance

Milan Ther and Leslie Thornton in Conversation

Milan Ther Throughout the four decades of work presented in your Kunstverein Nürnberg and MIT List Center exhibitions, there has been a persistent thread: an interest in science, language, and the formation of knowledge. *Ground* [2020] was largely shot at CERN, the mechanical world of the European Organization for Nuclear Research. How did you end up there?

Leslie Thornton There are stories that are too big to believe. Like when you learn that your father, a young technician in the army during World War II, signed the atomic bomb that was dropped on Hiroshima. People used to sign bombs, and he was told to erase the signatures right before the atomic bomb was loaded onto the *Enola Gay*. He did this with a soldering iron and then put his own name along with his mother's and father's names—who were involved with the Manhattan Project in different ways (my grandmother's participation was as someone who worried about the silence of her husband and son).

I first went to CERN because of an anecdote about Val Fitch, an American nuclear physicist who was awarded the Nobel Prize in Physics in 1980 (along with his coresearcher James Cronin). Using a linear particle accelerator, they proved in 1964 that certain subatomic reactions do not adhere to fundamental symmetry principles (calling it CP violation), thus upsetting a foundation of physics that natural laws are governed by symmetry. This is what the scientist in *Ground* is talking about and why we sought him out. We wanted to meet someone at CERN who was willing to talk about Fitch's work—not so much because I was interested in or understood the science particularly, but because of a story Fitch tells about how he came to be a physicist.

My father, who was Norwegian, was an avid skier, and when he was working as an engineer in Los Alamos during World War II, he was in a ski club that included some of the renowned physicists. Val Fitch, a young chemist, arrived at Los Alamos at the same time. As Fitch relates it, he grew keen to meet the European physicists, and one way this could happen, since they tended to keep to themselves, was to go skiing on the mountain slopes near the Los Alamos facility. In his own narrative, learning to ski from his Norwegian friend helped open the door to his future life in physics.

Val Fitch, quoting Lewis Thomas—whose essays on science could just as well speak of art—has described his vocation as follows: "You measure the quality of the work by the intensity of the astonishment."

MT So it was also the personal genesis—their interests, motivations, and rationales behind becoming scientists—that interested you?

LT Yes, to some extent, but *Ground* goes beyond any personal, romantic vision into a much bigger, suggestive space that I am currently engaging. In a way, it is about nothing, but it's also *not* about nothing. The effort is to manifest that which is *nearly* not there, unknown and knowable, simultaneously. There is believed to be a particle; physics does that. There is perceived to be a person; we do that.

What I found affecting in the scientist depicted in *Ground* is that he moves fluidly between outlining the scientific research he has conducted—talking about how hard it is to pull off these kinds of esoteric, no-guarantee projects—and also speaks about moments of inspiration, often in dark moments ... in the middle of the night. And he is so proud of the fact that people from all over the world work together in science. There is joy in his voice when he is talking about the collaborative nature of the work at CERN, which is a tremendous break from what we usually hear transpires between countries and in politics—that is, conflict, repression, ignorance, and greed. Truth is not stable, and that is profoundly the case in science and part of what draws me to it and the people I have met this year. They are so passionate, concrete, honest, and not afraid to try, experiment, and be wrong. And then, to go on.

Ground seems to teeter on an apocalyptic precipice. When it was first presented in public at Kunstverein Nürnberg in late February 2020, we were heading into the Covid-19 cataclysm, and it absorbed this specific reference.

MT Your film series *Peggy and Fred in Hell* [1983–2015] features two children, initially in a bunker-like, postapocalyptic space. The audience doesn't know where they are or why they are there. Their link to the "outside" world is through mimicking television. Somehow, the world of Peggy and Fred seems connected to the universe of CERN...

LT I do think of *Ground* as related to *Peggy and Fred*. In part, this is a structural relationship because I'm entering another cycle of works that also feels like it will be cumulative over time. I have the same feeling I had when I began *Peggy and Fred*—of exploring a very open, broad terrain.

I'm going to stick my neck out now and tell you the backstory I had in mind when shooting and finally completing *Peggy and Fred in Hell*. It's not particularly evident in the film itself, and any aficionado of science fiction would see it as well-trodden territory. *Peggy and Fred* can't be unraveled into a linear, speculative fantasy. And it is not fiction; it's something else—though it does have a somewhat narrative engine operating over the whole of it. I'm making a distinction between fiction and narrative here. For me, fiction relates more to constructing a story, and narrative relates more to rhetoric, form, and the devices used to configure or propel a story.

Peggy and Fred in Hell ends beyond apocalypse, if what we care about is all forms of carbon-based life. In the end—and this is why I was able to finally say the work was complete—the machines (that we have made) fail, close, shut down. People, represented by the children, died long before that. It is in the final episode, *The Fold*, that the suggestion for what caused the penultimate desolation occurs; it's in the last line: "Oh, the storm!" It occurs when the earth is drained of all resources. Maybe this happens thousands of years in the future. Machines can be smart, but even they have their limits. By eating up the last resources to keep running, they eat themselves up. Eat themselves alive.

Peggy and Fred in Hell: Folding ends on a bittersweet note. The AI voice that started entering the scenario about two-thirds of the way through the film is benign, even comforting, but not in a familiar, domestic, Alexa™ sort of way. It's something more like the opposite of HAL in Stanley Kubrick's *2001: A Space Odyssey*. It is intelligent enough to have developed an appreciation of the human. It has studied human emotion for a long, long time, and because the humans have died off, this AI hasn't been monetized into producing predictive algorithms. Rather, it keeps learning by watching television (and subsequent media)—the peculiar place where the thing called "human" can be observed and data processed.

It feels like these two works speak to each other, like they come from a contiguous space, as if *Ground* is a grown-up, present-day landscape of hope yet with ominous, apocalyptic threads; as if *Peggy and Fred* is now a substrate, where there is still light ... and it is bound to the earth, and we can touch it. We can imagine the world of those young people (at least in the first half of the film). We can relate to them as subjects.

MT Being more than thirty years in the making, how clear was the ending of *Peggy and Fred* when you began the project in 1983? How did the different episodes influence the overall structure, and how did you approach each episode?

LT When I met the real children, what was extraordinary was that they were gifted, natural mimics. They saw my equipment as I was moving into the apartment downstairs from them, and they wanted to record their voices right away. So, we just sat down on the front steps, and they began performing—they were incredible. The young boy liked to mimic Jack Nicholson, and they could both repeat long sequences from their favorite films. But they also just told stories—kind of like summer camp and bible school stories, the sort told around the campfire. Their real names are Donald and Janis. I wasn't used to being around children, and I was very taken by the mannerisms of their speech. I loved how they related to language. It was so vivid observing how they were becoming social beings; in their exposure to media and social exchange, you could just feel them becoming the subjects they were going to become. I didn't have children, so it was, perhaps, especially salient and present. When I began filming, this is what I looked for. I didn't want to interfere with their feelings of autonomy and space because I needed to hear them just being themselves in an environment that allowed for their own comfort. It needed to stay in a play-like context, and it felt like "serious" play when we agreed to film that first day—it was fun for all of us.

In the first episode, which focuses strongly on the voice and speaking, I asked them both to sing a song. Fred starts singing and doesn't stop. The longest take one can make when shooting on 16mm film is eleven minutes, so every second counts, but I couldn't stop filming because he didn't stop singing! What was so enchanting was that he was six years old here. He didn't know all the words or even the meaning when he was singing about lovers, for instance. He gets the words wrong. They are deformed, nonsensical, but they hold place as a bridge to keep singing.

When babies are born, their crying is symmetrical. When it is recorded, it sounds exactly the same whether running backward or forward. At about a month, you can hear a change in direction: vocalization becoming linear, giving it a shape. What is apparent in Fred's singing is a latent trace of this linguistic dissymmetry. Peggy is older, and she has a different self-awareness in her singing.

As the series progressed, I began to introduce a more eccentric, less linear form of cutting. This first occurs in the episode *Dung Smoke Enters the Palace.* The last linear passage occurs at the beginning of the episode *Paradise Crushed*, in the form of an amalgamation of mythological origin stories drawn from diverse cultures—from the Bible to early Chinese, Indo-European, Semitic, and Native American tales. All of these accounts contain floods and light. This passage occurs toward the middle of the work and is, ironically, the most linear and coherent narrative moment. After this, the rational configuration collapses. There is more fragmentation, discontinuity, and enigma; there is a growing sense of another presence, a different mentality; the children begin to dissolve into an incoherence. It's the first time the logic of the work completely changes, and there is no return to stable ground. *Paradise Crushed* was made in the aftermath of 9/11. Around this point, my own sense of *Peggy and Fred in Hell* as science fiction dropped away. It became more like a disturbed reflection of the present.

MT In *Jennifer, Where Are You?* [1981], you also worked with a child, younger than Fred or Peggy. What kind of relationship does Jennifer have to the camera and the voice from offstage?

LT Jennifer, whom we assume to be the child we are seeing, is voiceless. Her power lies in the fact that she is hidden. She is playing, even being naughty, and she is out of sight. As the film progresses, other forces enter, at times quite literally. We see that she is handed matches. Again and again. It is not her space anymore. She grows depleted as the larger world seems to play out around her. Even though we hear a man's voice repeatedly calling for her, she is, at first, fine and has her own imaginary space, which she maintains, and then she does not. I saw this film as being about coming of age and becoming conscious of the outside world. That was the narrative for me. Her moment of consciousness comes in the last few seconds, when she stares back—hard—at the flame. She gets it. She is gaining another level of awareness, an awareness that includes surviving. To be somewhat colloquial: she goes through her teens! It's tough. And she will probably survive. That's the allegory of the film, for me, at least. Of course, it's doing a lot of other things as well, formally, structurally.

MT How do you think language relates to the process of becoming a subject?

LT What first occurs to me in trying to respond to this question is a memory of my own nascent, idiosyncratic awareness of language as a child. And years later, this perception became a core part of my work. I seem to have a way of witnessing speech—which is the best way to say it—that is pretty primal, and it is absolutely central in my work. It is there in *X-TRACTS* [1975], in *Jennifer*, in almost everything except the *Binocular Menagerie* series [2010–14]. And if speech ever became absolutely, almost frighteningly, dominant, it is in *Ground*. We cannot own that speech—the speaker can; we can't. We can't consume or possess it. We can barely understand him, except for his anecdotal comments. It's a real display of modes of address. And all of it is intensified by what is removed or taken away, which is the sense of a physical context. Isn't that like this digital world that thrives around us every minute?

But this figure is not a thief. He seems quite wonderful to me, in fact, but we can't fully apprehend him, and that becomes part of the conscious experience of the work. It is not our space, and we may feel compelled, disturbed, and/or comforted by his words and his demeanor of speaking and that we are in a place of absolute otherness. What is that place? Well, for one thing, it is trying to imagine the unimaginable—the origin of the universe, a pandemic, an apocalypse, our survival, a nice guy, passion, cooperation. Not isolation, not competition. It is a terribly human space, in a way that we can feel but not occupy. It does not yield to the viewer. For me, it creates both a feeling of longing and fear. I thought I was making a film about an apocalypse at first, and it became a film about trying. Not erasing. And all of the hope is in the voice. Nowhere else.

MT Where does the footage in your films come from?

LT I shoot most of the material myself. A lot of people think I use found footage, but I am always producing my own "archive," and it is composed of material I film myself. I create a pool of material, and sometimes it's very focused, like in *Peggy and Fred in Hell*. There are no accidents in the filming. There is a certain kind of behavior I look for, and I keep the camera running for that. Because it's expensive to shoot on film, and almost all of *Peggy and Fred* was shot on 16mm film, one has to be very discerning, and even careful, while filming, and this affects the form. I also work in a deliberate way with appropriated material. In *The Prologue*, there are a number of appropriated sounds and images. The opening shot of vocal cords, for example, was filmed at Bell Labs in 1926. I found it in an archive and had it copied. Ironically, it's silent. The opening vocalization is of two women's voices, one from Handel's opera *Rinaldo* and, mixed over that, a song by Yma Sumac, who was an American singer with a range of seven octaves. In the next scene, a voice-over asks what the preferred pitch is for men's and women's voices. I pitch-shifted the male voice down, making it deeper, lower, exaggerated, and more ominous. The female voice was already squeaky and high, so I left it as it was.

MT Voices seem to have the ability to rupture linear time in your work. While the image moves forward, voices can appear fractured and disconnected, sometimes non-diegetically, but also in relation to the physical act of speaking, like in *Cut from Liquid to Snake* [2018]...

LT In *Cut from Liquid to Snake*, there is a passage in the soundtrack that was first recorded on the morning that Donald Trump's election to presidency of the United States was announced. It's from a phone conversation with a friend who usually has a broad historical take on things, and often, I would call him at stressful times. All I did to that material was leave his side of the conversation out—chronologically ordered, it is one side of a phone call. I edited out a few lines, mainly the word "Trump." In retrospect, I would say there was even a prescience about wiping out that word. I didn't want to pronounce that name; I didn't want to give it any more power. I was marking a crisis, and to a US audience, the reference was clear, at least at the time. What I felt and wanted to establish was that this was a crisis of an unprecedented, terrifying, unpredictable nature. In this soundtrack, you hear me talking about how we were watching television in the middle of the night. And then something happened, and it felt like a conspiracy, because the television feed cut out exactly at the moment the election results were announced, at 3:25 a.m. Did that just happen in my house, my street, in New York City, or was it everywhere? It was so precise; was it intentional? What had happened? *Cut from Liquid to Snake* registers the anxiety of an isolated voice.

In the history of my work, this project was a major turning point. There is no escape in *Cut from Liquid* from a kind of horror or breakdown. If there is a moment of hope, it is in the conversation about thought. I felt a great sense of responsibility in making this work. As someone who has been working in a way that you can't pin down too tightly, this was a more direct sounding of an alarm. *Cut from Liquid* constructs an environment of trepidation and apprehension. It also addresses a historic moment of great horror—the deployment of the atomic bombs.

When a media work is made for looping in an installation context, something interesting can happen as one watches through more than a single cycle. In the case of *Cut from Liquid*, a shift occurs, such that the historical material seems to get drawn into our present. The woman speaking about secrecy is my aunt, who is reminiscing about my father, grandfather, World War II, and the atomic bomb. Her memory is resonant with current nuclear concerns.

Cut from Liquid leads directly into *Ground*. *Ground* looks like an abyss, but the inflection of the primary voice—the dimension brought forward in this more or less unedited, linear commentary—

is so far-ranging and such a detailed representation of the work that this scientist and his research group have been doing, it almost feels like ideas coming to you in the middle of the night, ideas that rouse you but you can barely decipher. The voice can't be located in a natural body—his figure is rendered as waveforms, a wireframe schematic, a diagram that loosely follows the form of a real body. However, as you hear his voice, there is some solace in that presence. If *Cut from Liquid* addresses only a darkness, an end of days, in *Ground*, you may feel hope; there are people who are trying to figure things out. You think, "Thank goodness someone is trying." And without meaning to, this directly attaches to the current circumstances surrounding the coronavirus pandemic. Furthermore, to carry that identification along, we do not see these people; they seldom appear in the media frontline, but we know they are there.

When I made *Ground*, I was worried. I didn't—still don't—want this to be a negative image, and I am not sure whether or not it is. At the same time, there is an element of nihilism to it. *Ground* is beyond our capacities, more like a video game on the surface, perhaps. I don't know. I'm not sure what it is. I feel like it's nothing, but there's still a gesture in there, in a man's voice, to hold onto. But the experience of it should be like nothing. Beguiling, a somewhat startling image, a sense of movement through an unseen space, but little to retain past the moment of sitting there. Nothing to take away, no resonance, mostly noise if it leaves any trace in the memory. Because it feels so far away, when actually watching the piece, it can be particularly engaging in those few minutes. That longing for meaning, understanding can set in. Or maybe it's not that deep, but we want our minds to be occupied somehow. And it is erased once we walk away, like most of what we see in our world. Except this is/was done on purpose. This is an artwork doing its particular work. It's supposed to self-annihilate. That's what this artwork is meant to do.

MT You utilize abstraction but also grids to organize visual elements, like *Strange Space* [1993] and *The Last Time I Saw Ron* [1995]. The main scientist in *Ground* is translated into some form of visualized radiation, wavelength, or frequency. It is as if the grid has come alive and broken up the spatial regression...

LT When I began working as an artist, I was painting, and I was organizing paint into gridlike structures. I played back and forth between measured forms—a grid or a rectangle within a rectangle—and the fluidity and gestural materiality of the medium. Within the grids, there were dashes of color, dripping paint, textures from the brush—in excess of the pattern holding the whole together. I was working between an analytical sensibility and a joyous, excessive exploration, using the same material. Coming from that orientation, making a film like *X-TRACTS* (my first film, made with Desmond Horsfield) was perfectly consistent and made complete sense: the precise structure of images, shots, and sequences was like a net, catching the unruliness, patterns, and excesses of life.

In later works, the relations between structure or framework and living/being become even more complicated and subtle. Bringing in the gridlines in *Strange Space* is, on one level, an instruction on how to look, a reference to a scientific eye. In *Strange Space*, the grid is laid over NASA documentary footage of the moon and outtakes. In superimposing the grid over NASA footage, you are being asked to be more cognizant of what you are seeing. There is an inference of the analytical eye, of the objective medical gaze. This is the strange space.

MT In this selection of films, there are different ways in which music has been deployed. In *Jennifer, Where Are You?*, the music is almost painful and foreign to the image, a force upon the character, while in *The Last Time I Saw Ron*, the music by Richard Strauss is genuinely beautiful and very close to him. In *Ground*, I get the feeling that the music is very digital—like listening to the metaphoric sound of data.

LT In *Jennifer*, I am using it as "movie music," as "upping the ante" of effect. However, I am not making a narrative film, and that is significant. I may use music or sound as a manipulation, like in a conventional narrative film, where it is an additional layer outside of speech and plot that underscores an emotional register. In my detournement of movie music, what I want, on some level, is for you to stick around. I use some of the tropes of conventional cinema to intensify engagement. It is an instance of my thievery from the norms of dominant forms of cinematic storytelling. I also play with continuity in editing. In *The Last Time*

I Saw Ron, it's music as music. It's with him, with Ron. In *Ground*, the music is meant to drive a visceral overload. What the feminine voice is referencing, while that frenetic music plays, is absolutely phenomenal: it is the locus of data processing at CERN. It feels like things are getting faster and faster, to the brink of failure, yet she is speaking in real time. The only thing that speeds up and grows in density is the music under her voice. It makes our hearts beat faster. It's a metaphoric, rhetorical use of sound design to intensify the mass and velocity of information being processed.

MT So there are ways in which the music establishes different proximities to the material. There is also another formal decision that appears in your work: the inverted use of black-and-white film.

LT It denaturalizes the image so that focus shifts to another register. It's a few steps before turning an image into waves, noise. These are strategies, just like using my own persona on occasion. I don't make works about "me"—this is only a "way in." It's a deliberate manipulation, as is the use of "movie music." It's in quotation. It's also not hidden. I am interested in performance; the figure is a construction. I don't work with actors—when a version of "Leslie Thornton" appears, there is an immediacy, and it is expedient in establishing a site of vulnerability and perspective. In *X-TRACTS*, there is the line: "Of necessity, I become an instrument." I use myself as an instrument. It is not about the drama of my personal history; I don't like that. There is no romance in this.

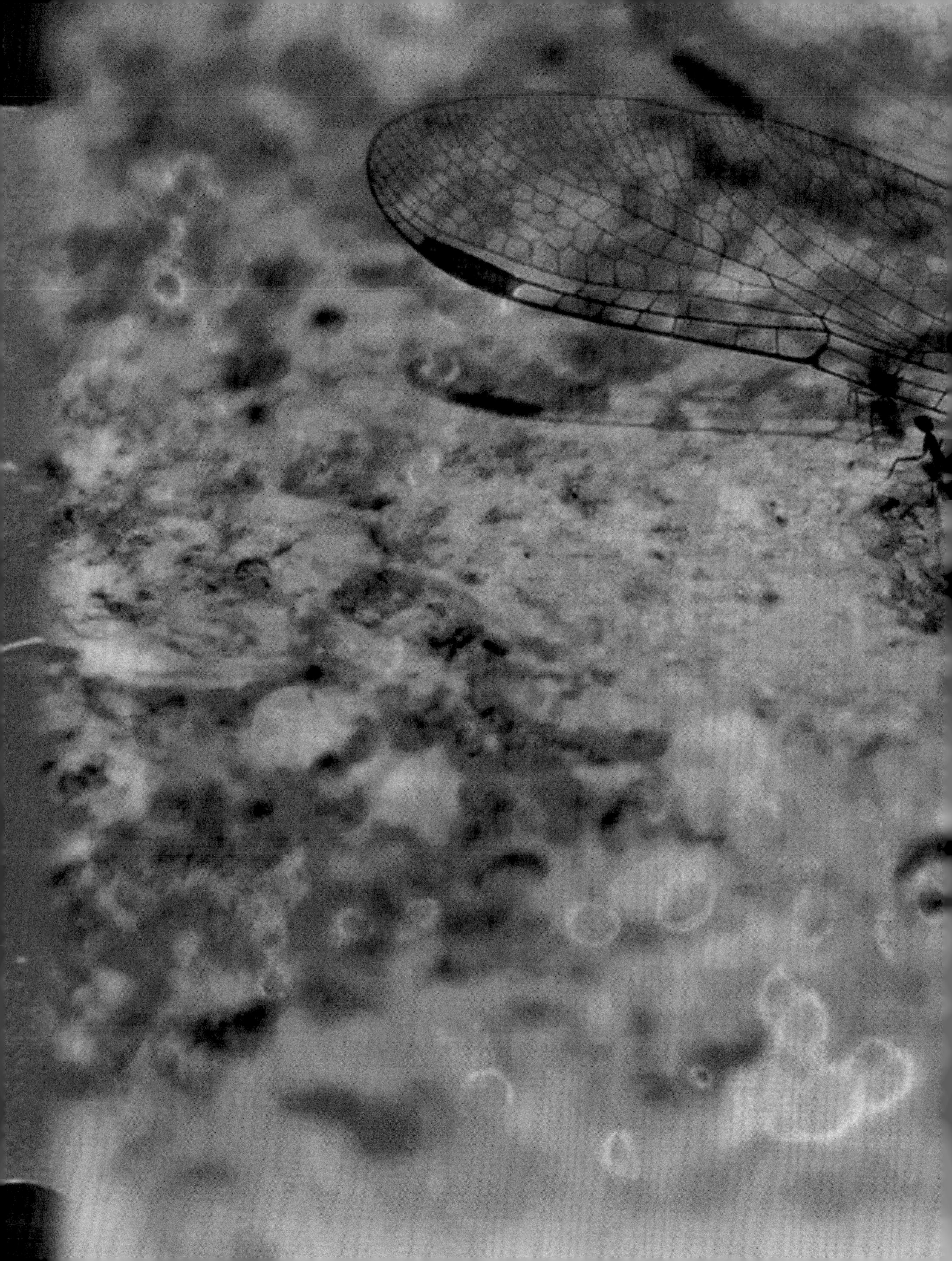

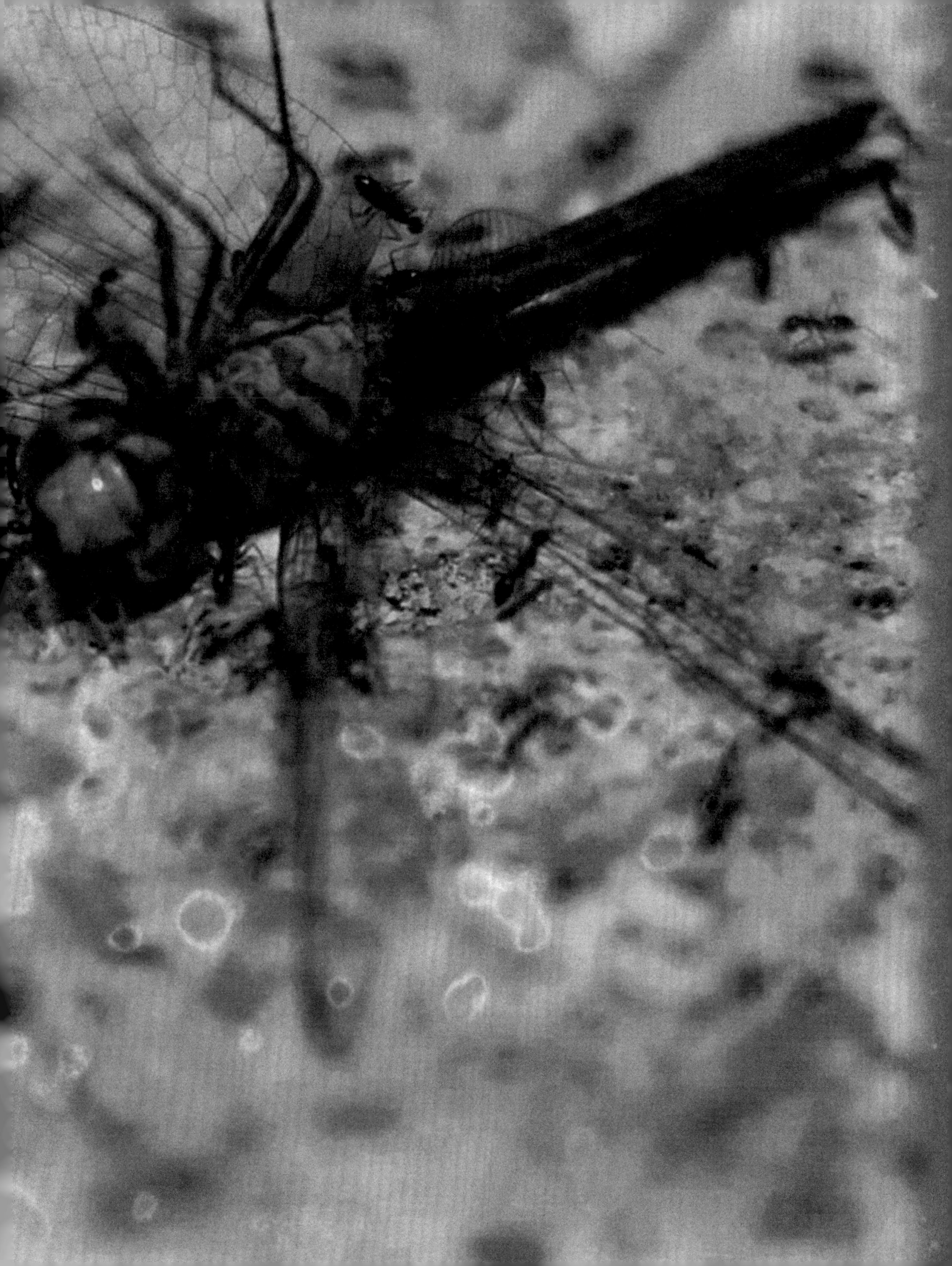

Where Does the "I" End?

Chrissie Iles on *X-TRACTS*

In 1975, Leslie Thornton made her first film, *X-TRACTS*, an enigmatic black-and-white composition whose rigorous conceptual inquiry into the conditions of representation is structured through an elusive staging of the self. Filmed that winter in collaboration with her fellow student Desmond Horsfield[1] in their rural home outside Hartford, Connecticut, the piece was generated as "a structural or indexical system of sound/image relations."[2] As Thornton explains:

> For the image we created a gridded score of movements, both within the frame ("subject moves right to left") and between the camera and the subject (zooms, pans, tilts...,) using this as a shooting script. The sound was derived from an old journal, read out loud and then cut-up into the same units of time as the image, ranging from 3 seconds to 1/4 second. Assembling the material was largely mechanical, following the predetermined score. That a tonal portrait of a person emerges was an after effect; [...] and [we] viewed the soundtrack as a linguistic experiment, working with the building blocks of speech.[3]

Every element of *X-TRACTS* demonstrates an operation of this indexical system, starting with the opening section of the film, in which a dark screen is accompanied by a male voice counting from one to six at three-second intervals. This slows down and reverses the direction of the countdown leader that typically precedes a film and obliterates the numbers that announce the beginning of the narrative. Instead, the disembodied voice is identifying the six sections that structure the film, of which this is the first. The black screen prevents one of the primary purposes of the countdown leader—the synchronization of sound and image—thus introducing not the film itself but the material process by which its conceptual meaning is formed.

The verbal counting continues, drawing our attention to the material and conceptual site of the film's production as its content. This time, in the only synchronization of sound and image that occurs in *X-TRACTS*, each number is matched with a close-up shot of Thornton's naked body: pubic hair ("one"), thigh ("two"), foot ("three"), back ("four"), knees, and torso. The segment introduces the eroticized female body as the tool by which filmic coherence is gauged, with Thornton's body arguably standing in for the ubiquitous Girl Head or China Girl, an image of a white woman, absent in the final film print, against which film laboratories measure correct contrast, color, chemical balance, and general quality control. Coupled with the mechanical counting, each image of Thornton's body confronts how, as Genevieve Yue argues of the China Girl, "the woman's vanishing into sheer materiality is necessary to the transformation of her into an instrument fundamental to the operation of the film

1 A British artist with a BA in sculpture and film, attending art school at Leicester, Norwich, and Wolverhampton Universities.

2 Leslie Thornton, "X-TRACTS," Letterboxd, accessed April 9, 2021, https://letterboxd.com/film/x-tracts/.

3 Thornton, "X-TRACTS."

4 Genevieve Yue, "Introduction," in *Girl Head: Feminism and Film Materiality* (New York: Fordham University Press, 2020), 3.

5 Yue, 5.

laboratory."[4] This, Yue proposes, renders the China Girl "a pre-representational image. [...] It imports gender into the film image before representation ever occurs."[5]

The six shots of Thornton's body occupy a similar status, embedded within the film's "leader," until, at the fourth image, her voice utters a phoneme—the smallest unit of sound—right after the male voice's declarative "four," and just before the fourth image moves on to the fifth. This linguistic signal evokes the "2-pop" in film production—a beeping tone one frame long, inserted at the end of the countdown leader, which allows the alignment of image and sound to be checked during the making of the film print. In *X-TRACTS*, the tone emanates from the artist's body as a fragment of speech, underscoring Yue's argument regarding the inscription of the female body into the materiality of film production. But here, the artist's voice signals not alignment but separation, in a rupture that punctures that inscription. Right after Thornton's utterance, the male voice disappears, and her body begins to move, rolling away from the camera as if refusing its gaze and shifting from a passive to an active performative presence, opening up a literal and associative space in which her body shifts from object into subject, transitioning from materiality into representation.

After her body turns, Thornton can be heard uttering the word "breathe," and from this point on, she takes control of that representation in a series of actions scored for the camera, each edited according to the strictly controlled timing of the gridded score. Her movements fall into four loose groupings: staged gestures, ordinary actions, close-ups of her face, and extended movements. In each section of the film, clusters from each grouping are edited together. In the second section, for example, rapid edits show fragments from the artist's daily life—getting out of the bath, sitting with her left foot resting on her right knee, reading, sitting cross-legged on the bed. These quotidian domestic scenes are followed by a more staged sequence, in which she appears in a dress wearing lipstick, raises her arms, and leans over from the left of the frame to kiss an unknown man with his hands behind his head. The kiss is filmed through a window, indicated by the glint of light on the surface of the glass. This shot is immediately followed by a close-up of her face on the right of the frame, her left hand holding a camera lens that she moves slowly downward, away from her closed eye.

The following section consists almost exclusively of close-ups of Thornton's face from different angles and in different light exposures, smiling, smoking, talking, looking downward, pensively into the distance, through her hair, or seductively at the camera. Some of the randomly collaged soundtrack fragments matched to these images include references to the self: "Sometimes I..." / "entering my..." / "to be contained..." / "thought that I'd be frozen." A sequence of sweeping movements of the camera follows, panning, zooming, and tilting upward, filming Thornton in chairs, surrounded by plants, against a window blind, framed from a distance through a doorway, wrapped in a shawl, talking, petting the dog, unpinning a large Warhol poster from the wall, and walking across the kitchen.[6] Throughout these sequences, the author of the gaze remains ambiguous; Thornton positions herself as subject whilst simultaneously staging herself as an object of desire and loving observation.

After a sequence filmed outside in which Thornton appears walking down a snowy lane, the final chapter displays a rapid-fire, barely legible montage of earlier gestures, before the film ends abruptly, as though mid-sentence. This progression is mirrored in the soundtrack, which shifts from a syncopated rhythm of disconnected words and phrases to indecipherable syllables and, as the interval between each grows

6 Pinned to the wall next to the large-format practice silkscreen print by Warhol is a small hand-printed photograph of a woman in a wooly hat, holding an open book. The photograph reappears two more times in increasing close-up, so quickly that it is almost as if a photographic record of the soundtrack's original recording had been subliminally embedded. Another enigma occurs in the presence of a third person throughout the film; the man kissed by Thornton appears outside the doorway through which she is being filmed, sits next to her, deep in conversation, and stands by her side as she is filmed through an open window. He could also be the male voice counting to six at the beginning of the film with an American accent—Horsfield is British and only arrived in the US the year before.

shorter, occasional words punctuated by silence.[7] Yet, throughout the film, Thornton's halting speech, with its interrupted sentences, half-completed words, morphemes, and other tiny linguistic sounds, proceeds in a sustained flow of subtle intelligibility, despite being filtered through three sets of intervals. One is between the sounds themselves, one created by the decoupling of Thornton's speech from her image, and the third by the gap between her audible words and the ones she speaks silently on-screen, since, in almost half the film, she is talking. Even when she is not talking on-screen, her voice can be heard on the soundtrack; apart from the beginning of the film, she is never not speaking. That her audible speech is a cut-up of her private journal whilst her filmed conversation is muted underscores the creative process, and not the artist, as the subject of the film. Midway, with her eyes closed, she speaks the only complete phrase in the film: "I / of / necessity / have become / an instrument."

Thornton's translation of her journal notes into aural fragments disperses traces of an earlier stage of her creative thinking across the surface of the film as material:

> Left to right...interrelated...of the material...all that red has... / darkness...implied movement... to be contained...a self-successive moment...in myself, each...speak only...feeling...and from and around and with...subtleties implicated... where does the "I" end...where is the language... darkness...syl / lable...ceremony...alone.

The translation of her thoughts into a collage of speech belies the influence of feminist linguistic theorists such as Hélène Cixous, Julia Kristeva, and Luce Irigaray. The latter's critique of masculine language systems calls for "an examination of the operation of the 'grammar' of each figure of discourse, its syntactic laws or requirements, its imaginary configurations, its metaphoric networks, and also, of course, what it does not articulate at the level of utterances: its silences."[8] To undo the erasure of women, one must "work at 'destroying' the discursive mechanism," which requires "a jamming of the theoretical machinery itself."[9]

The gaps between Thornton's words create the sensation of a hiccup occurring within the machinery of the film projector, as though from an irregularity in the material surface of the print. This rupture, caused by the translation of her writing into a randomly encoded spatial and linguistic alterity, opens up the film into what Giampaolo Bianconi has described as the conditions of an open site.[10] This openness is, by its nature, ambiguous, collaborative, nonhierarchical, and fluid, reflecting Thornton's self-described "refusal to be located."[11] It is also apparent in the film's title, in which one letter is missing and a gap is created by a connective hyphen, indicating the process by which Thornton's words, extracted from her private writing, have been further removed from their original source by their translation into the spoken and recorded word, and again by their random cutting into physical fragments, just as the film's images are extracted from a larger whole, reassembled, and reordered.

In *Glitch Feminism: A Manifesto*, Legacy Russell argues that "the glitch creates a fissure within which new possibilities of being and becoming manifest"[12] and "[celebrates] failure as a generative force."[13] Russell's arguments, addressing the contemporary, nonbinary Black body in digital space, resonate with the liberatory potential indicated in *X-TRACTS* by the falling apart of meaning that occurs through its conceptual, linguistic operations. Each fissure points to the gap and the fragment as a radical, generative space through which new futures can be built.

7 This dissonance evokes what Paul Sharits, Thornton's teacher at SUNY Buffalo's Department of Media Study, described in his own work as "a 'heterodyne effect' between vision and hearing—i.e. two separate systems which are similar enough in *structure* [...] so that when they are experienced together they 'interweave' into a new-emergent, percept-mixed 'whole.'" Sharits, letter to Klaus Kertess, 1971, in Melissa Ragona, "Water-to-Film, Image-to-Sound: Paul Sharits's 'Locational' Installations," in *Paul Sharits*, ed. Susanne Pfeffer (Kassel: Fridericianum and Walther König, 2015), 191. In Sharits's work, this occurs through a fusion between randomness and structure that is also present in *X-TRACTS*, in the random collaging of the soundtrack onto the predetermined score for the image.

8 Luce Irigaray, *This Sex Which Is Not One*, trans. Catherine Porter (Ithaca, NY: Cornell University Press, 1985), 75.

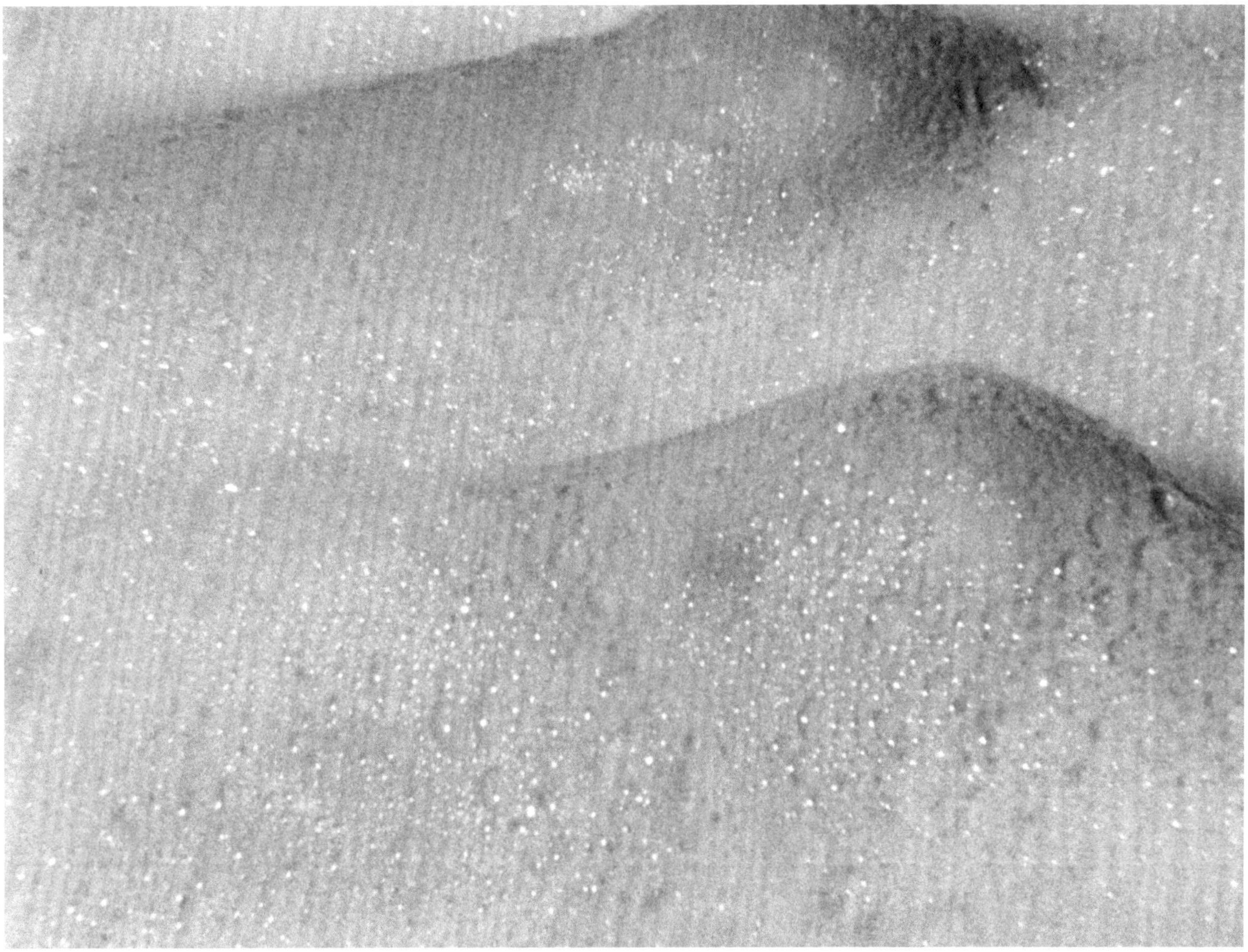

X-TRACTS, 1975

9 Irigaray, 78.

10 Giampaolo Bianconi, "Confusing Boundaries: Two Films by Leslie Thornton and Desmond Horsfield" (unpublished MA thesis, Columbia University, 2013), 23–24.

11 Jonathan Rosenbaum, "Leslie Thornton," in *Film: The Front Line 1983* (Denver: Arden Press, 1983), 202.

12 Legacy Russell, *Glitch Feminism: A Manifesto* (London: Verso, 2020), 11.

13 Russell, 28.

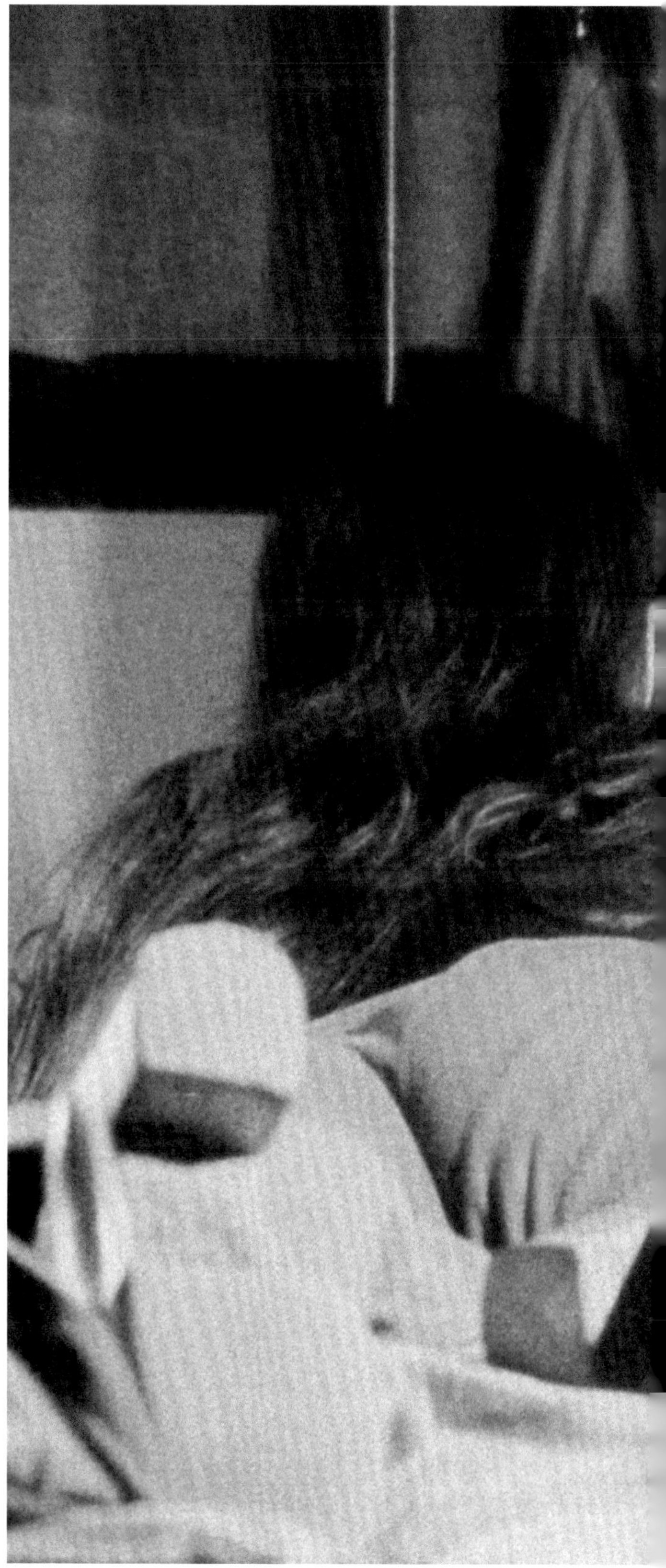

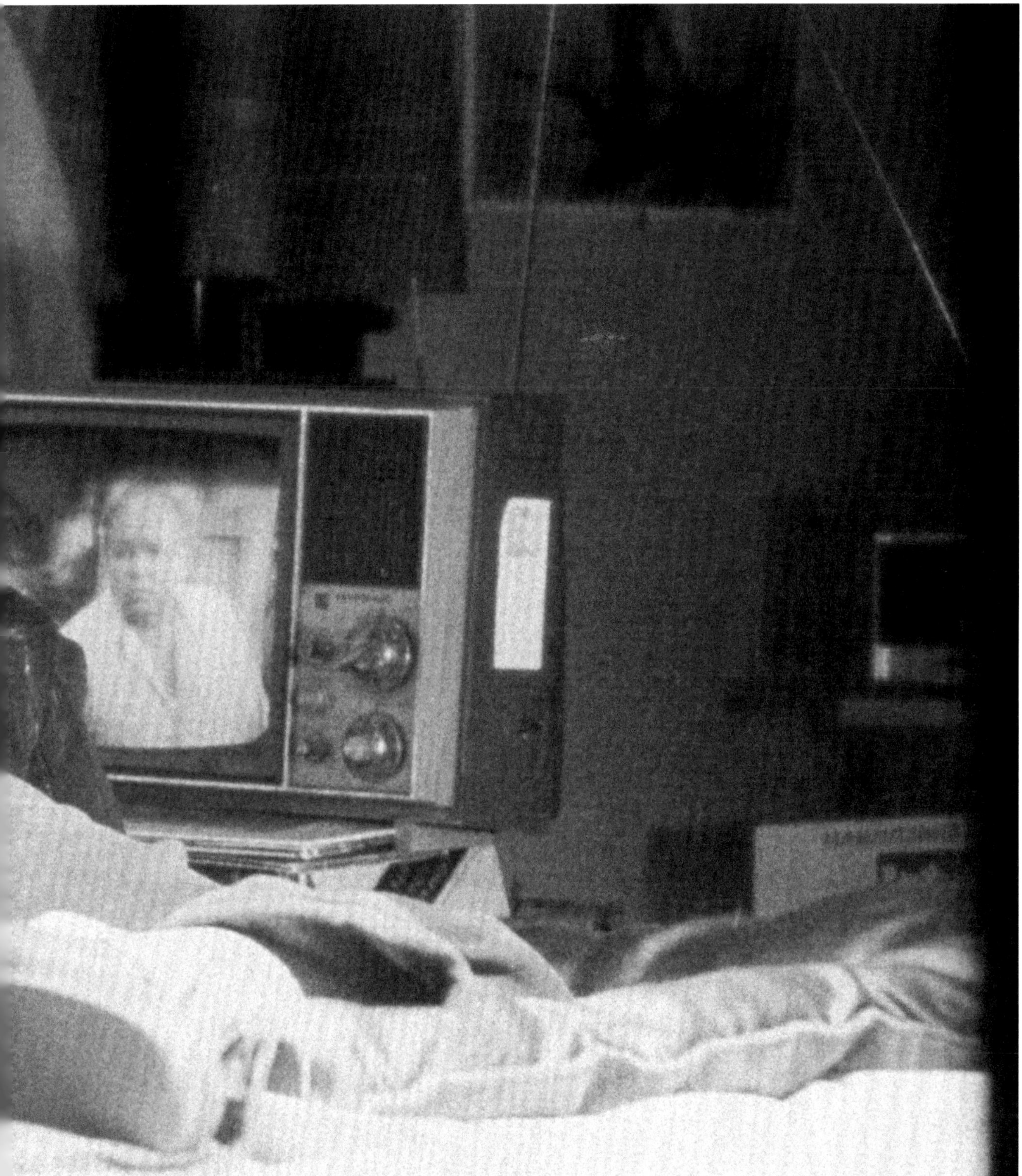

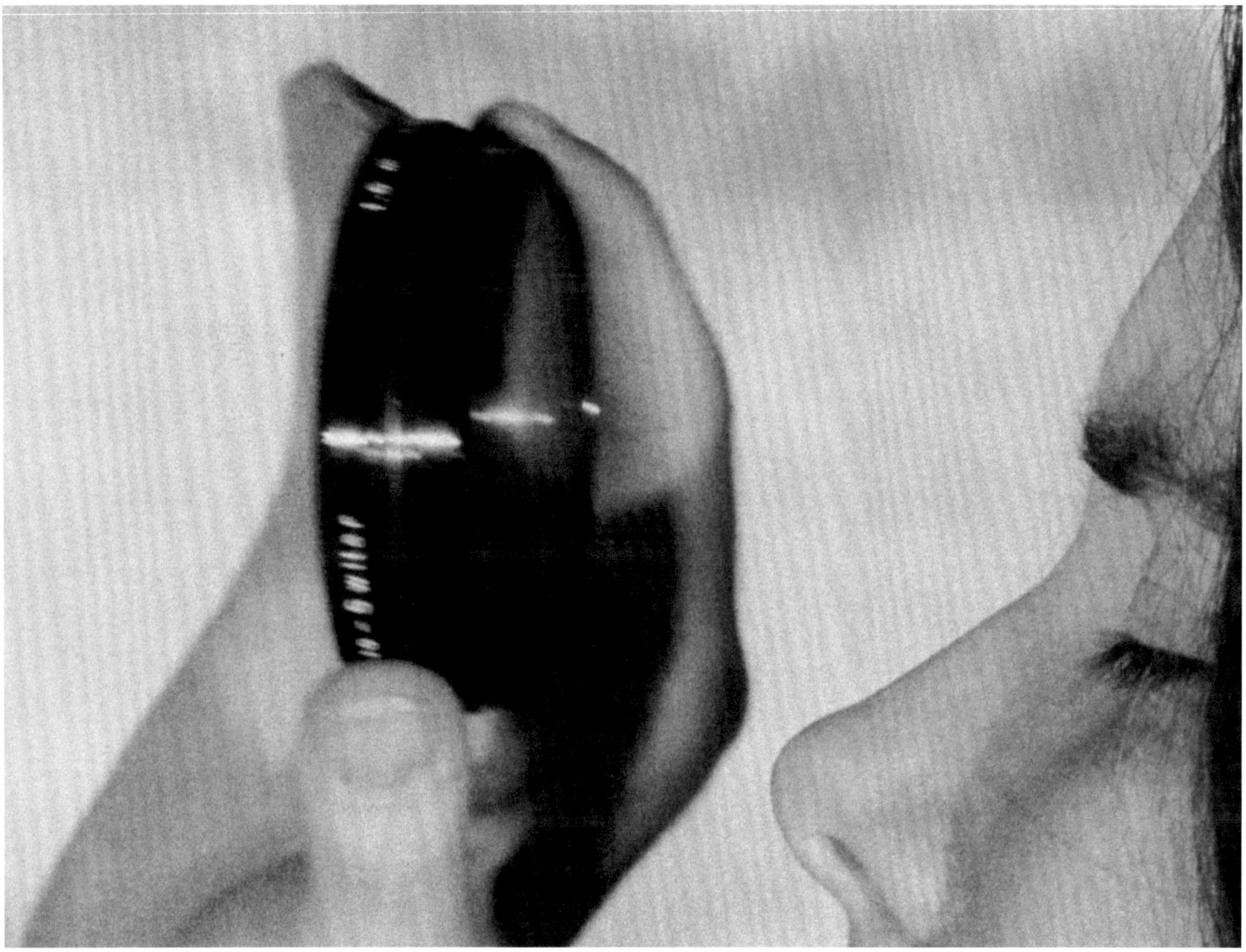

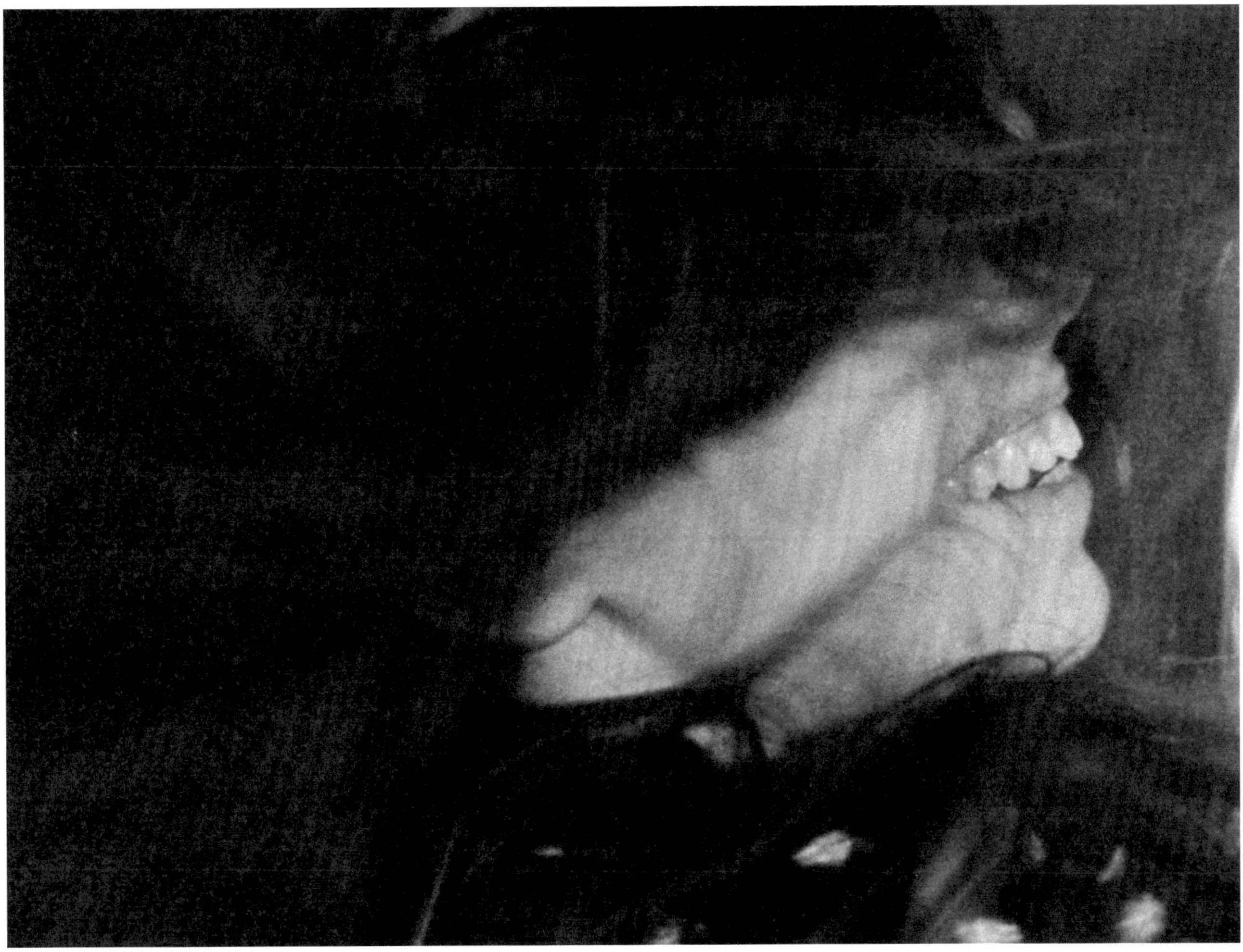

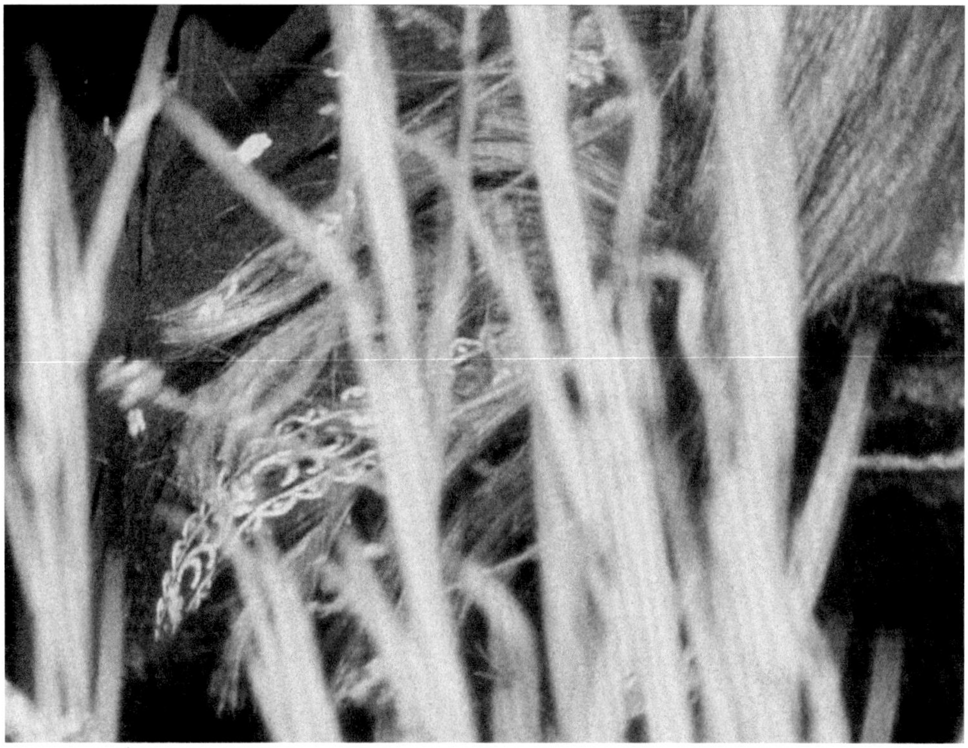

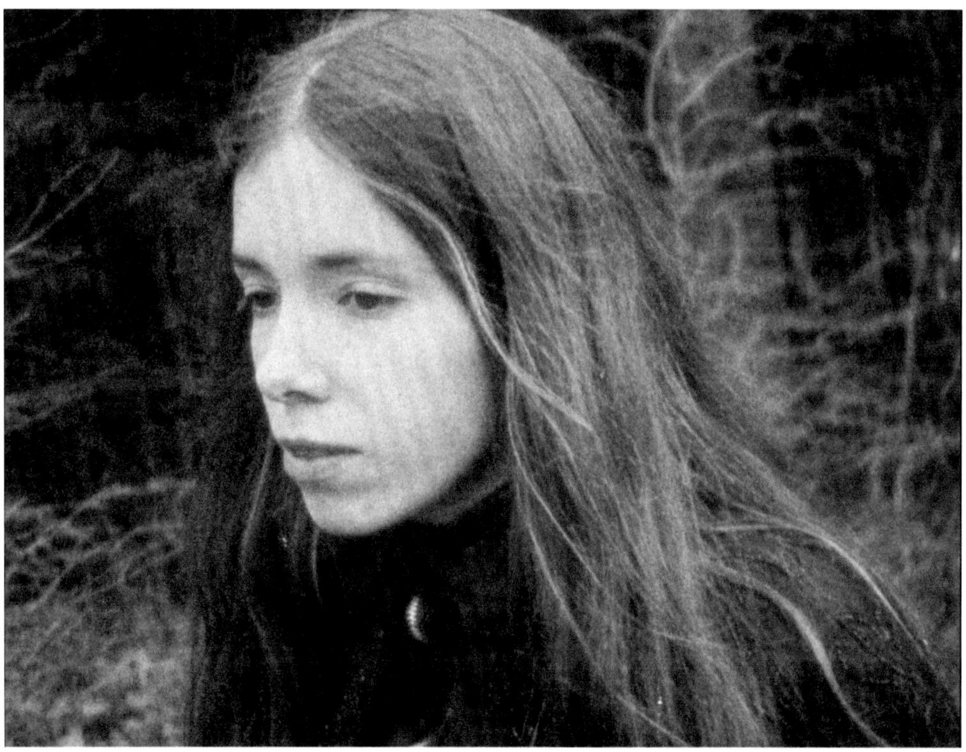

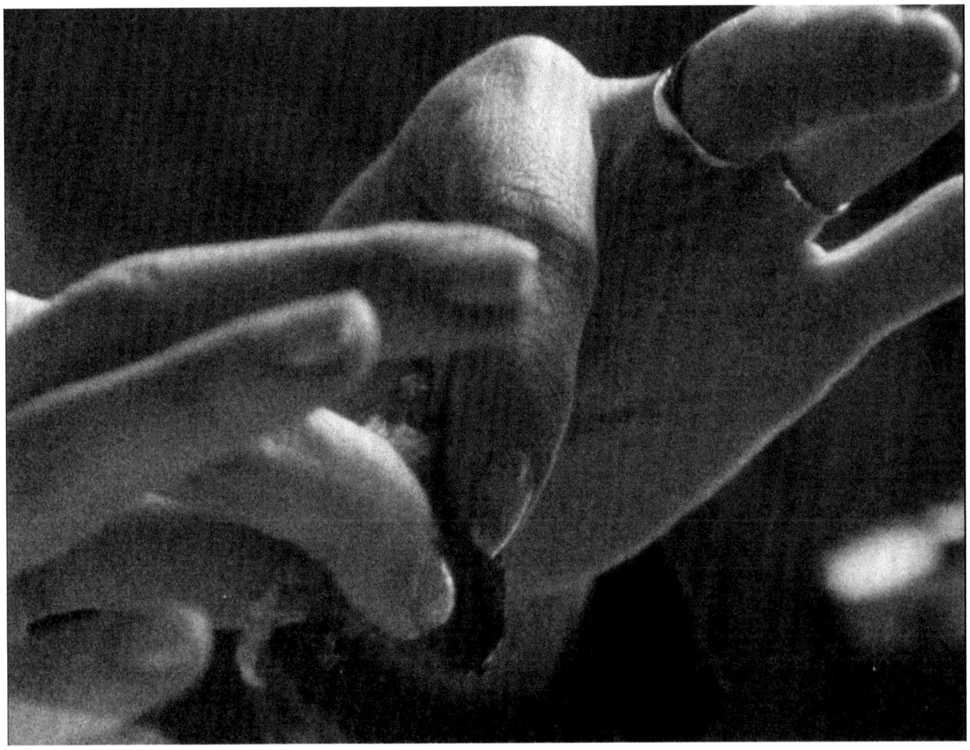

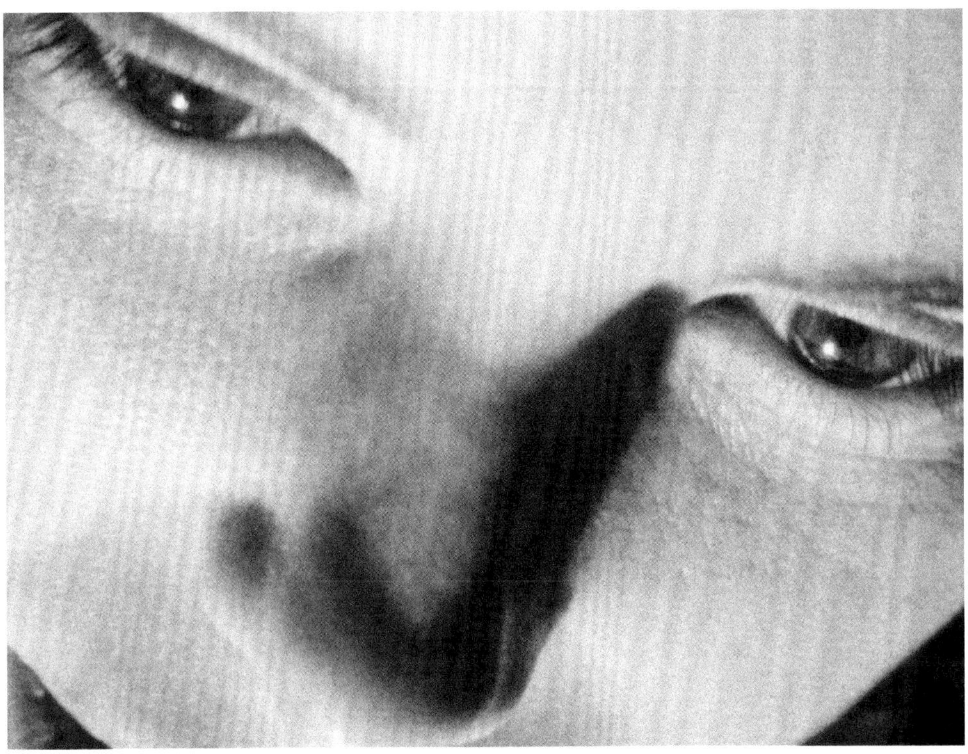

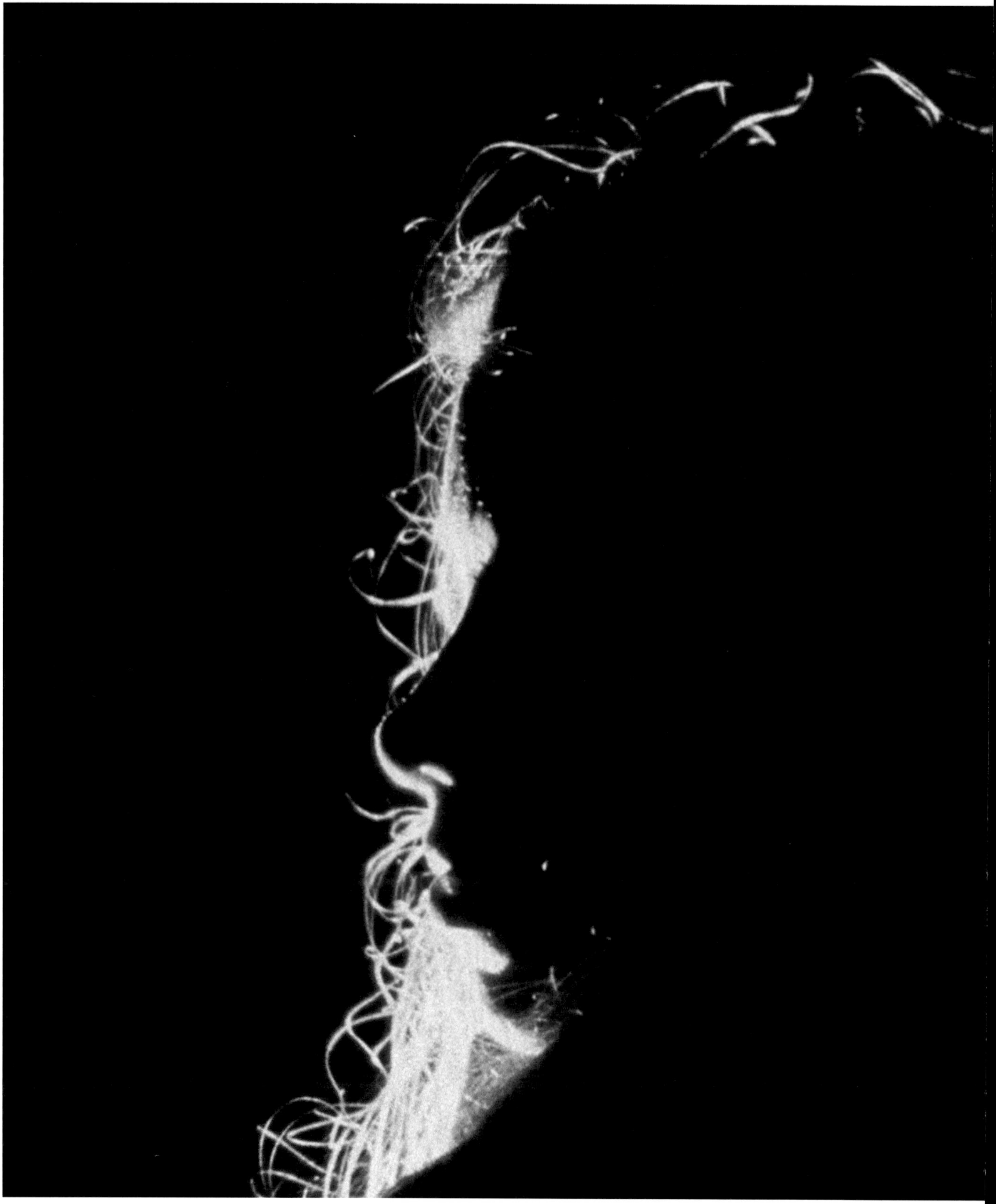

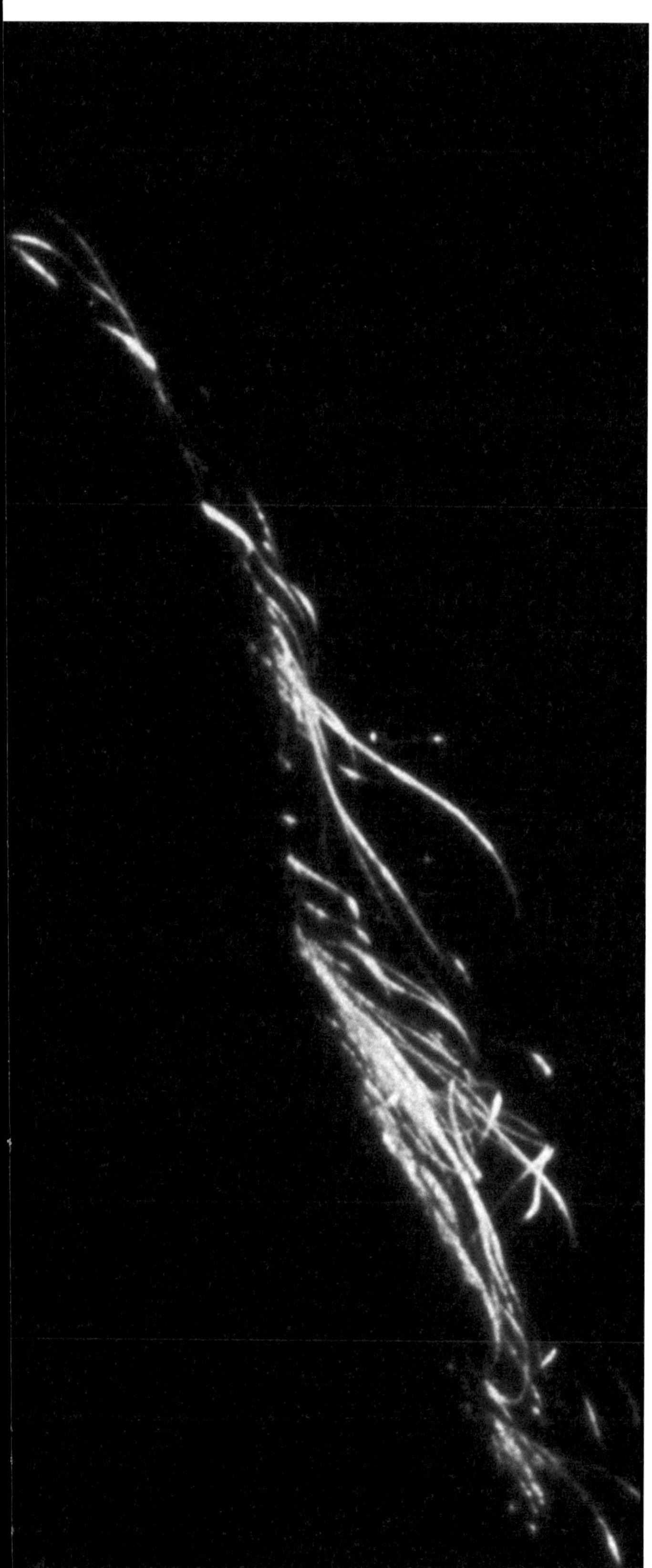

All Right

You Guys

Intimate Cruelty

Chris Kraus on *All Right You Guys*

Shot in beautiful black-and-white 16mm film almost five decades ago, *All Right You Guys* (1976) appears archaic in ambience, but its approach and conception feel very contemporary. It begins the first of its six sections with a close-up of Eleanor Thornton, the artist's sister, describing herself: "Have big teeth and fat lips, and, uh, my face is always moving around," she says, "even when I don't mean for it to." The camera zooms in for a mid-shot of her sinking back, legs outstretched, into an upholstered chair. She's a young woman, about twenty-one years old, with pale skin, wooden hoop earrings, and thick blonde hair. Eyes cast slightly upward, she seems dreamy and speculative as she forages around for the right words: "Uh, a lot of freckles, feet that always crack, uh, belly button, suntan mark on my skin. I look like a healthy girl," she concludes with a laugh. She's maybe a little bit spacey or high and also tentative, mildly embarrassed. "I look like Eleanor. And that's a goofy person who looks sad most of the time, but then sometimes she looks happy." Off-camera, Leslie asks Eleanor why she's not going out with any more men. "I'm never stable when I'm going out with men," she replies. "I'd rather get myself together, I guess."

In the next scene, she's tap dancing. A flared knee-length skirt, a cardigan sweater over a leotard, sheer black stockings, and shiny silver shoes. When she dances off-screen, her shadow cast on the back wall moves across the frame. The rapport passing between Leslie and Eleanor from both sides of the camera is focused and intimate, as when cutaways of Eleanor show her in profile exhaling invisible smoke, and yet the movie's depiction of her is, finally, clinical. Her actions are never continuous. She is bisected, dissected by jump cuts of herself in other poses and moods, suggesting another side to the story that's being withheld.

Scene four, "Liz," follows a young woman around a loft or apartment as she carries and plays with an oversized infant. Her partner, Terry, explains how Liz's body has changed since having the baby: "She's looser and yet she's also more, like, together. She's sharper sometimes and more conscious of what she's doing." The TV is on, and the baby fusses and gurgles. "She used to be very tight, but she also used to rumble along, like, her ass used to stay in one place and her legs used to go round ... and now she's a little more conscious of what she's doing." The film cuts repeatedly to an image of the young mother getting dressed. Liz herself interjects with a laugh as he continues: "Where there was sharpness around her, you know, hips, there's now like a softness, like a freshness. Ahh. Her tits have got bigger, and her ass has changed shape from like a pear shape to a more rounded, you know, 'u' shape. She's got more fleshy."

The matter-of-factness with which the scene unfolds is bracing, almost shocking, to a contemporary viewer. Liz—and, by extension, the filmmaker—doesn't seem to take any particular exception to Terry's fetishization of her maternal body. It's true; it's not true; it's the kind of thing people say. What Liz says is more interesting. Sitting down, finally alone on a daybed, Liz speaks to the question completely differently. Oblivious, obviously, to the shape of her ass, she's searching inside: "I'm trying to think of, like, real changes. All I can think of is projections, you know ... it's all projections." And then, later: "I know what it's like. It's like being held in the middle. In limbo, like it's waiting to continue."

Rather than being refuted, Terry's dumb comments about the maternal body are allowed to just hang in the air. It's all just ambient talk. The baby fusses and whines. Thornton's question to Terry and Liz—how Liz's body changed—is edited into the film long after we hear his opinions. In the next scene, as the two dance, a harpsichord composition can be heard. He holds Liz's back in his hands protectively, suggestively. Bare-chested, his jeans bump against the lap of her crêpe-de-chine vintage dress as they move, casting shadows. It's such a (hetero)sexual dance. The camera pulls back to reveal the environment they're living in: a cramped, unfinished loft with kitchen equipment, clothes racks, a desk, and a collapsing tin ceiling. She lets her head sink onto his shoulder; she's holding a beer can.

Thornton's earliest work, this film included, has been praised for its marriage of structuralist filmmaking techniques and feminist consciousness, but I think that's selling it short—the film is so much more. Thornton and her collaborator Desmond Horsfield set out to make a kind of anti-documentary documentary, probing, as Thornton recalls, "between the seams, locating an ambience around these people, sans the narrative backbone that most documentaries had then and now." But in its brief fifteen minutes, *All Right You Guys* examines the nature of persona, presentation, and identity.

Eleanor returns in the next scene, but not as we would expect. Pieces of footage from the start of the film are cut up against a scene in which Liz and Terry discuss what they're having for dinner. Spinach omelet? They've been eating nothing but eggs for a week. "What do you have with pork chops?" Terry asks. Liz answers, "Potatoes."

It's unclear whether Eleanor and the couple are actually adjacent to each other in real space and time. Probably not, but Thornton's relentless, deliberate editing creates that illusion. More than simply capturing the atmosphere of pre-digital artistic/bohemian life, Thornton's weaving together the life of a single woman with that of a problematic couple—all of them close to the artist—experiments, dangerously, with how close one might come to a subject while maintaining a critical eye. The film is the first revelation of Thornton's talent for intimate cruelty.

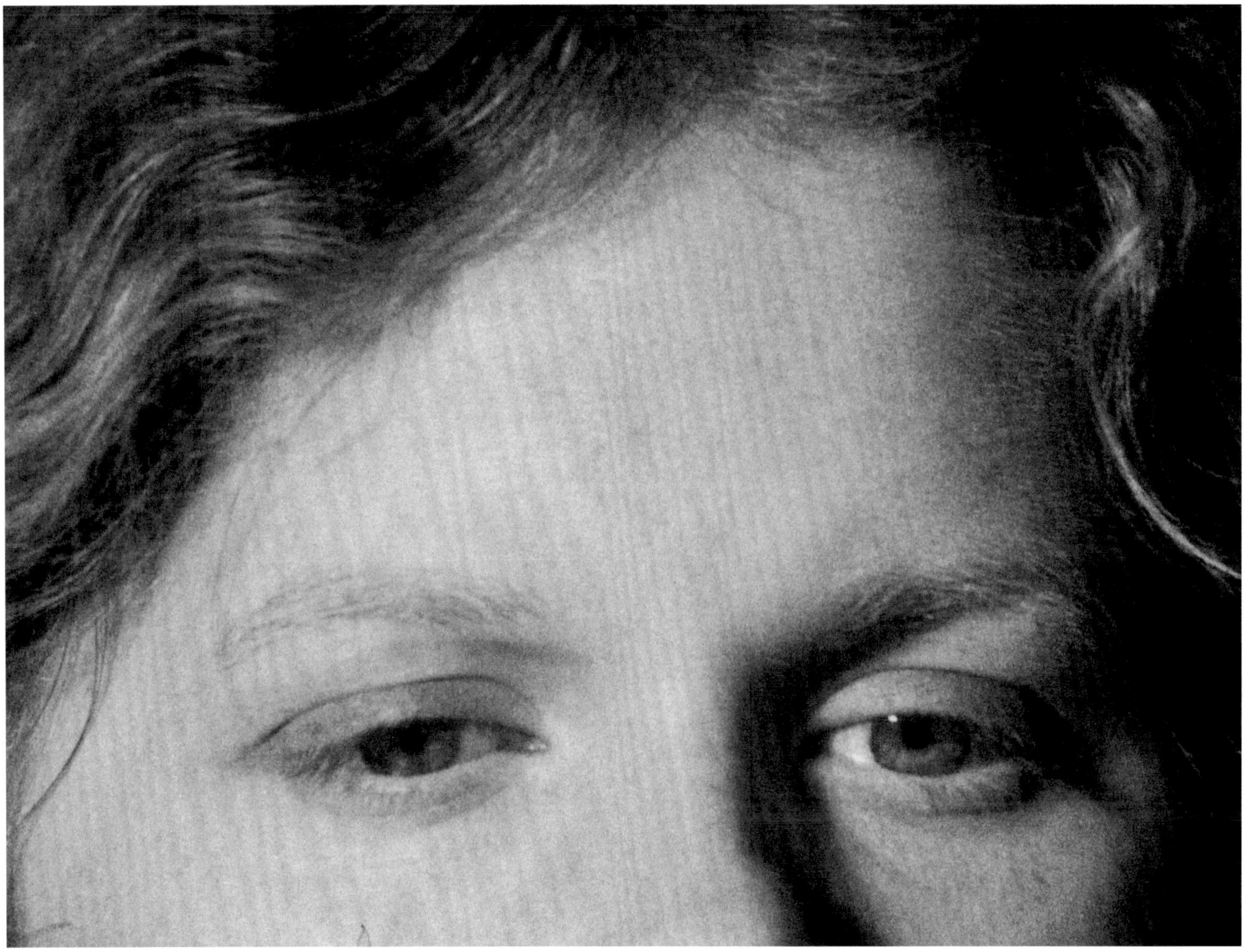

All Right You Guys, 1976

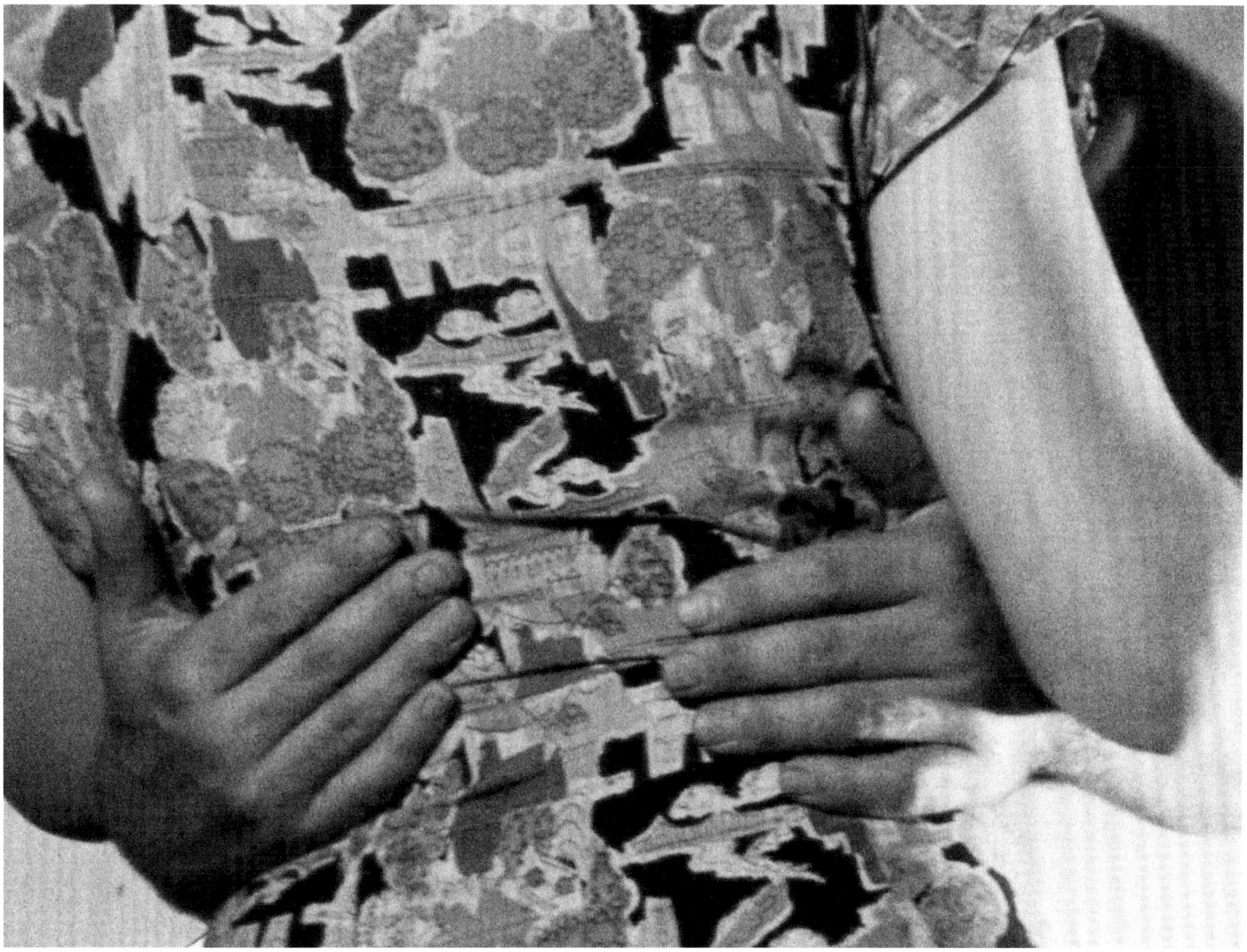

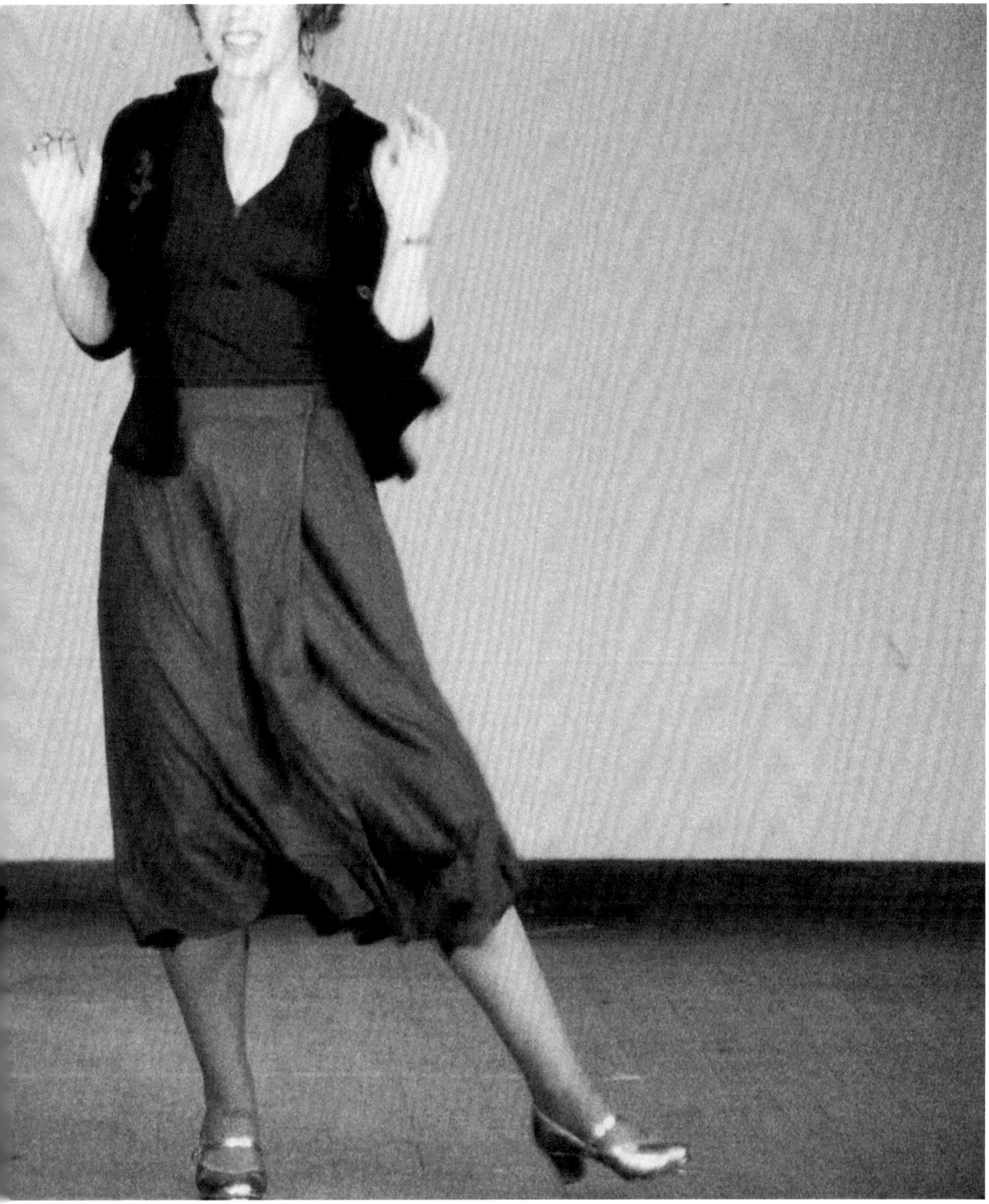

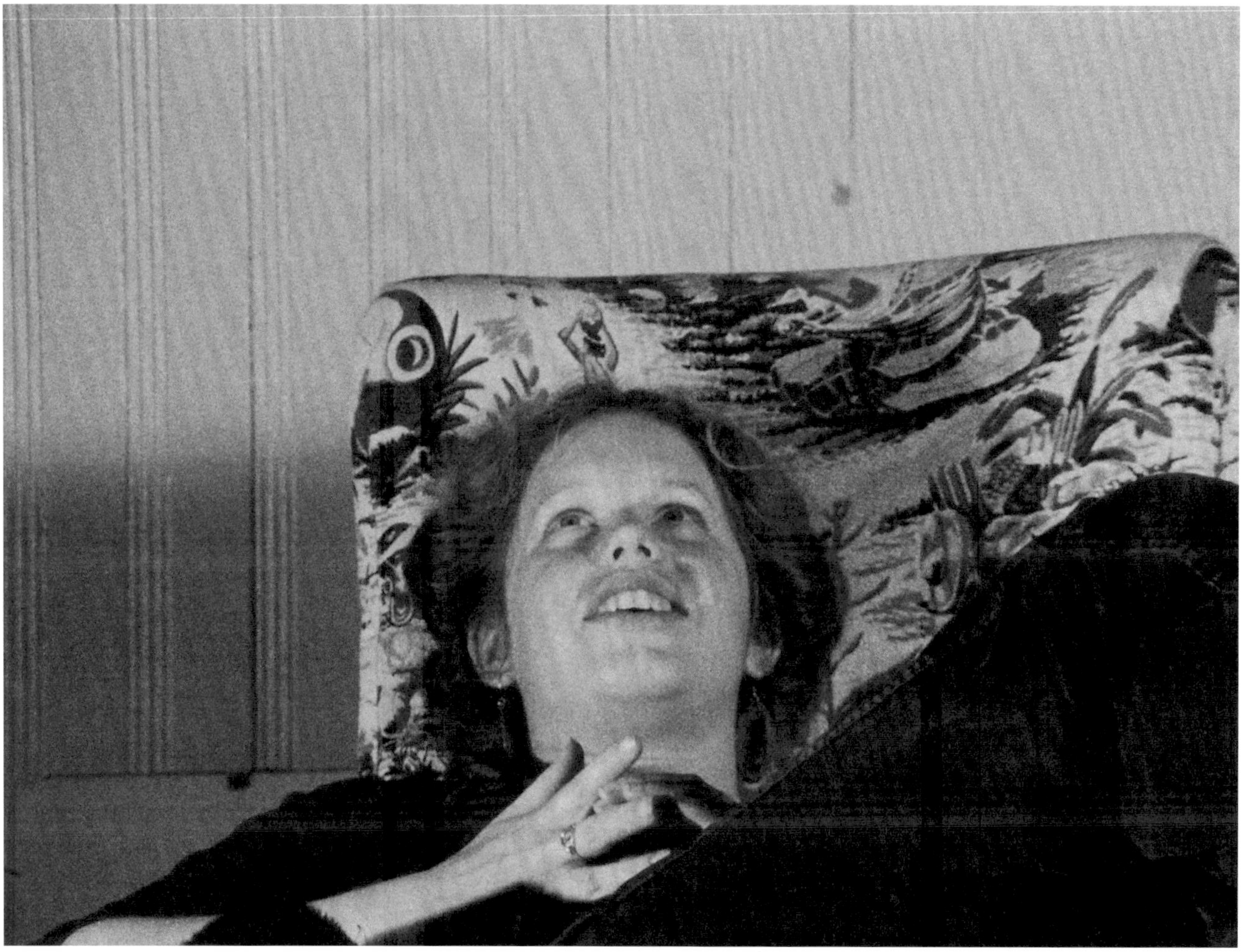

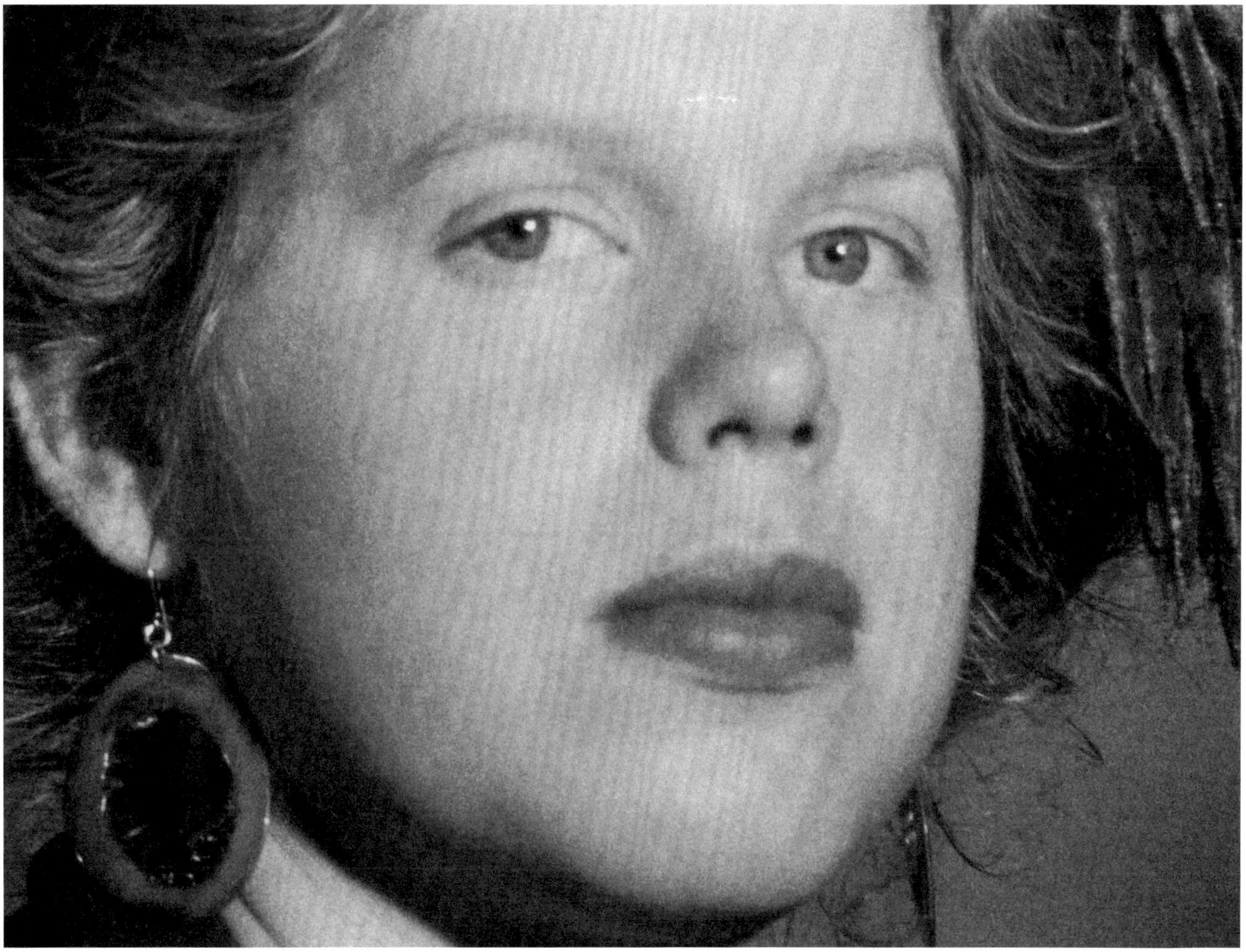

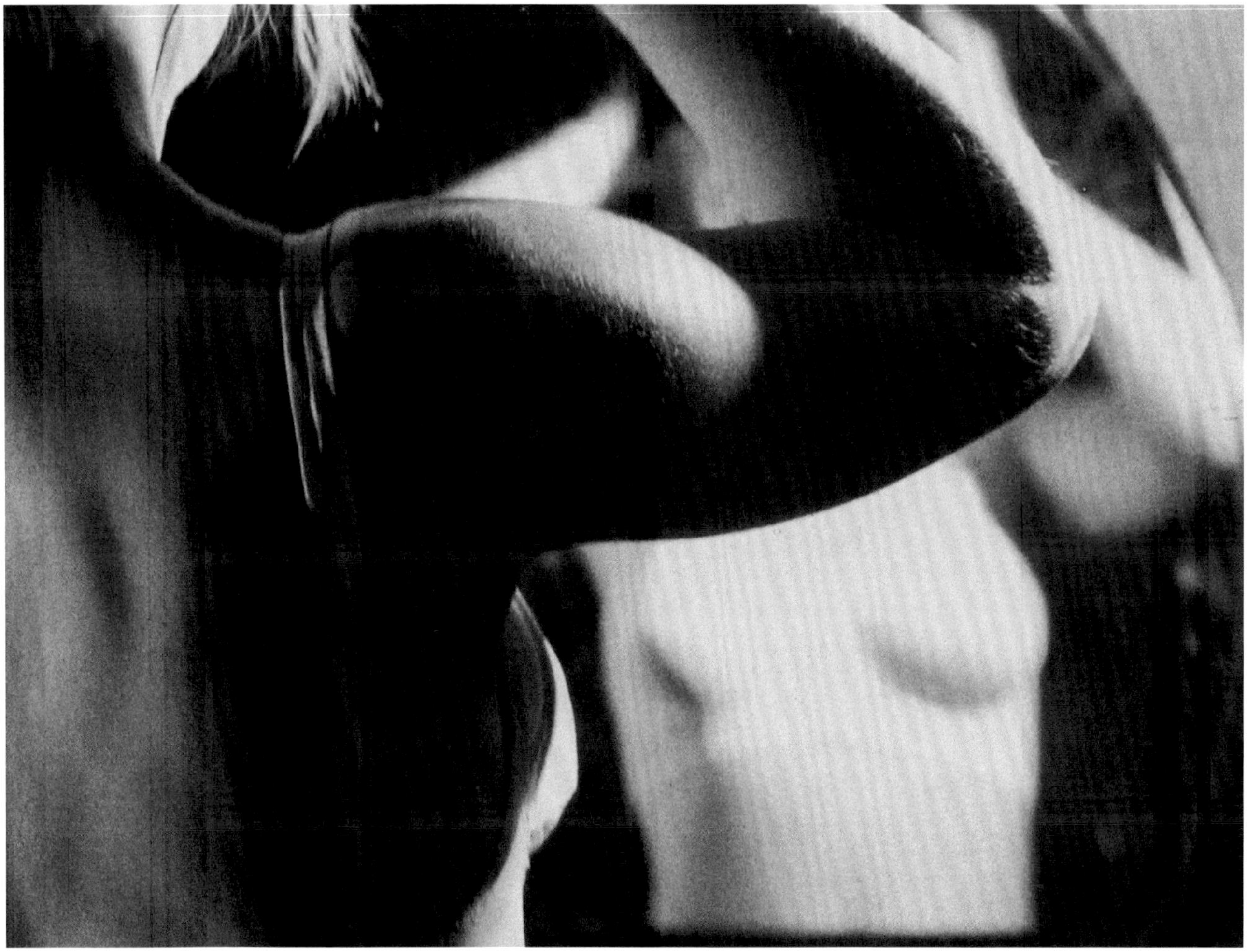

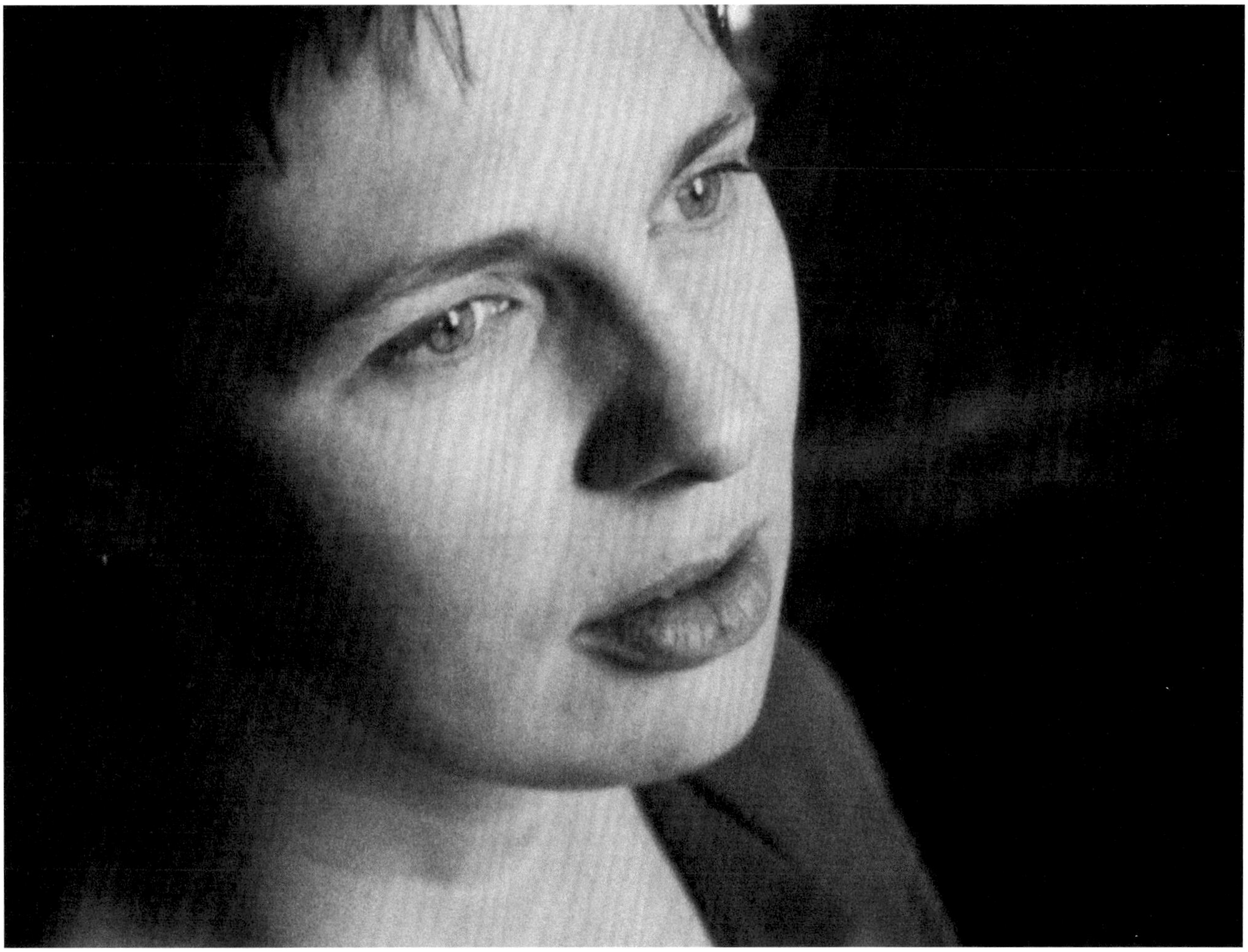

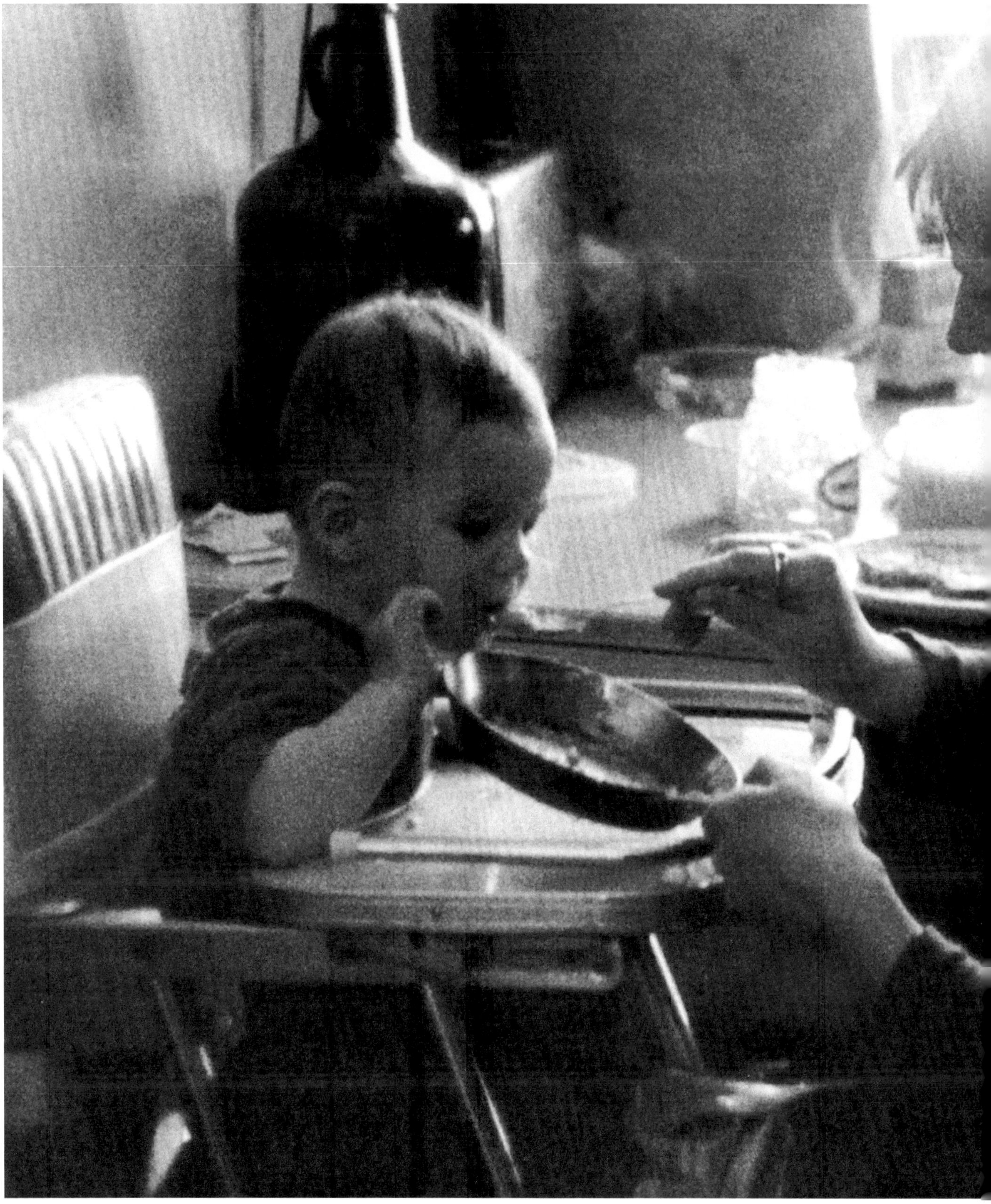

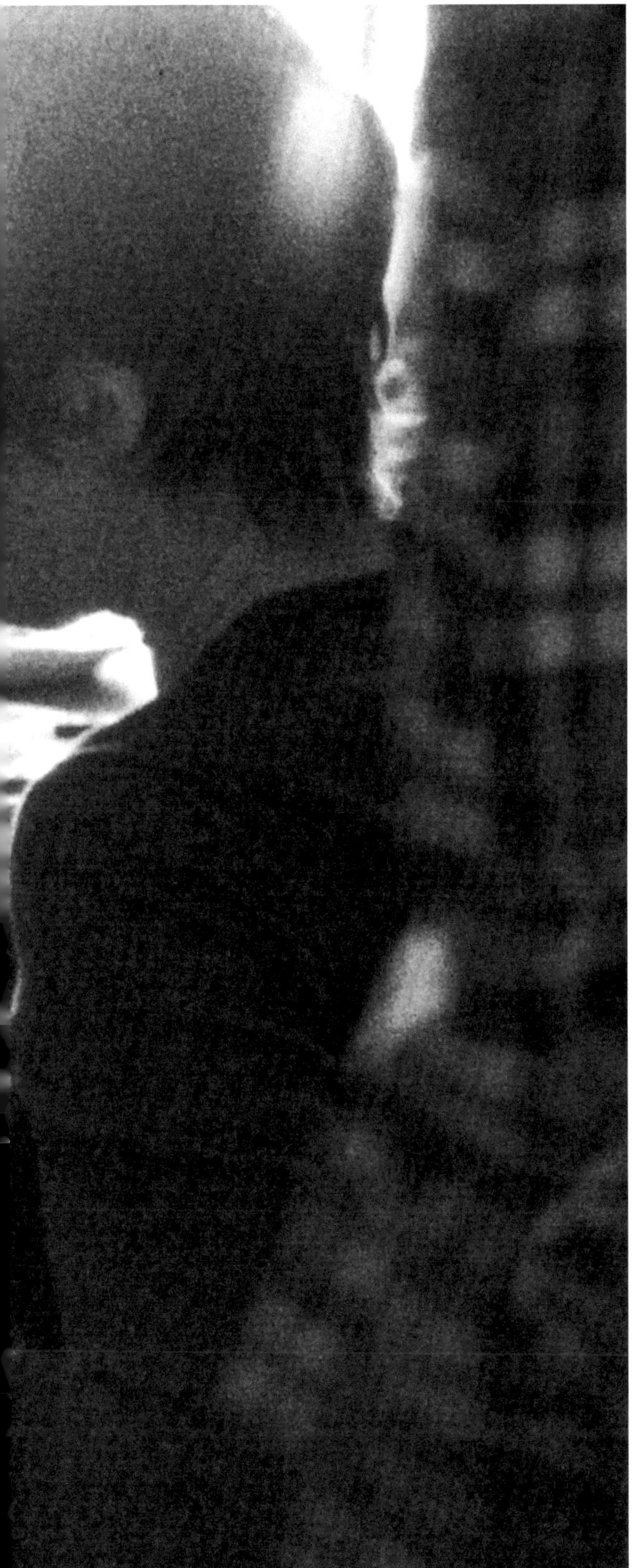

Jennifer, Where Are You?

Jennifer No Name

Su Friedrich on *Jennifer, Where Are You?*

The dominant image in Leslie Thornton's *Jennifer, Where Are You?* (1981) is a tight close-up of a small girl engaged in various activities: playing with lipstick, a mirror, matches. These shots are separated by black leader from other upside-down images. The soundtrack consists of music, natural sounds (footsteps, water, etc.), and a man's voice repeatedly asking the title question, "Jennifer, where are you?"

Some have said that they don't understand the film. "Nothing happens." Does "nothing" happen when a little girl smiles out of fear? Does nothing "happen" when a man's angry voice haunts the face of a young girl? Does "nothing happen" when a little girl looks aside—for a split second—at you—at her reflection—at the camera—before deliberately doing something "wrong"?

"Jennifer...?" Every thirty seconds, a man demands to know.

"Jennifer, where ARE you?" Jennifer stops, looks up, looks out at someone we can't see, bends back to the mirror, proceeds.

"JE-NNI-FER WHERE ARE YOU?" Jennifer, whose name *isn't* Jennifer, enlarges the oval of her mouth, smearing the lipstick in wider, messier circles around and around her grin.

"Jenni-FER whereareyou?!" But she can't hear him; he wasn't there; he wasn't looking for *this* Jennifer; and I am trapped in the midst of their absence.

So we are given this simple coincidence of Man's voice and Girl's "innocence." But throughout, his harsh command is surrounded by a cacophony of sounds. Music is reduced to noise while noise is elevated to the musical, and it prances and grunts with and against his constant refrain. And throughout, the camera moves against and with this Jennifer of no name: it demands her direct gaze; it tries to catch her through the mirror's reflection; it closes in too tightly, and always her eyes stare through and through all of us. It *is* the gaze of innocence. Of wisdom? Of both.

Perhaps this convergence of elements is a deceit of the film, and of the filmmaker. Each are filmic fabrications, having been taken out of context (his shout is looped to repeat itself ad nauseam; she was originally filmed for a fire-prevention commercial). But then how is it that they complement each other so well while belonging to such separate events? It isn't simply a marriage of image and sound (a perverse chemistry that makes almost any juxtaposition thick with meaning): because of Thornton's fine control of the materials, it becomes the wedded bliss of authority and fear. The one necessitates the other; the other bolsters the one. This may appear to be a static relationship, monolithic and one-dimensional, but the filmmaker doesn't allow for such a coarse reading. The subtleties of power, far more tenacious than its obvious forms, weigh on the film, drag us in, lead us through precarious detours, and leave us unsure of even our most certain responses.

Why does the spellbinding range of emotions expressed by this girl during such a commonplace activity provoke so much anxiety? And why do we feel so anxious when faced with the realization that his voice, although it is a loop, never sounds the same? It is through this chameleon-like quality of the film's two major elements that we sense the damning complexity of their relationship. And then the context for these elements—the other sounds and images of the film—extends our journey into the maze of emotions and questions that are being provoked.

Jennifer unnamed is bracketed by black leader and interrupted occasionally by other upside-down images. Twice, a man. Once, two smiling women, their faces close together. Twice, painfully red images of fish: one is sinister and sensuous; the other seems stricken and silly. Once, a house, above which leaves blow across a grassy sky. These images suggest terror, nostalgia, isolation, awkwardness, and mystery. Each sensation has its place in the film, and each corresponds to some aspect of the sounds used. Three dominate: a high-pitched and distant siren, the man's question, and a frantic piece of Baroque piano music. The siren never ceases to wail, his question recurs every half-minute, and the too-boisterous piano music is used to shift direction, offer solace, make elegant that which is too raw. There is a discrepancy in feeling and volume between the sounds, which, when used most aggressively, creates a heartbreaking mood. The siren seems to become a *memory* of warning, the piano takes on that awful quality of forced laughter, and there, again and again, is his question, made ridiculous, menacing, indecent, or ordinary by its surroundings.

But a muteness prevails. I'm interested in silent films that are LOUD, but here is a film that is deadly quiet despite a chaos of sound. This too-tangible sense of things being left unsaid or unexplained seems to emanate from the amorphous space (does sound occupy space?) between the siren and his voice. And her gaze. Surely she isn't hearing his command to make a present/presence of herself. And surely he doesn't understand why Jennifer refuses to make herself present. His voice assumes that his need is sufficient explanation, while her glance admits that she is subject to circumstances that she can control only through minor disruptions and delays.

Until the end. Until exhaustion coincides with instinct, and even as she musters all her will to "perform," she cannot. As Jennifer-still-with-no-name tries once again to blow out the match, flashes of white appear to slash her, mimic the flame, and suddenly, with a terrifying suction and a piercing outcry of sound, the screen is black. This "failure" is her first real success.

This "failure" is also one of the many (necessarily) partial answers to the film's central question. It isn't the whereabouts of Jennifer that obsesses us and that man; it is her relationship to the question of her place and her being. The film is a question(ing) of authority and authorship, of the power implicit in authority, of the balance between her fear and her will to disrupt, of the balance between his angry question and his inability to understand her (lack of an) answer. We are led to fear greatly for the separate ground that each of the "characters" maintains. We are also led to fear greatly for the absolute entanglement of the two, which is as dominant as their separateness.

So maybe "nothing happened." No one got killed, no one got kissed, no one even got an answer. But the last match wasn't blown out—at least not by her. Maybe nothing can happen if we watch too closely; people put on their best faces. Maybe nothing happens if we watch too closely: it dissolves into rhetoric. Perhaps if we sit perfectly still and bear witness to the dance between interrogator and interrogated, we can begin to disembody that dance. Jennifer No Name can only *offer* us her true name; under his circumstances, she cannot be known. As long as her gaze slips into the mirror and he shouts so mechanically, there remains this coexistence in mutually exclusive space where image and sound, flesh and voice, feed on each other and meet only to seduce, terrorize, and be divided, again and again. And *that* is where "everything happens." And that is where one might think nothing happens. But we might begin to ask, as we are entrapped by this strange dialogue, why we are so relieved to find that "at least *something* is happening."

By forcibly conjoining Her gaze and His voice, the film makes us consider the implications of the film medium and our given environment, both of which can create such an agonized resonance between two disparate elements. The fact that we are each victims of our individual and shared memories complicates the effort to expose and analyze the dialectic between authority and resignation as it constructs our selves and our world. We are saturated by it; it is embedded in every institution and every relationship. Most people would admit its existence: some to condone; others to condemn.

If one is to condemn it, the question is how to make its function present, and its presence dysfunctional. To be spoon-fed a "politically correct" analysis of the seductiveness of power and resignation, and to be told that we must despise and renounce that darkest part of ourselves, is to be left with little understanding of how arduous and gradual the process of change really is. In order to push us past a rhetorical knowledge and acknowledgment of this dialectic, we need something that traces its existence to our deepest memories: our childhood. A film such as *Jennifer, Where Are You?* works because it makes us afraid, not in the interests of confirming our fears, but in the hopes of making us so vulnerable that we finally become angry about the questions, the noise, the camera, and the presence that belies an essential absence.

In the last shot, Jennifer not Jennifer stares at the flame so stubbornly, with such absorption, that for the first time, we find ourselves removed from her, by her. Until then, she had made "eye contact" with us. We had established a compassionate "dialogue" with her through her gaze. Now, as her seductive and playful gaze crumbles into a silent and angry mask, we are staring *at* her and feeling the full weight of her resistance. The situation is critical. She cannot leave, *but she can no longer participate.* The best she can do is not move, not respond, and not look anywhere but into herself for the strength to ignore his command and break the cycle.

As we witness the subtle assault on this child of no name yet, and her first stubborn avowal of self, we become part of her struggle against the chaos of authority and fear. Do we all hear certain voices as Jennifer No Name "hears" his command? Does his incessant questioning of the "real" Jennifer reflect our own solipsistic moments? Are we as vulnerable to daily assault as we are to his voice and her fragility? Perhaps we demand of the unseen and respond to the imagined (which are both seen and real) more often than we realize.

Throughout *Jennifer, Where Are You?*, Thornton makes it clear that terror and evasion are an inadequate but nostalgic sublimation of the need for genuine communication. And she makes it clear that we must break the cycle, or be broken.

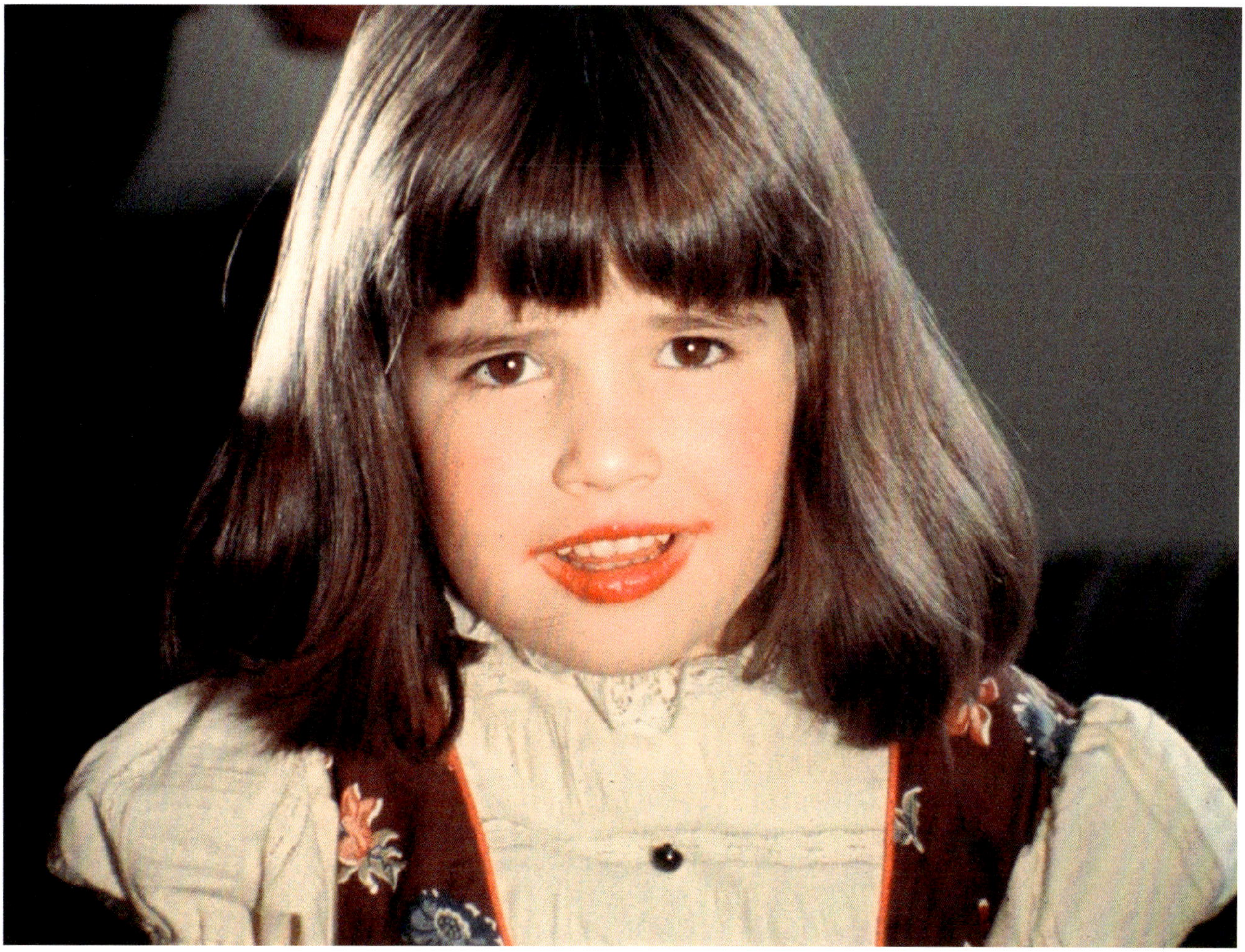

Jennifer, Where Are You?, 1981

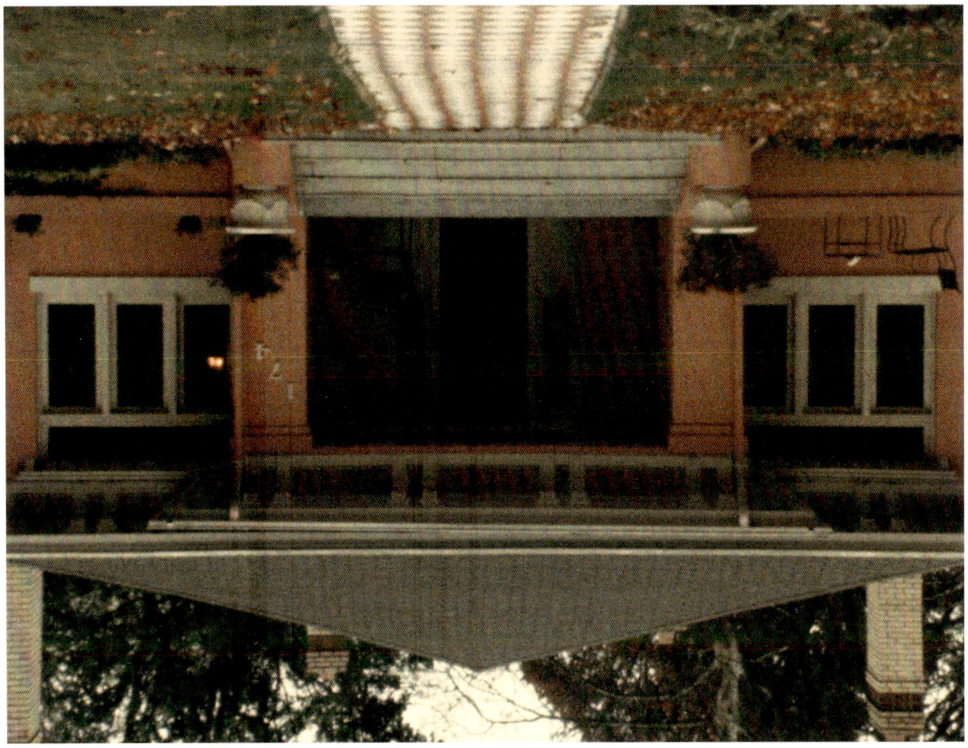

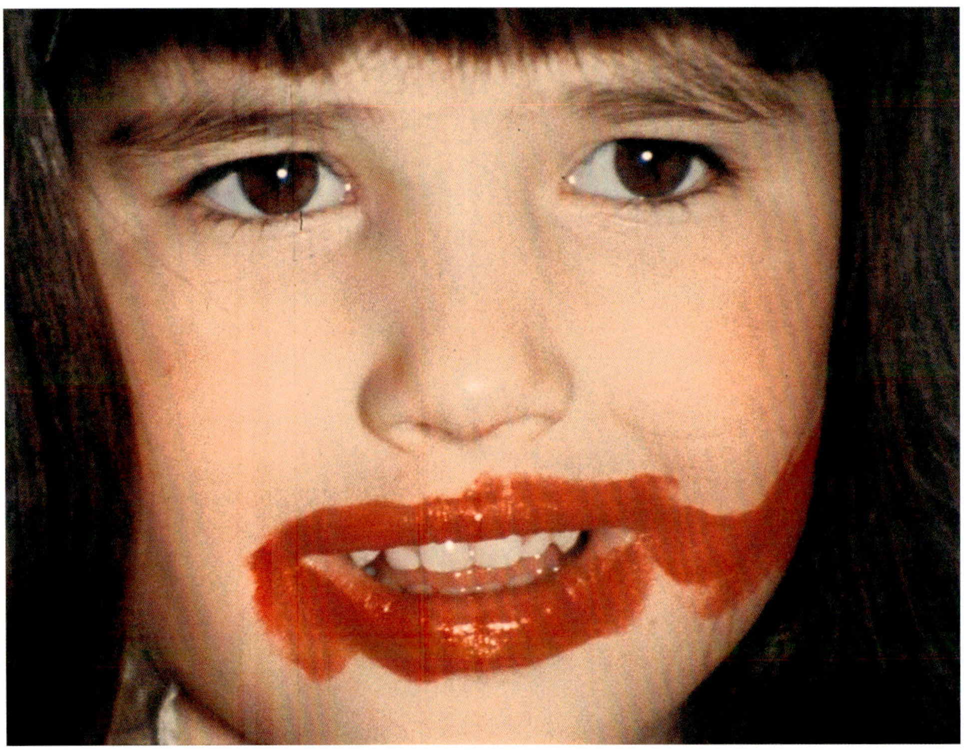

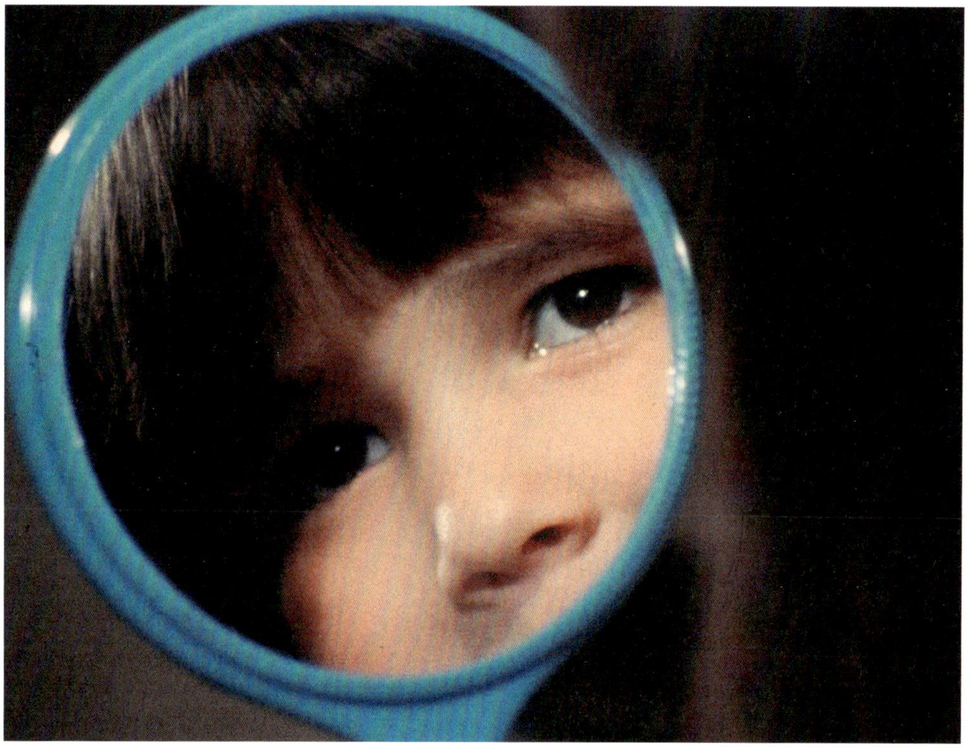

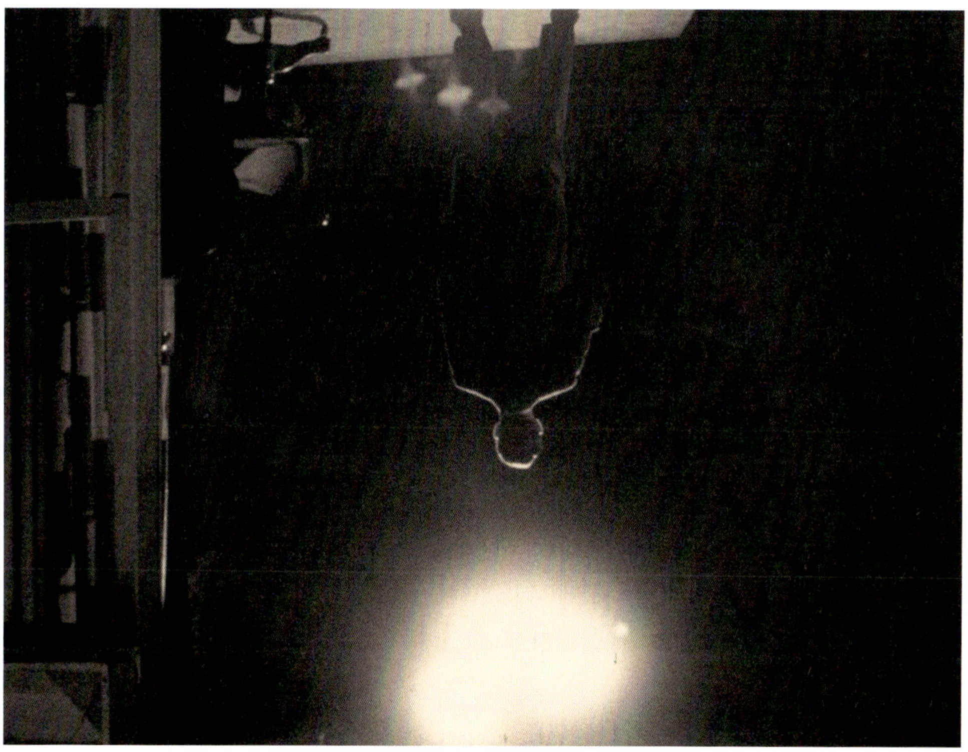

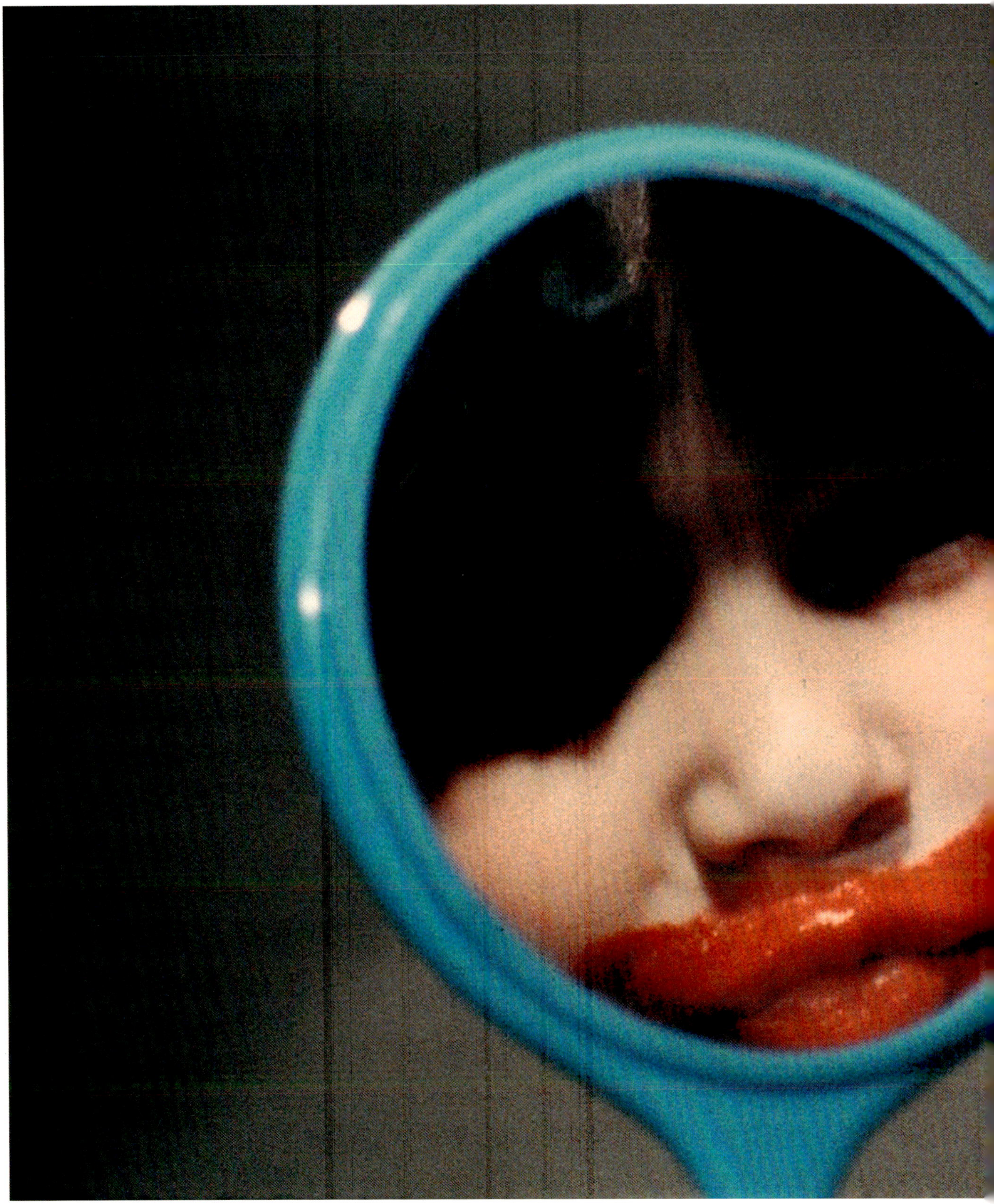

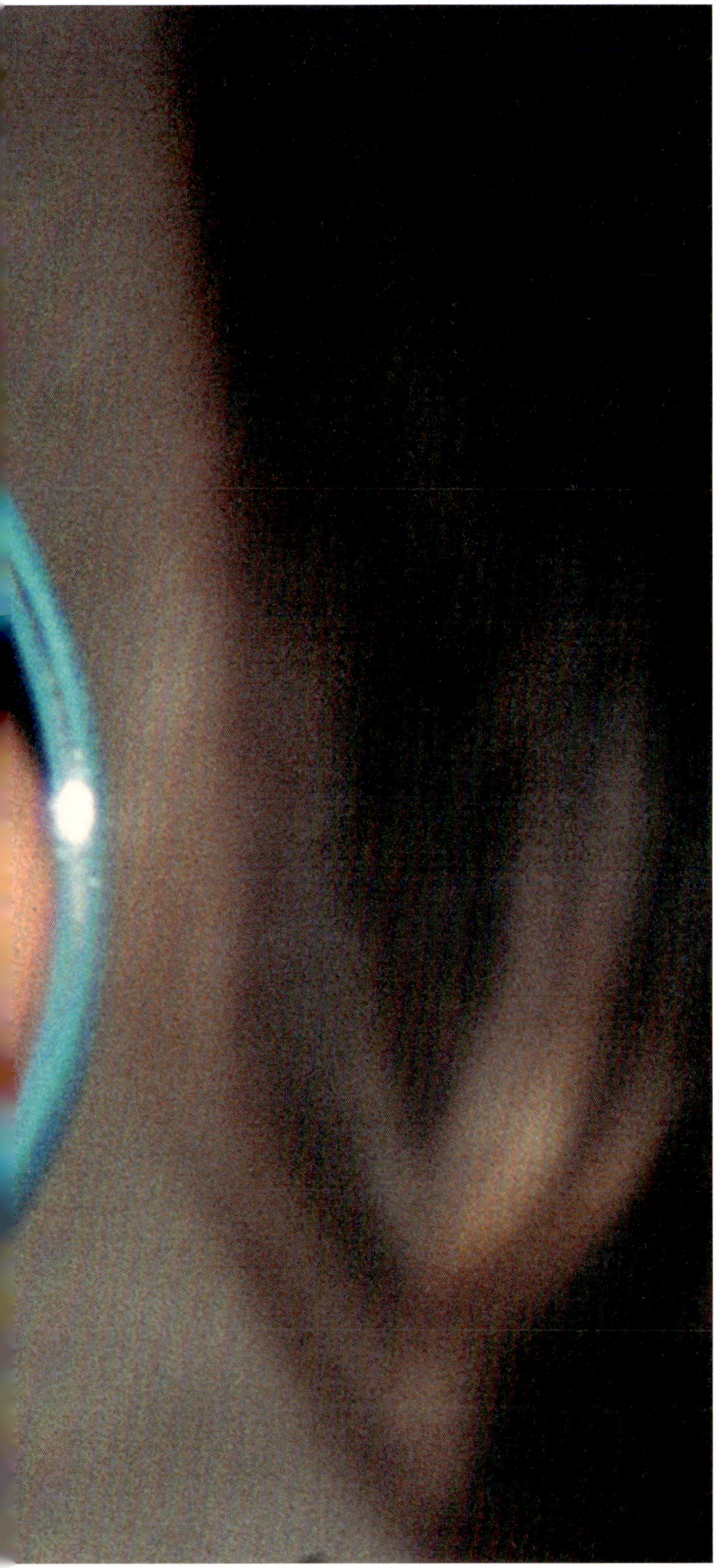

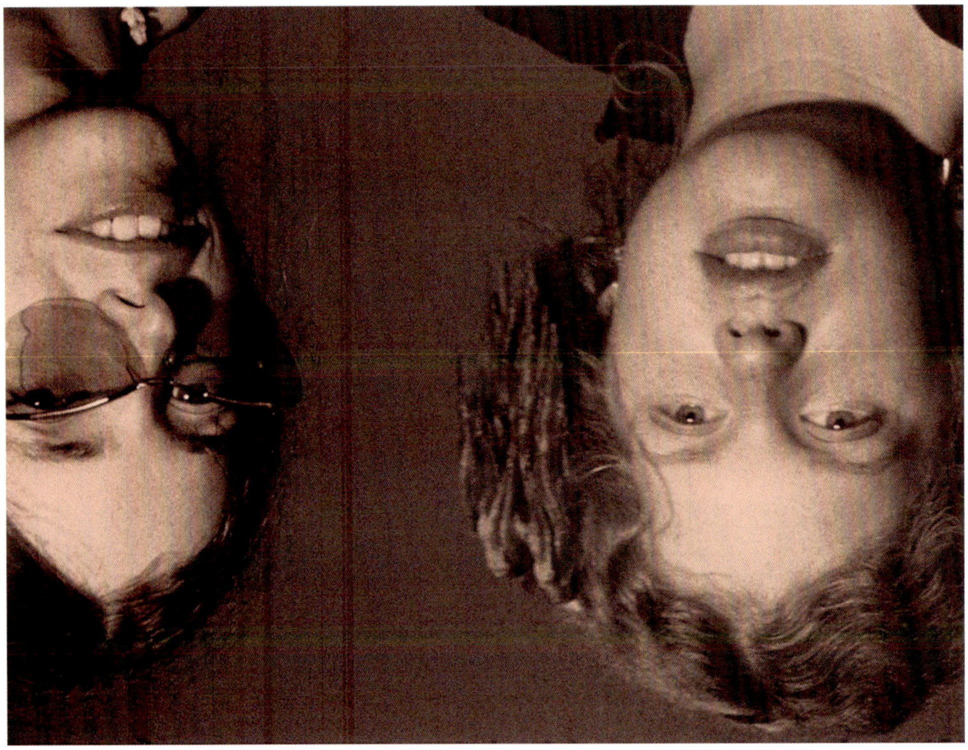

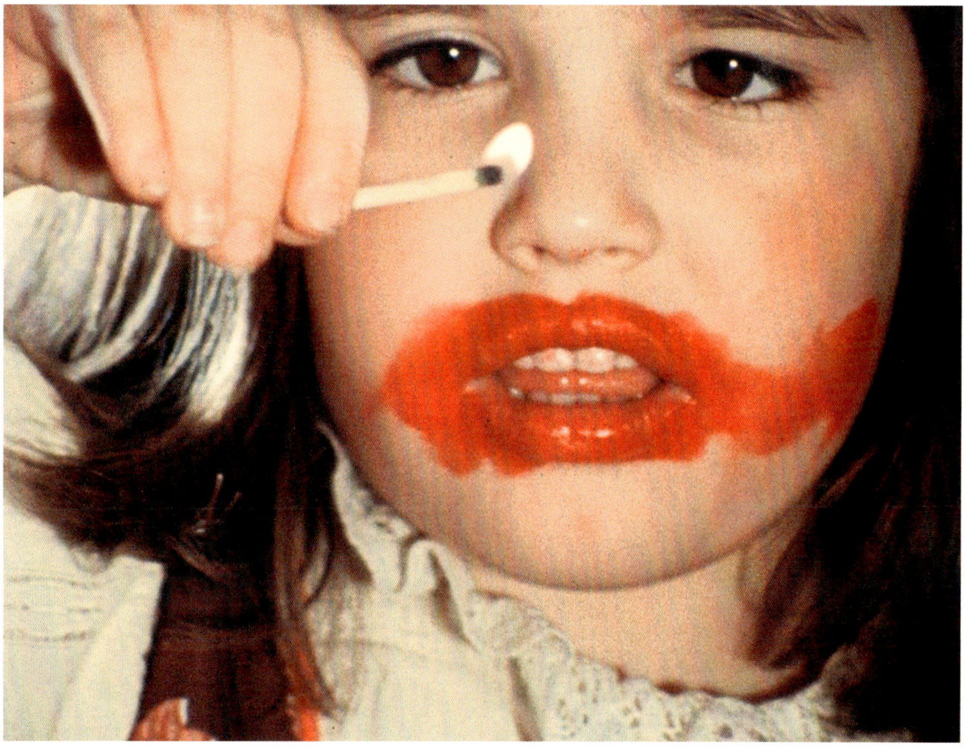

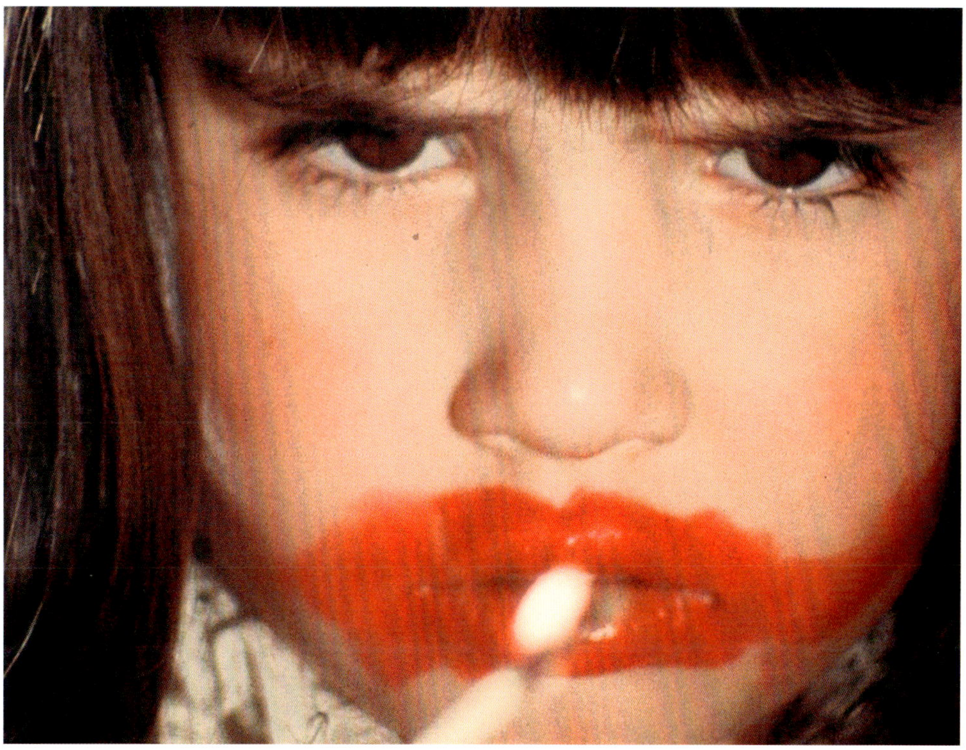

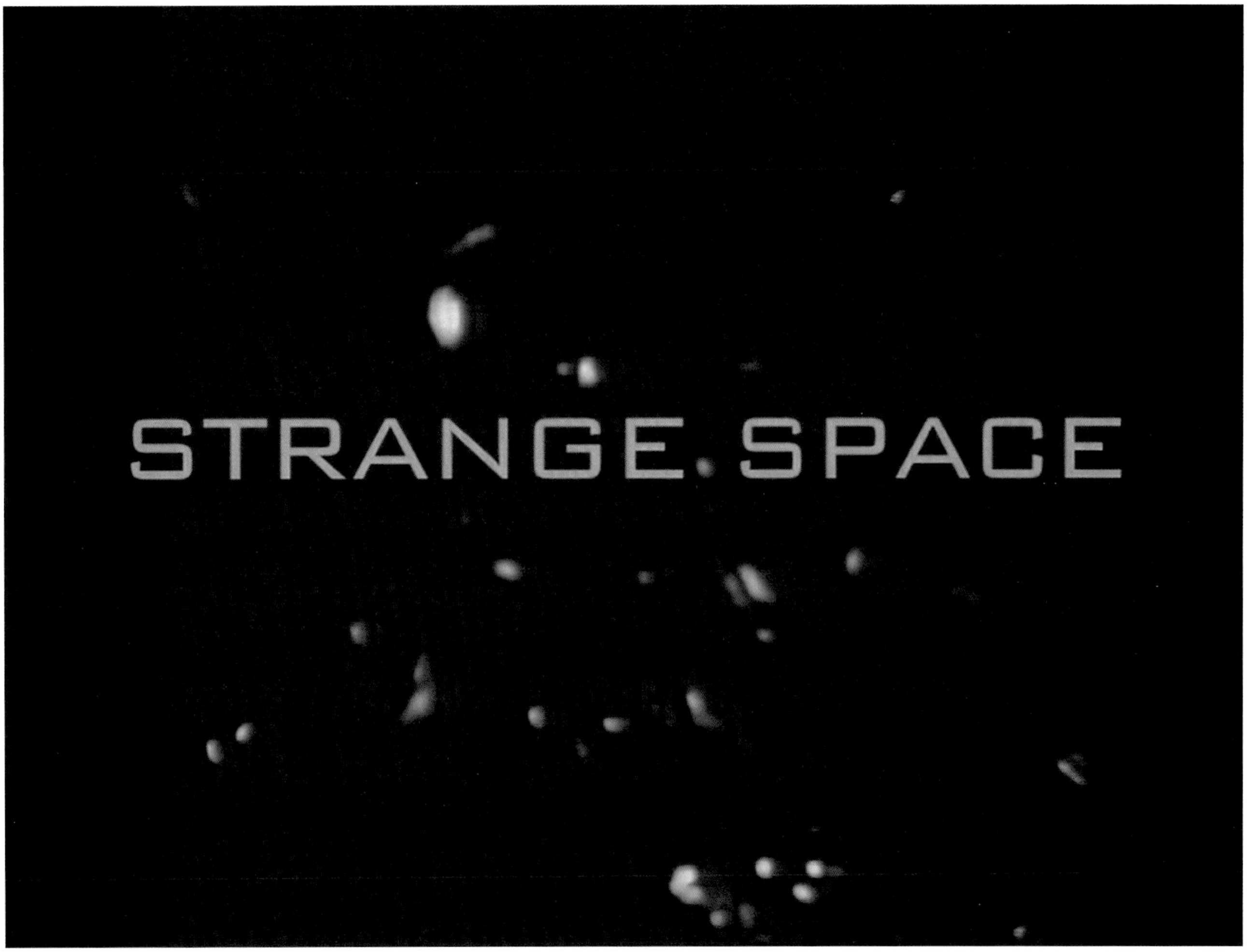

Strange Space, 1993

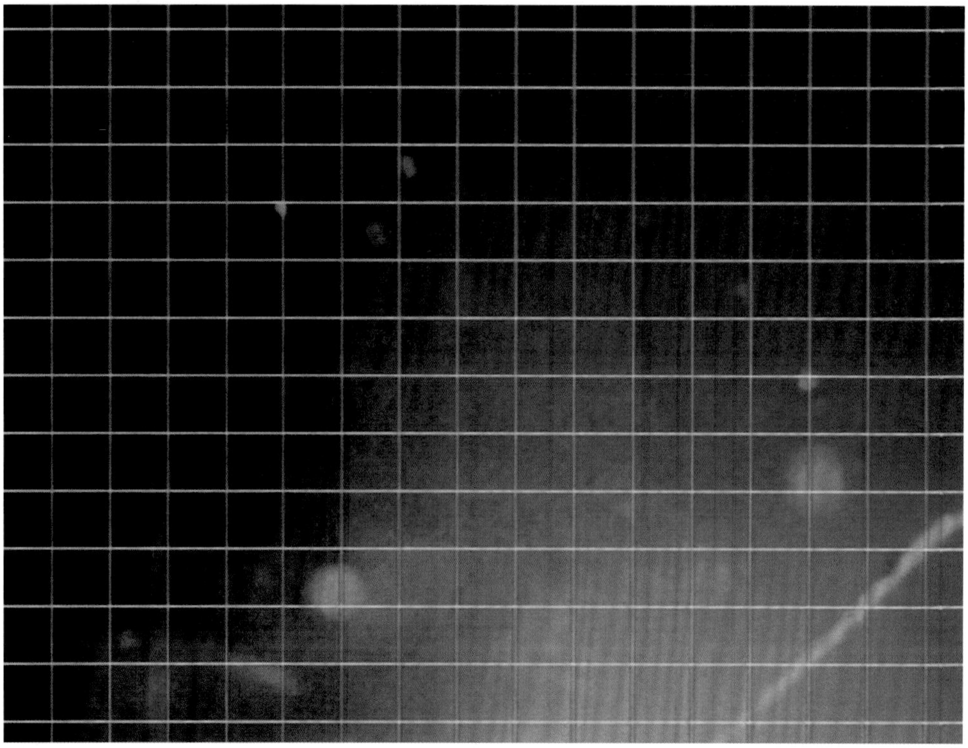

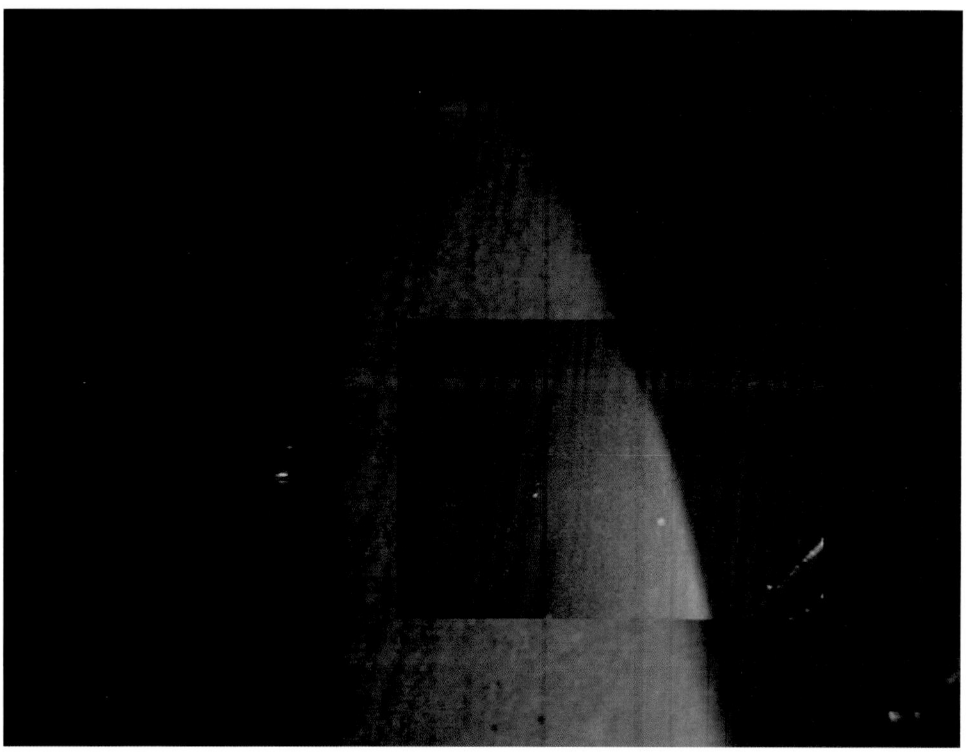

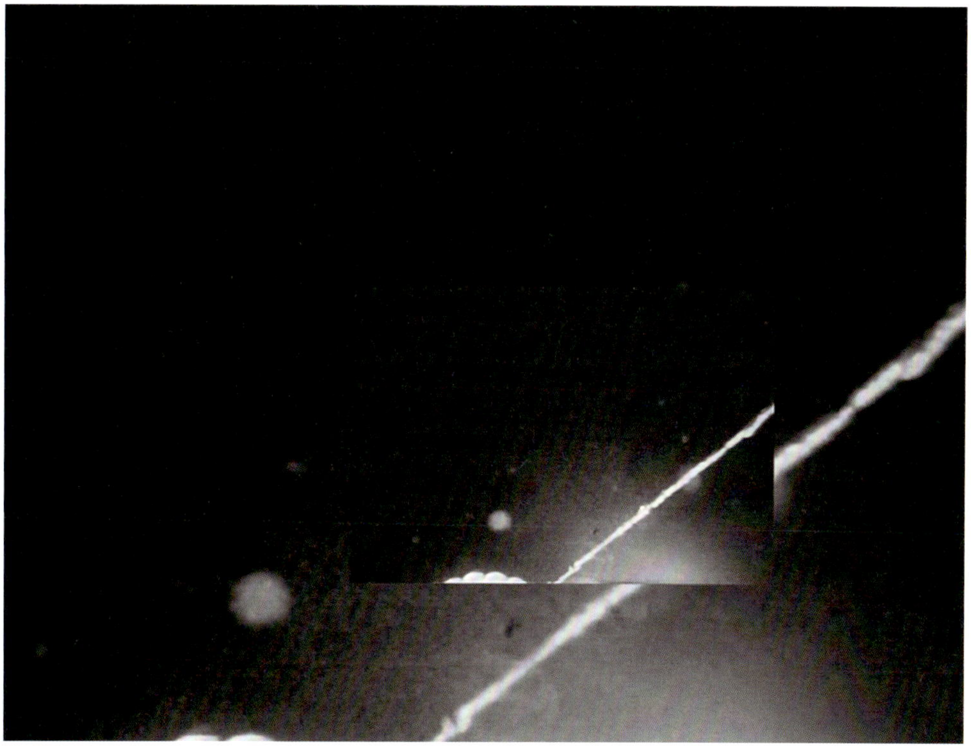

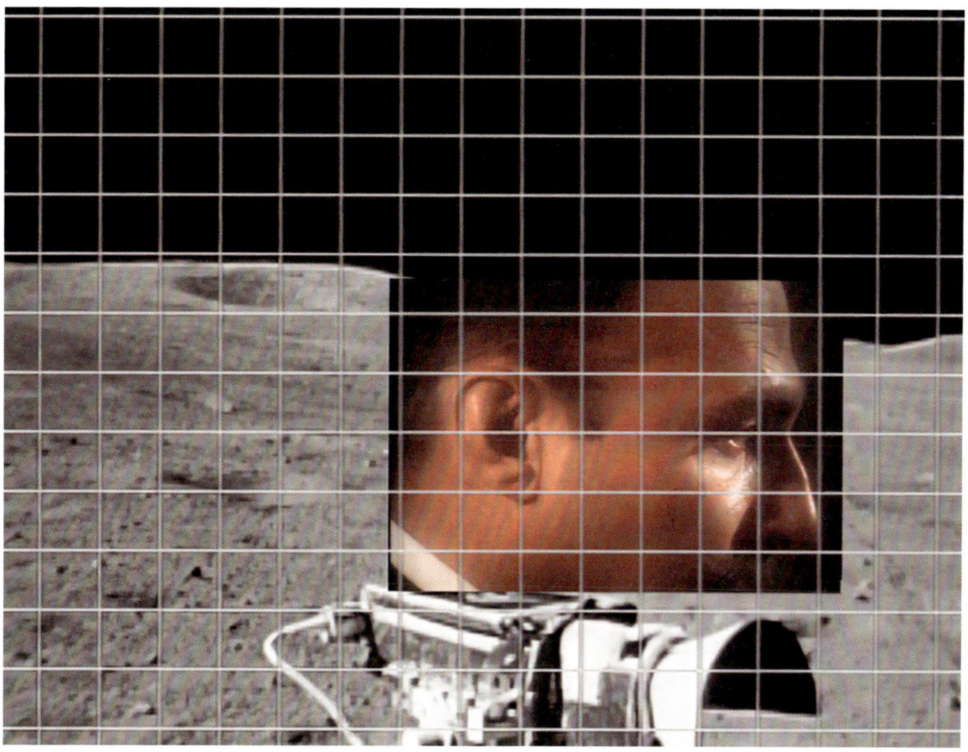

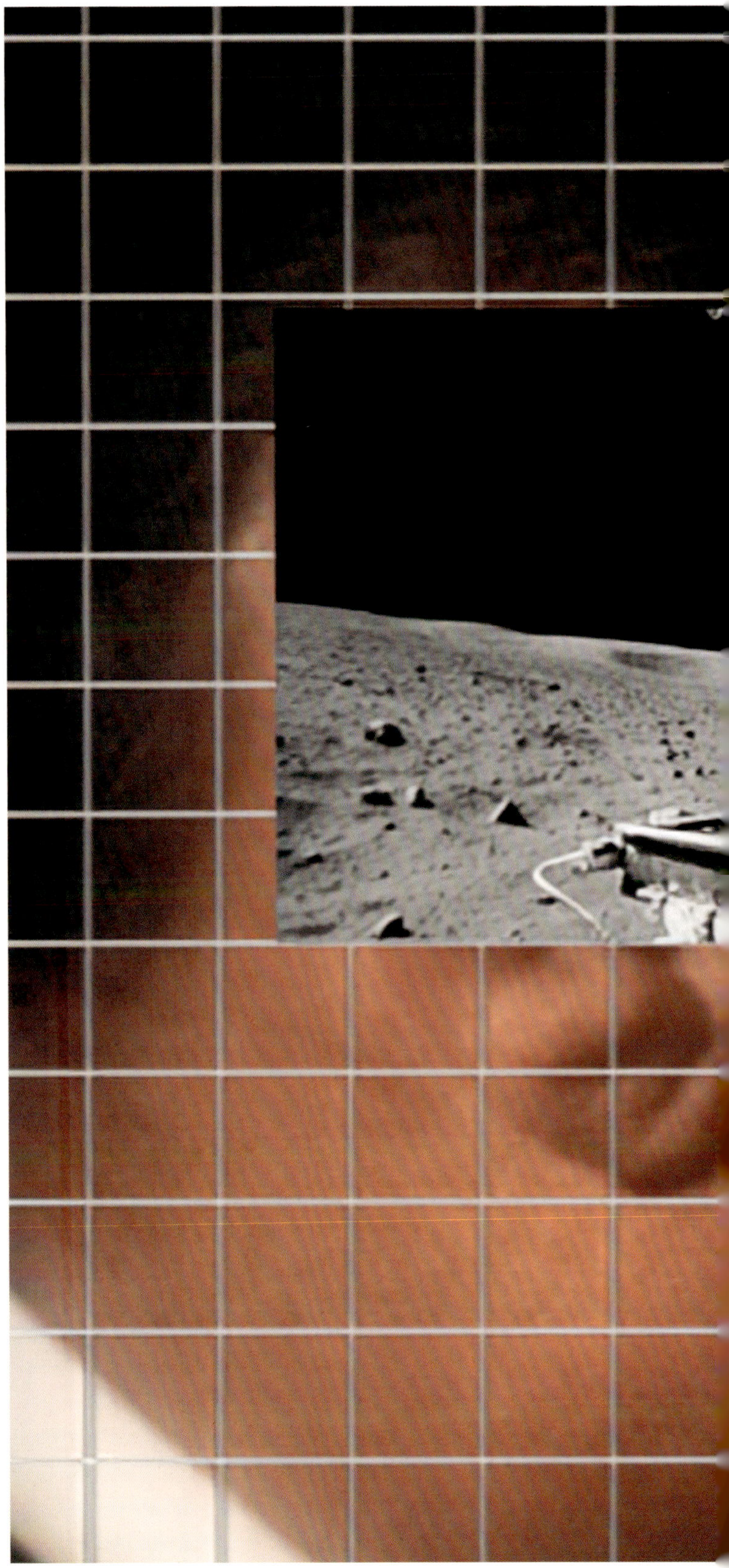

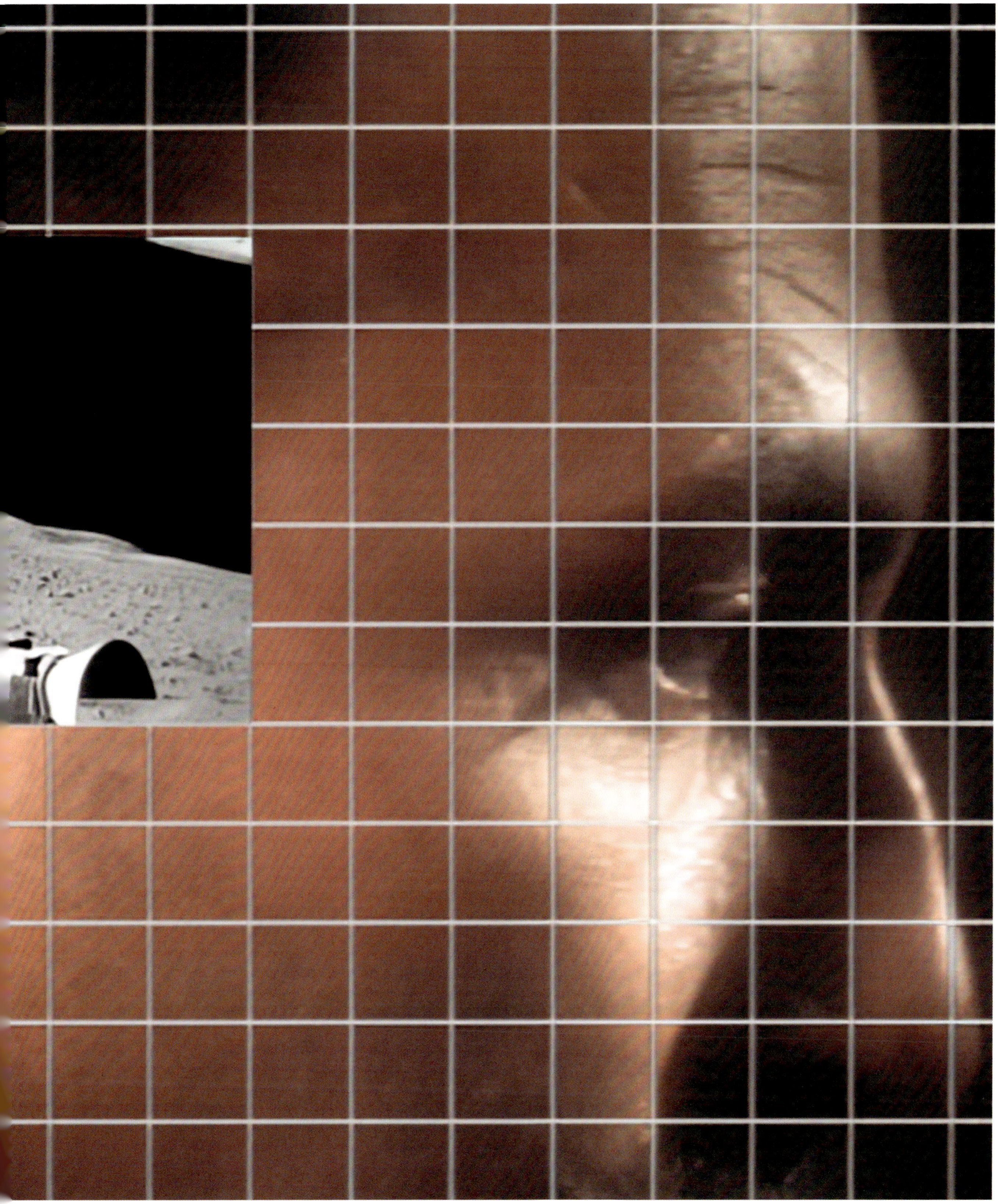

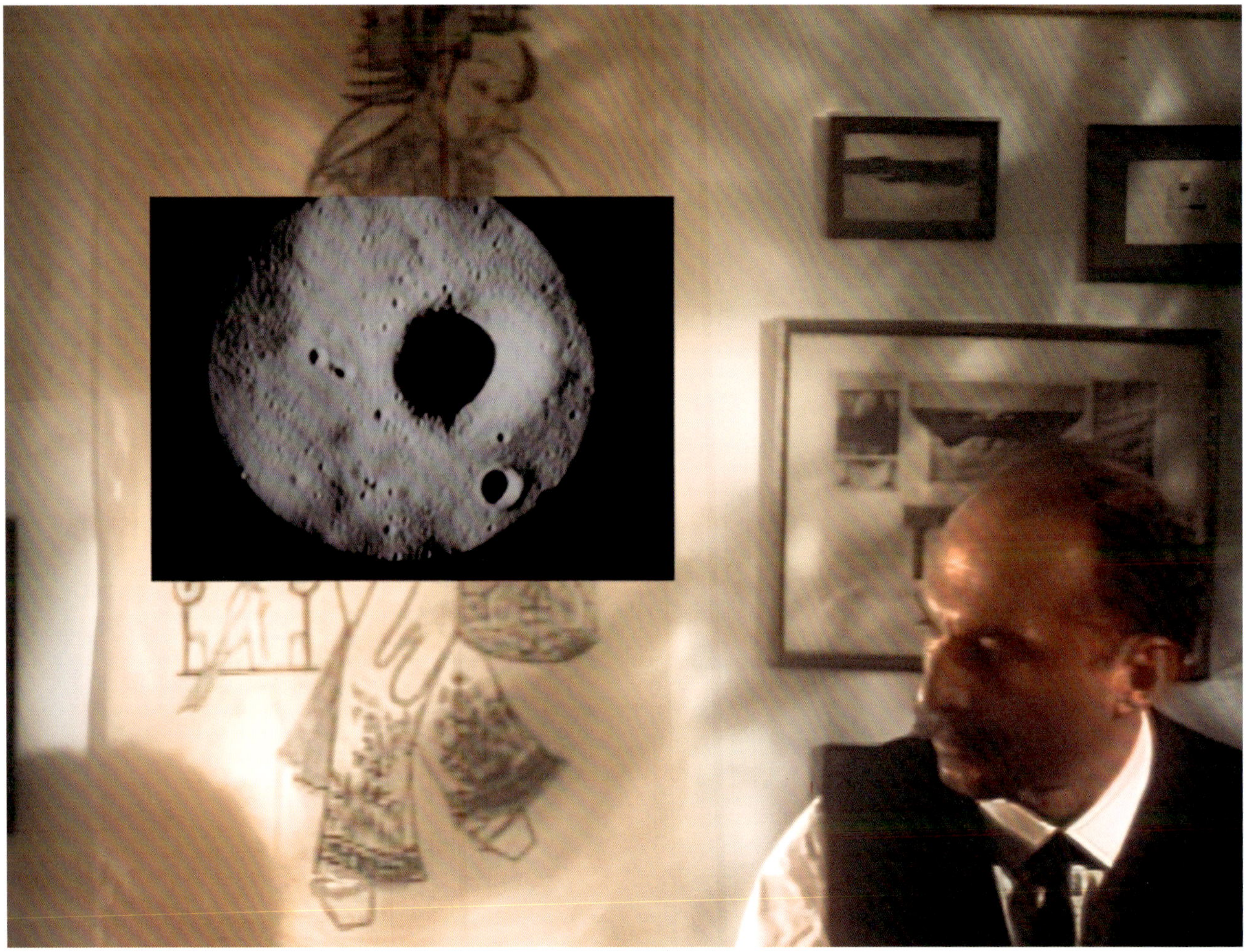

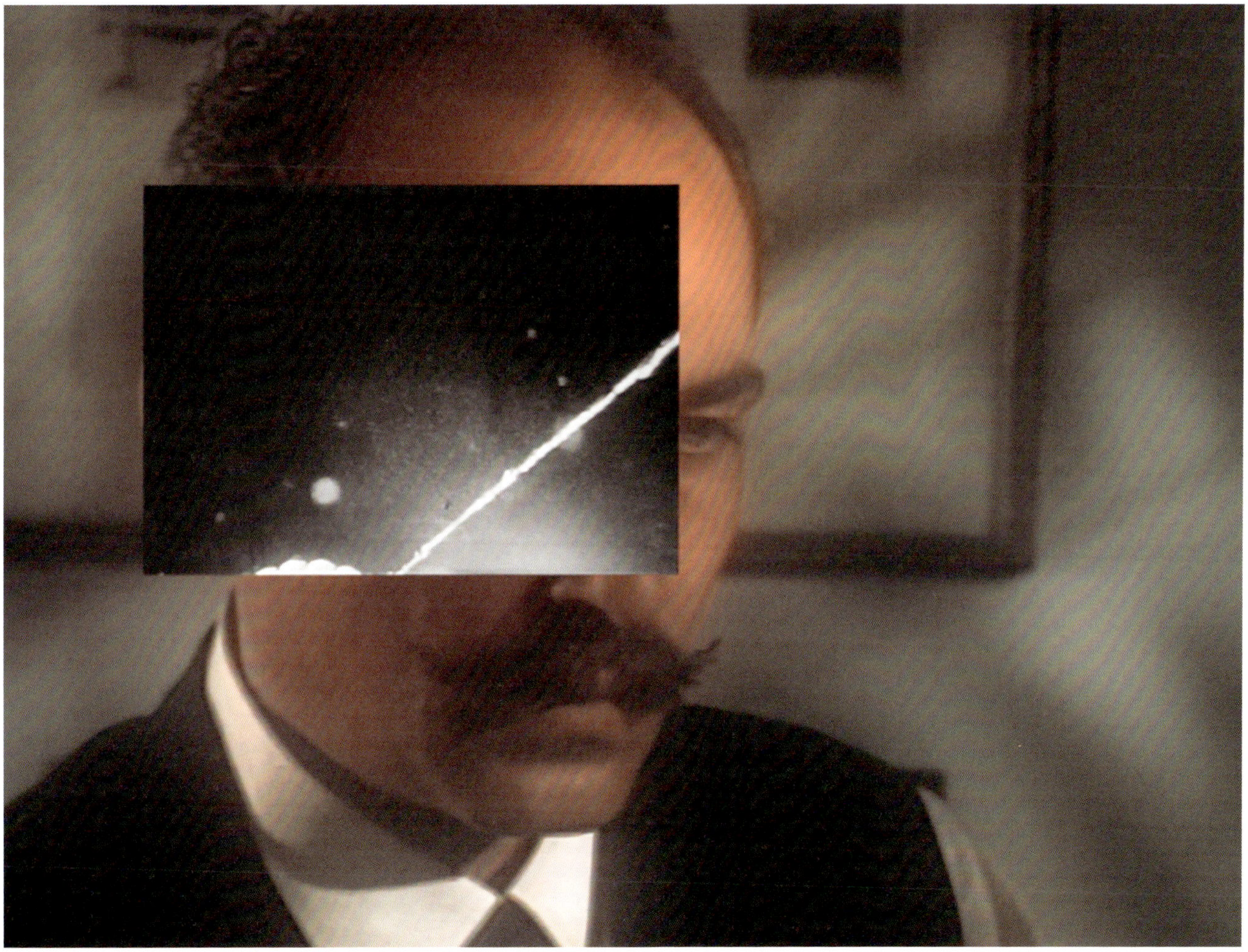

Life Force

James Richards on *Strange Space* and *The Last Time I Saw Ron*

I first encountered Leslie Thornton's work in 2005, working as an intern at Electronic Arts Intermix. In the afternoons, my errands completed, the higher-ups would let me watch anything I wanted. Such was my education in American video art, an intuitive browsing of the archive rooms, which led me to a startling and moving encounter with Thornton's *Strange Space* (1993) and *The Last Time I Saw Ron* (1995). Both pieces feature the actor Ron Vawter, a friend and collaborator of Thornton's as well as a founding member of the Wooster Group, an experimental theater collective in New York City.

Elegiac and forensic, incidental and precise, raw and highly synthesized, these brief works do so many things at once and hold images together in a taught, crisp way. Vawter, in the early 1990s, was undergoing treatment for what proved to be a fatal struggle with AIDS, and around the time, he suggested that Thornton record him reading from *Duino Elegies*, the 1923 lyric poem by Rainer Maria Rilke, and combine it with audio taken from his doctor's visits. Thornton agreed, and from the beginning of *Strange Space*, the contrast and layering of these two overlapping voices are its most commanding features—one procedural, objective; the other, an interior rumination on being itself.

The Last Time I Saw Ron came out of a collaboration around *Philoctetes Variations*, a 1994 theater production at the Brussels Kaaitheater based on the Greek tragedy. It starred Vawter, in his last role, as the injured Philoctetes, who was banished to the uninhabited island of Lemnos because his infected wounds had become so noxious. From the beginning, the actor's body was the focus of the production. Thornton's collaboration was, in part, to shoot footage of a nude Vawter with the Kaposi's lesions that covered much of his skin, which was projected during the performances. (Vawter also greeted the audience each night with a direct address: "I am dying. I am on my way to the grave but am just doing this performance on the way.")

Today, it still strikes me that these works could be about technology—or better put, somehow be *of* technology—and still deeply rooted in the body, the physicality and mortality of being human. *Strange Space* opens with a clinical voiceover—a female voice lists Vawter's symptoms—as Thornton combines imagery from NASA's film archive with shots of her friend's face, creating a flicker between layers of voice and image. Vawter reads a rendition of Rilke's poem that fades in and out as we hear electronics bleeping, and a nurse instructs him as she looks inside his body during a radiographic scan ("OK, sir, again, push your stomach out," she imperiously repeats). Hovering over Vawter's face, as a kind of porthole into the inner mechanics of his mind, a grainy frame of glimmering found footage is placed. We see a satellite catching the light as it wobbles and wiggles against the black infinity. Vawter's spoken words could be describing the satellite or his own finitude: "Strange to see all that was once relation, soullessly fluttering hither and thither in space." Here are two worlds existing at once, an inner mind and outer space, receding into a mutually constituted invisibility.

Intensely metaphysical, Rilke's *Duino Elegies* describes a state of becoming disembodied, and the passage Vawter reads most explicitly addresses the strangeness of one's own death. Yet, because of the audio track of raw medical details, the tape oscillates between the existentially vast and the administered and functional, periodically bringing us back to sensations of care and empathy. I keep returning to the idea of a life force suspended in expert hands, and the tape relays a mixture of intimacy and unsentimental detachment in Vawter's hospital care. Just as Rilke described the strangeness of being on the cusp of death, on the edge of not being, Vawter similarly described the "strange space" of the hospital—where a patient is somehow more object than subject, more life force to be preserved than person to be met.

While Thornton's hard-edged compositional grammar in these works draws on the history of structural film, it also extends beyond into something more lyrical and adamantly electronic, something proto-digital. In *Strange Space*, we witness Thornton grappling with a new language—grounding the image with a grid. I later learned from Thornton that, in making these works, as she sat with the technician in the editing suite, she felt distracted by the many options that early-nineties technology offered. So Thornton parsed it down to two: the frame within a frame (a smaller image inside the main video frame) and the grid. The grid was, in fact, a ready-made measuring device within the editing program, but transposed here into a formal device, she created an instant shorthand for technologically mediated vision.

In *Strange Space*, the recurring motif of the grid juxtaposes the living world that Vawter inhabits and the technical space in which the camera operates. In this work, the grid functions as a viewfinder, a scientific way of breaking down the visual into something rationalized and quantified—atomization and overview. It seems relevant, too, that GRID, or Gay-Related Immune Deficiency, was also an early acronym for HIV when it was afflicting primarily gay men (an acronym chosen by nascent research and communication teams to suggest a networked system of viral movement). In both *Strange Space* and *The Last Time I Saw Ron*, image modifications also propose scientific or medical modes of viewing, of collecting visual data for functional use for medical care or forensic research. At the same time, the extreme enlargements, fleshy textures, and scientific disorientations show us just how tactile moving images can be, how hands-on editing can feel.

For me, *The Last Time I Saw Ron* also stands out for its use of inversion (the negative effect), which Thornton applied to moving images culled from her research trips to the National Archives in Washington, DC. Throughout *The Last Time I Saw Ron*, we register that these images are handled lightly, a sense fortified by the slippage between different types of imagery (various explosions, waves crashing, trees waving in the wind). The black-and-white filter applied to much of the imagery gives an artificial feeling of consistency, yet, simultaneously, the diversity of material brings forth the full emotional poetics of the project.

The inversion of black and white—as with the grid—similarly speaks to a kind of analytical or scientific image with suggestions of an X-ray or thermal camera. Once color is drained from an image, and its whites and blacks are inverted into a kind of negative silhouette, it becomes, somehow, more general, unspecified. The registrations of the tree species don't matter—rather, we focus entirely on the feeling, the shock of the event, the pure force of the bomb hitting the veiny, bodily sky. We see only impact and internal structure, and a bypassing of detail opens up a sense of existential vastness that haunts both works. "When he had to use a wheelchair, sometimes we tried to see right through it and into the universe," Thornton recalls in her narration—revealing the act of summoning her own X-ray vision to peer beyond a physical apparatus, out into the vast, strange space.

The Last Time I Saw Ron

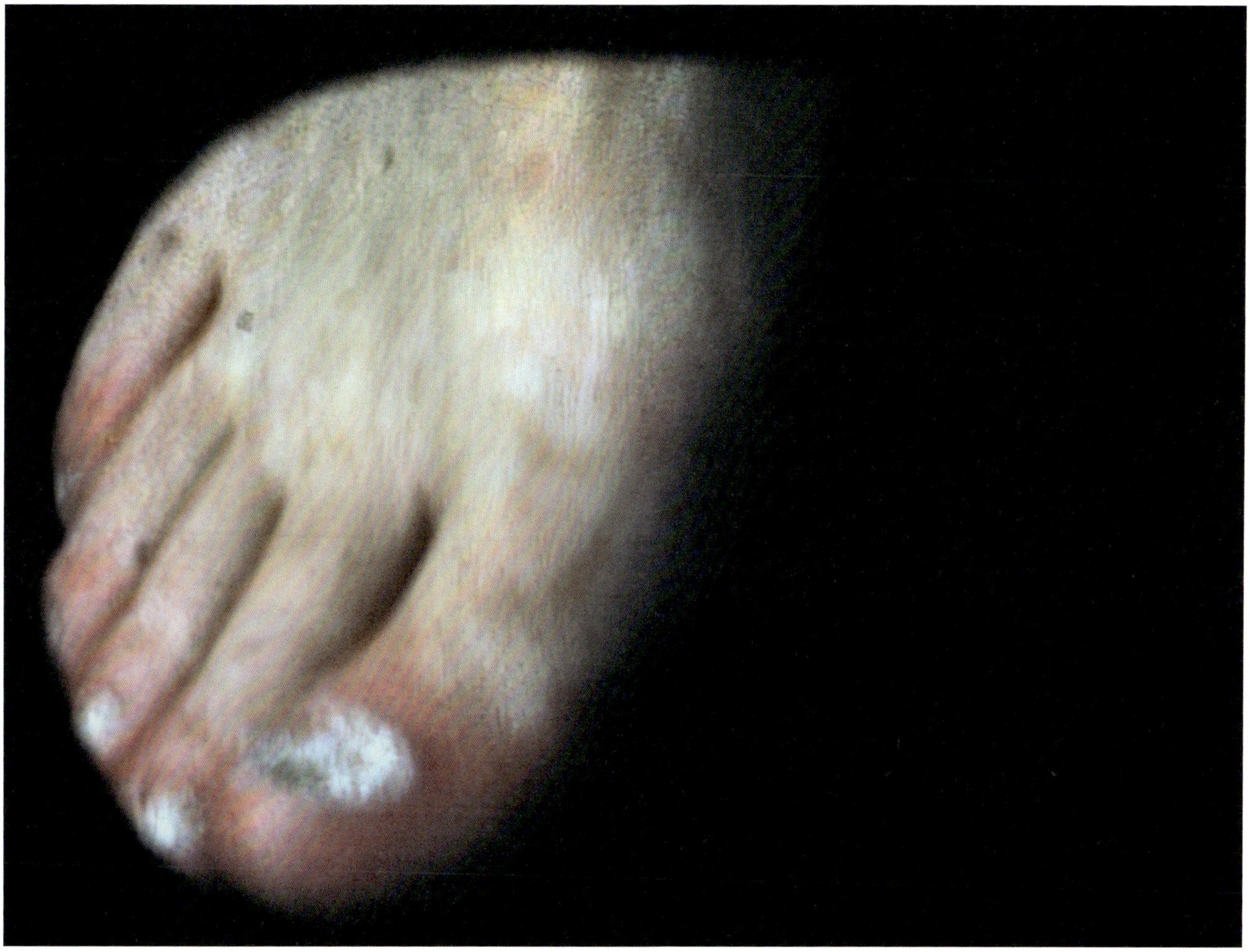

The Last Time I Saw Ron, 1995

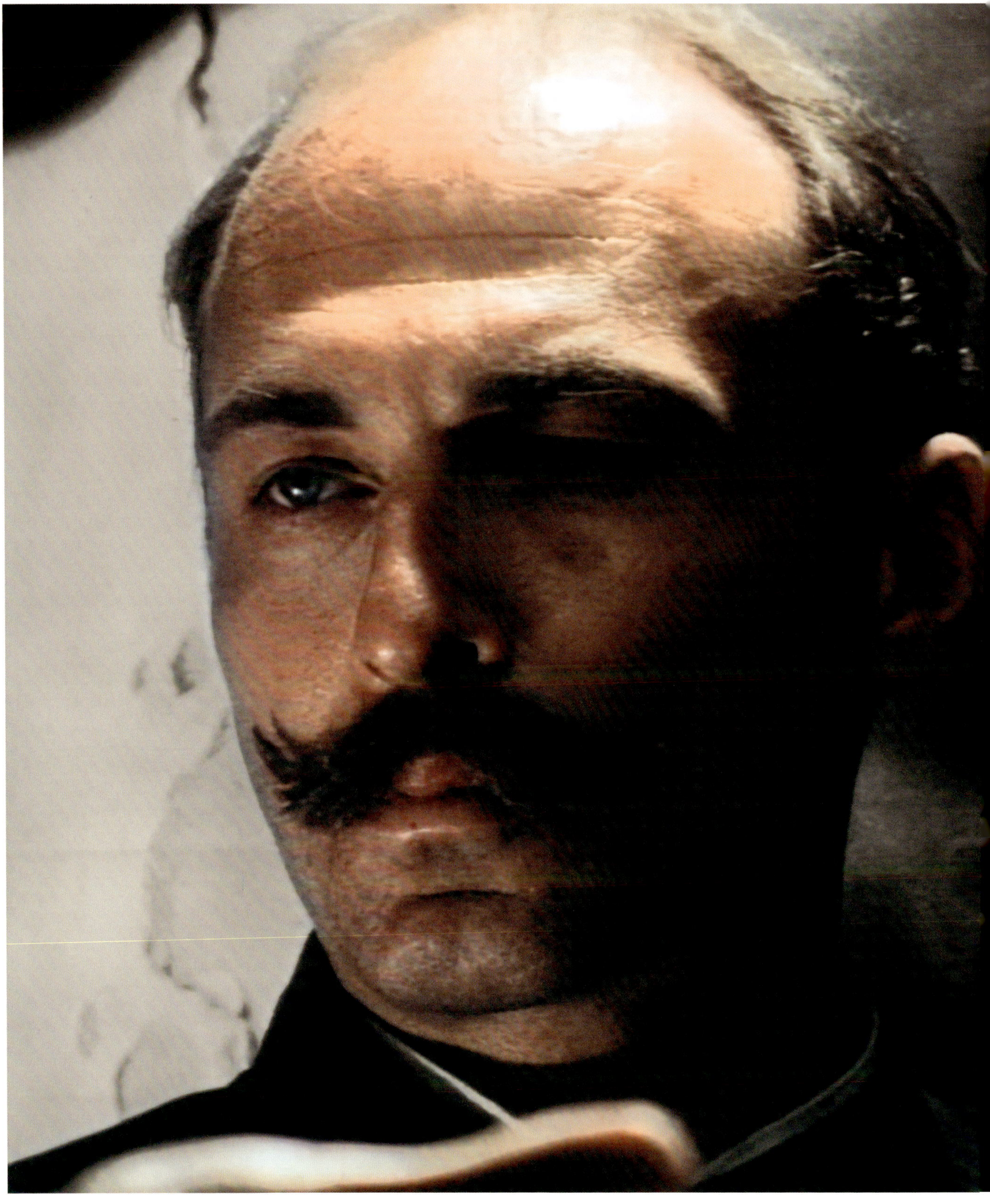

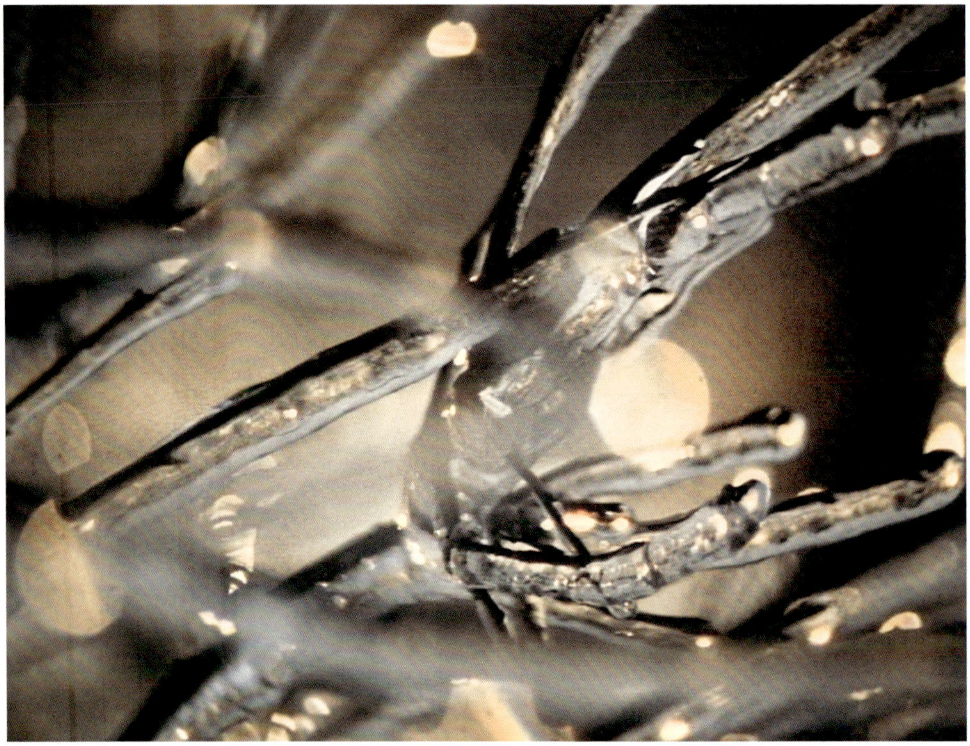

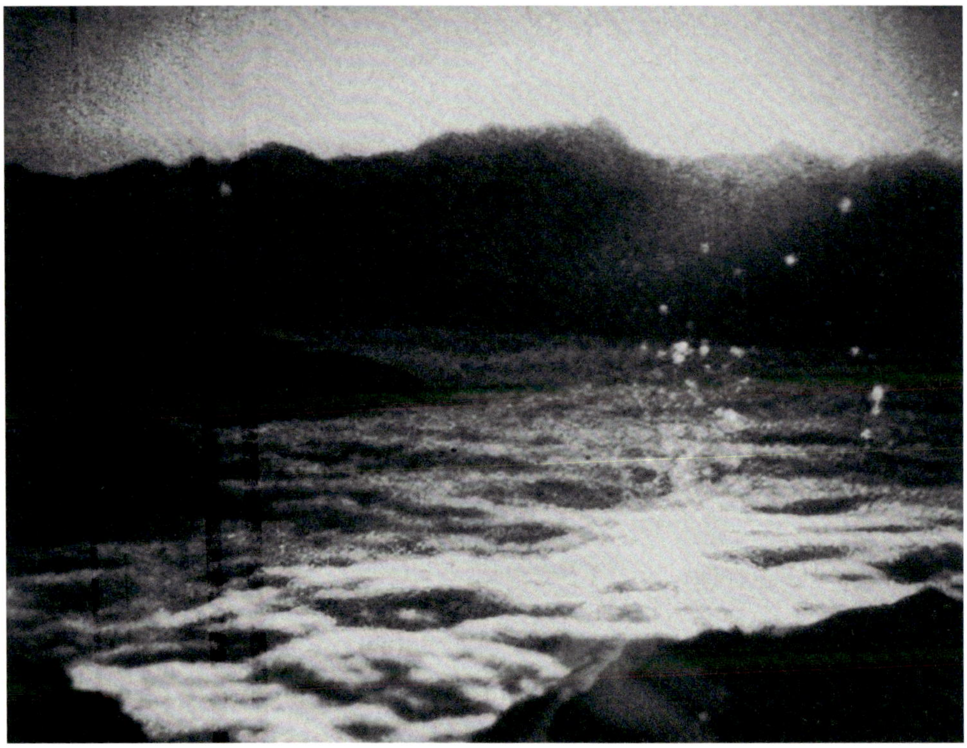

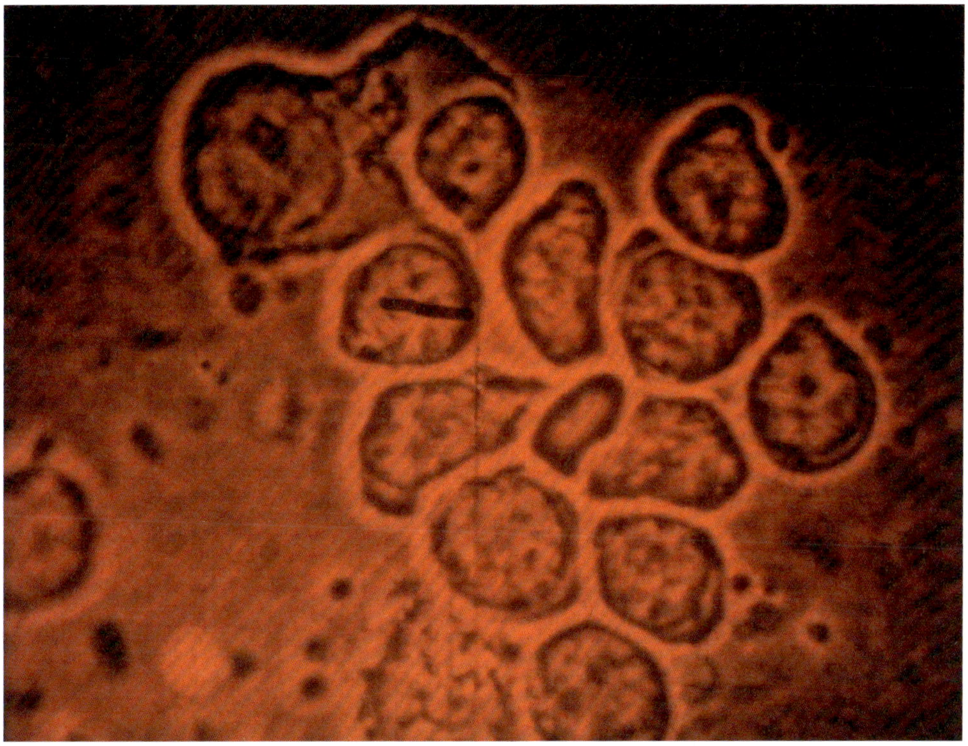

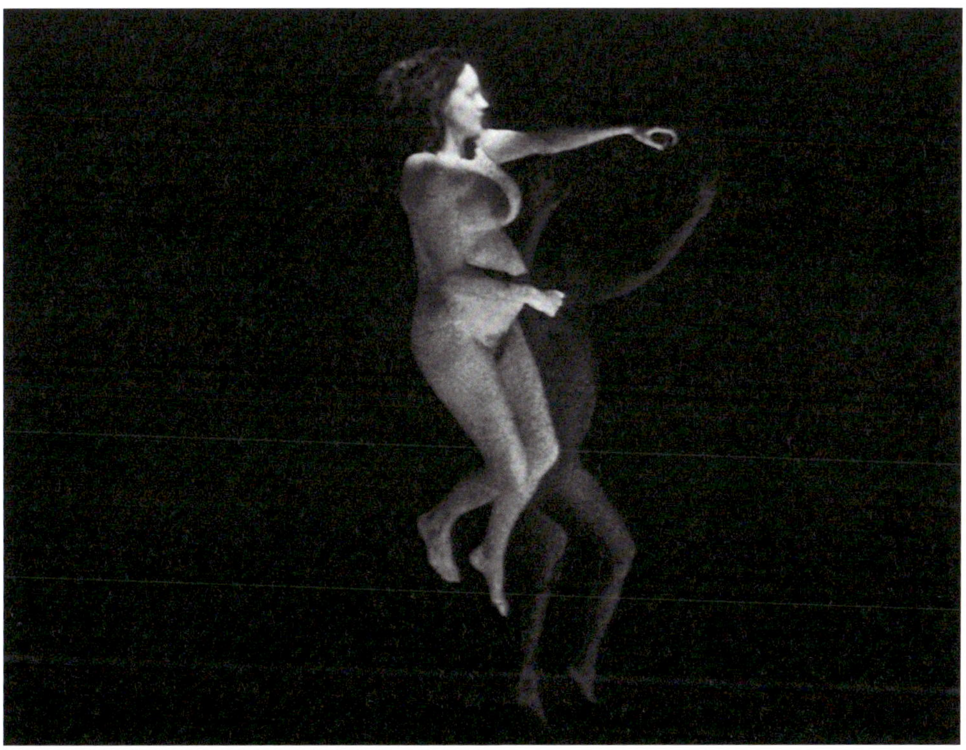

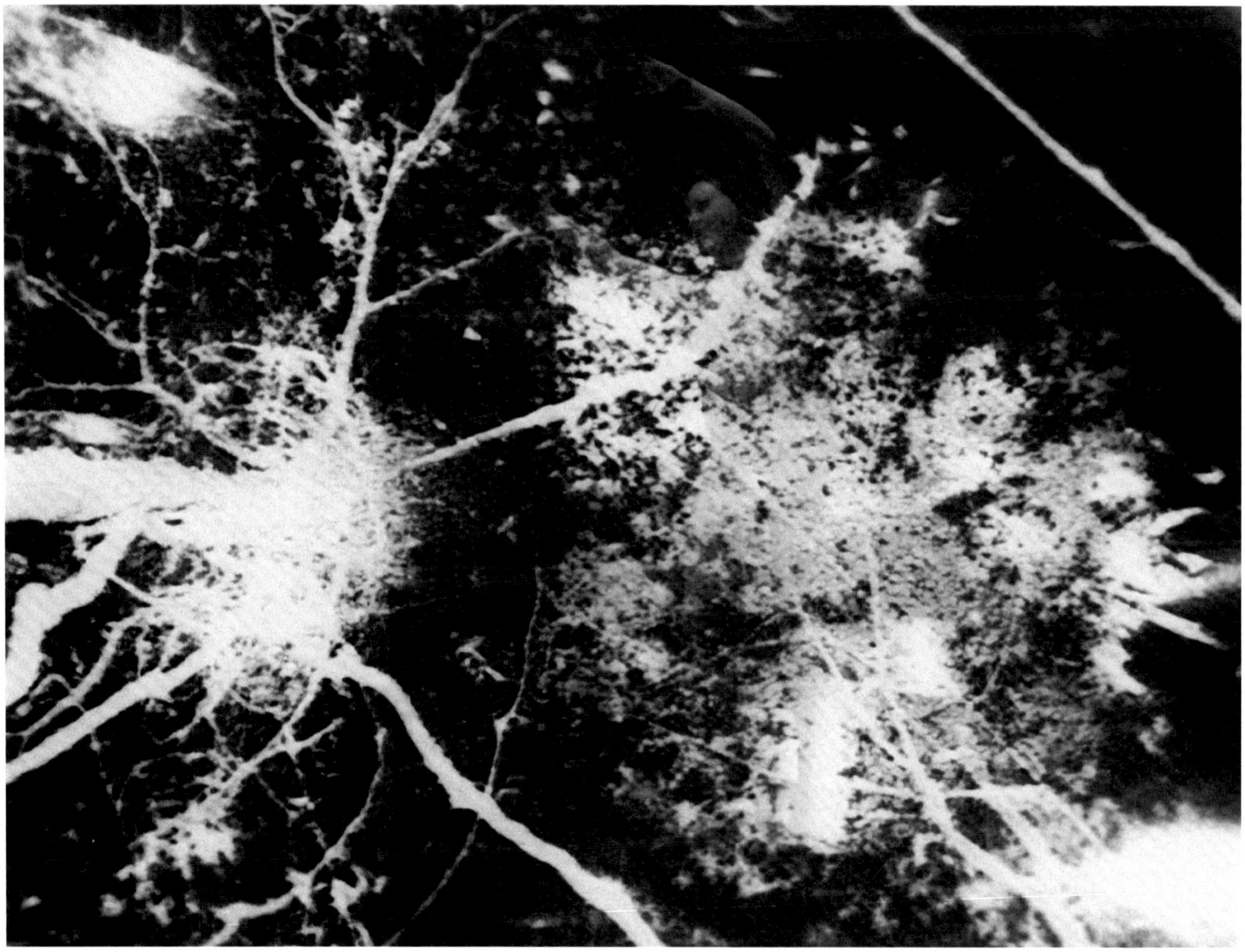

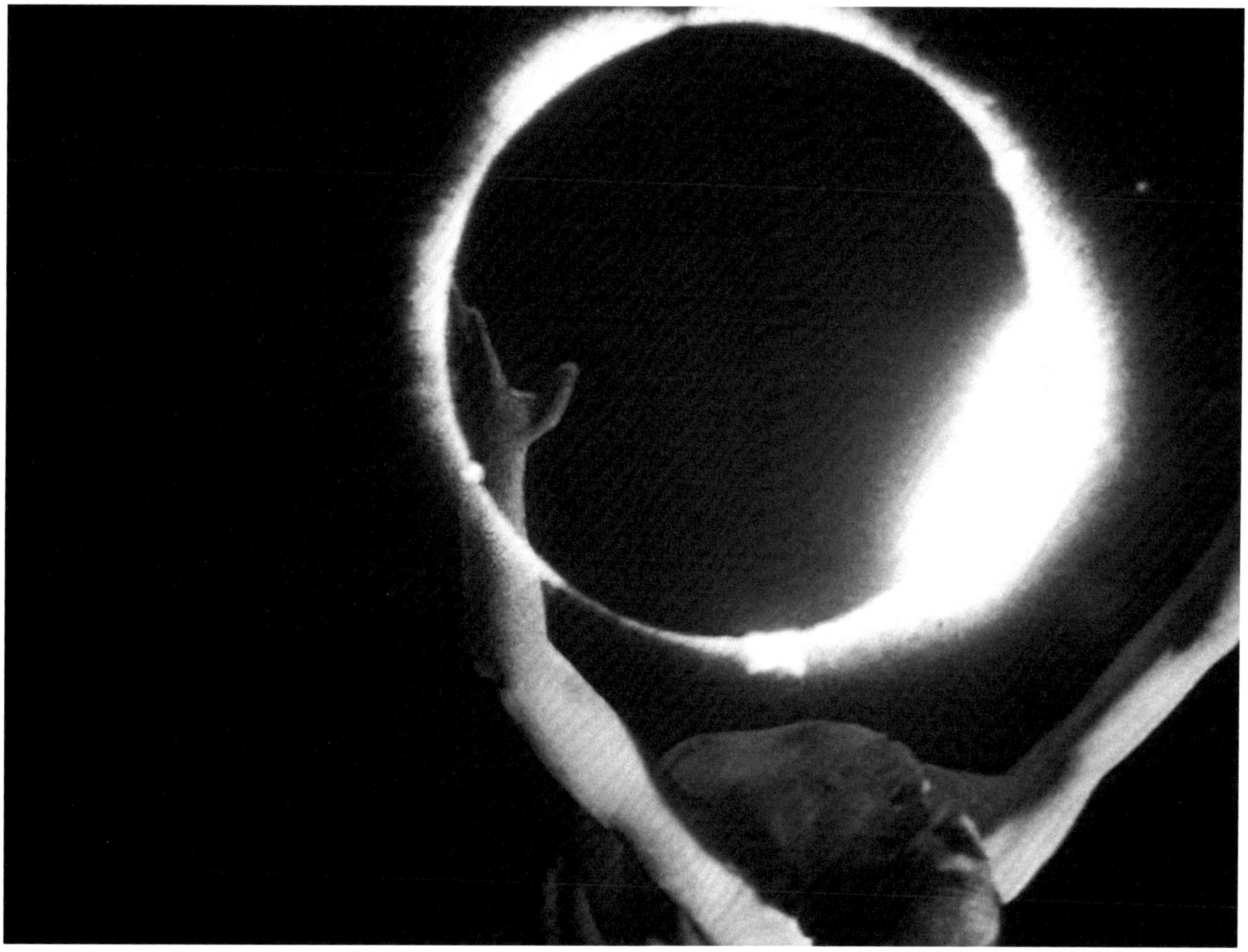

Peggy and Fred in Hell

Oh, the Storm

Dan Kidner on *Peggy and Fred in Hell*

Originally conceived as both a "feature" and a cluster of shorter "satellites," to be shown separately or configured as an installation, *Peggy and Fred in Hell* (1983–2015) is a radically open-ended, unstable cycle of works.[1] When Thornton began working on *The Prologue* in 1983, she wrote in a production notebook of her desire for the project to become "modular" and of its assault on narrative:

> *Peggy and Fred in Hell* is a disturbance. It disturbs narrative form; it disturbs our understanding of action and fiction. It disturbs the way we regard children. It disturbs our complacency as viewers, the expectations we have for comfort and resolution. It stirs up ideological biases. It disrupts linearity, it disrupts cause and effect.[2]

Although the sprawling project is difficult to describe and categorize, it is possible to reconstruct an origin story. The names of the two nominal protagonists were an inheritance from a previous film, *Minutiae* (1979). This earlier film, which contained many of the techniques that Thornton would go on to employ in *Peggy and Fred in Hell*, was shot in a cinema-verité style but conceived and edited in the manner of a structural film.[3] *Minutiae* focused on the gestures and speech of a couple (whose real names were Peggy and Fred), their daughter, and their parrot. The artist was planning to make a new film returning to the two adult subjects, exploring "the danger of technology that had grown to exceed the human grasp," and even had the title *Peggy and Fred in Hell* in mind.[4] But after meeting two children, Donald and Janis Reading, she reconceived the idea around "mass media as a social technology" and developed a fictional scenario involving two feral children raised by television, alone in a postapocalyptic world, save for the mysterious presence of an artificial intelligence.[5] In 1983, Thornton moved into a house in the Mission District of San Francisco and immediately forged a connection with the two siblings, Janis and Donald, who lived next door. Intrigued by their new neighbor and the audiovisual equipment she hauled out of the trunk of her car, the children began performing and asked to be recorded. Cycling through popular songs, impressions of movie stars, and improvised stories, they presented themselves as willing participants in what would become one of the most unique, compelling, and searching artworks of the late twentieth century.

In Janis and Donald, Thornton found not only muses who would collaborate on a suite of works dominating her practice and life for the next thirty

1 The complete cycle of *Peggy and Fred in Hell* consists of sixteen short works, ranging in duration from two to twenty-three minutes, and one final "feature-length" film, *Peggy and Fred in Hell: Folding*, with a running time of ninety-five minutes.

2 Leslie Thornton, "Afterword: Annotations on *Peggy and Fred in Hell*, Circa 1983–84, Excerpted in a Notebook by Leslie Thornton," in *Peggy and Fred in Hell: The Complete Transcript*, ed. Leslie Thornton and Thomas Zummer (New York: Mono No Aware, 2017), 62.

3 Thornton was schooled in both structural film and cinema verité but rejected both. As an undergraduate at SUNY Buffalo in the early 1970s, she was taught by a group of artists—among them Stan Brakhage, Hollis Frampton, and Paul Sharits—who influenced the development of what became known as structural film. As a graduate student at MIT in 1975, she was taught by two of the pioneers of cinema verité and direct cinema, Richard Leacock and Ed Pincus.

4 Leslie Thornton, email conversation with the author, May 2021.

years but also lifelong friends with whom she has maintained contact. Their father, Don Reading, was involved in the West Coast music scene of the late 1960s and early 1970s, knew Janis Joplin (after whom he named his daughter) and members of Jefferson Airplane, and served three tours in Vietnam with the US Air Force.[6] After this, he made his living as a part-time prospector and drew on his Native American heritage through his silversmithing. Thornton and her partner, Thomas Zummer, grew close to not only the children but also their father—regularly venturing out on adventures together, foraging and prospecting. The artist would always carry her camera and the children's costumes (a white suit jacket for Fred and red printed dress for Peggy) waiting for what she deemed a "Peggy and Fred moment"—something she described as an occasion when the scenario she had sketched out could be overlaid onto what the children were doing naturally. Observations made during filming and details about the family gifted the project some of its themes, being fed like data into the Peggy and Fred imaginary or mythos. But it was Janis's and Donald's hunger to perform, their striking looks, struggles with language, and feral energy that imbued the project with a jittery unpredictability, which the artist harnessed to maximum effect.

In the first film of the cycle, *The Prologue*, it is the scenario rather than a plot that is foregrounded. The hell in which our eponymous protagonists find themselves is, seemingly, a postapocalyptic future in which the technological detritus of the twentieth century provides at once a playground, a means of survival, and, as becomes more apparent in later works, a laboratory in which Peggy and Fred are being surveilled and studied by the AI.

In reality, hell is a makeshift home studio constructed in the artist's living room, across which she has strewn an old GE television set, an overturned office chair, a toaster, a broken lamp, a vacuum cleaner, some doll parts, and a tumbleweed brought back from the Mojave Desert. Thornton traveled to the desert with Don and the children on one of their trips to shoot footage used in a later episode, *Peggy and Fred and Pete* (1988). Pinned on the back wall is a print of a Jack Goldstein painting—the streaks of light across the surface of the print (made even more dramatic in the monochrome world of Peggy and Fred) might depict a fireworks display or bombing raid above a generic city, represented by a church steeple and some rooftops in silhouette.[7] Another Goldstein work pops up in a later episode, *Introduction to the So-Called Duck Factory* (1992)—an un-stretched, unfinished canvas of a silver moon—which serves as a backdrop to a sequence in which Peggy tapes two lightbulbs to Fred's head.

The Prologue features a passage much commented on in the literature on *Peggy and Fred in Hell*, taken from two main sources: a Bell Laboratory education film from the 1920s, documenting the vibration of vocal cords, and an education film about pitch and gender. Further close-up footage of fleshy tissue vibrating and flapping originates from an unknown film. Mary Ann Doane draws attention to the vocal cords' resemblance to female genitalia and cites Luce Irigaray's influential (and controversial) writing on sexuality, which, for Doane, describes the "development of a morpho-logic whereby a psychical sexuality mimics a bodily sexuality and in which the phallus is no longer the supreme arbiter of sexual difference."[8] This logic for Doane and other commentators is enacted by what Ed Halter has called "the female-male dyad of Peggy and Fred" through their conforming or otherwise to gender roles.[9]

5 Thornton, email conversation, May 2021.

6 Reading was largely solely responsible for raising his children. During the period Thornton was closest to the family (between 1983 and 1985), she had infrequent contact with an independent older sister and never met the mother, who was absent from the children's lives at the time.

7 Goldstein's paintings of this period, made using acrylic spray-painted onto canvas, depict volcanos, lightning strikes, and fireworks. The painting (Untitled, 1983), from which the print in Thornton's living room was made, was worked on by Zummer, who was an assistant to Goldstein in the 1980s (as were a number of other young artists during that period, including Ashley Bickerton) and fabricated several works for the artist.

8 Mary Ann Doane, "The Retreat of Signs and the Failure of Words: Leslie Thornton's *Adynata*," *Senses of Cinema*, no. 22 (October 2002), https://www.sensesofcinema.com/2002/leslie-thornton-experimental/adynata/.

9 Ed Halter, "Close-Up: Hell Is for Children," *Artforum* 51, no. 1 (September 2012), https://www.artforum.com/print/201207/-31962.

However, for those looking for fixed coordinates, Thornton is already laying traps. Punching through the potentially heavy symbolism of this opening sequence is a crunching soundtrack that marries the rambunctious exotica of Yma Sumac's "Gopher Mambo" with the soaring aria "Il Vostra Maggio" (The Mermaid's Song) from Handel's *Rinaldo*. Irigaray's famously essentialist theory of the formation of gender identity has been critiqued by successive generations of feminists since the early 1980s, including, most recently, those writing from a queer and trans perspective, and Thornton here is clearly more interested in multiple ill-disciplined voices, including those of the protagonists themselves, which refuse or elude conventional enunciation.[10]

Thornton's editing of these opening sequences also sidesteps the conventions of voicing or giving voice often enacted in feminist experimental film and video art through the use of voice-over and critiques of verité and opens onto what Pooja Rangan calls "the parallel domain of voicelessness that lurks in the shadows of legitimate, articulate speech."[11] Thornton cuts from this opening sequence to the set of *Peggy and Fred in Hell*, where the old GE television is broadcasting live and the children roam, giving impromptu performances to camera. But despite appearances, this move isn't from one cinematic idiom to another, where montage and voice-over give way to verité. For Thornton, neither of these film forms necessarily gives a coherent voice to either filmmaker or subject.

After the voice of authority is heard from the education program, carefully enunciating that "the pitch most people prefer for the male voice is around low C," we see and hear Fred run through a number of half-remembered folk songs. First up is a schoolyard parody of the Appalachian folk song "Old Smokey": "I went to her funeral / I went to her grave / People threw flowers / I threw a grenade." He follows this with "Mr. Noah," popularized by Dave Van Ronk and adapted from a song in Frank Shay's *My Pious Friends and Drunken Companions* (published in 1927) and the schoolyard song "There Were Three Jolly Fisherman." Each rendition is as spirited as it is wayward. If one is looking for meaning, then it is there to be found—"Mr. Noah," with its dark lyrics predicting a storm, is especially resonant.

However, everything and nothing are meaningful in Thornton's hell. *The Prologue* opens with a shot of a cog, soundtracked by a low, ominous, rumbling sound. This is actually a slowed-down image of the high-speed motion camera used to capture the vocal cords in the Bell Labs film, but could be read as a subtle allusion to both the Moloch machine in *Metropolis* (1927) and the scene in Charlie Chaplin's *Modern Times* (1936) where Chaplin's Little Tramp is dragged into a machine and spat out the other end. Internalizing the logic of the Fordist assembly line, Chaplin's character continues tightening bolts (his assembly-line job) even where there are none, and this assimilation to the logic of capitalism sends Chaplin's character straight to the asylum. We might also think of Milton's Moloch, the Canaanite god who was said to have sacrificed children and appears in *Paradise Lost*: "Their children's cries unheard, that passed through fire."[12] Watching this sequence another day will bring other references to mind and resonate differently or just drift past, before something else catches the attention and another connection is made.

As much as these references, details, and items can be indexed, they do not provide a reliable legend with which to navigate and decode the series of short videos, multimedia installations, and final, longer edit that make up the *Peggy and Fred* family of works. In an important sense, *Peggy and Fred* as a project is not navigable at all. There is what the artist has called a "circulating logic"—different kinds of connections that *can* be made between scenes,

10 For Irigaray's writing on sexuality, see "This Sex Which Is Not One" and "When Our Lips Speak Together," published in 1979 and 1980, respectively. And for a critique of Irigaray's essentialism, see, among others, Judith Butler, Monique Plaza, Christine Delphy, and Monique Wittig.

11 Pooja Rangan, "In Defense of Voicelessness: The Matter of the Voice and the Films of Leslie Thornton," *Feminist Media Histories* 1, no. 3 (Summer 2015): 95–126.

12 John Milton, *Paradise Lost: Book 1* (London: Taylor and Francis, 1968), 85.

13 The first four episodes were edited on a Steenbeck then transferred to video. All subsequent works were edited on video or digitally.

14 Openness was a key concept in literary theory from the 1960s and was structured around ideas of multiplicity and

objects within the scenes, and the project's apparent themes and subject matter—but there is no center. The works are charged with a kind of nervous energy militating against meaning. In a number of scenes, although not exactly scripted, the children are consciously furthering a narrative that has been sketched out in collaboration with the artist. But more often than not, their words sound like accidents in a maelstrom, and connections between scenes or separate satellite works are contingent upon an elusive logic.

Another possible way of reading the project would be through its use of different media. Much of the footage of the children is shot on 16mm film, and most of the found footage is from 16mm reels bought from national archives, while all episodes after *The Prologue* are edited on video. After the first few works, the episodes are also almost entirely constructed in the editing suite, using and reusing found footage in combination with material shot by the artist during those early encounters.[13] As such, despite the fact that over thirty years separate *The Prologue* and the last work in the cycle, *The Fold* (2014), the children barely age.

Through the many iterations of the project—multichannel installations, monitor presentations of single episodes, film and media festival screenings of collections of episodes, or longer "feature-length" edits—Thornton's interest in media is not only evident but also constitutive of the complex meanings and pleasures to be taken from the project. Although many of the animosities that fueled debates between experimental filmmakers (who valorized 16mm as a medium and rejected video) and video artists (who drew closer to both broadcast television and the emerging form of the music video, on the one hand, and a punk DIY aesthetic or community activism on the other) now seem rather archaic, the terms of these debates are still legible as a critical context for the project.

Reflection on both the history of media art and its attendant discourses in the late twentieth century will only get one so far, however. Thornton's relationship to this history and those ideas, as well as to thematic foregrounding, is much the same as her relationship to plot and narrative continuity: antagonistic. But these contexts are important, nevertheless, and they ground the project in a complex network of themes, questions, and discourses that now seem prescient: ecological catastrophe, nuclear annihilation, forced migration, language formation, gender identity, and the use of AI technologies to surveil and harvest information.

Her scenario, these themes, and this art-historical context provide a backdrop against which both her protagonists and viewers are encouraged to plot their own journey. In this sense, *Peggy and Fred* could perhaps be seen as an "open work," although this may also be a trap.[14] Any attempt by viewers to complete the work or ascribe their own logic to a sequence of events will inevitably be frustrated. The world of Peggy and Fred is one of simultaneous movement and stasis.

Over the years, the episodes become ever more elliptical, enigmatic, and, in Thornton's words, "nonlinear." She notes that this decoupling from linearity occurs midway through *[Dung Smoke Enters the Palace]* (1989). Linear cutting does feature in later episodes, though with less and less frequency. After *Paradise Crushed* (2003), not only is there less reliance on linear cutting, but there is also very little footage that isn't digitally manipulated in one way or another or recycled from previous episodes, almost as if the project is devouring or destroying itself.

This is felt most acutely in the crowning work of the whole project, *Peggy and Fred in Hell: Folding* (1983–2015), a "feature-length" edit that incorporates many of the satellite pieces in addition to some new footage secreted between episodes.

the structuring of a relationship between reader and text. Prior to his conversion to semiotics and poststructuralism, Umberto Eco explored these ideas in his book *The Open Work* (trans. Anna Cancogni [Cambridge, MA: Harvard University Press, 1989]). See also the expansion of these ideas of openness and the relationship of author to reader, and of the author-function, in Michel Foucault's "What Is an Author?," and Jacques Derrida's deconstructive criticism. Although beyond the scope of this essay, it would be interesting to trace Thornton's relationship to these theories and her own idiosyncratic and original application of them.

The experience of watching all the way through can feel like half-waking from a dream, only to be dragged back into the dreamworld, now the same but different. Discretely sandwiched between the end of *Introduction to the So-Called Duck Factory*, with its poor-quality recording of Amelia Earhart speaking after crossing the Atlantic, and the all-out visual assault of *Paradise Crushed*, Thornton has inserted footage of urban architecture she shot while visiting the Royal London Hospital in Whitechapel, London, in 2015. It is at odds with much of the other footage, but by this stage, the project has become so expansive and sibylline, this kind of contamination has become part of the organizing principle.

Some motifs repeat throughout *Peggy and Fred*, and sections even migrate to other works in the artist's catalog. This creates the impression of a logic internal to Thornton's practice: an ever-expanding universe of worlds. Yet, the radical discontinuity and fragmentation of *Peggy and Fred* frustrates attempts at interpretation. You may pay attention for a second and catch a moment of continuous editing that seems to produce narrative coherence, but you are soon cast adrift again, like Peggy and Fred, picking up a piece here, making a connection there, and then moving on. In a 1999 interview, Thornton maintained that the "main thing to get is that there is nothing to get. [...] You're going through something. You drift and you have moments."[15]

This porosity, instability, and resistance to meaning are constitutive of Thornton's method. But, for the artist, making the final satellite work, *The Fold*, followed closely by *Peggy and Fred in Hell: Folding* a year later, really did constitute the conclusion of the project. Over thirty years after meeting the children and reorienting her practice, Thornton reached the edge of this particular world. Peggy and Fred moments may creep into other works as rediscovered reels are turned into standalone postscripts, such as in *High Heel Beloved* (2020), but the project was concluded in 2015. At the end of *Folding*, a computerized voice, which has been sparring with and guiding our protagonists, utters the devastating yet strangely soporific line: "Oh, the storm." Expressing both alarm and resignation, it is somehow at once matter-of-fact and strained—and is the artist's own voice, digitally manipulated.

As the project that sustained Thornton for over three decades comes to an end, a line is drawn in the sand, and a view of the wreckage of our world comes into sharp focus. From the turn of the millennium, with the production of the episode *Have a Nice Day Alone* (2001), the artist began to contemplate the end of the project and understand how the amassed fragments might reflect on "our slow-motion apocalypse, our own self erasure."[16] The specter of climate catastrophe and the demise of our species in the early episodes had the dramatic status of premonition or speculation, but in the later videos become lived reality for the spectator. As the artificial voice intones toward the end of the 2001 episode: "The people made a fire. Then they entered the last house. They had a nice day alone."

Although radically discontinuous, Thornton's magnum opus frequently returns to the idea of beginnings and endings. References to creation myths pepper the later works, and death and destruction are frequent motifs. Immediately prior to the AI announcing the arrival of the storm in *Folding*, it stumbles through a monologue; its thoughts or logic at odds with human reasoning, or maybe attempting then failing to mimic it: "To reach this emotional state, there have been contact moments too many to count. Or animals. A viral eradication. Denied. Error. Begin. Begin. Begin again. Again. Again!" We may have escaped viral eradication this time, but the storm has arrived.

15 Irene Borger, "An Interview with Leslie Thornton," in *The Force of Curiosity*, ed. Irene Borger (Santa Clarita, CA: CalArts, 1999).

16 Leslie Thornton, "Leslie Thornton's 35 Years of Radical Filmmaking," interview by the author, *Frieze* (August 23, 2018), https://www.frieze.com/article-leslie-thorntons-35-years-radical-filmmaking.

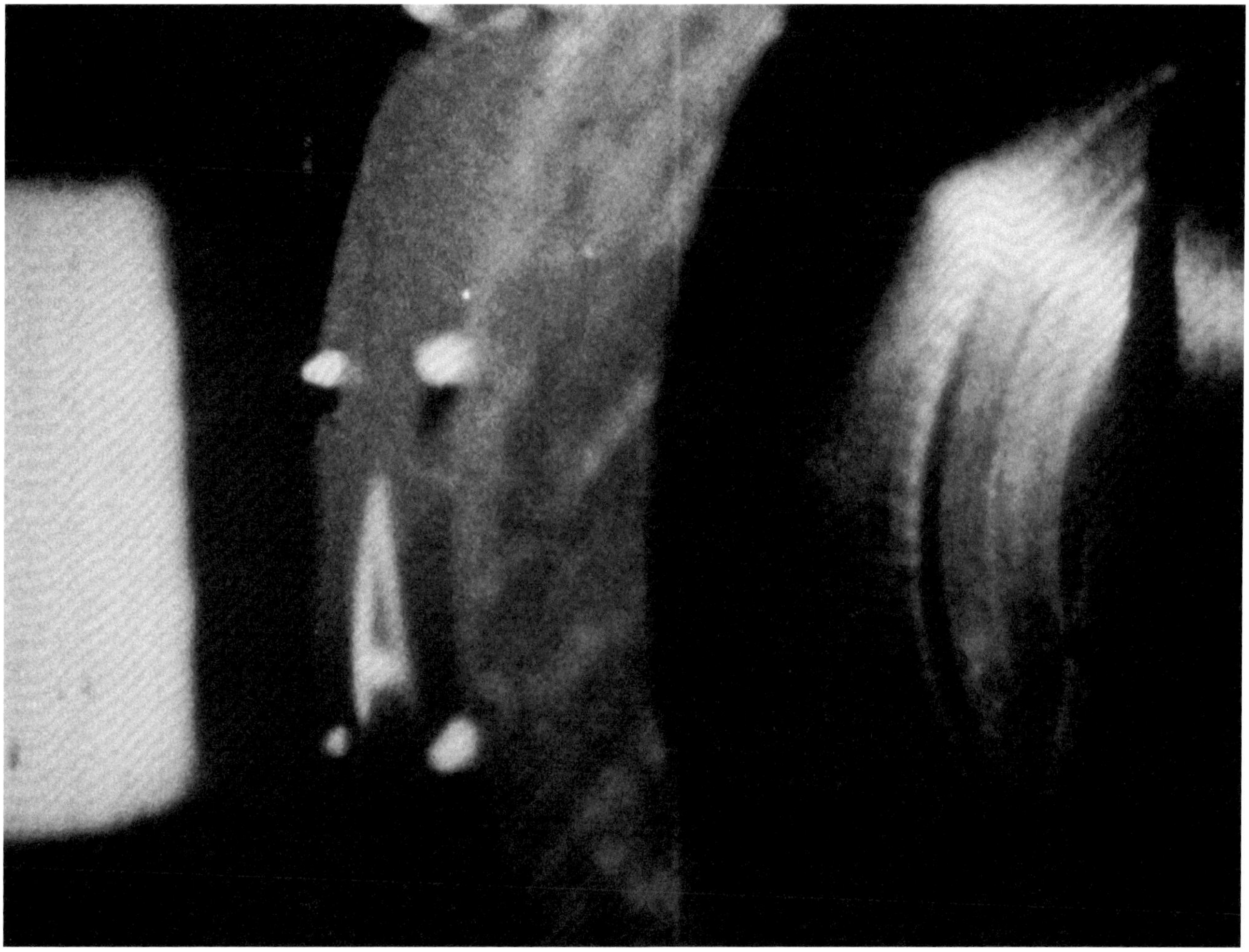

Peggy and Fred in Hell: Folding, 1983–2015

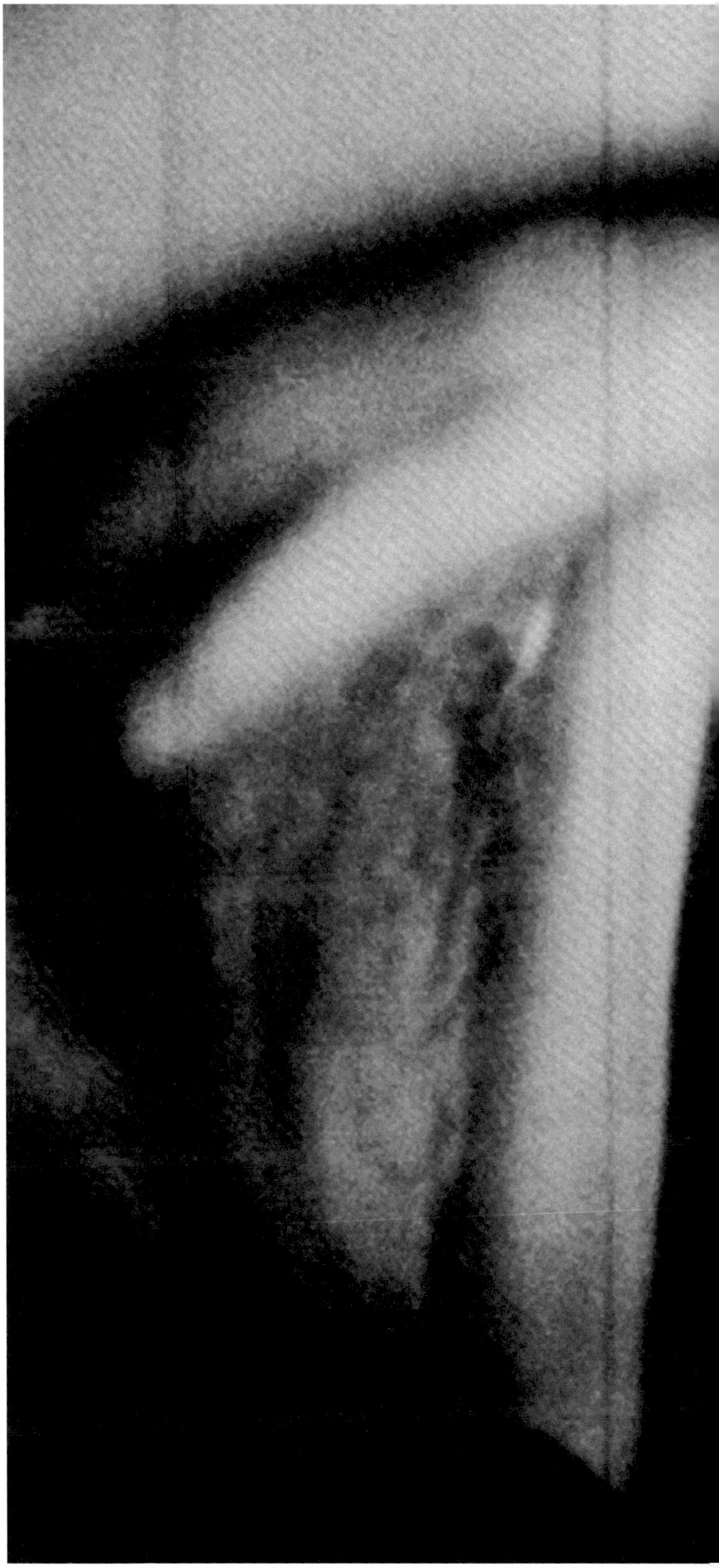

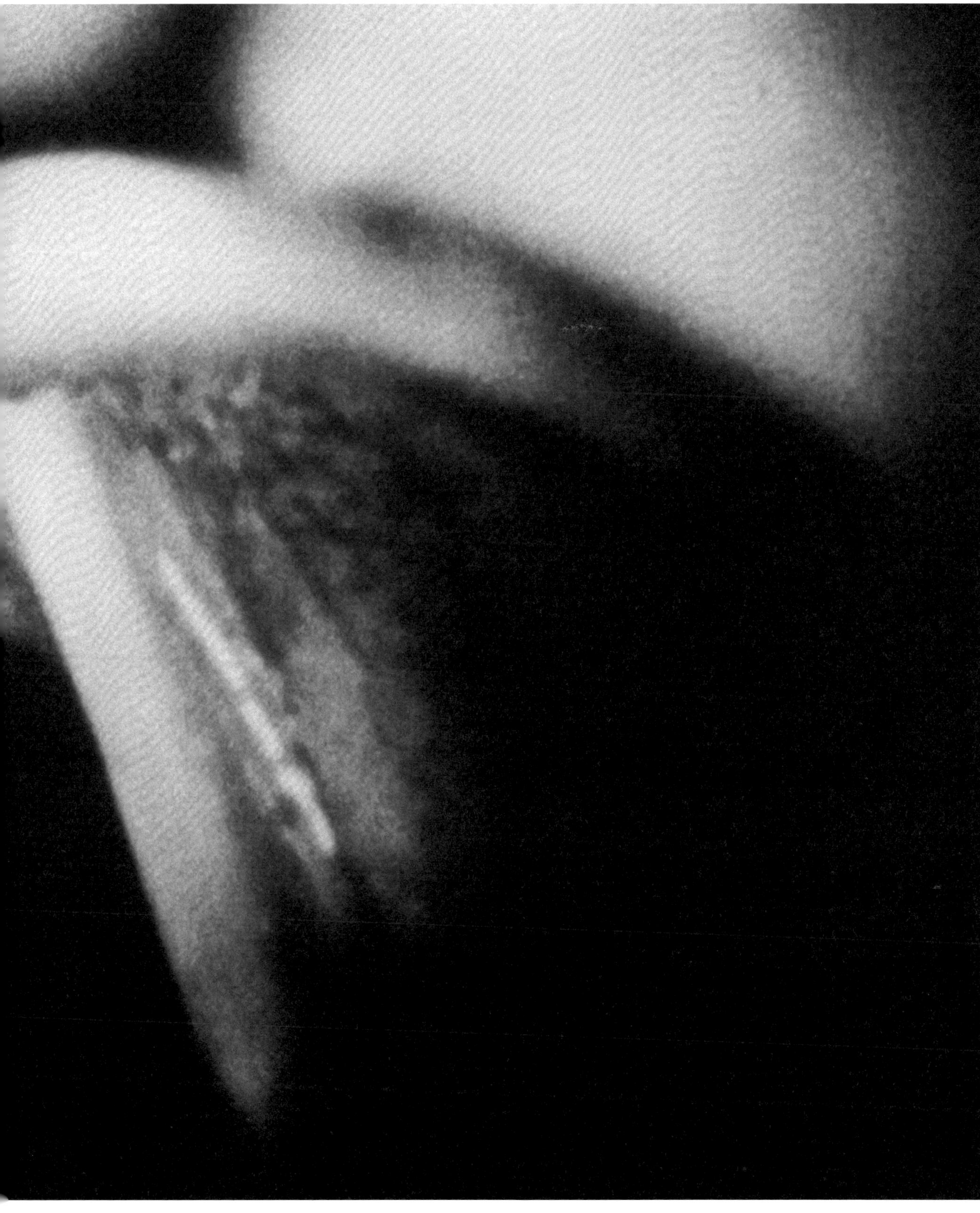

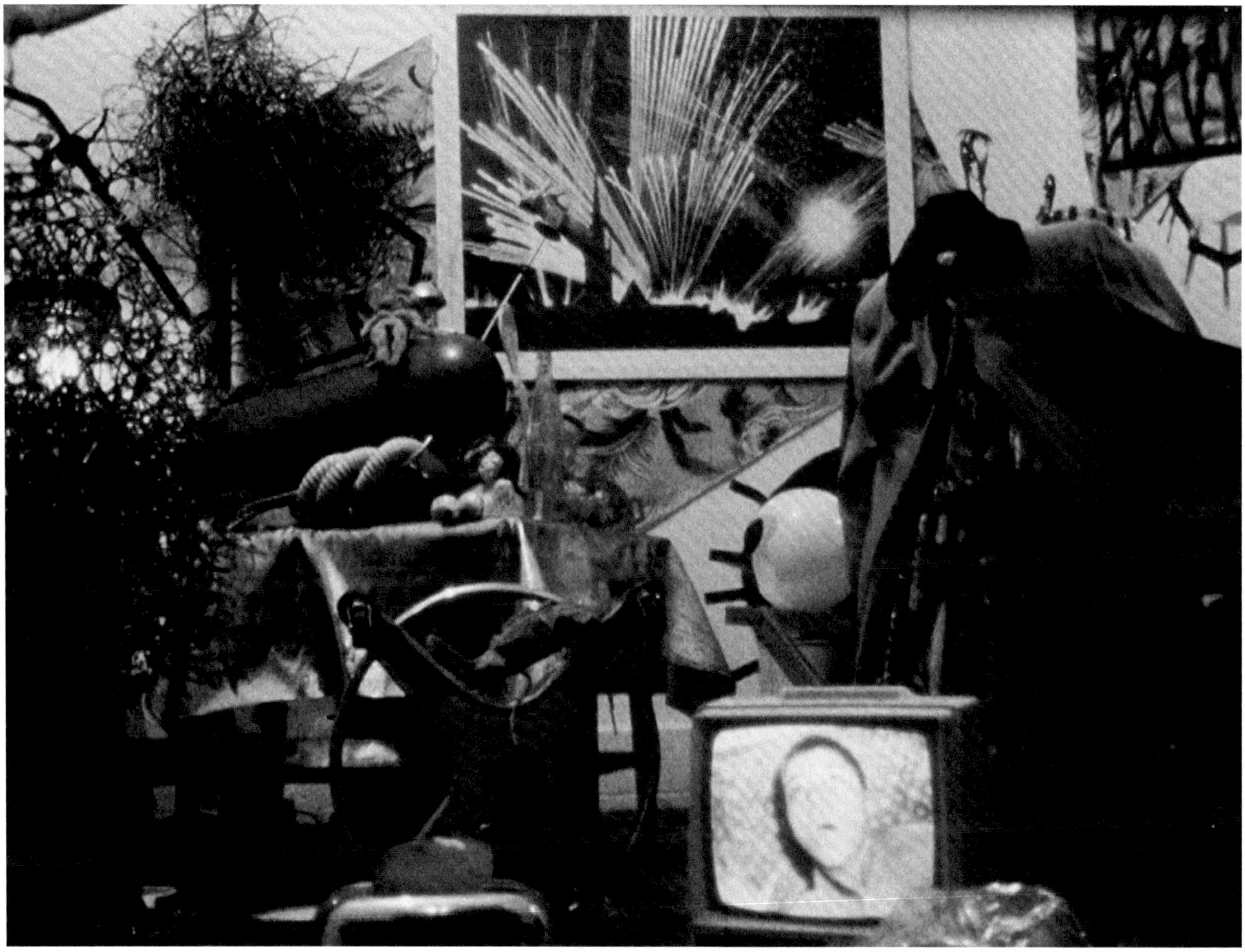

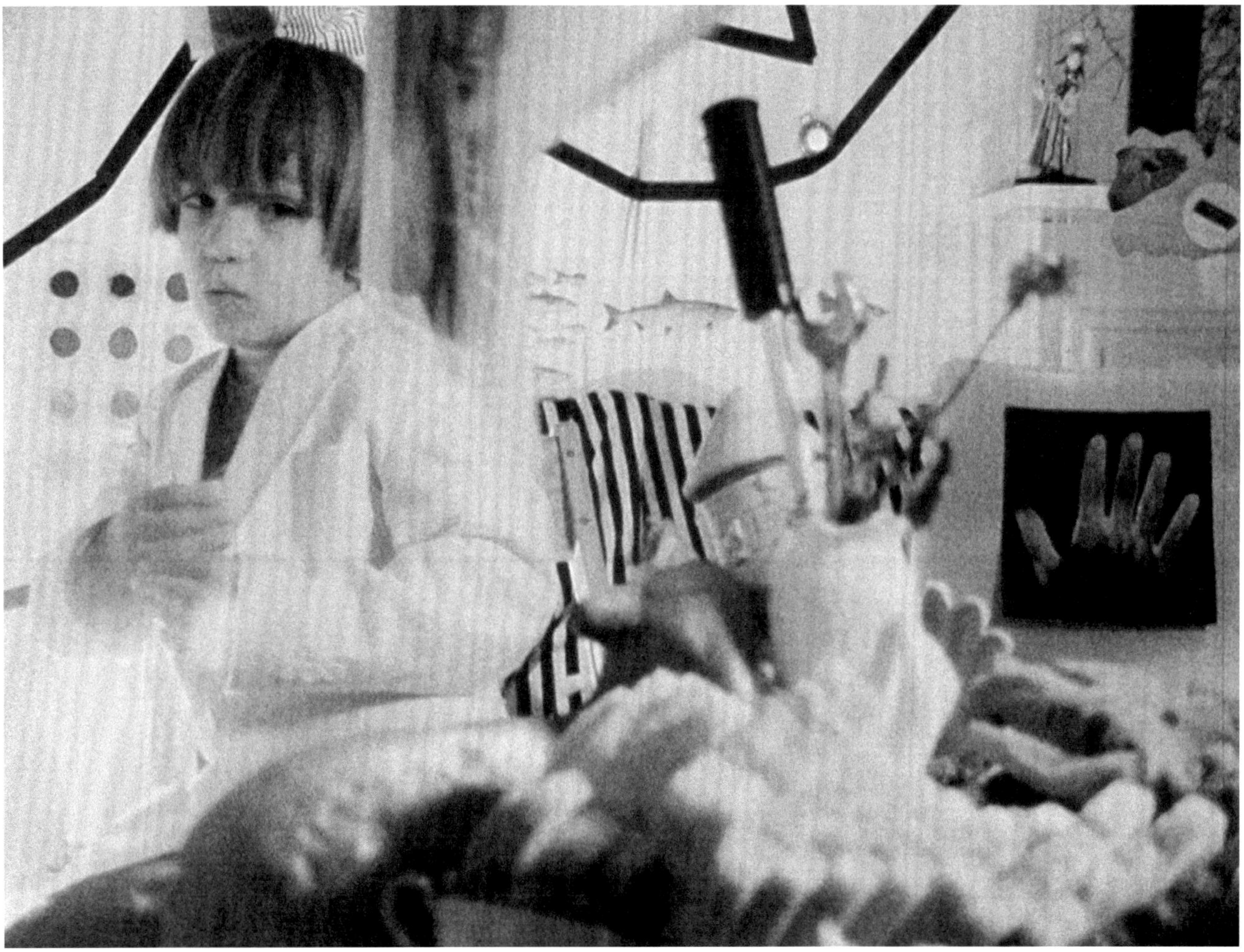

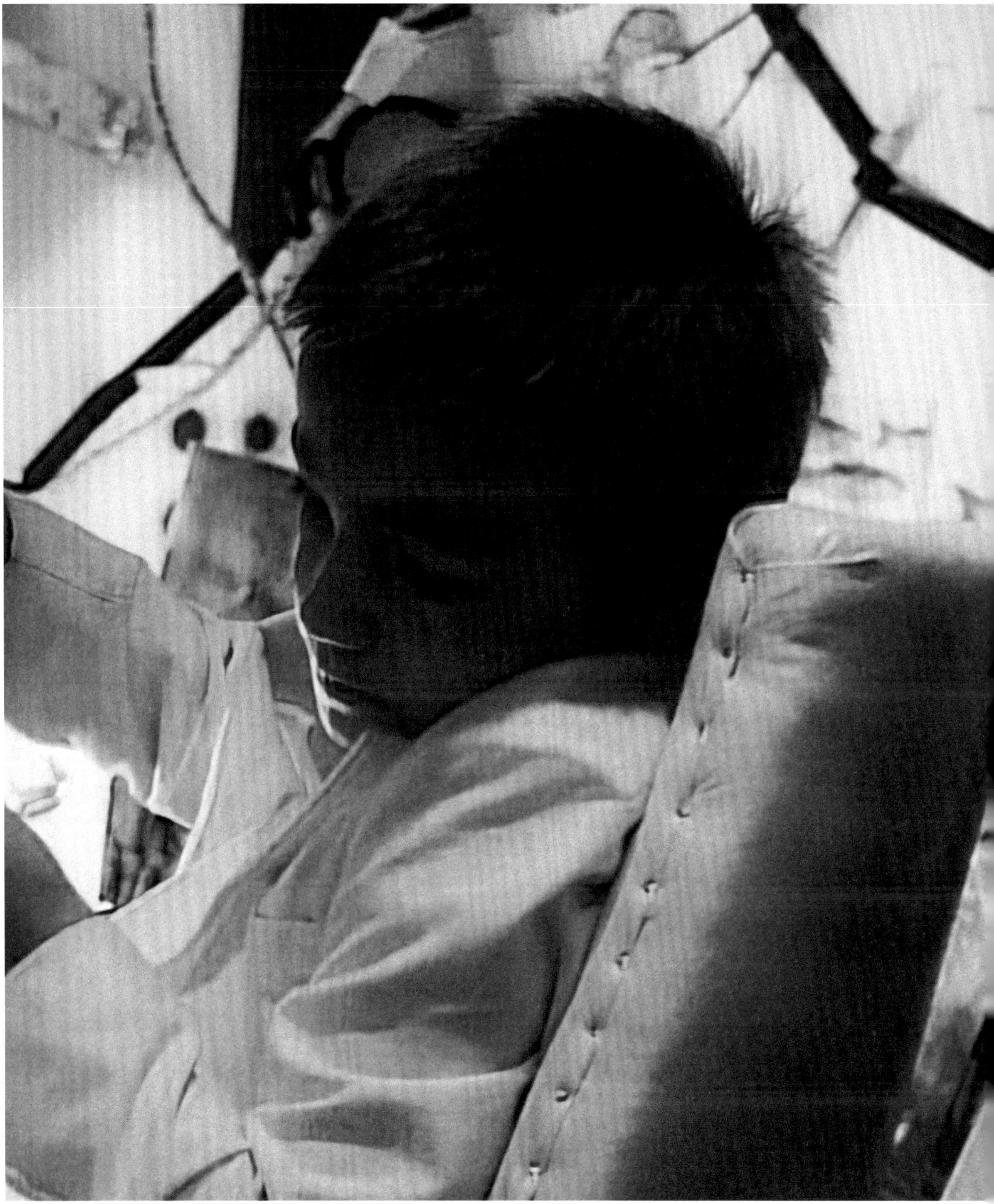

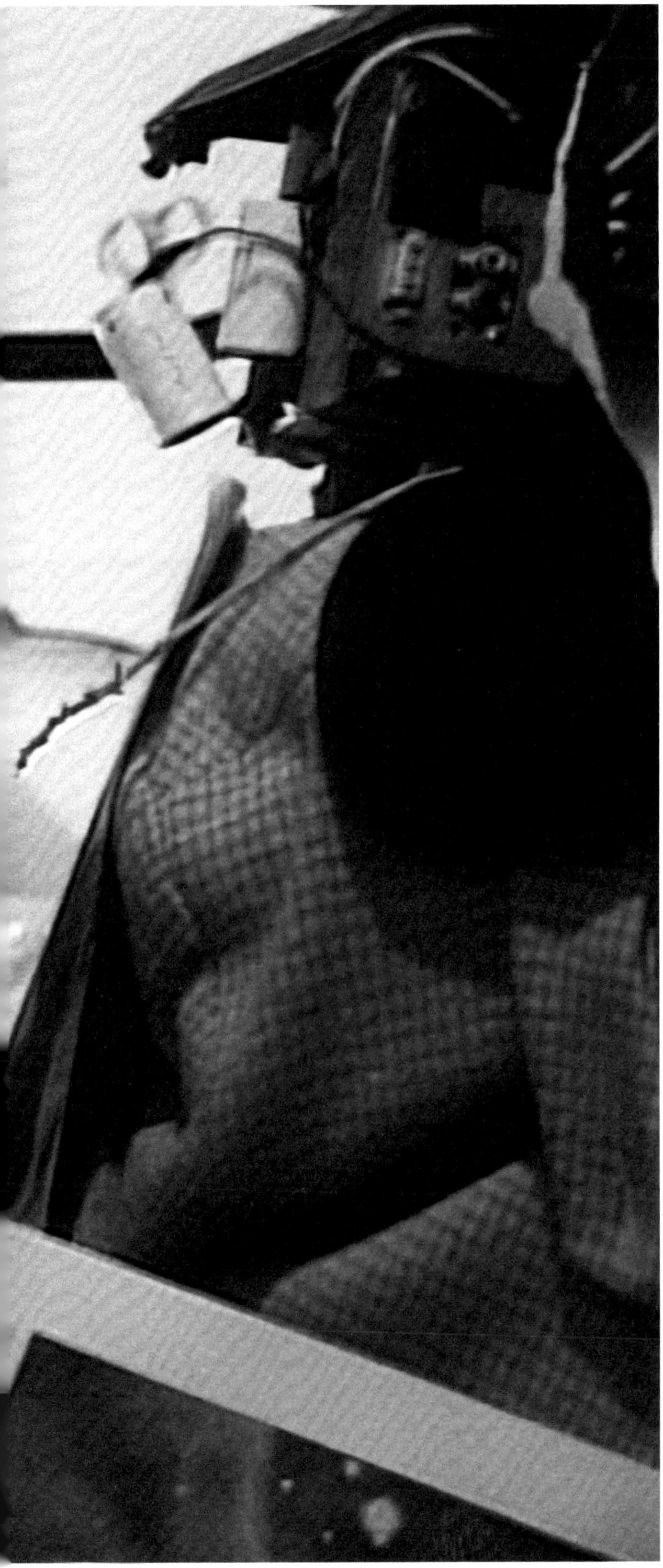

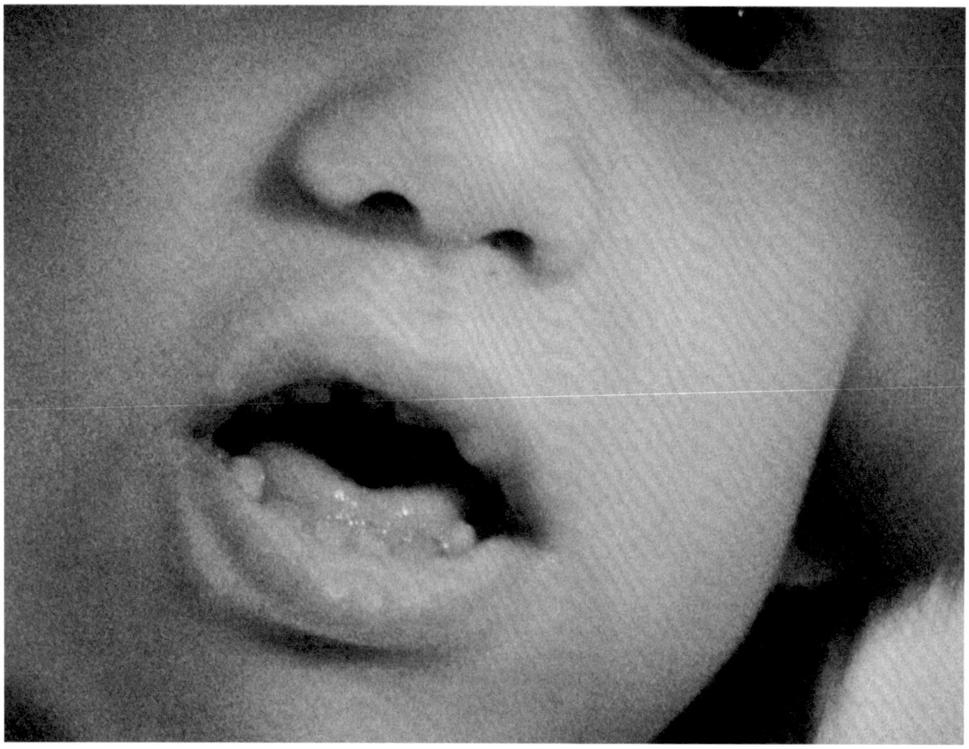

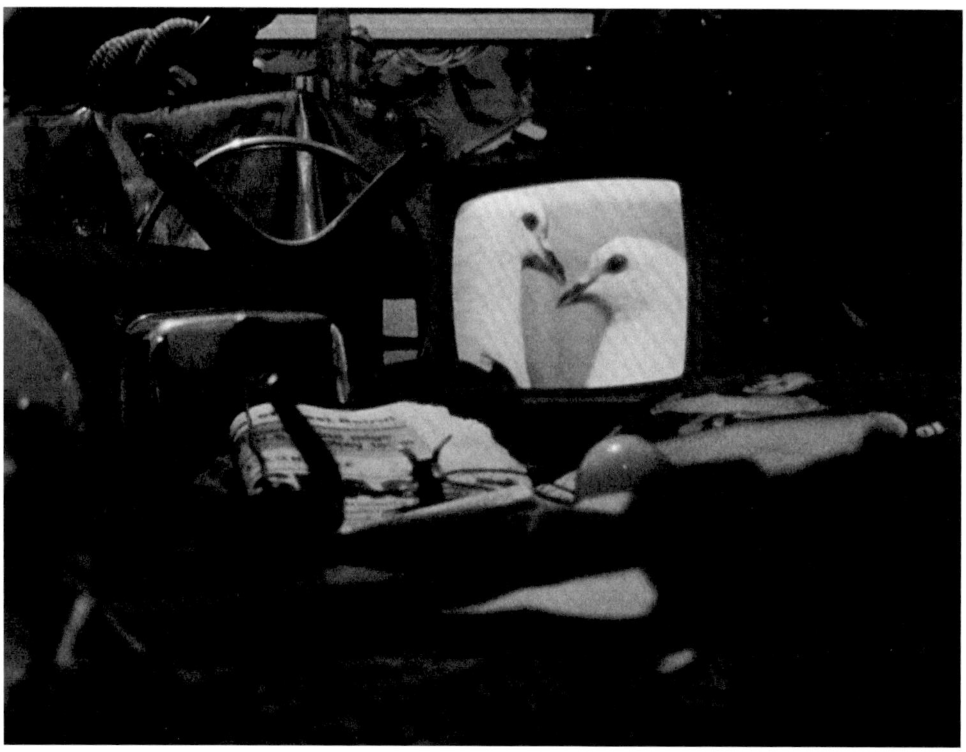

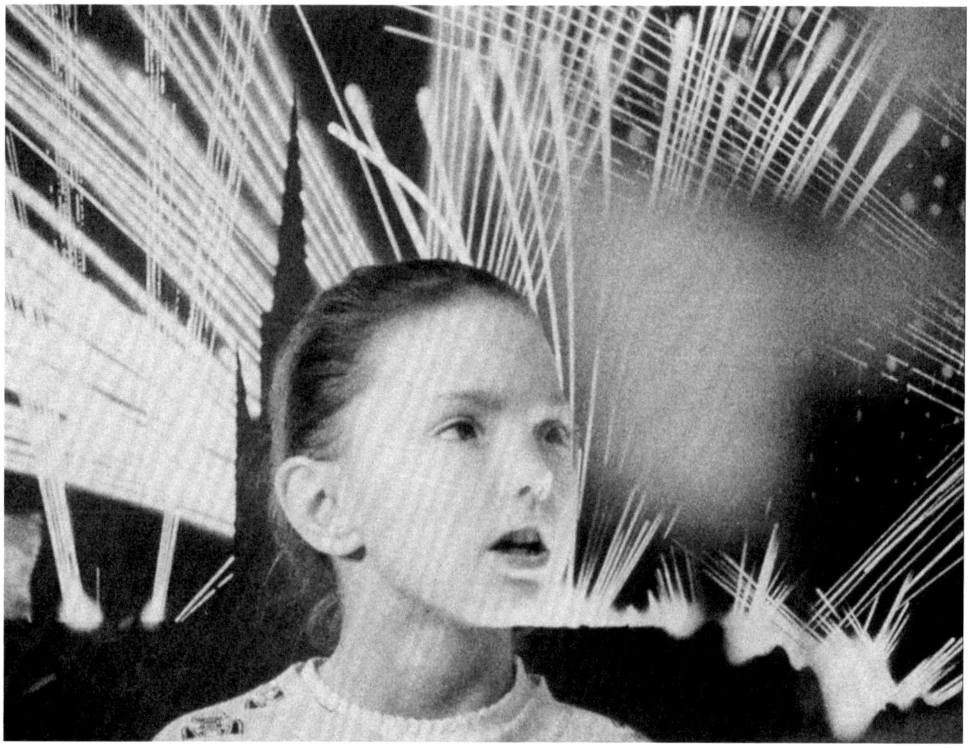

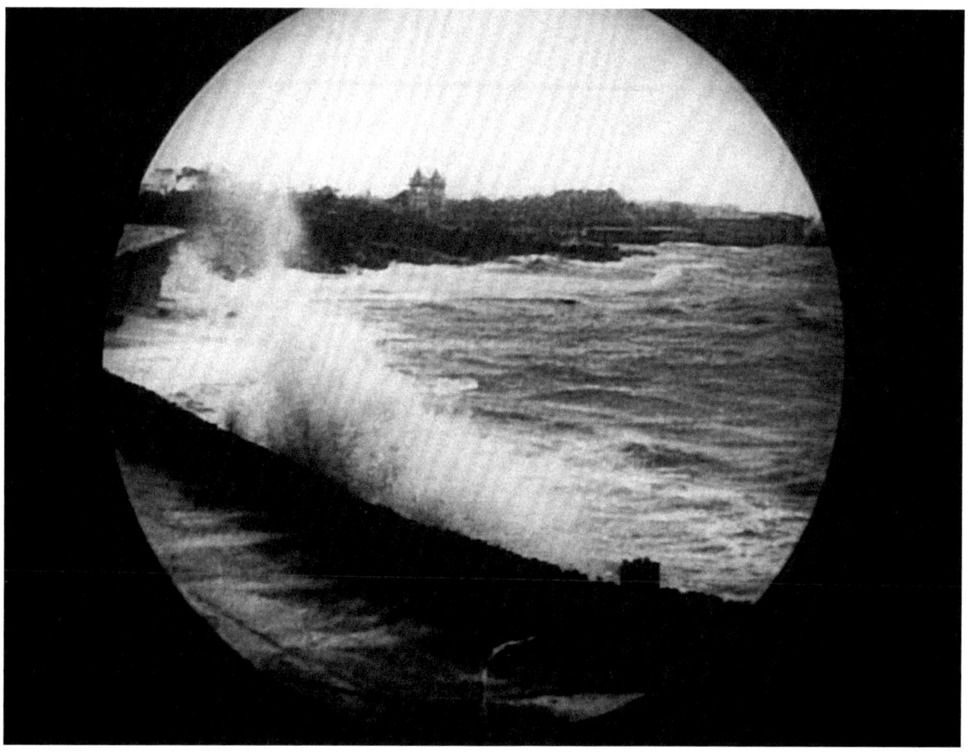

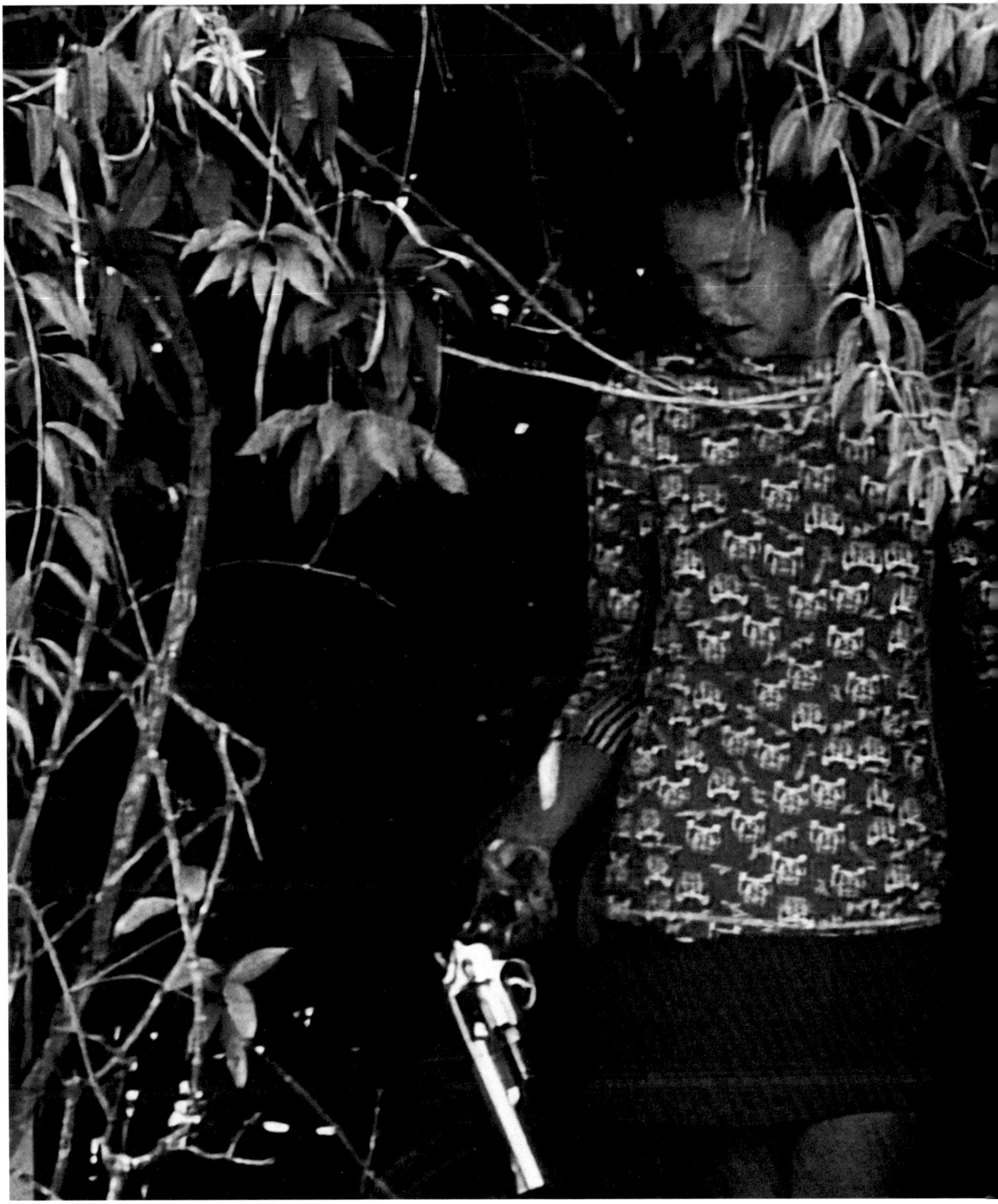

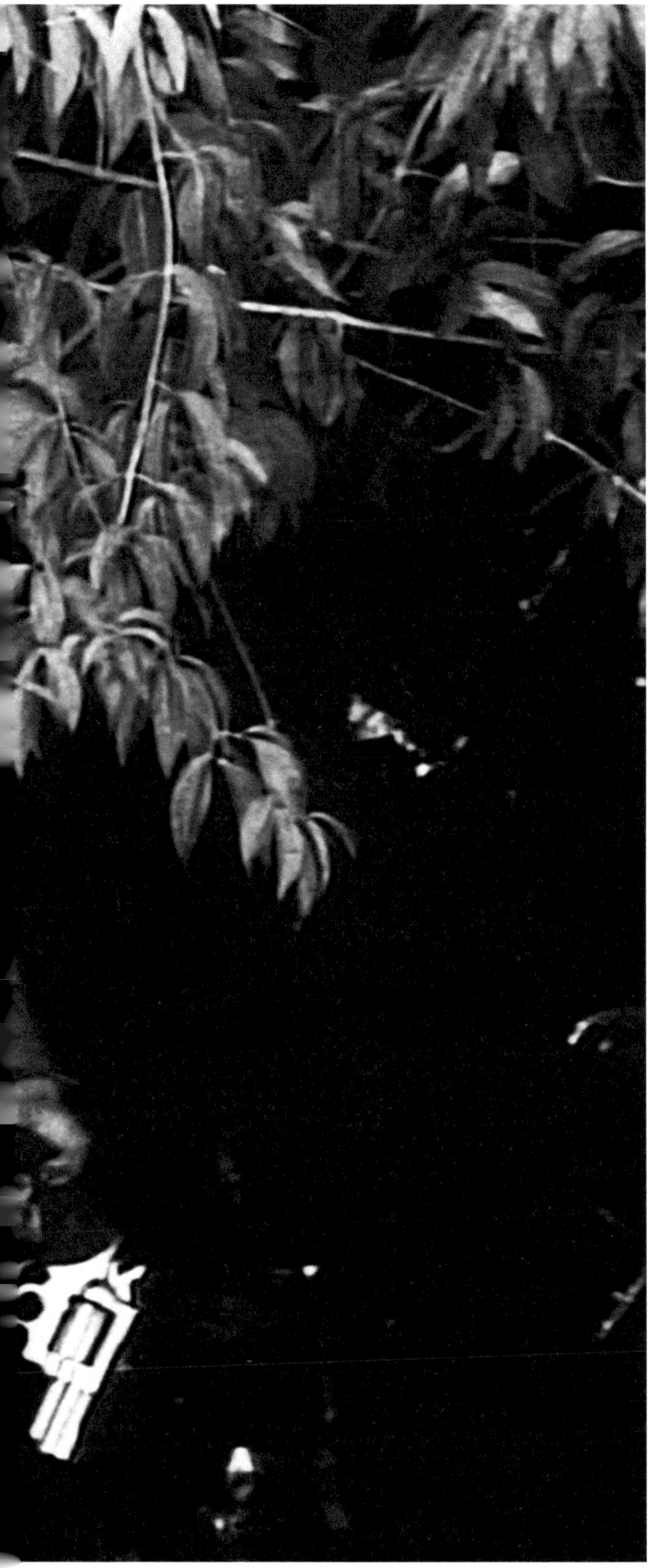

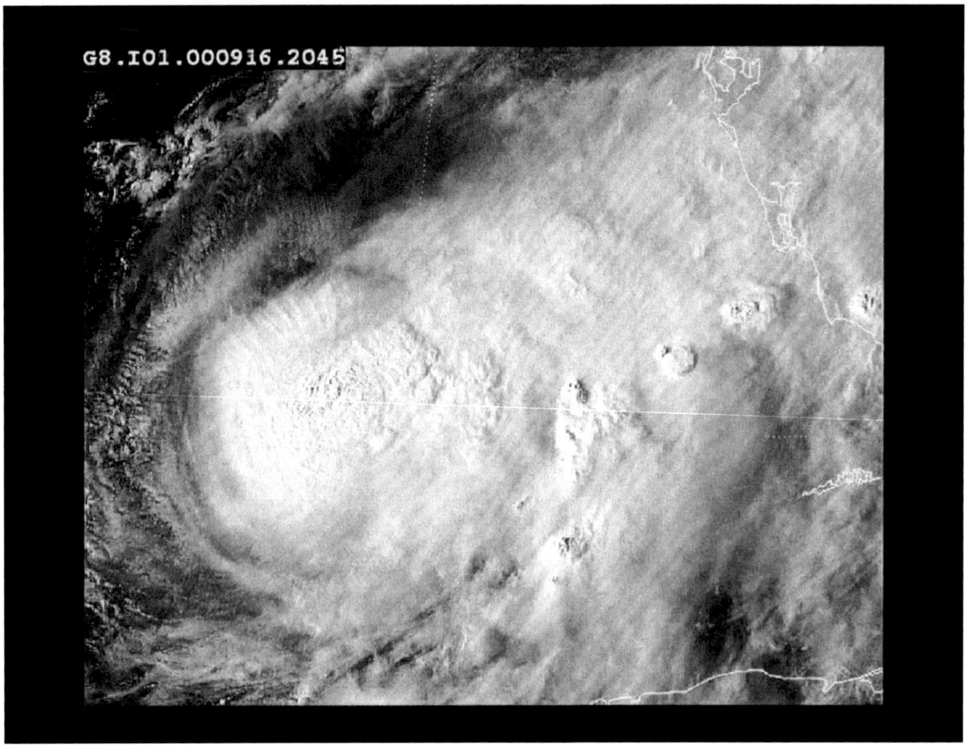
G8.I01.000916.2045

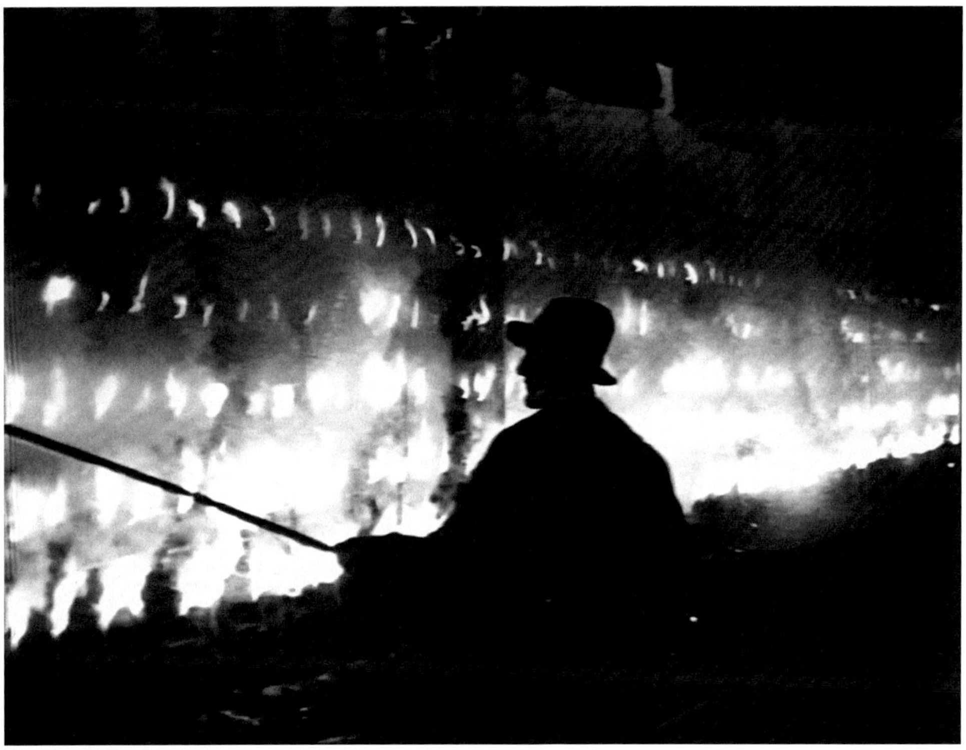

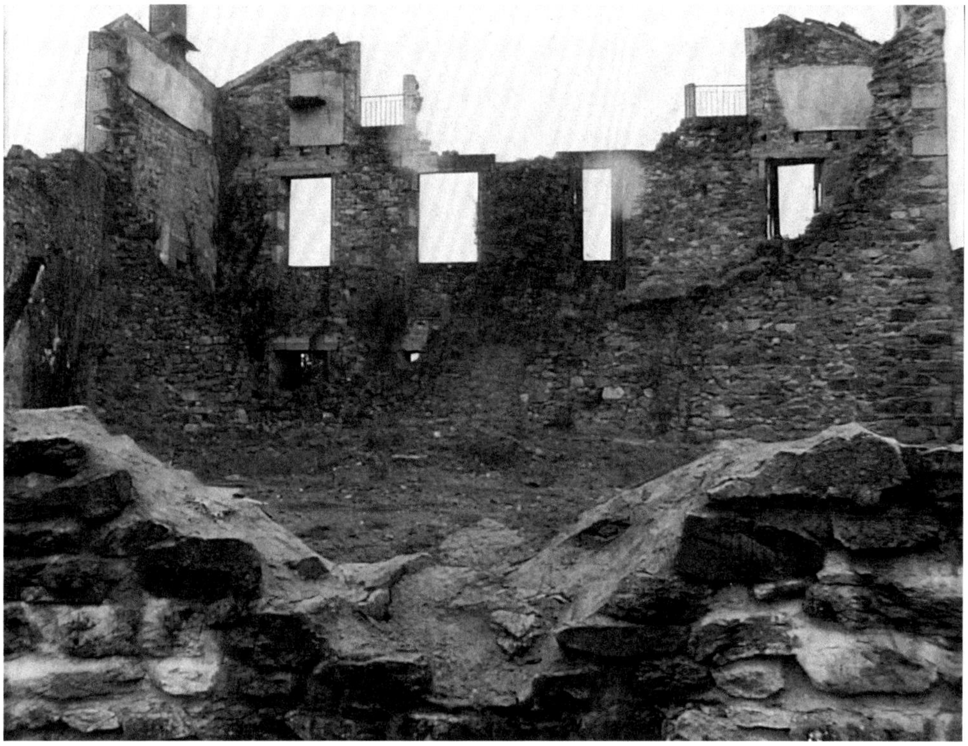

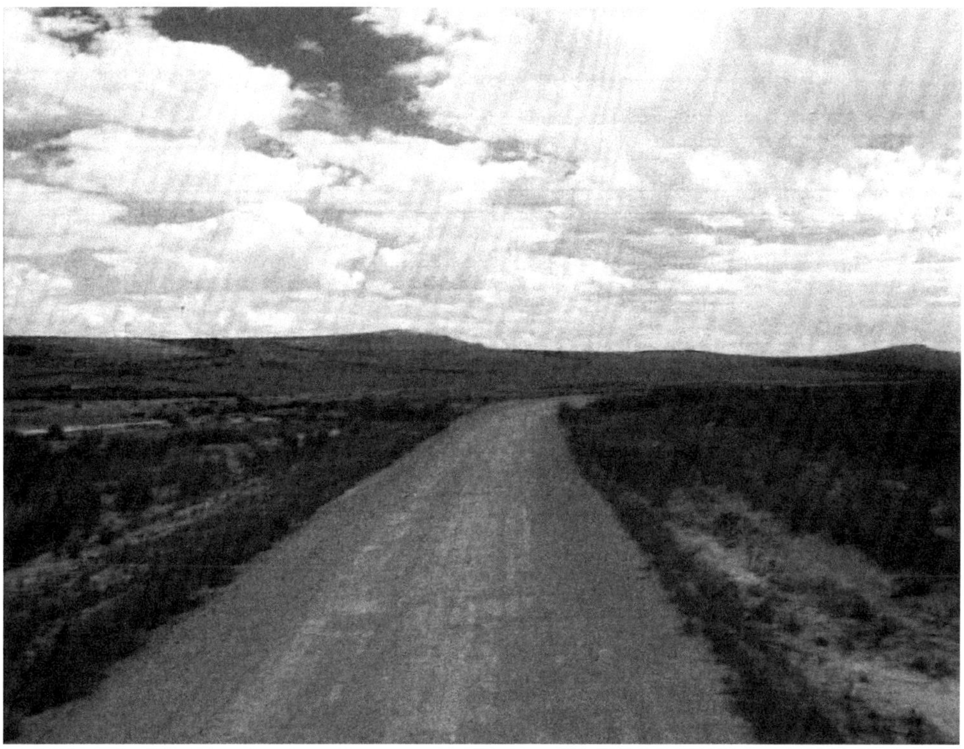

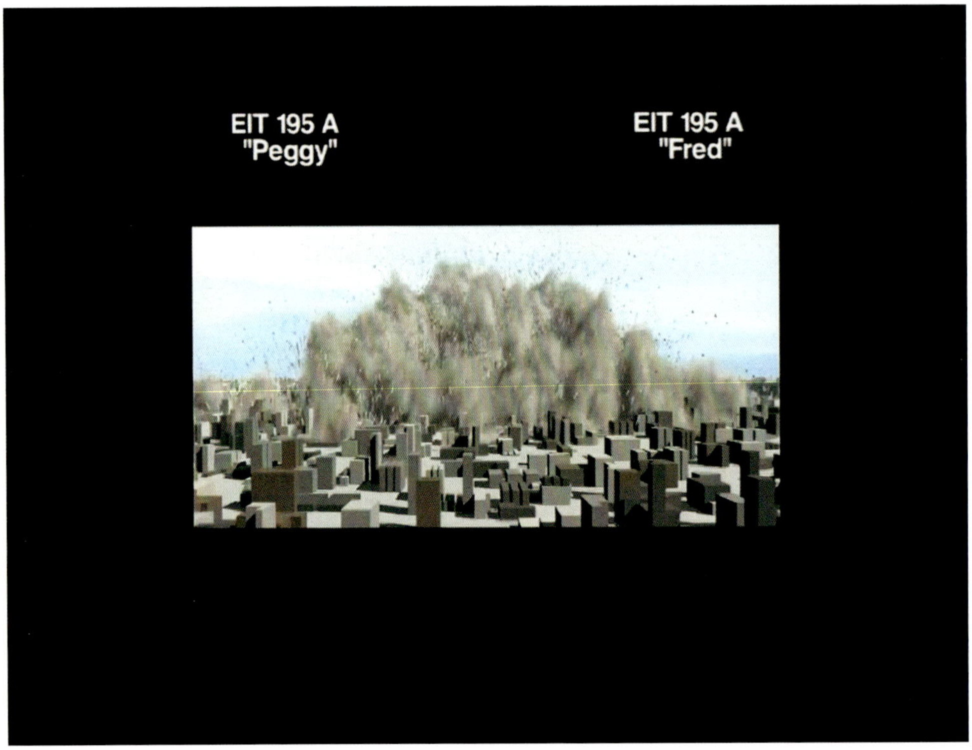
EIT 195 A
"Peggy"
EIT 195 A
"Fred"

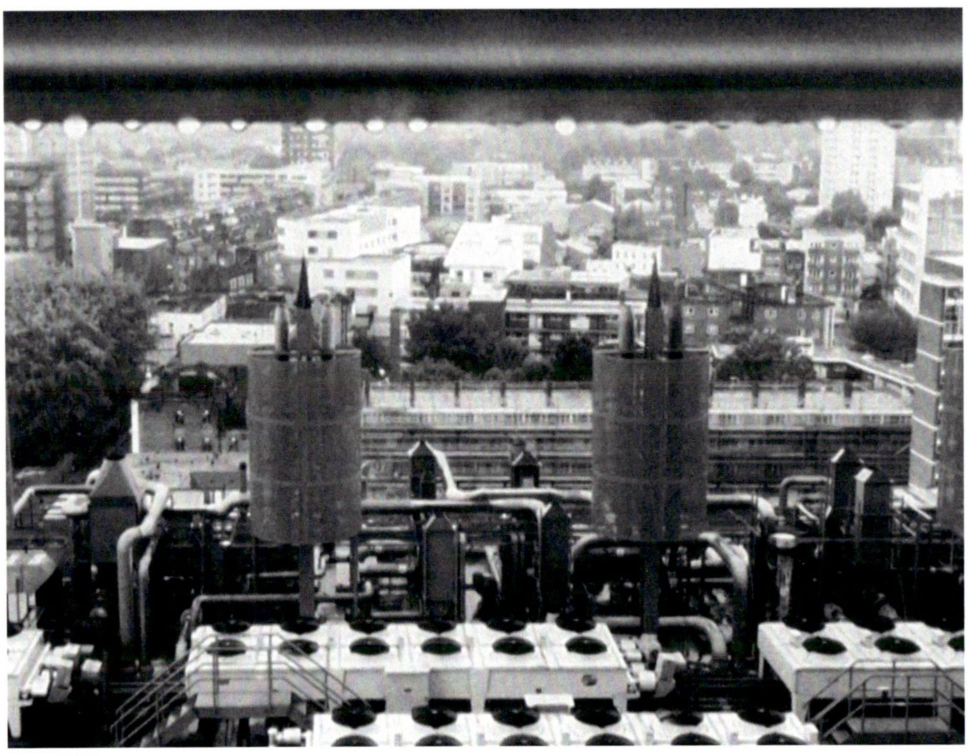

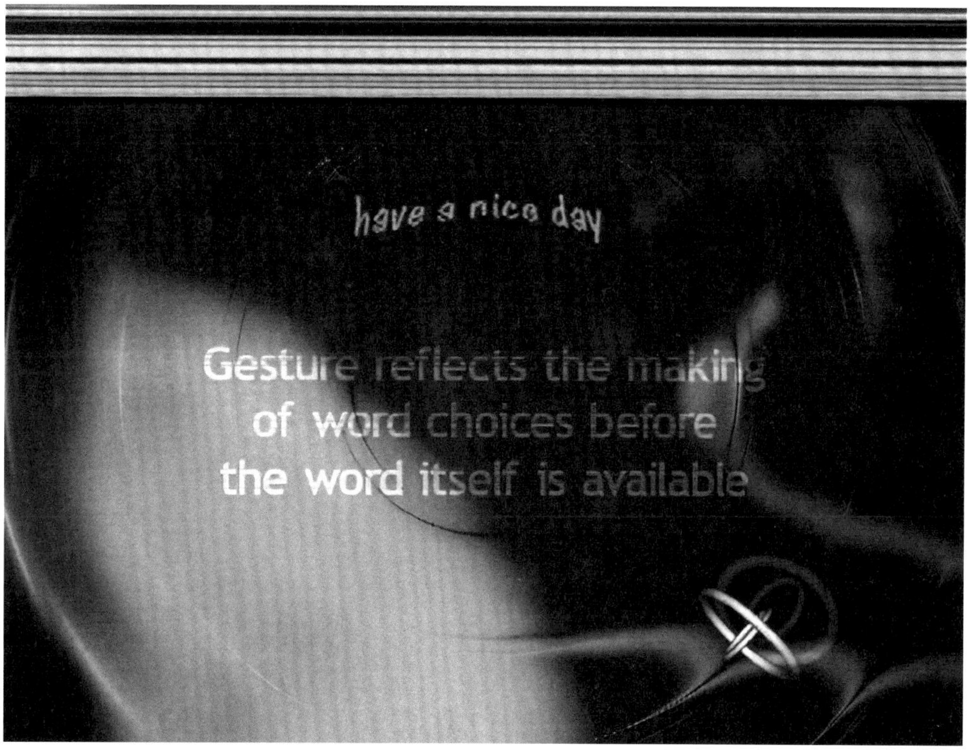
have a nice day
Gesture reflects the making
of word choices before
the word itself is available

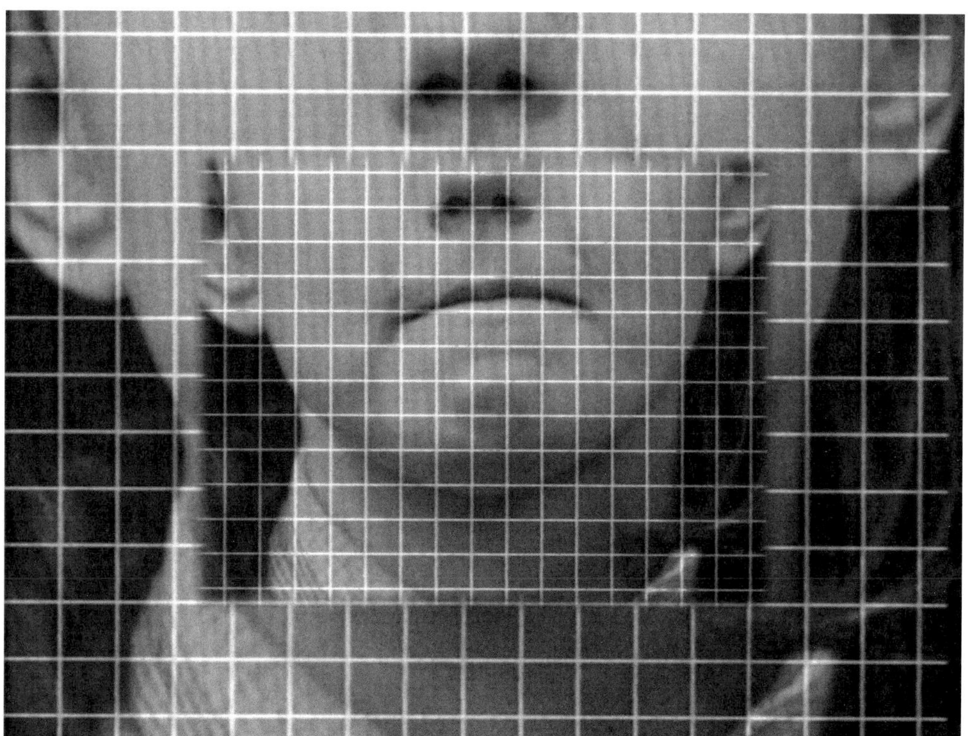

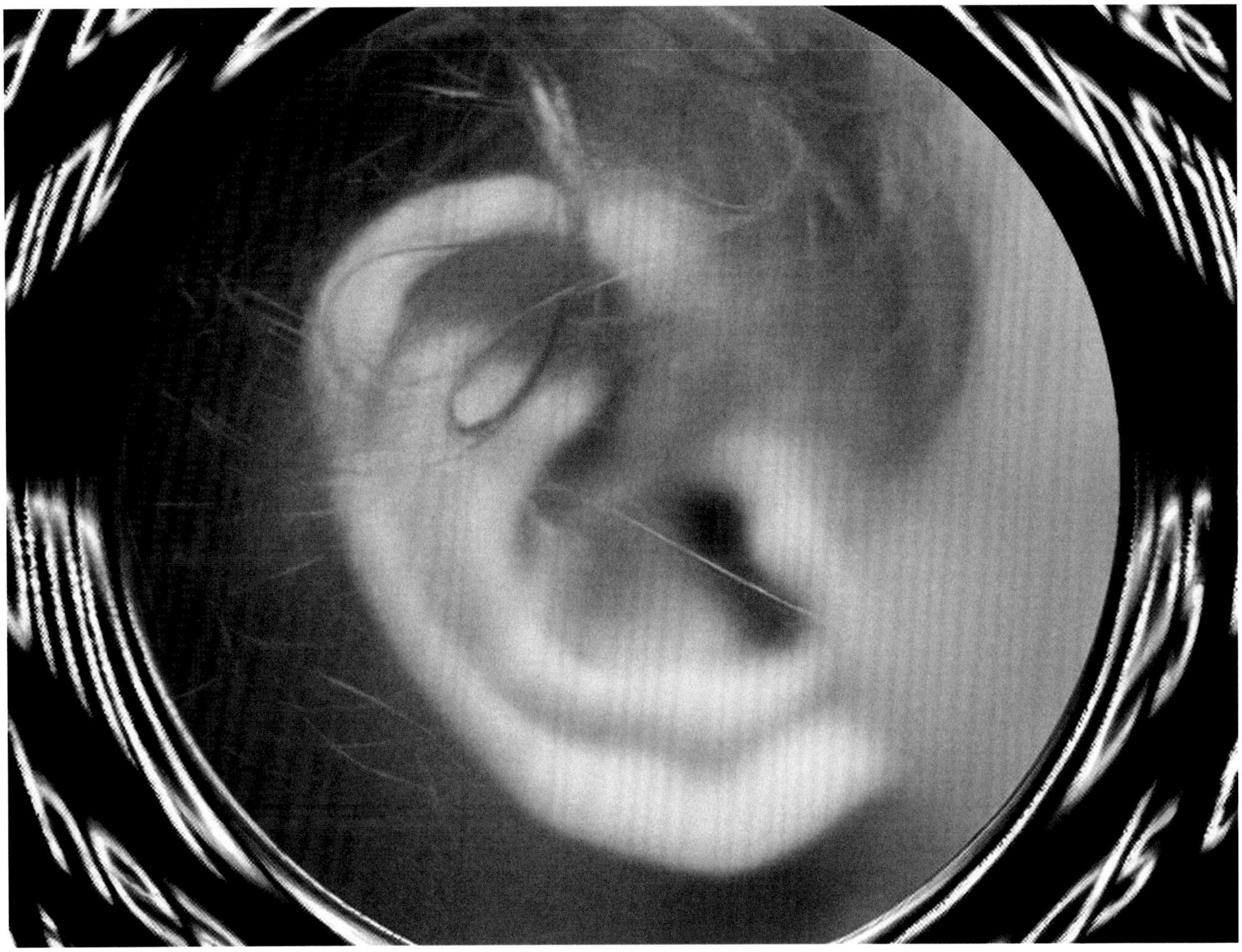

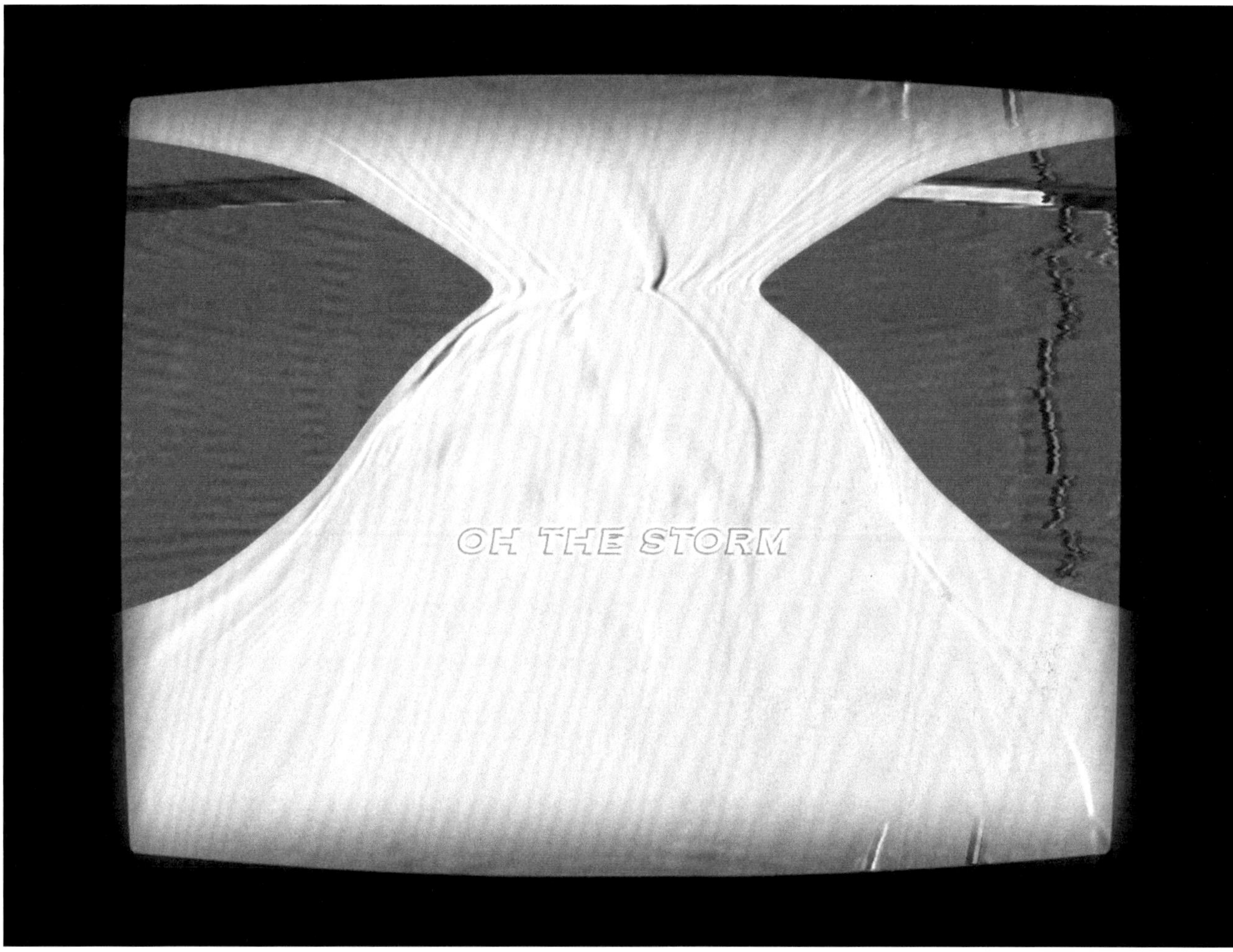
OH THE STORM

Let Me Count the Ways

Love and Death

Rosalyn Deutsche on *Let Me Count the Ways*

Groups, said Freud, citing churches and armies as examples, are held together by emotional ties that can arise from either common identification with a leader or common devotion to an abstract idea or concrete object. Perhaps, even, to a bomb. Such passionate identifications and devotions are expressions of libidinal or loving impulses, which seek to preserve, and unite with the aggressive impulses, which seek to destroy and kill. The coupling of the two is embedded in the title of Leslie Thornton's video *Let Me Count the Ways*, which, taken from the first line of Elizabeth Barrett Browning's "How Do I Love Thee? (Sonnet 43)"—a poem that itself combines references to love and death—also invokes a countdown to a bombing.

Thornton released the first section of *Let Me Count the Ways*, titled *Minus 10,* in 2004, one year after the invasion of Iraq. Since then, she has added four segments; the final, *Minus 6*, was completed in 2008. My discussion here focuses on the first two segments, *Minus 10* and *Minus 9*.

Let Me Count the Ways combines archival imagery, original footage, and text, a process that results in an essayistic work that produces meaning through montage and editing. Before seeing anything, however, we hear a countdown: the voice of an American man prepares for a recorded interview with a Japanese-speaking woman, a survivor of the atom bomb, a *hibakusha*. The Japanese voice-over continues as the visual track of *Minus 10* emerges, beginning with an old, presumably re-edited 8mm film, the kind once used for home movies. The shaky, faded footage shows a group of men taking pictures and indulging in horseplay on a hiking trip in, as a title informs us, the countryside outside Los Alamos, the New Mexican town where the first atom bombs, Little Boy and Fat Man, were made. This home movie is followed by a second, badly deteriorated one, in which we see members of Project Alberta, also known as Project A or the Destination Team, the group that developed the means of delivering the bombs and dropping them on their target cities. In Thornton's video, the men of Project A lightheartedly photograph each other as they prepare to load Little Boy onto the polished-aluminum intercontinental bomber that will carry it over Hiroshima. During both home movies, the word "Dad" repeatedly appears and floats over one of the figures, identifying him as the artist's father, a nuclear physicist and engineer who participated in both the Manhattan Project and Project A.

This montage element—the autobiographical word "Dad"—inscribes the artist and, with her, the viewer into the scenes depicted in the home movies, inserting subjectivity into the representation of the past and undermining our status as objective viewers. "Dad" also relates the nuclear-bomb-making groups pictured in the home movies to the nuclear family, which Freud considered the prototype of all groups. For the men in Thornton's home movies, including Thornton's father, who is listed in the closing credits as the source of the movies, and for Thornton herself, who presumably saw the movies as a child, the footage constitutes a personal archive of the past. Because, however, the found footage depicts collective historical events and comes from a public archive, it combines Thornton's past with that of the nation, merging two levels of remembrance: individual memory and wider social and political history. The video's troubling proximity of cozy domesticity and historical atrocity is paralleled by an equally disturbing juxtaposition of the playful conviviality of the members of the Manhattan Project and Project A groups and the catastrophes these groups played a critical role in perpetrating.

Like flashbacks, the home movie footage in *Let Me Count the Ways* renders history as subjective experience and simultaneously casts the artist and viewer as subjects in history. At the same time, the recorded voice-over of the Japanese woman, which mediates the image and bears witness to the consequences of the activities referred to in the home movies—the making, assembling, loading, and dropping of the bomb—places a hibakusha in the position of narrator of history, dividing the formation of subjectivity at the opening of the video. In conjunction with the voice of the Japanese woman, the word "Dad" establishes a human scale against which to measure the historical catastrophe of Hiroshima, but it also evokes and disturbs the innocence of American domesticity that characterized the United States in the 1950s. Like Sylvia Plath's famous poem "Daddy," in which the poet associates her father with Nazism, *Let Me Count the Ways* juxtaposes the intimate domestic sphere with a historical atrocity, bringing together two fields that, at first, seem far apart but are, in fact, closely related. Like Plath's Daddy, Thornton's Dad carries the weight of individual and collective memory and guilt.

At the end of *Minus 10*, the home movie of Project A gives way to footage of another group: an audience of US sailors and soldiers, some taking pictures, watches a female Asian dancer. A superimposed title informs us that, after delivering the bomb to Tinian Island, Thornton's father was among the group of scientists who watched from an accompanying airplane as the *Enola Gay*'s bombardier released the bomb: "August 6, 1945, 8:15 A.M./Dad observes the bomb drop on Hiroshima." The image shows a female Asian body made to connote sexual and racial otherness, as well as exoticism and spectacle, so that Orientalism is aligned with scopophilia, or pleasure in looking, which Freud counted among the sexual drives. Under the influence of the title, the look of the sailors watching the Asian dancer—and the photographic look—is tied to the look of the father watching the bombing of the Japanese city, hinting at the sexualized mania that often pervades war violence. And, conversely, under the influence of the image, the purportedly neutral, scientific look of the title is invested with desire. Because the scientists' airborne vision is affiliated with the acts of sighting and taking aim at a bombing target, both looks are implicated in the annihilation of their objects. The closing scene of *Minus 10* thus forms a bridge between the video's opening section and its next segment, *Minus 9*, in which Thornton draws a relationship between vision, especially photographic vision, and the violence of war.

For Paul Virilio, who has explored the way in which cameras form part of the equipment of war, this relationship constitutes the significance of Hiroshima—a significance that links Hiroshima to contemporary technowarfare. The blinding flash of the atomic bomb—what the Japanese call the *pikadon*, a brilliant light followed by a thunderous blast—represented, according to Virilio, the complete merger of observation and destruction. For this reason, the atomic bombings, which were made possible by aerial photography of the bomb's targets, and whose effects were photographed from accompanying planes, was a climactic moment in the history of what Virilio calls a developing "war of light."

Like Virilio, Akira Mizuta Lippit, a scholar of cinema and Japanese culture, has added to the meanings of Hiroshima by linking the event to light. In *Atomic Light (Shadow Optics)*, Lippit argues that, in addition to unleashing the potential for total destruction, the light of the atomic bomb inaugurated a crisis of visuality, of, that is, social and historical sight. First, the detonated bomb initiated an "excess visuality," a catastrophic light, which, in conjunction with nuclear heat, annihilated the bodies it touched, reducing them to ashes. "There can be no authentic photography of atomic war," writes Lippit, "because the bombings were themselves a form of total photography that exceeded the economies of representation."[1] Which is to say that only symbols can represent atomic warfare, symbols that bear witness to the avisuality, that is, the unrepresentability of the catastrophe.

The most common displaced referent for the obliterating force of atomic weaponry is, of course, the so-called mushroom cloud, which became the quintessential image both of a dangerous technology and, ironically, of the promise of science. Blanchot describes the mushroom cloud as a public image of the death drive. Thornton, however, forgoes the clichéd image, which has been criticized for its depoliticizing organicism, and, in keeping with Virilio's and Lippit's depictions of the atomic bomb as a light-weapon, she substitutes found footage of, first, a flashbulb going off, which serves as an emblem of the pikadon, and then, of a self-developing Polaroid camera, which figures the bomb's immediate effects. The Polaroid camera is a fitting symbol not only because, like the bomb, it produced instant photographs but also because the invention of the Polaroid in 1948 was greeted, like that of the atomic bomb in 1945, as a technological "miracle," a kind of scientific "magic," as the voice-over of *Minus 9* describes it.

Whereas the *Minus 10* segment of *Let Me Count the Ways* portrays preparations for the atomic bombing, *Minus 9* represents the bombing itself and its immediate effects, just as *Minus 8* and *Minus 7*, which deal with mutations in irradiated plants, might be read as an allegory of the bomb's longer-term effects, what Kenzaburō Ōe describes as the "haunting question of genetics." Like *Minus 10*, *Minus 9* begins with a black screen and a voice-over of a 1945 interview with a Hiroshima survivor. This time, the speaker is a "Miss Palchikoff," who, though not American, was a white woman who provided the only English-language eyewitness account of the bombing in the National Archive. Palchikoff gives an account of the effects of the atomic bombing that is inconsistent in at least one important respect. Asked by the interviewer whether white people suffered any burns, she emphatically replies, "No. Not one white person was burned. They were injured, but not burned." Soon after, however, she insists that not only did no white people lose their hair, but that "not a single white person was injured in any way." Testifying that white people were unaffected by the nuclear flash and atomic radiation, she voices a fantasy about the invincibility of the Western body, even as her contradictory statements attest to an underlying insecurity about that body's fragility.

Directly following this portion of the narration, the visual track shows an aerial shot of New York City taken before September 11, 2001, in which we see a tiny World Trade Center, the very buildings and the

1 Akira Mizuta Lippit, *Atomic Light (Shadow Optics)* (Minneapolis: University of Minnesota Press, 2005), 95.

very bodies inside it whose fates challenge such a triumphalist discourse. With this shot, Thornton links the terror bombing of Hiroshima to the terrorist attacks on the Twin Towers, acknowledging how, as in Palchikoff's description of the bombing of Hiroshima, the vulnerability exposed by the World Trade Center attacks has been collectively denied. This denial is apparent not only through plans for rebuilding, in which architects mobilize images of security, but also through the subsequent launching of the "war on terror" and, especially, the Iraq War, with which the Bush administration sought to bury trauma by taking refuge in triumphalism—in, that is, heroic masculinism, or what Freud identified as a defensive fantasy of omnipotence.

Let Me Count the Ways: Minus 10, 2004

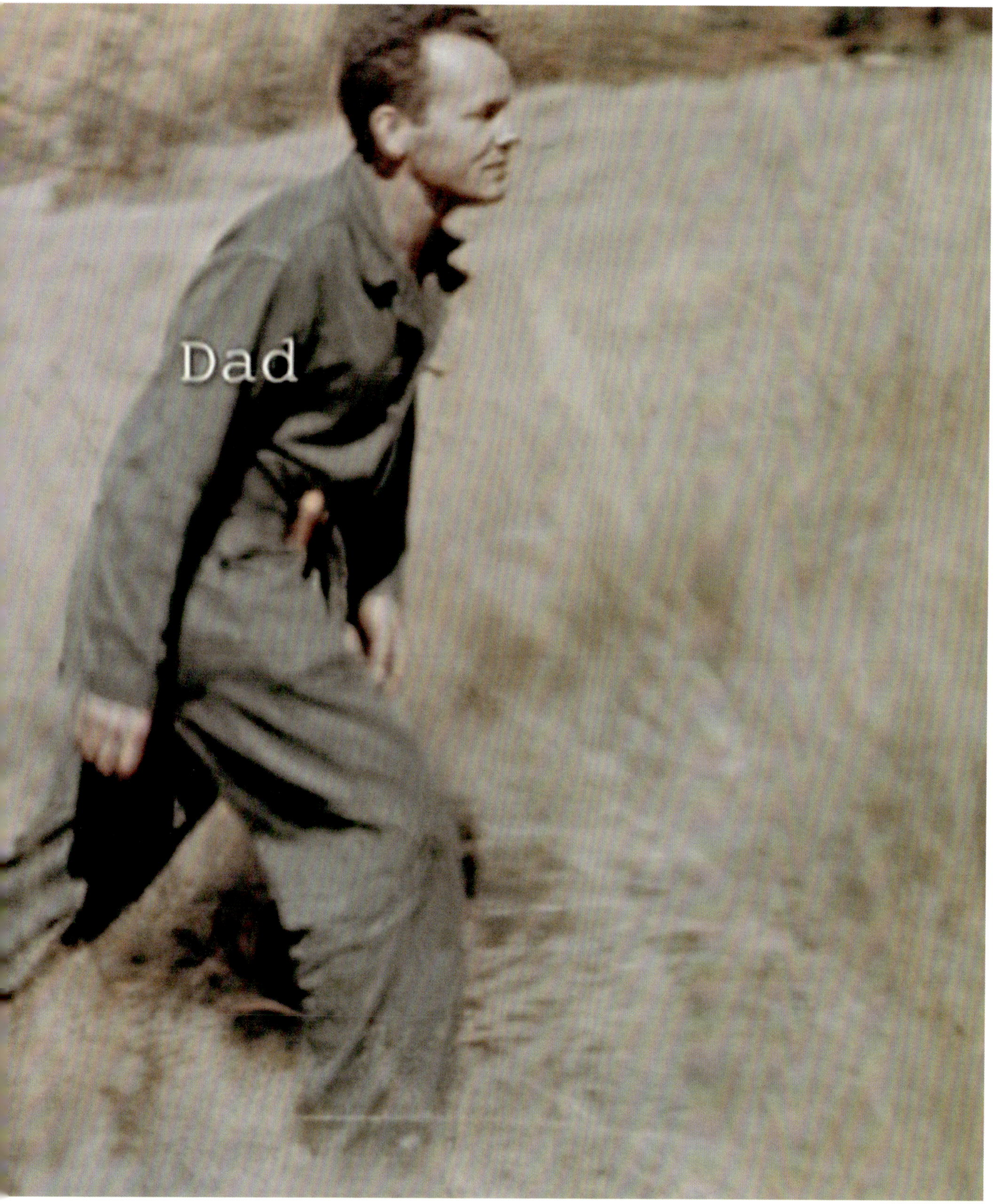

Dad

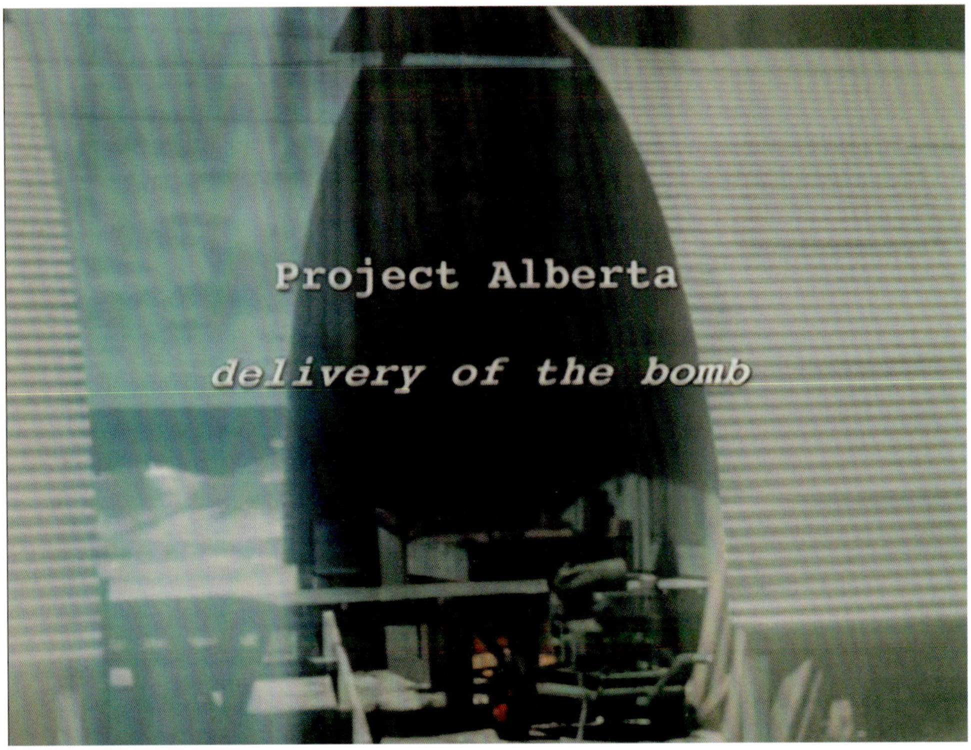
Project Alberta
delivery of the bomb

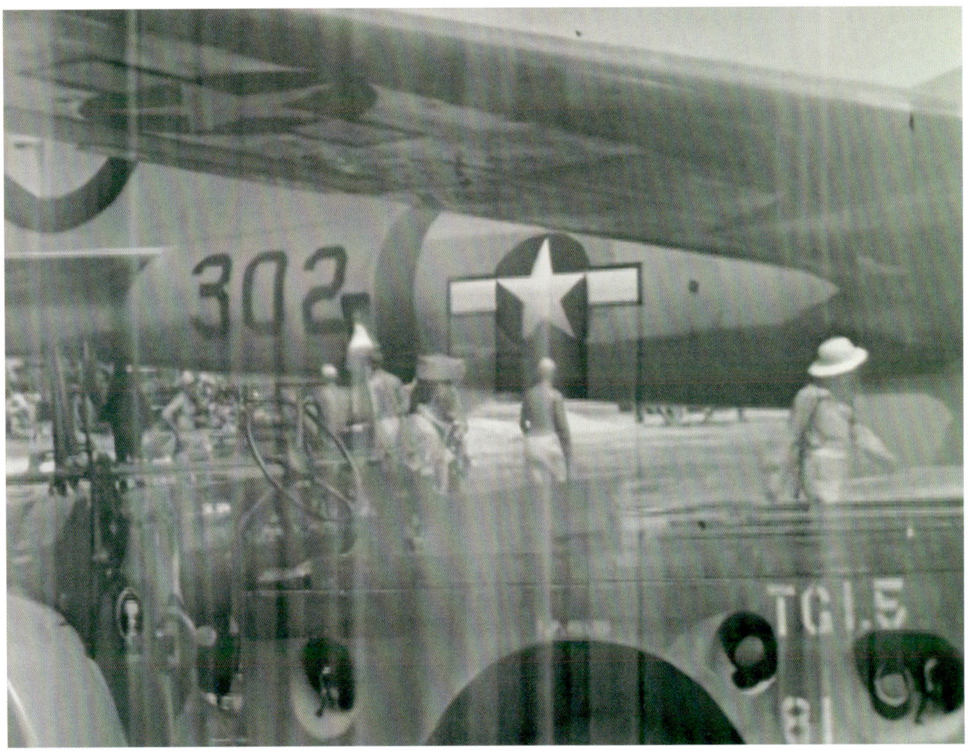
302

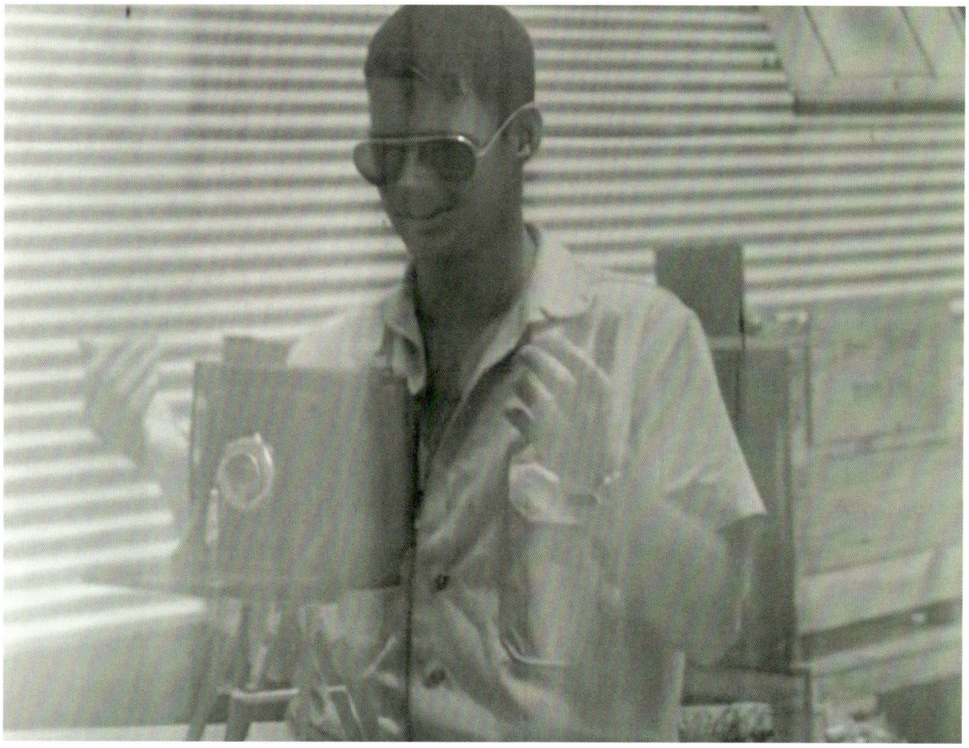

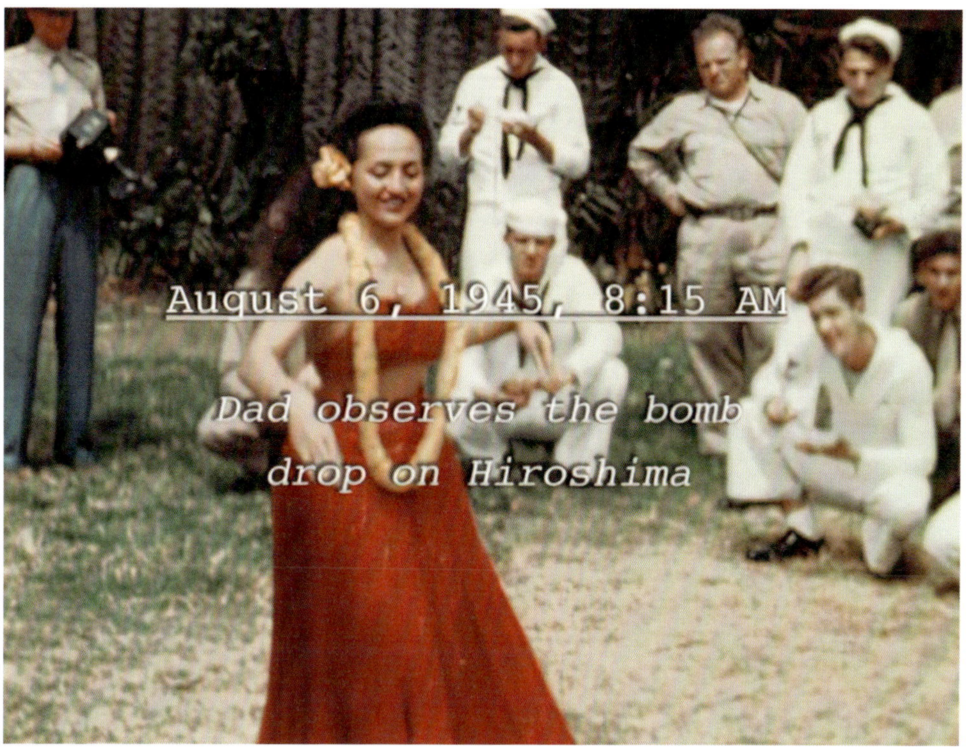
August 6, 1945, 8:15 AM
Dad observes the bomb
drop on Hiroshima

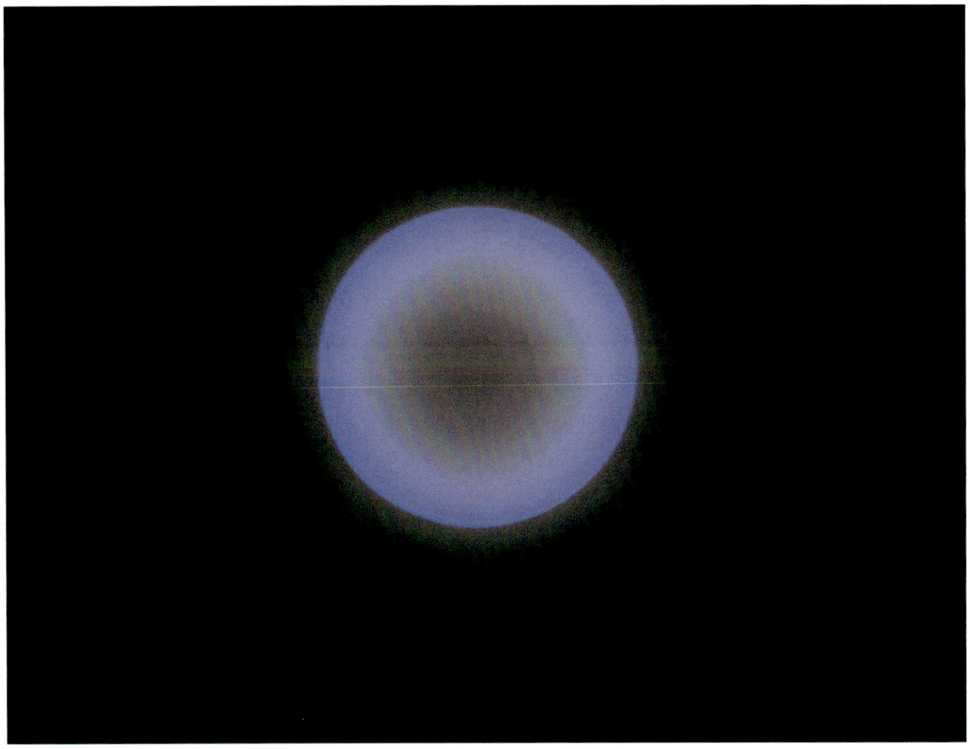

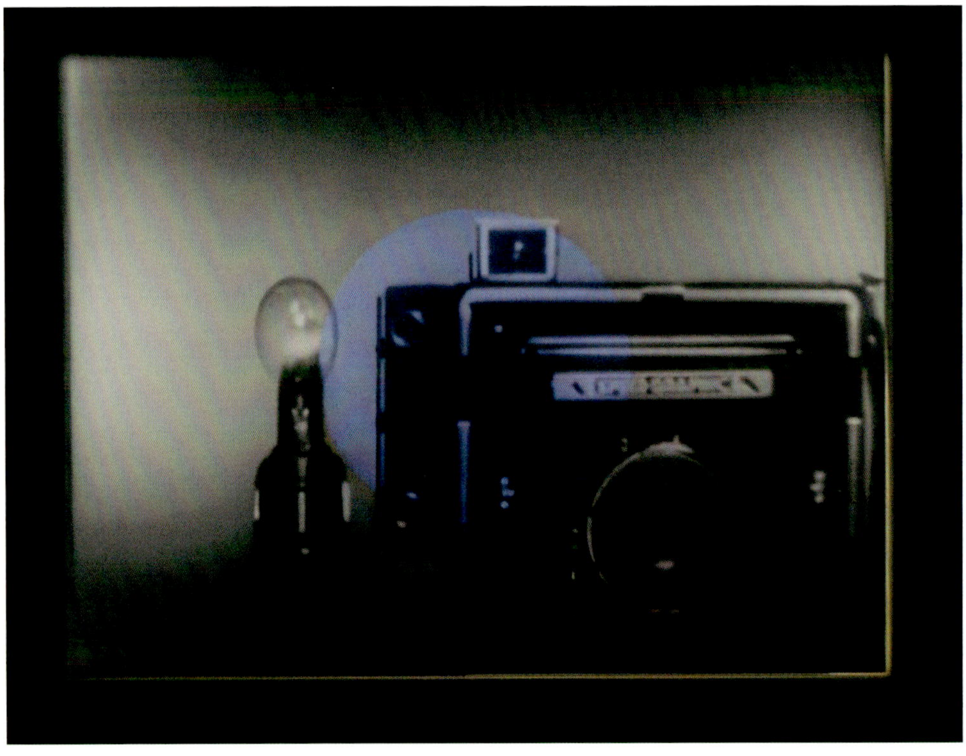

Let Me Count the Ways: Minus 9, 2004

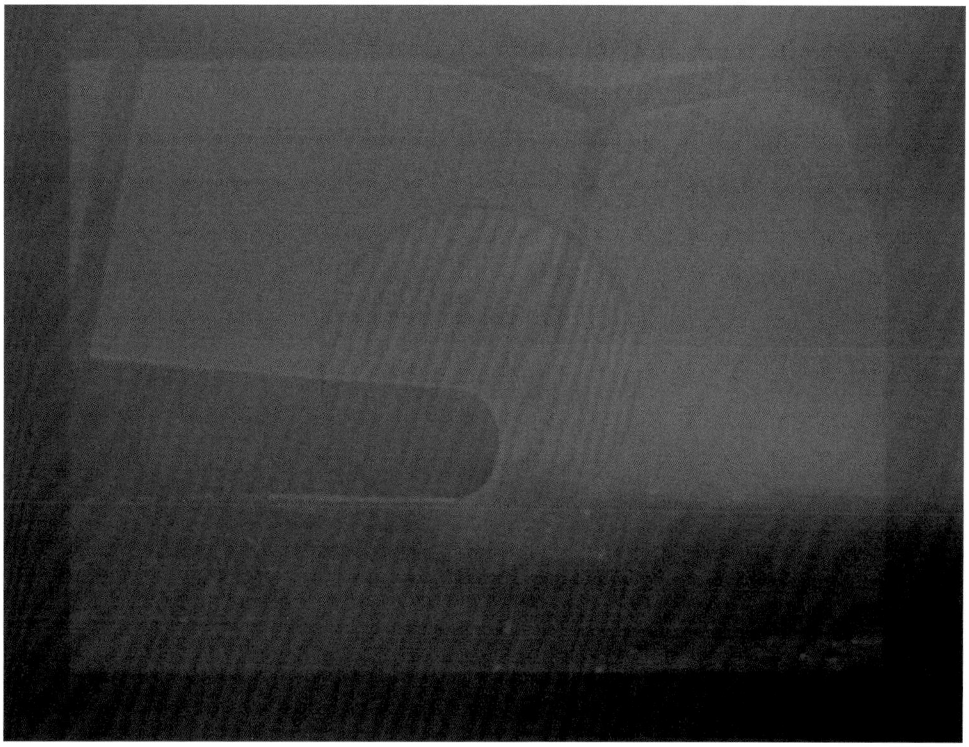

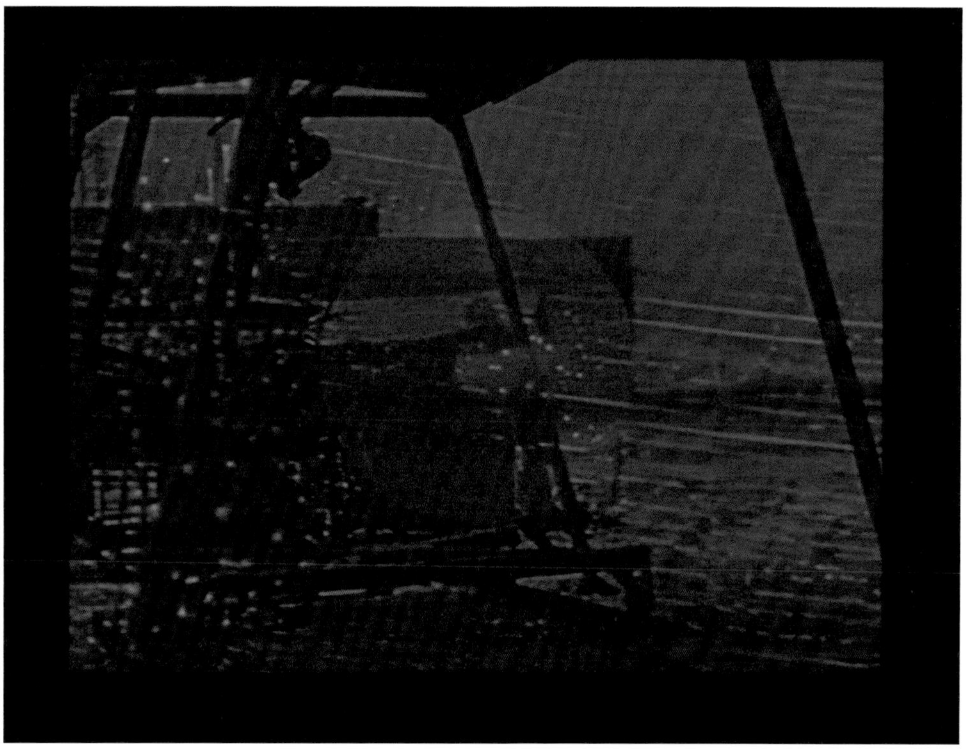

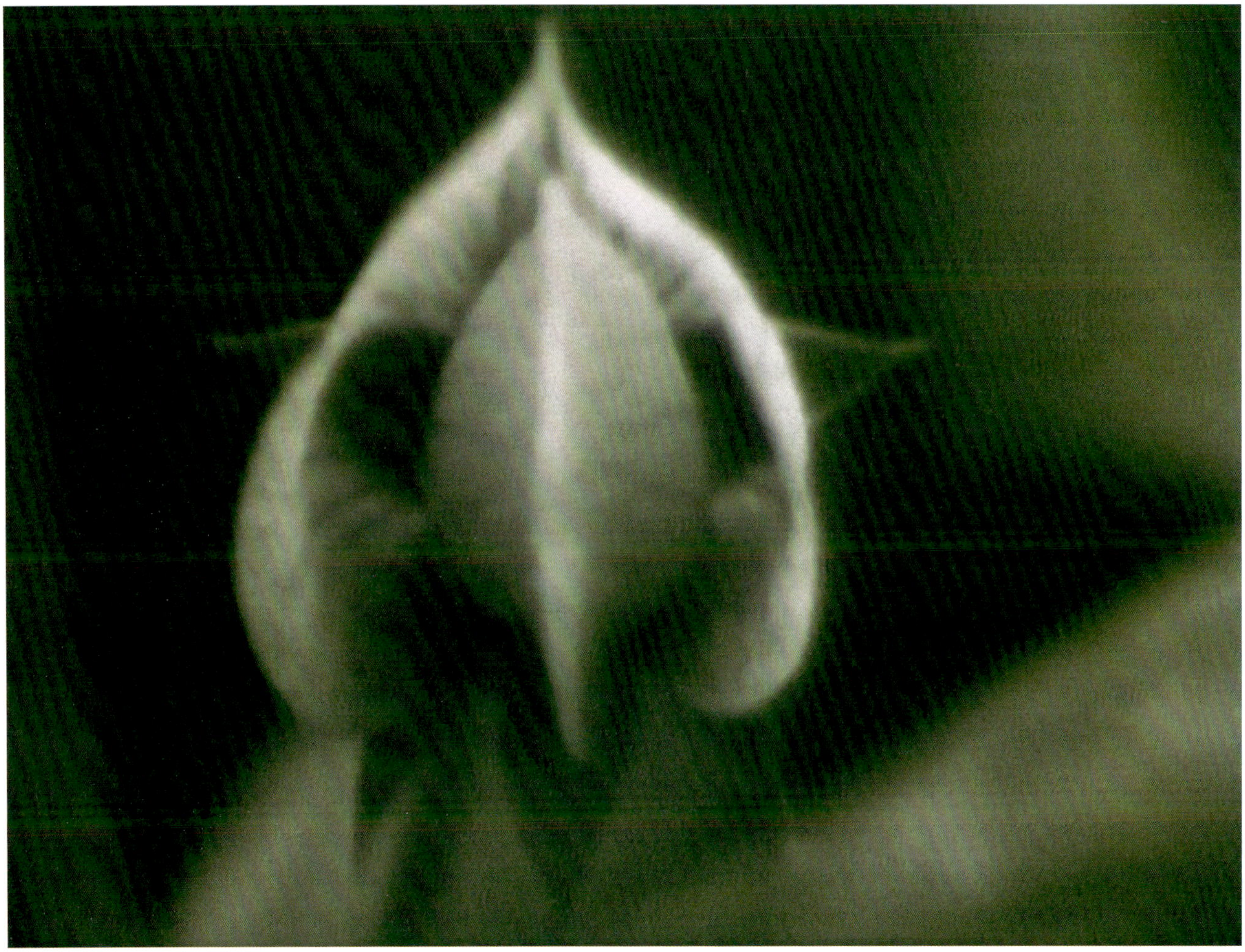

Let Me Count the Ways: Minus 8, 2004

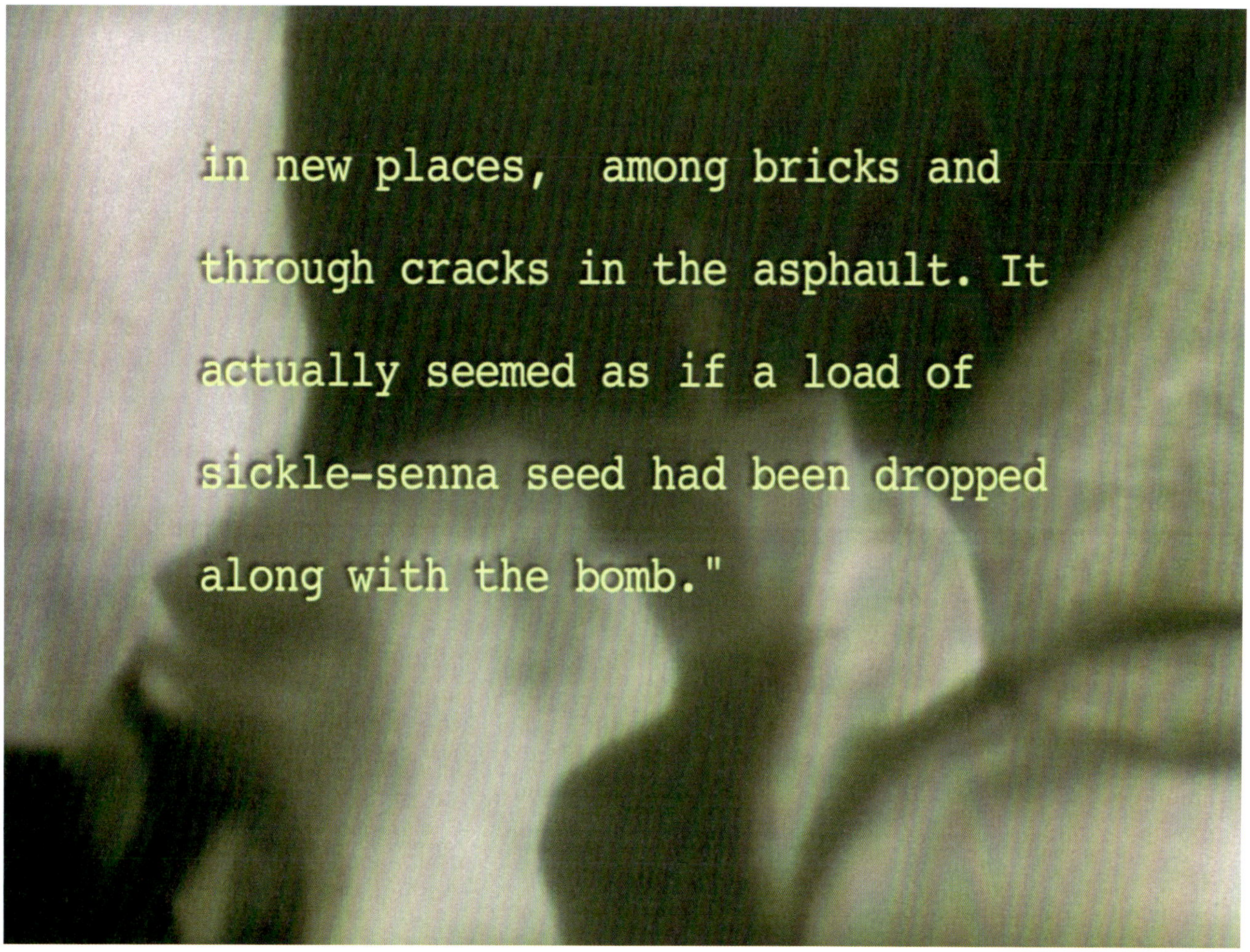
in new places, among bricks and
through cracks in the asphault. It
actually seemed as if a load of
sickle-senna seed had been dropped
along with the bomb."

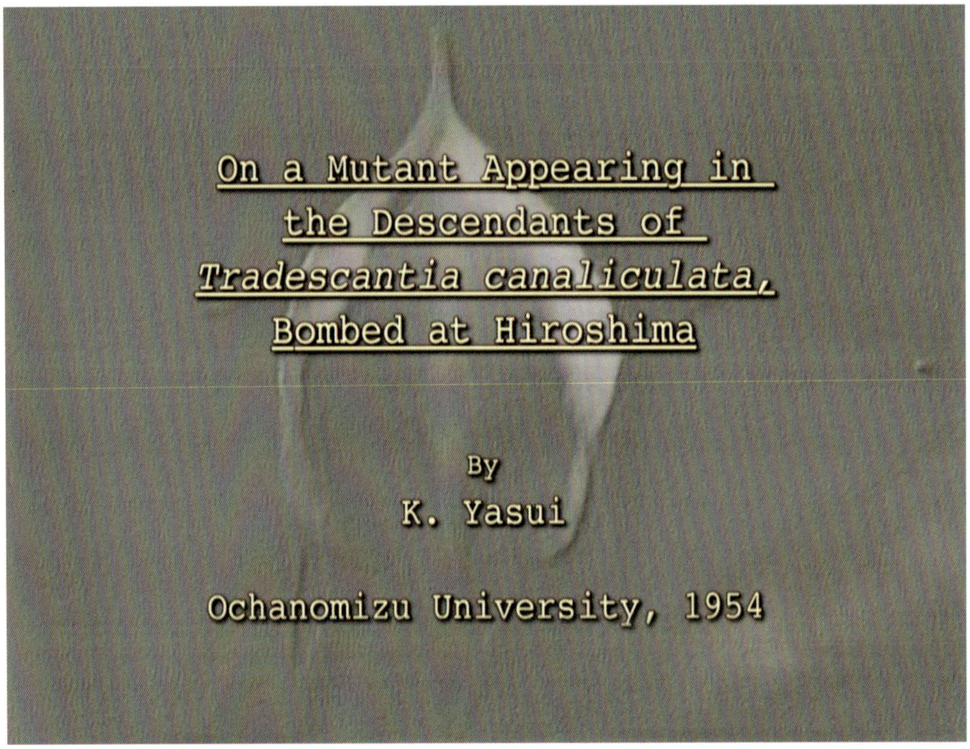

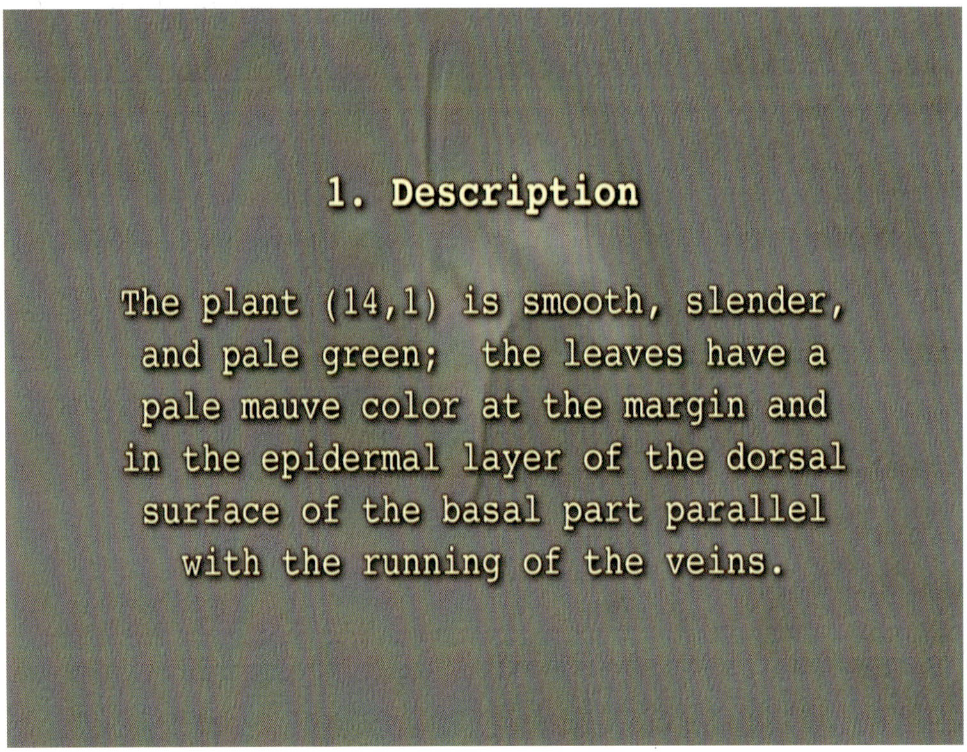

Let Me Count the Ways: Minus 7, 2004

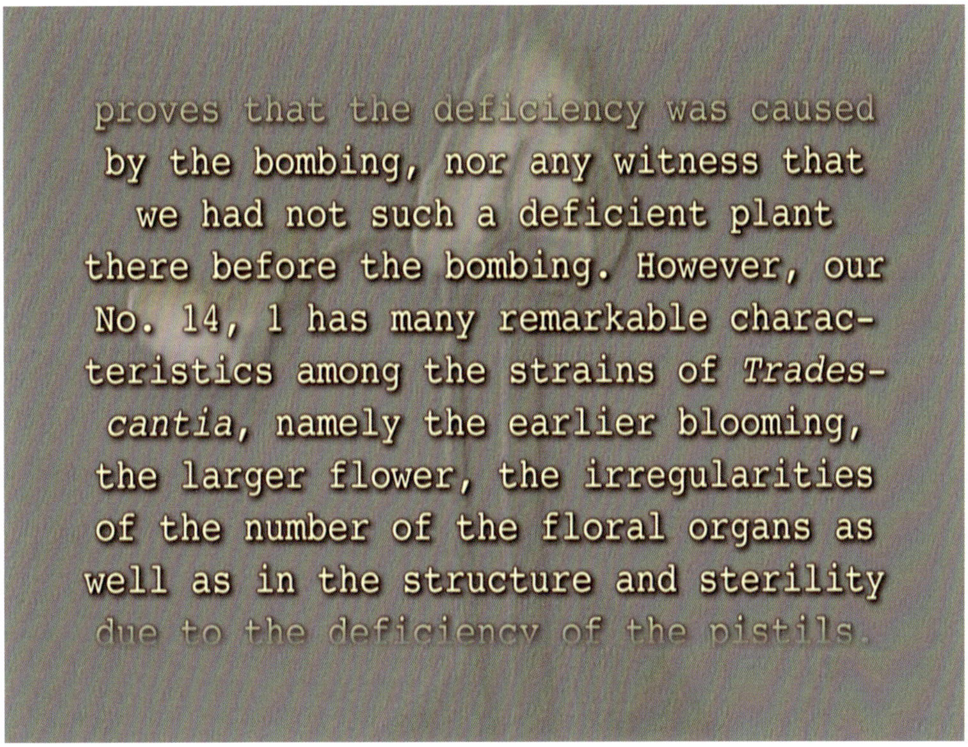
proves that the deficiency was caused
by the bombing, nor any witness that
we had not such a deficient plant
there before the bombing. However, our
No. 14, 1 has many remarkable charac-
teristics among the strains of *Trades-
cantia*, namely the earlier blooming,
the larger flower, the irregularities
of the number of the floral organs as
well as in the structure and sterility
due to the deficiency of the pistils.

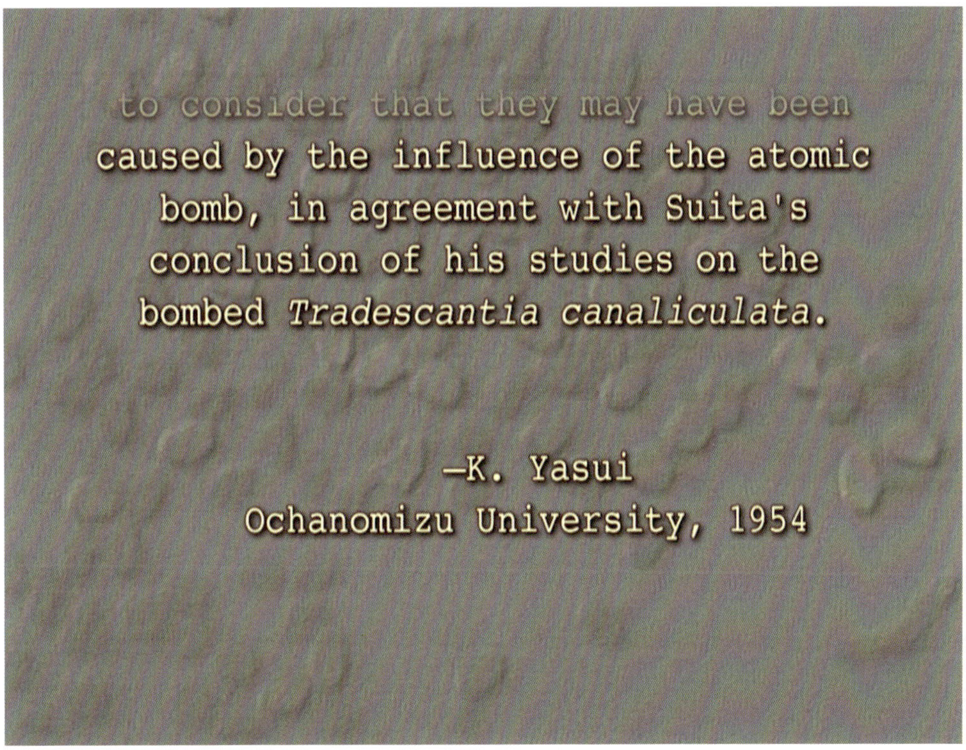
to consider that they may have been
caused by the influence of the atomic
bomb, in agreement with Suita's
conclusion of his studies on the
bombed *Tradescantia canaliculata*.
—K. Yasui
Ochanomizu University, 1954

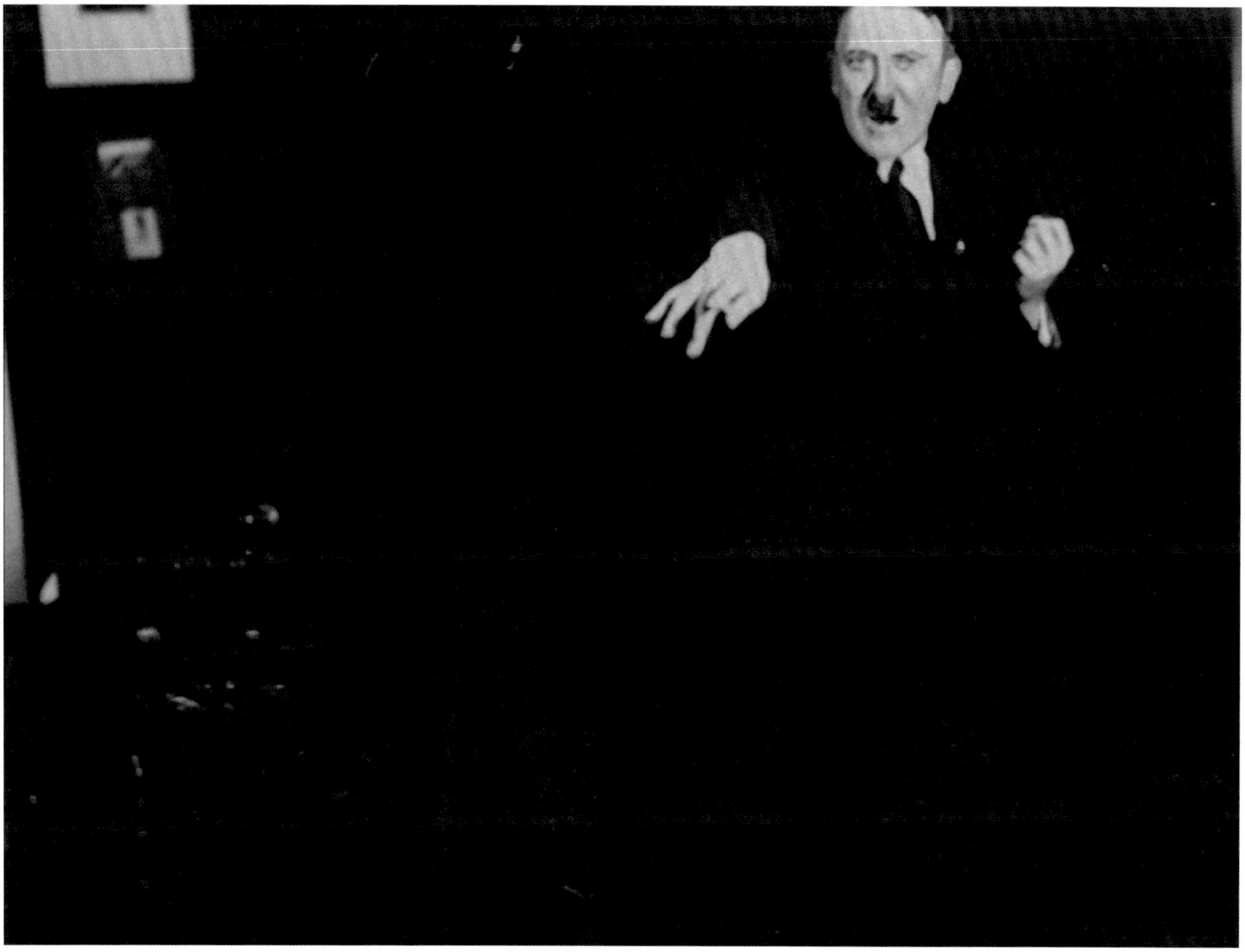

Let Me Count the Ways: Minus 6, 2006–8

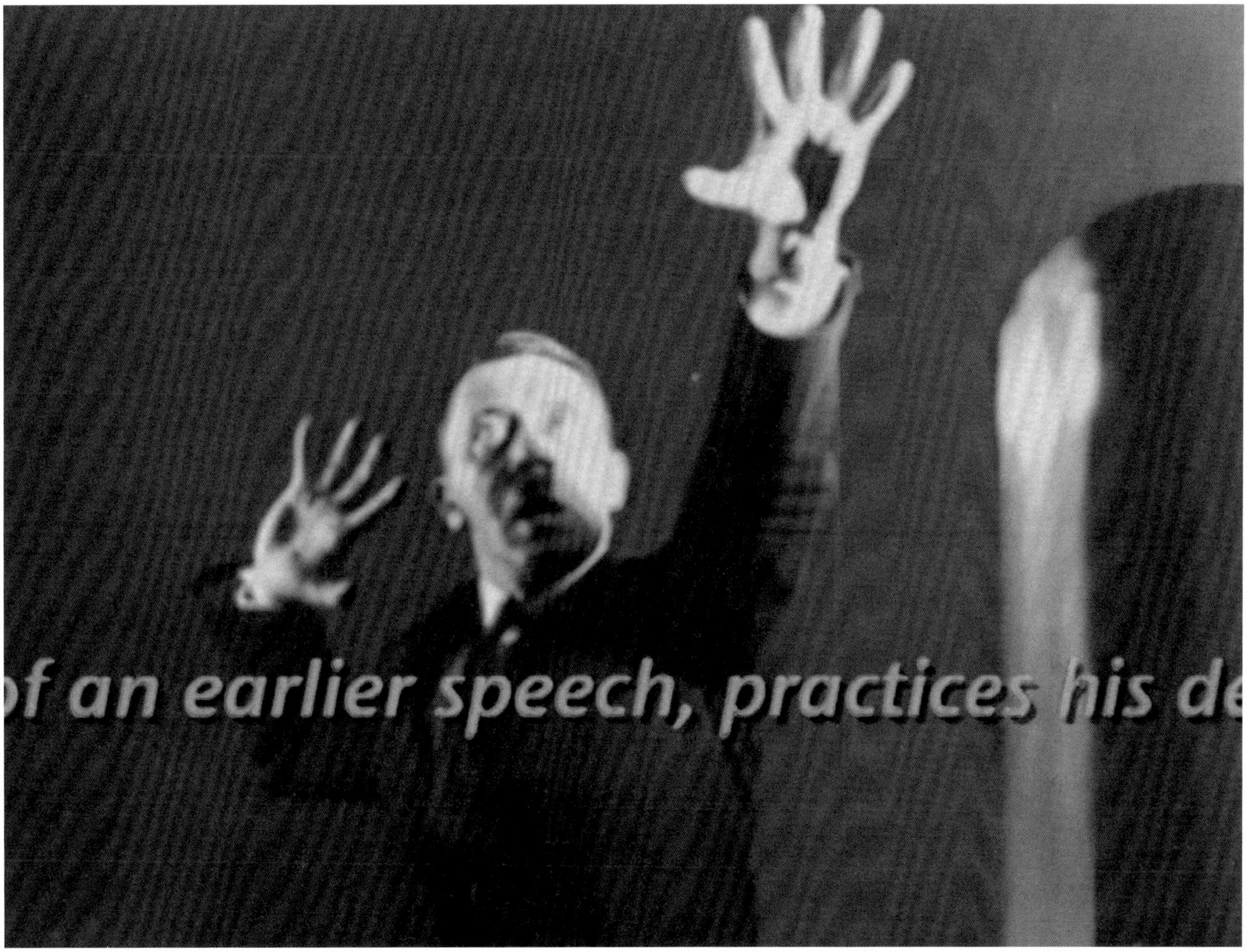
of an earlier speech, practices his de

Cut from Liquid to Snake

The Shock of Comprehension

Mason Leaver-Yap
on *Cut from Liquid to Snake*

The history of American film is inextricable from the history of surveillance. The advancement of one often serves the other. Both share a hunger for technological progress: improved fidelity, better environmental adaptability, lighter and faster devices for record and display. So, too, both industries purport complementary versions of truth. When one invents new ways to track and capture its subject, the other develops new narratives to fortify that subjective position. They are two poles of a technological feedback loop.

Film and video technologies, and their capacity for harm and pleasure, have long fascinated Leslie Thornton. Her career is suffused with Cold War anxieties, as represented in postapocalyptic works, such as *Peggy and Fred in Hell* (1983–2015), which stem from the filmmaker's formative experiences living in the world of the atomic bomb.

But Thornton's relation to nuclear foreboding has an intimate origin story—one that provided the inspiration for *Cut from Liquid to Snake* (2018). Embedded at the center of the film is a story narrated on-screen by the artist's aunt, who reveals that both the artist's father and grandfather (unbeknownst to each other at the time) were engineers in the Manhattan Project. It was Thornton's father who encased and fastened the last screw in the atomic bomb dropped on Hiroshima. Before loading it onto the plane, he wrote his name, his father's name, and his mother's name on the bomb casing—an inscription of familial dedication, legacy, and authorship. For Thornton, then, nuclear disaster is a story of kin and consequences—one that recalls theorists Gilles Deleuze and Félix Guattari's haunting refrain, "Weapons and tools are consequences, nothing but consequences."[1]

Through her interrogative style of work, Thornton continually pores over and attempts to comprehend consequences—of war and natural disaster, but also the claustrophobia of daily details that congeal and intensify with a sense of dread. Perhaps because of this, there is a persistent evidentiary quality to the filmmaker's footage. "Hey," says Thornton in *Cut from Liquid to Snake*'s opening address. Its immediacy sounds both startling and startled. Snippets of the one-sided conversation hover between trouble and tedium, as compressions in the audio speed provide an almost mechanical or algorithmic scan, lighting upon clear phrases such as "end of days," "something will happen," and "she's a spy" with an alarming suddenness. Framed as a kind of eavesdropping, suspicion and fear of endangerment seem tethered to the grain of the audio recording, sometimes revealing moments of dry surrender: "If anything happens, there will be a nice record of my last few moments. Wow." After all of the audio has been stretched, bent, and recompressed, it snaps off into murky silence. Comprehension of imminent danger is reduced to inference, not evidence.

In their book *A Thousand Plateaus: Capitalism and Schizophrenia*, Deleuze and Guattari discuss the

1 Gilles Deleuze and Félix Guattari, "Treatise on Nomadology: The War Machine," in *A Thousand Plateaus: Capitalism and Schizophrenia*, trans. Brian Massumi (Minneapolis: University of Minnesota Press, 1987), 398.

2 Deleuze and Guattari, 395.

3 Leslie Thornton, email to author, April 5, 2016.

4 Kevin McGarry, "Leslie Thornton," Crane.tv, published October 2013, accessed October 2020, https://web.archive.org/web/20131002235250/http://www.crane.tv/leslie-thornton.

constitutive parts of a weapons system or "assemblage," arguing that the primary component of such a system is speed. "The more mechanisms of projection a tool has," they write, "the more it behaves like a weapon, potentially or simply metaphorically."[2] Deleuze and Guattari's assessment of technology compellingly describes how the very apparatus of film might come close to resembling the characteristics of a weapon (cinema, too, is a "mechanism of projection"). It is this porosity between the technologies of annihilation and description that lends Thornton's work the capacity to represent and incite horror—in short, she draws on the shock of comprehension characteristic of both.

Nowhere is this more apparent than in the last ten minutes of *Cut from Liquid to Snake*. The video concludes with a long, sustained stereoscopic image of California's La Brea Tar Pits: on the left, the slowly blistering surface of the asphalt lake, and on the right, a prismatic refraction of the original image rendered as a kaleidoscopic abyss. Thornton extracted the accompanying voice-over from found audio, an oral testimony by "Miss Palchikoff," a Russian-born medical missionary, which describes the human trauma in the immediate aftermath of the atomic bomb explosion in Hiroshima, Japan, on August 6, 1945. In spite of Palchikoff's impassive language, her administrative account gradually reveals itself as a series of appalling abstractions of human suffering:

> And they turn very pale green, and they die off. [...] The people that were very badly burned, they vomited all the time, absolutely. No intermissions. Vomited and vomited. They couldn't take in any water or even ice. [...] Some doctors said it was the uranium effects with the sun rays, which passed through the body, and that would poison all the bones and everything inside the bones. That's how they explained it.

This section of Thornton's film was initially conceived by the artist in reference to *CROSSROADS* (1976), Bruce Conner's iconic 35mm film that drew from the US Army's own surveillance of the titular nuclear bomb test at Bikini Atoll, depicting the detonation in extreme slow-motion. Thornton describes the late artist's work as an "enabling force, a point of departure, a fundamental reassurance."[3] But rather than channeling Conner's singular, decisive moment of horror, Thornton's work instead builds from slow dread, confronting viewers with the persistent half-life of violent histories.

The effect is mirrored in the audio, as the viewer must strain to make out the details of Palchikoff's oral account, in part due to the archival chafes and abrasions to the record; her descriptions provoke a disgust of the imagination. What this eyewitness has to say, and the administrative ease and comprehensiveness with which she says it, is likely at odds with the eavesdropper's desire to hear completely. It brings home the horror of the atomic bomb and of Thornton's personal ties to its construction, embodying the difficulty of comprehension.

With oily pustules popping on the surface, the oozing La Brea Tar Pits intensify and provide a visual metaphor for Palchikoff's descriptions. Together, they portray a narrative of violence, and, rendered as a pair of eyes, the image stares back at the viewer, revealing only darkness, unblinking. Thornton describes her stereoscopic technique as "a mechanical gaze, [that] seems so full of life, [...] so intimately ocular, related to the way a binocular as a technical extension of our eyes isolates and frames."[4] Recalling Deleuze and Guattari's technological apparatus, Thornton's image of the pit is both an image of a void and its technological abstraction—a metaphor for the ineffability of the bomb and its refraction through the language of administration that obscures humanity. That such material of horror would appear in Thornton's work as a "readymade" is symptomatic of the times that the artist and her audience continue to live through.

Following spreads:
Cut from Liquid to Snake, 2018

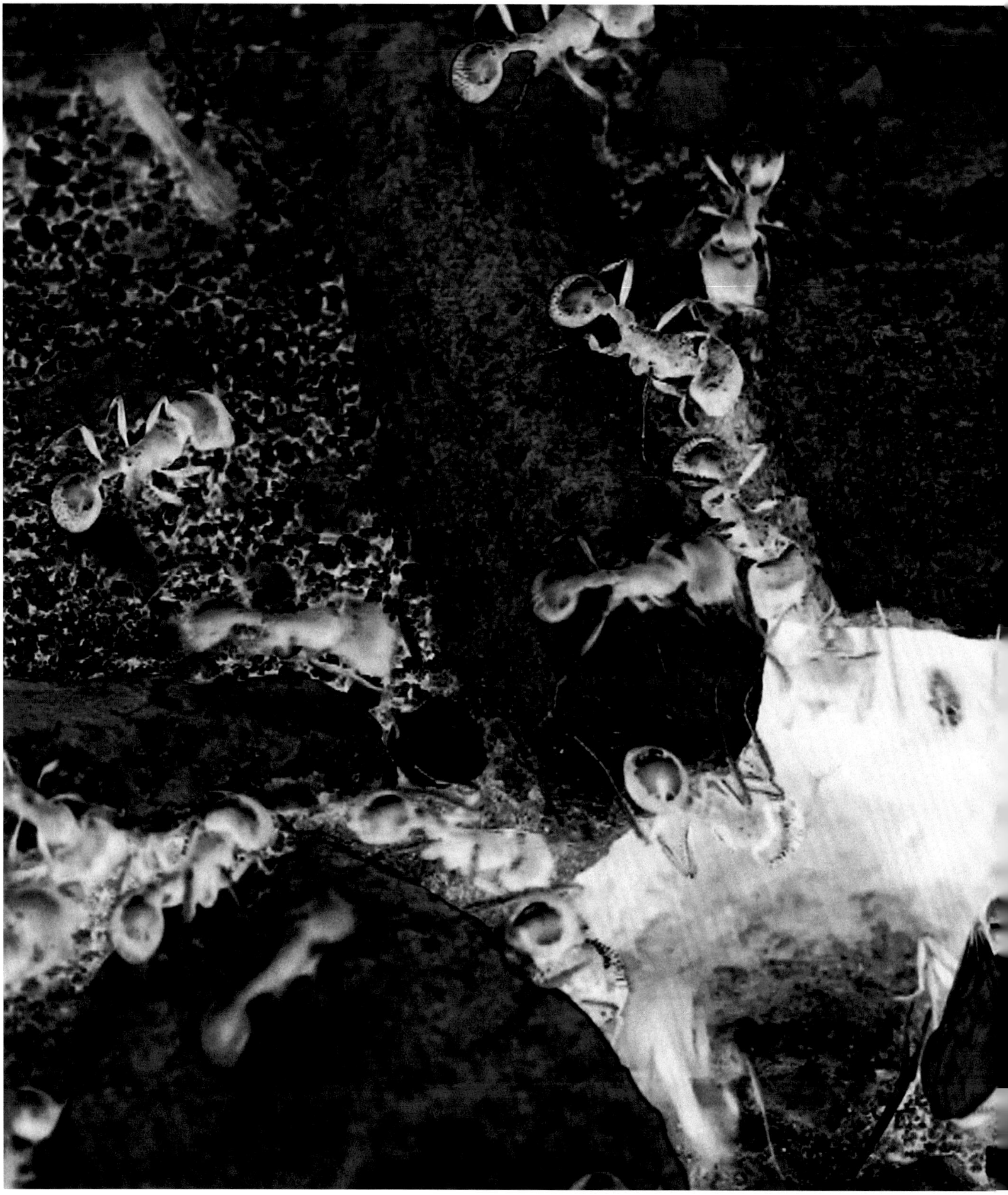

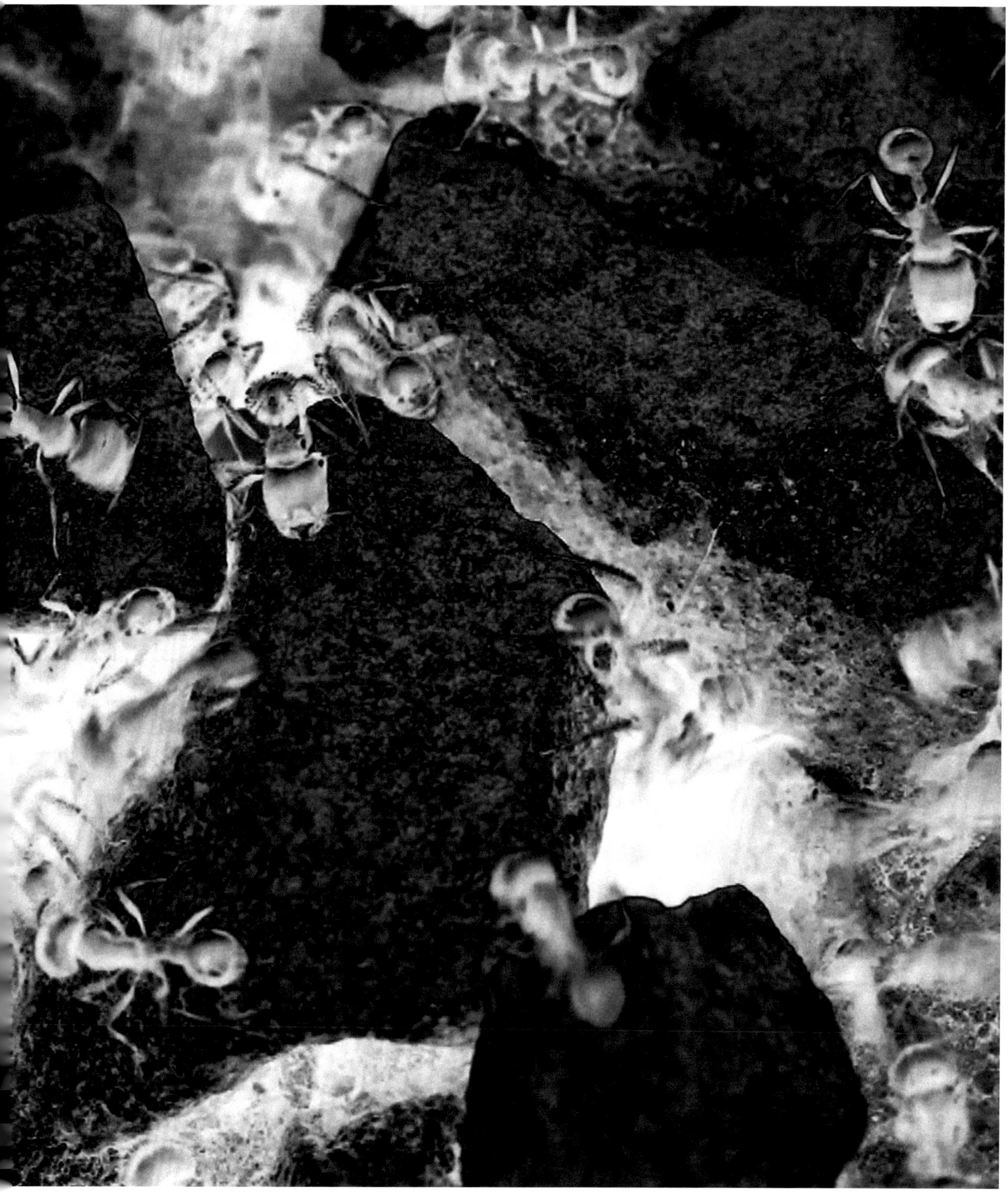

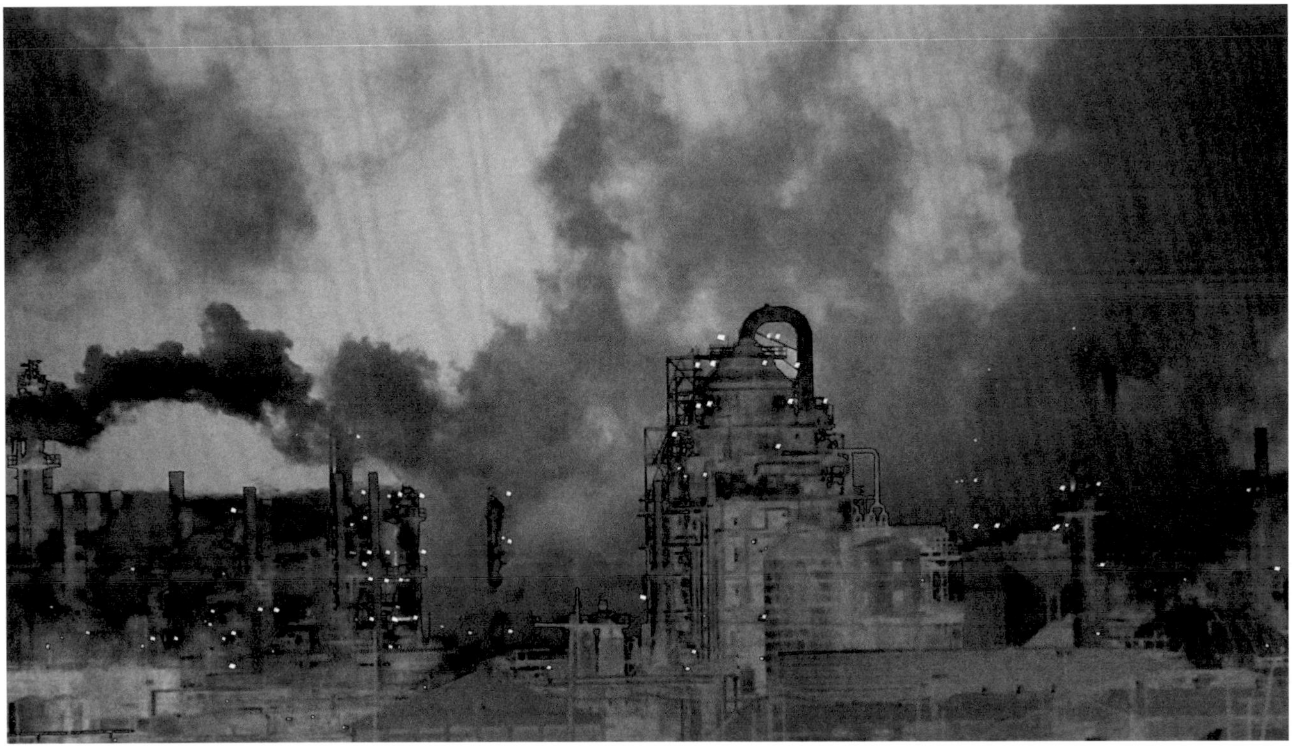

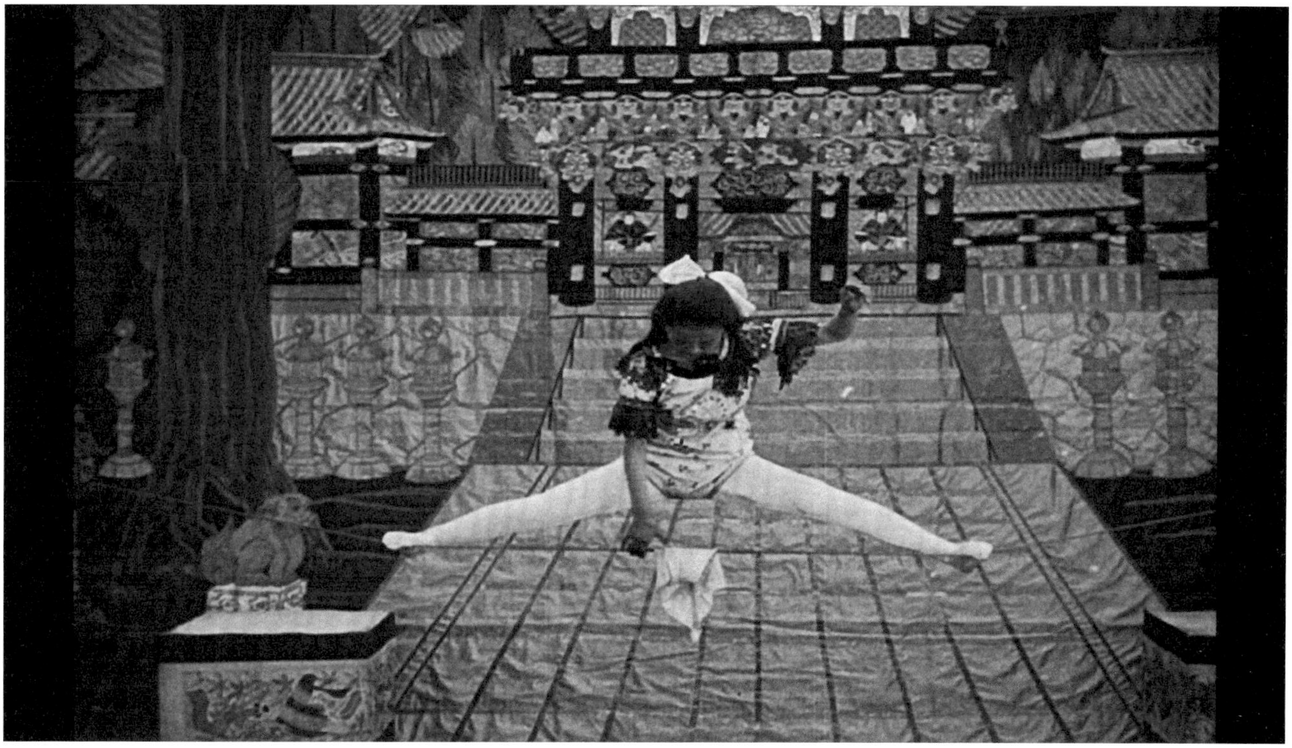

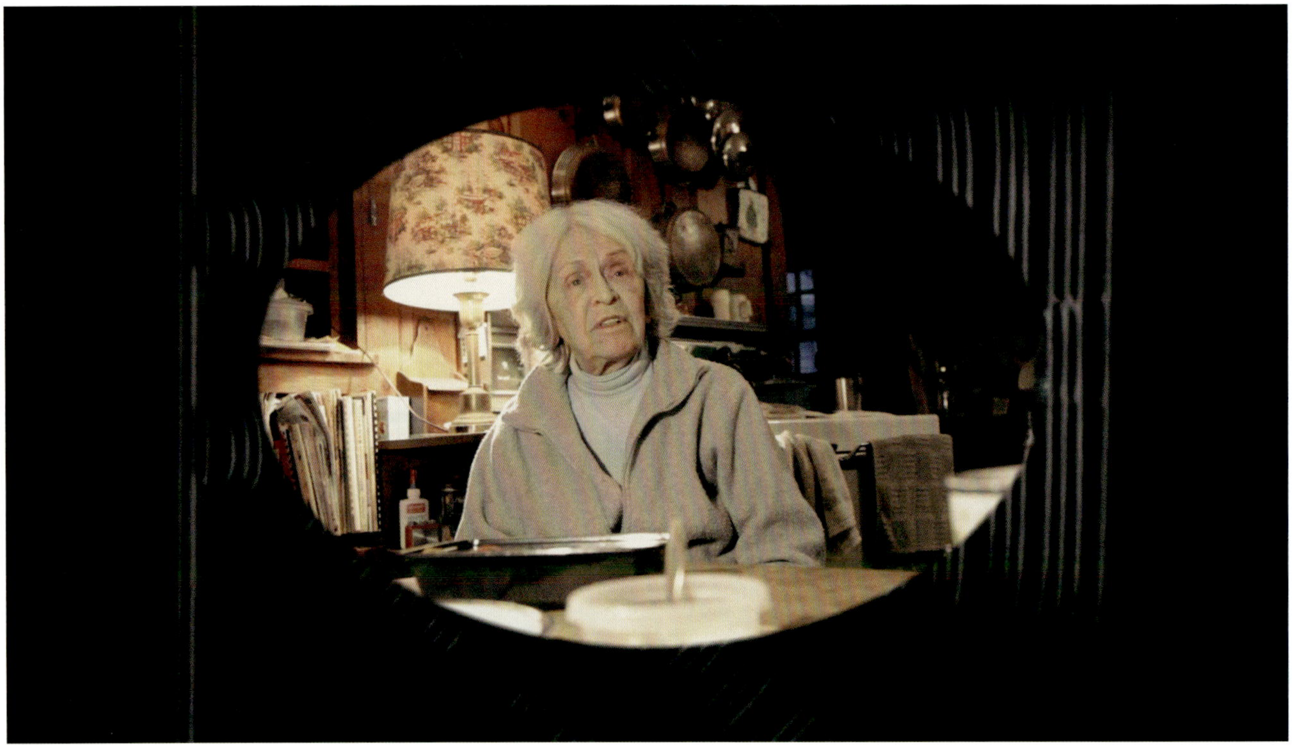

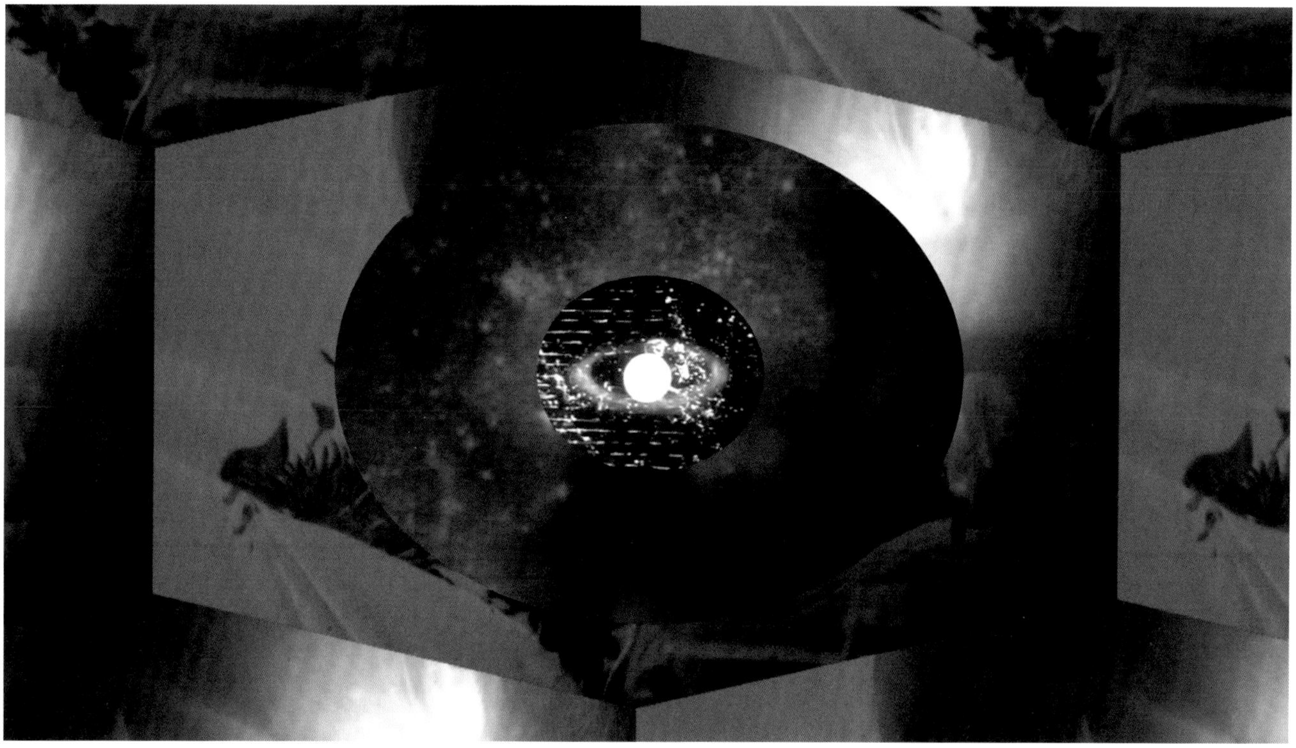

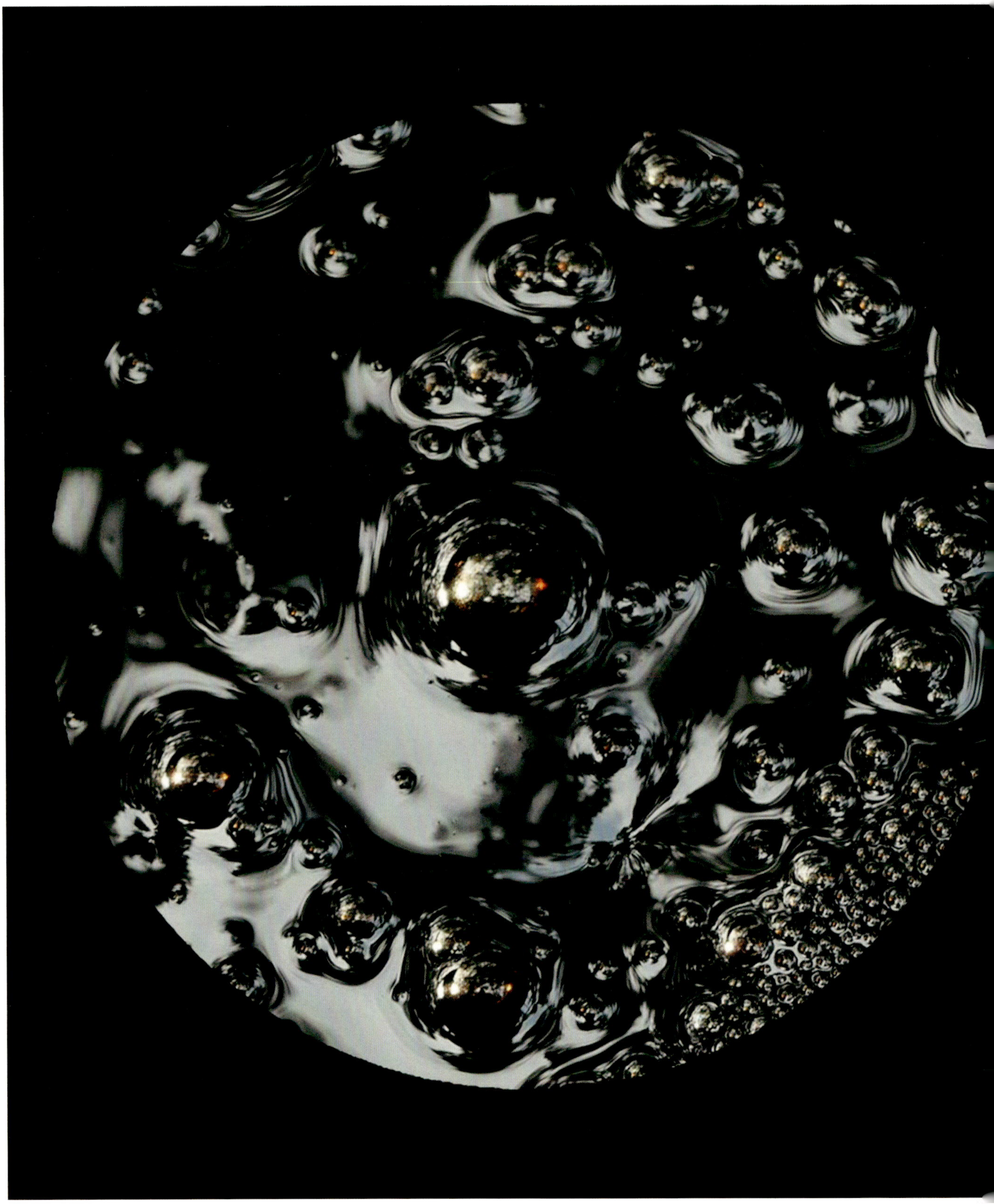

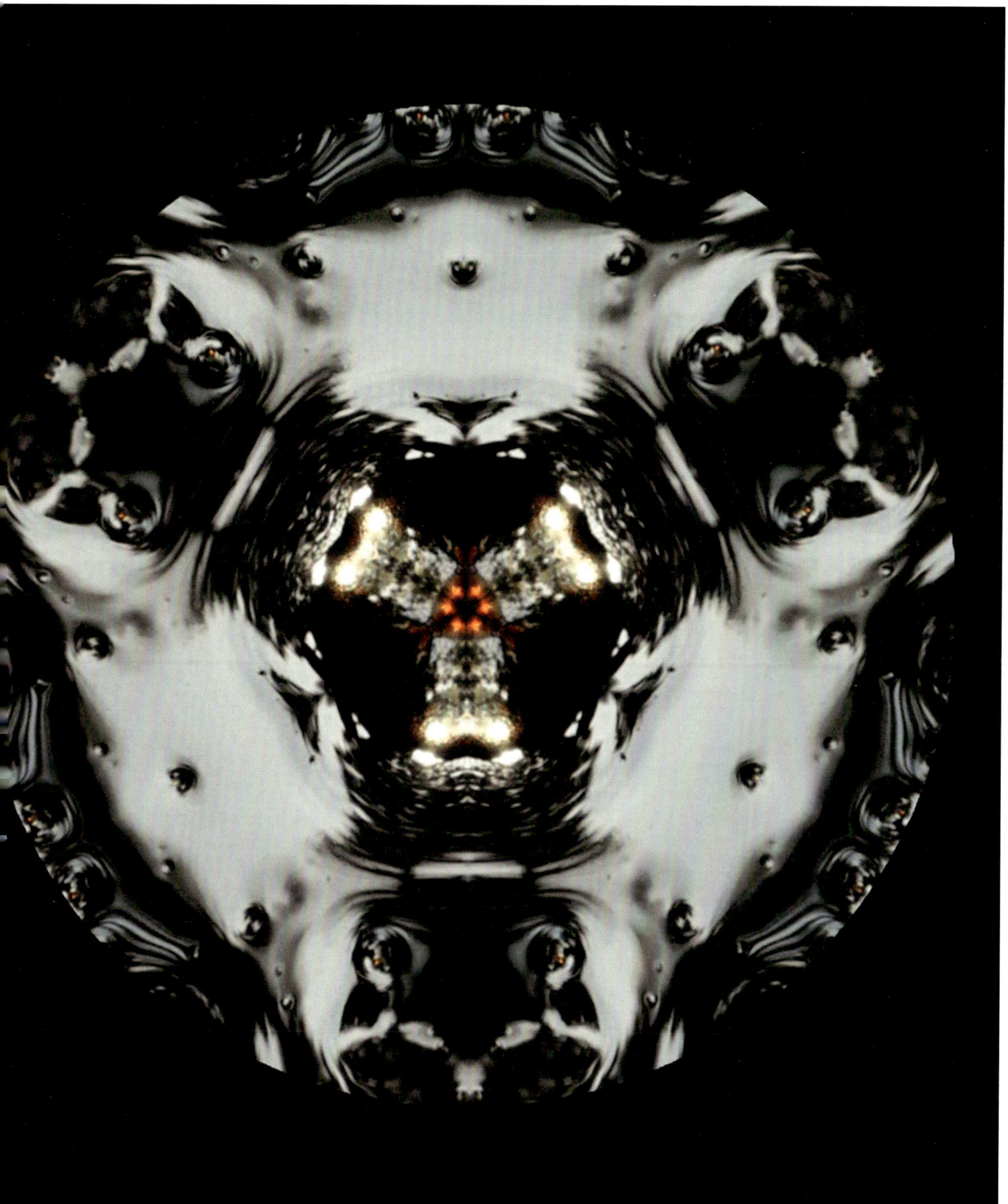

Ground

Out of This World

Milan Ther on *Ground*

Leslie Thornton's *Ground* (2020) traces, in a thirteen-minute loop, the undefined complexity of human knowledge production. It also tethers its inert, latent, or abeyant effects—at times beautiful and at other times disorienting—as they resonate into human existence. Thornton has described the space of the film as "terribly human [...] in a way that we can feel but not occupy. [A space of both] longing and fear."[1] Much of the film is shot and presented in black and white, digitally altered, and set in the dark, subterranean landscapes of cables and server stations of CERN (the European Organization for Nuclear Research). Through Thornton's use of digital effects, her figures are translated into grids with no beginning or end—floating wavelengths that collapse into surfaces. These distortions creep across the image space of the film like smoke or bacteria, obfuscating the legibility of the source footage while suggesting invisible objects of scientific study (such as wavelengths and particles) that occupy the figures.

The footage in *Ground* was filmed by Thornton during residencies at CERN and California Institute of Technology and visits to Los Angeles and Oslo. The film's leading motif is that of a landscape, and the frame is cut along the horizon line. The lower half establishes Los Angeles as the ground—a place defined by the pace of its traffic, the human automotive motion rendered in digital black and white, like chalk on a blackboard. At the front of this human-made geometry sits the by-now demolished DC Stages building that contained Hollywood sets like a city hall, courtrooms, and other spaces related to the regulation of social order and civic bureaucracy. On the upper half of the split screen, making a kind of sky above LA, is the digitally re-rendered footage of a scientist from CERN, a type of protagonist walking through what appears to be the metabolic machinery of the nuclear research institute. His figure and the background are depicted in white frequency lines against a black background. In this image-space that oscillates elastically between depth and surface at any given time, he mutters, "Resources, resources, resources." As the scientist moves, the effects momentarily render him indistinguishable from the machinery of CERN. With humming in the background, his voice resonates as unmistakably human. "My life has been dedicated to—" he says, pausing to let Thornton complete the sentence off-camera, "the decay." While he refers to specific scientific processes, such as elements of decay in CP violation,[2] the film seems to imply another process of deterioration—that of indexicality, through which "reality" has historically been consolidated. In prophetic reverie, he muses, "What really counts is the imagination."

His voice is audibly edited. Thornton's cuts interrupt his breaths at the end of sentences while he relays his life and work with a mix of inspiration and exhaustion, exhilaration and despair. When he

1 Leslie Thornton, "No Romance: Milan Ther and Leslie Thornton in Conversation," in this publication, 69.

2 Thornton outlines this anomaly in the laws of physics in "No Romance," 63.

3 Thornton, 63.

4 Thornton, 63–64.

mentions Val Fitch, a pioneer of CP violation (and a friend of Gunnar Thornton, the artist's father), the correspondence between his work as a scientist and Thornton's as an artist becomes tangible and real. This personal history is what drew Thornton to CERN in the first place, as she explains in an interview on the occasion of her exhibition "GROUND": "This is [...] why we sought him out. We wanted to meet someone at CERN who was willing to talk about Fitch's work—not so much because I was interested in or understood the science particularly, but because of a story Fitch tells about how he came to be a physicist."[3] Thornton continues:

> My father, who was Norwegian, was an avid skier, and when he was working as an engineer in Los Alamos during World War II, he was in a ski club that included some of the renowned physicists. Val Fitch, a young chemist, arrived at Los Alamos at the same time. As Fitch relates it, he grew keen to meet the European physicists, and one way this could happen, since they tended to keep to themselves, was to go skiing on the mountain slopes near the Los Alamos facility. In his own narrative, learning to ski from his Norwegian friend helped open the door to his future life in physics.[4]

With this information, Thornton's family history is woven into both the subject and mise-en-scène of *Ground*, which joins works like *Cut from Liquid to Snake* (2018) and *Let Me Count the Ways* (2004–ongoing) in retracing her father's and grandfather's engagements within twentieth-century science and the military-industrial complex and the ramifications of their work, both good and ill. In Thornton's thirty-two-year-long project *Peggy and Fred in Hell* (1983–2015), two children live through the transition from broadcast media to the information age, culminating with the advent of AI set against a postapocalyptic world. *Ground* is a further exploration of the space in which *Peggy and Fred* ends. It contains a similar dynamic: Los Angeles is presented as the center of an image-based media system—that is, the film industry—while CERN is a palpitating, formless structure run by humans and machines alike. One serves to place humans in the world through media—while the other, in a way, does the opposite. Discoveries made at CERN perpetually redefine how we understand our place in the universe, quietly but forcefully changing what it means to be human.

In the later stages of *Ground*, we encounter another, audibly younger scientist, who is visible only by the proxy of her hand as she gestures at a dark server room operated by a robotic rig. While offbeat, sped-up techno music thumps, she explains: "No humans are allowed here. Skin produces dust, which could interfere with the system.... So you take the human away and have a very effective setup." Then her voice fades into the noise. In mirroring the ominous server room of CERN, the film seems to ask: What leads humans to create spaces they cannot enter? As an allegory of both scientific progress and Thornton's, *Ground* captures the clash between belief and uncertainty. It maps an epistemological shift—and an ambient existential fear—that emanates from the increasing presence of machines and a type of cognitive inaccessibility to the complexity of the organization of human perception and thought.

Following spreads:
Ground, 2020

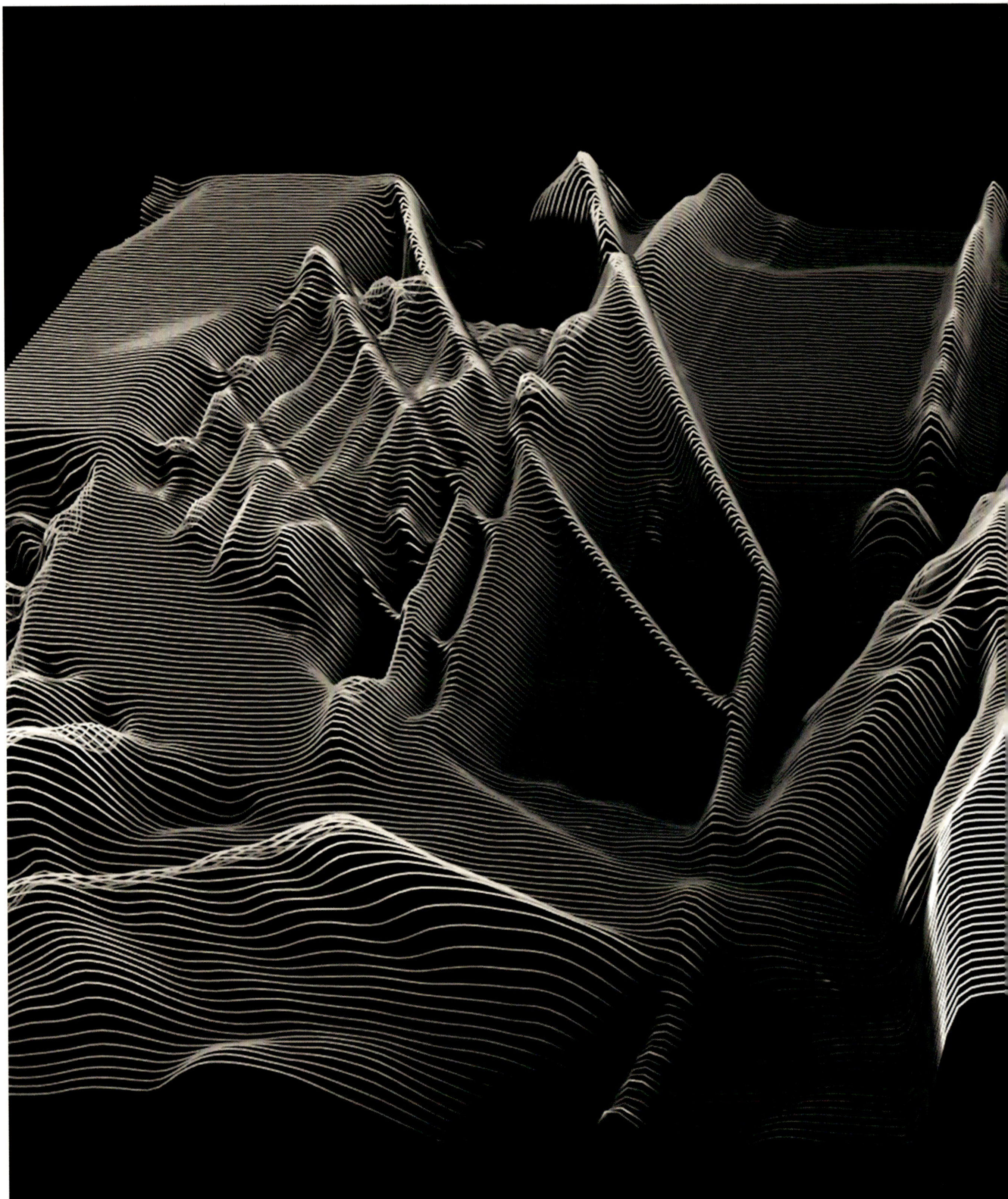

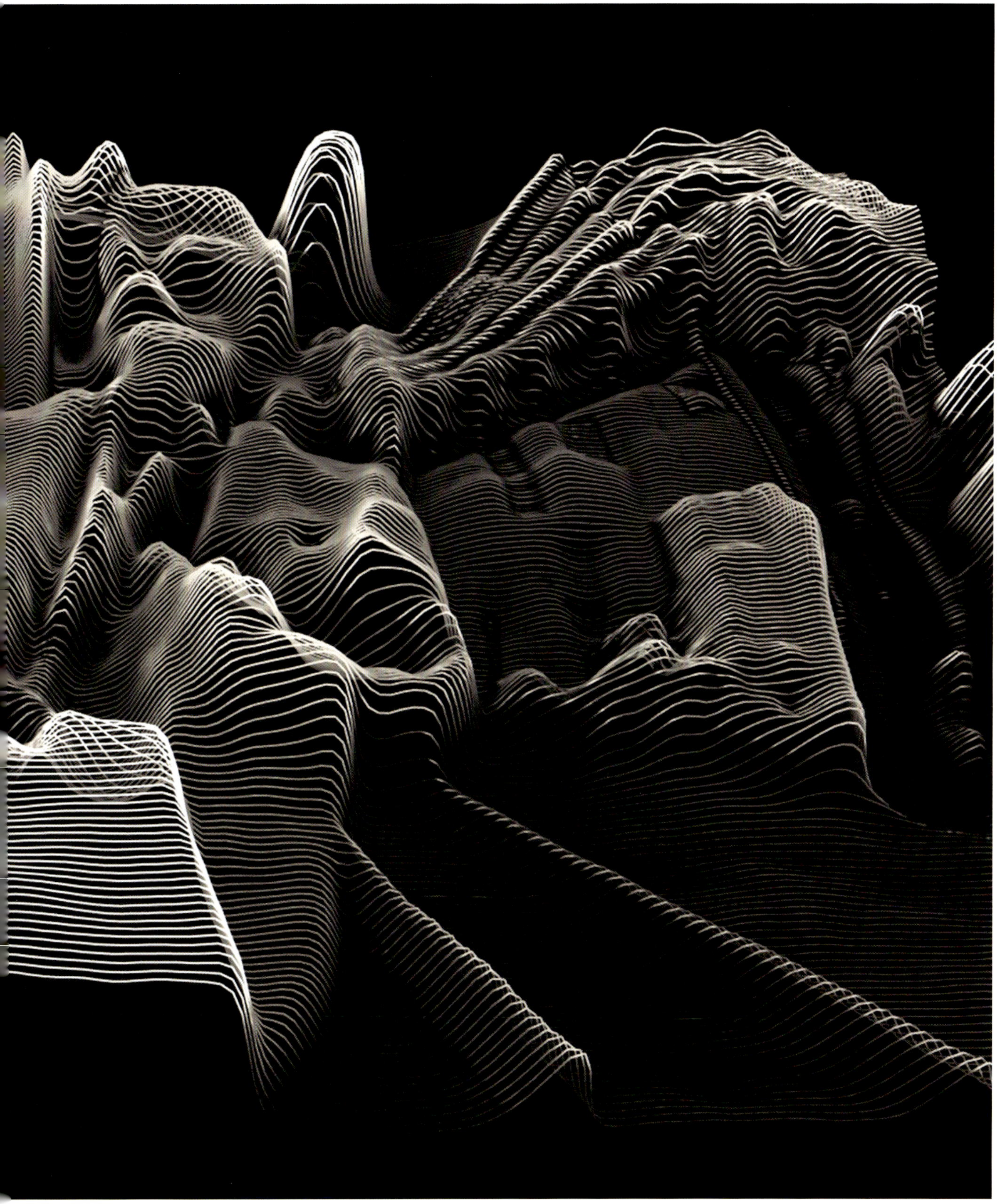

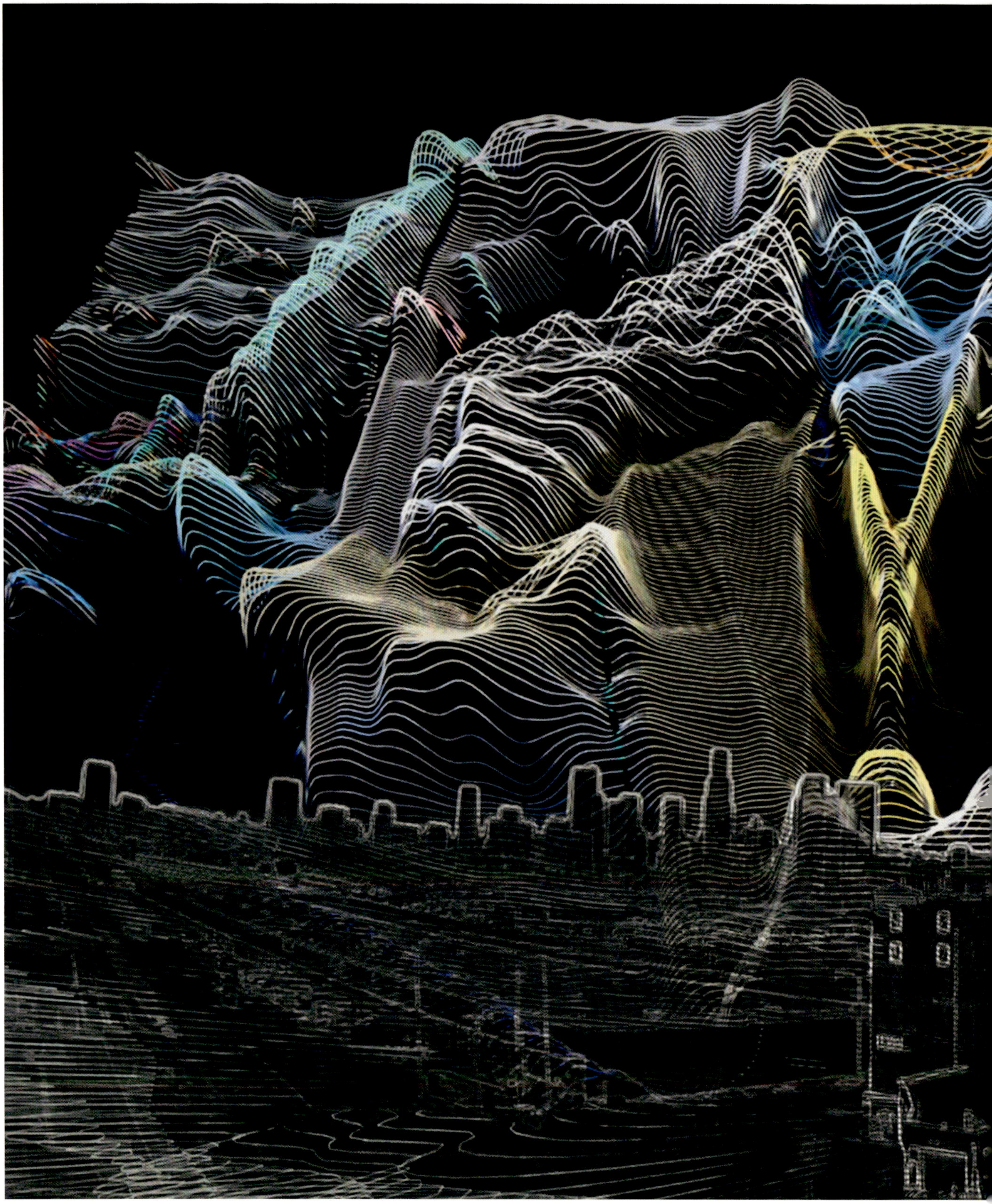

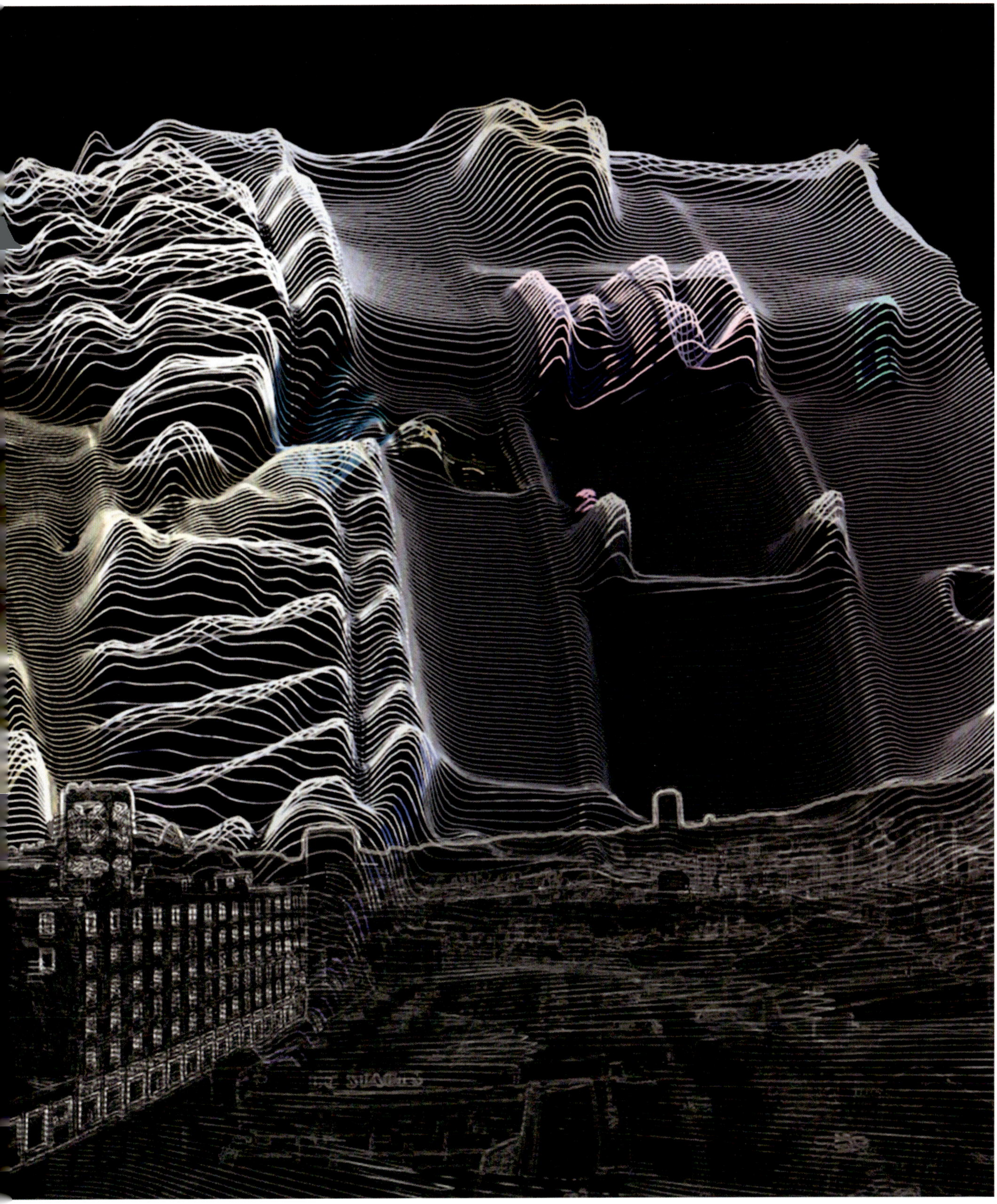

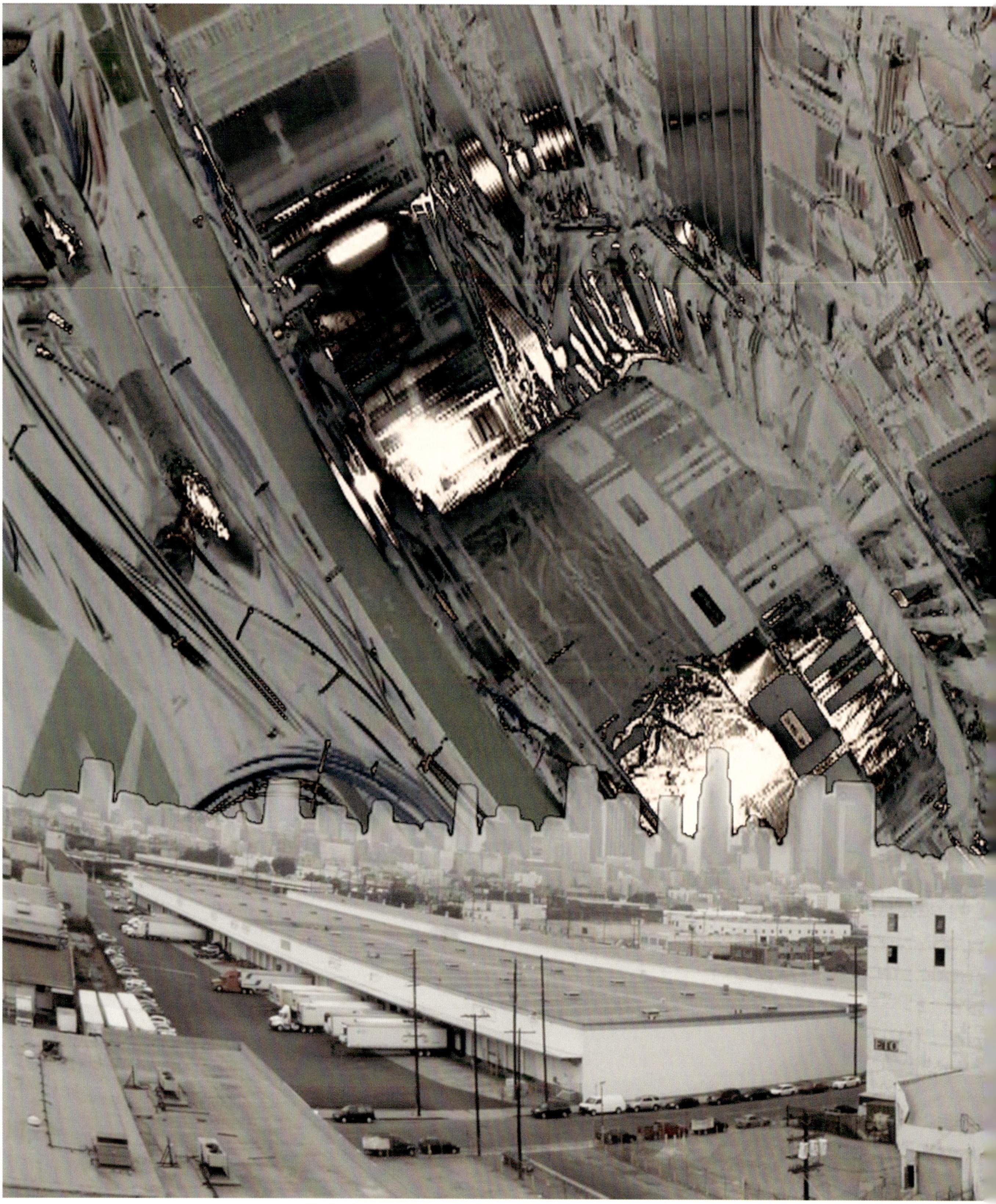

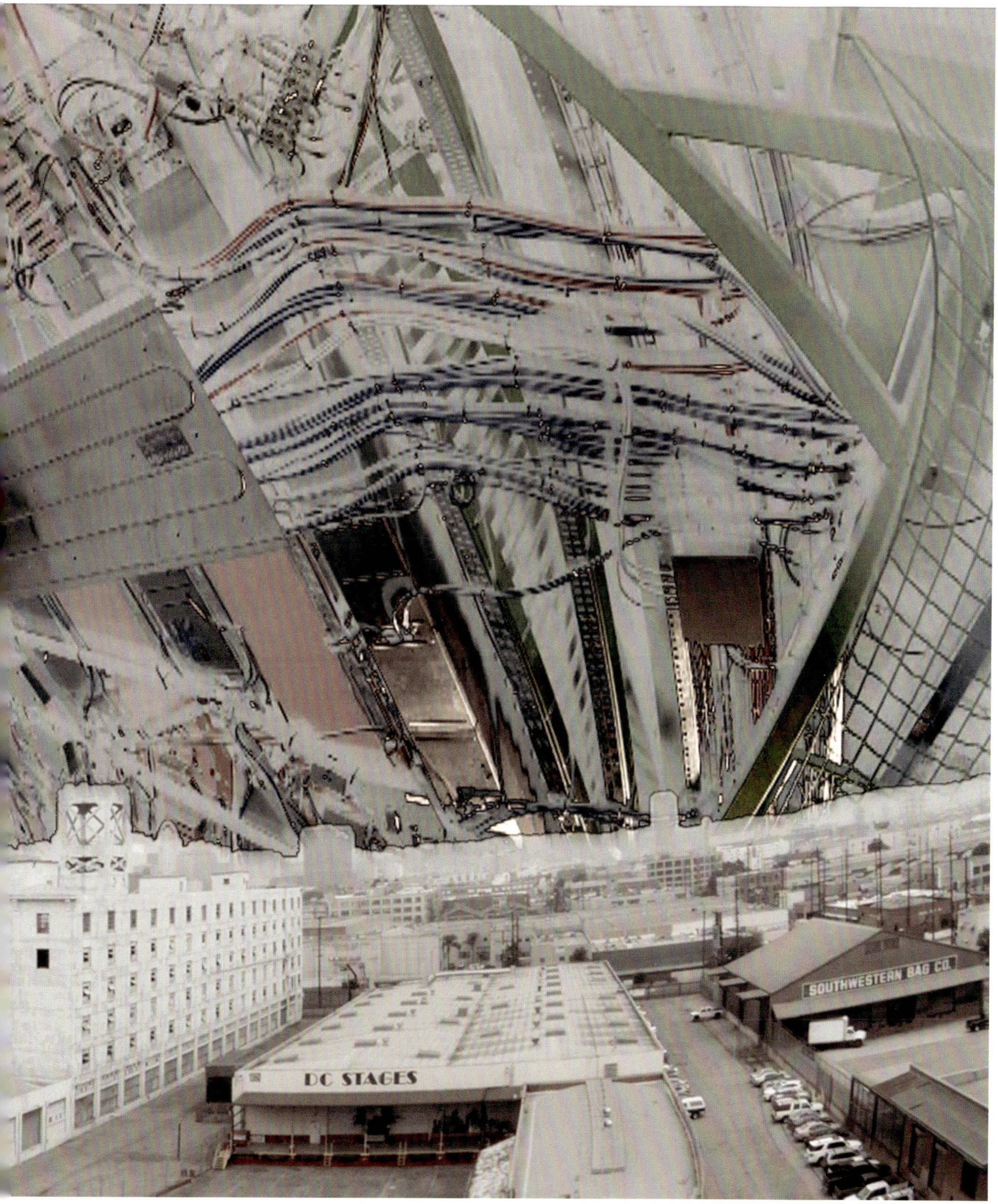
DC STAGES
SOUTHWESTERN BAG CO.

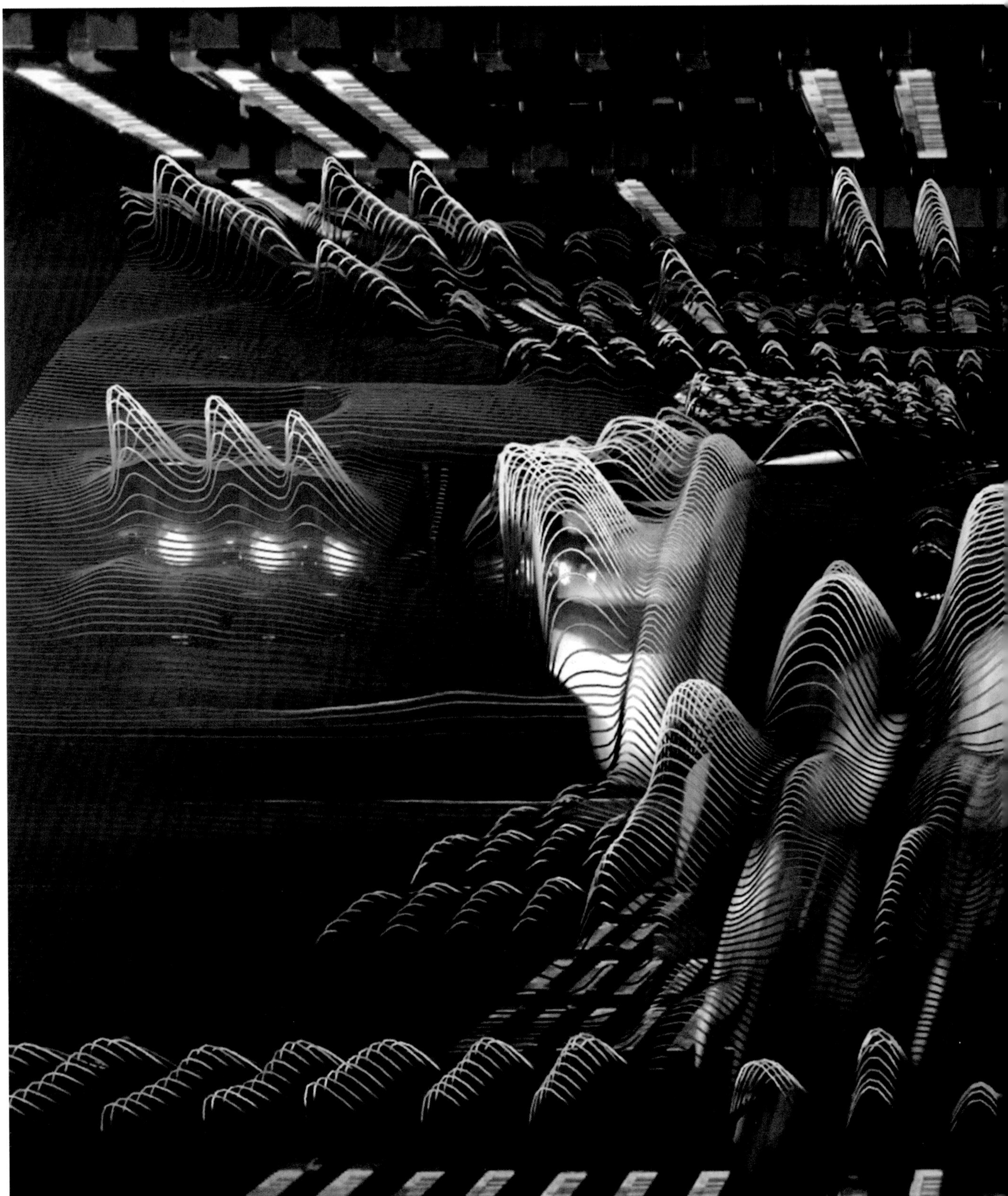

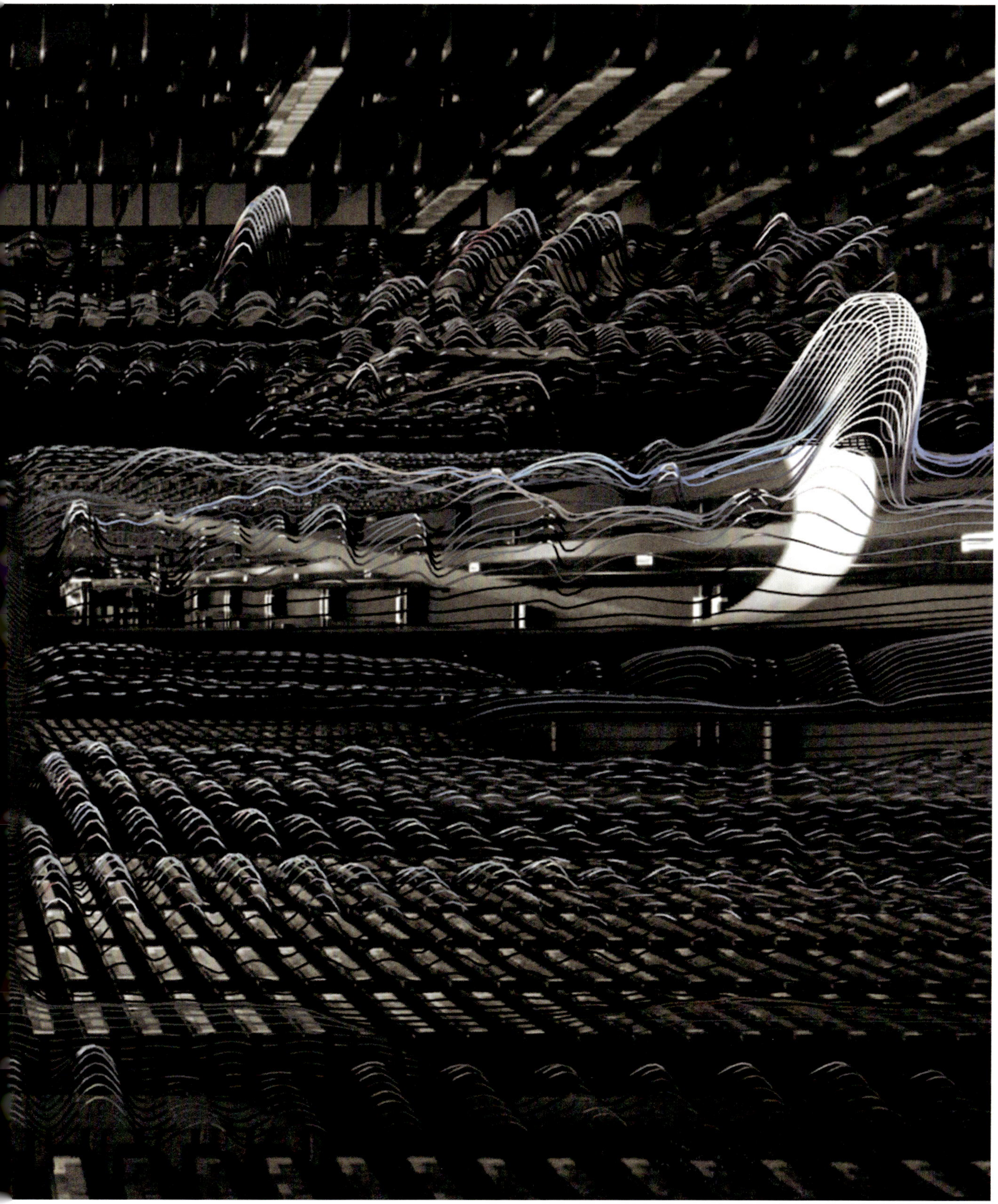

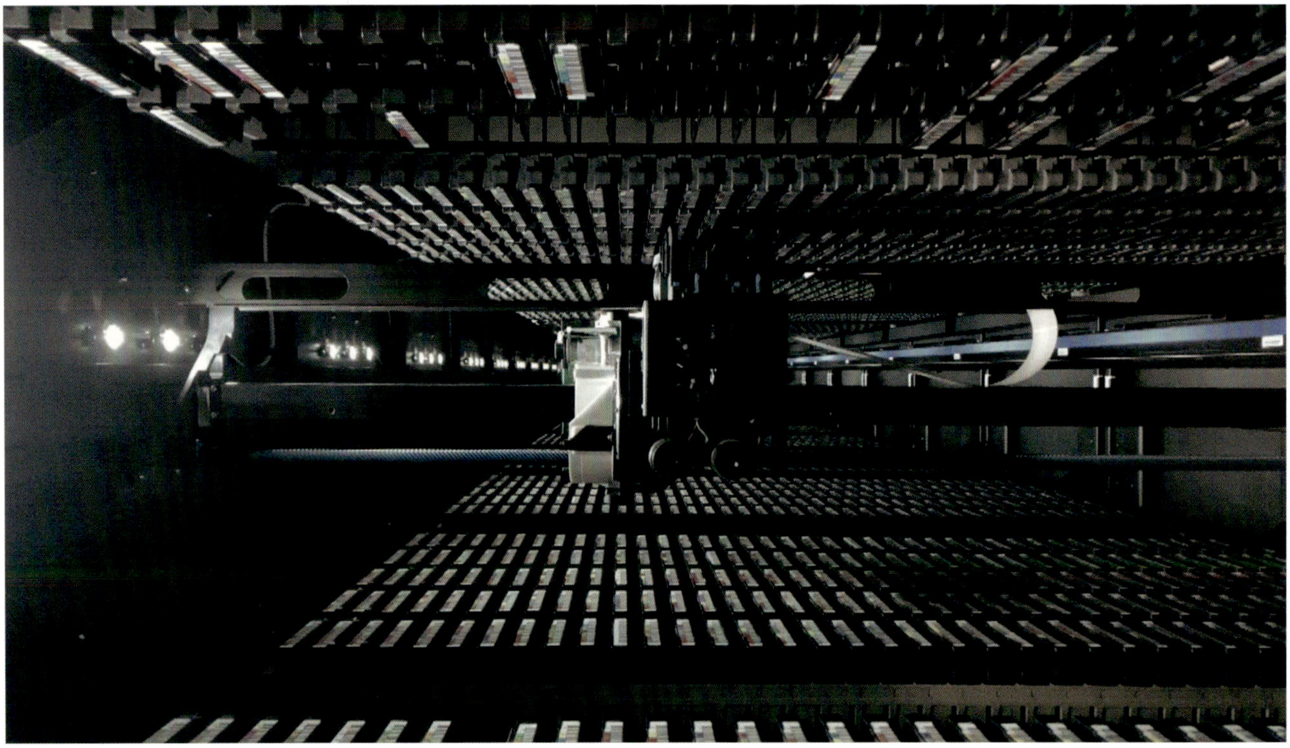

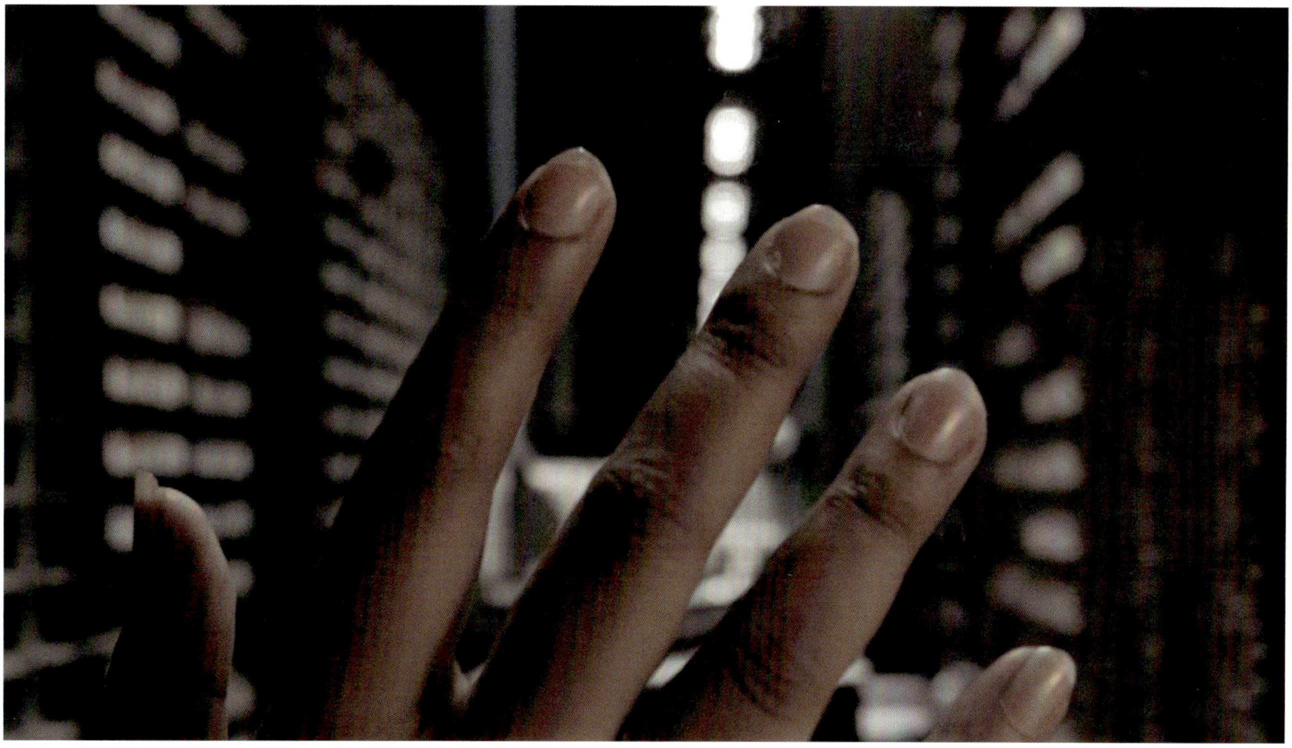

HEMLOCK Handmade

Touching the Abyss

Thomas Zummer on *HEMLOCK Handmade*

"Have you ever seen so many fallen trees?
I don't remember ever seeing so many fallen
trees. Ever."

—Leslie Thornton, Chesterfield Gorge,
New Hampshire, August 2020[1]

We are arguing, then laughing and sighing as we make notes together. I insist that one does not begin lost. She prefers to think that being lost is never a problem. As we walk into the woods, there are always figures, visual portrayals in and through language: a thicket, bramble, field of lines, marks, impediments, cairns, walls. In so many words: a dusky, gloomy image. Before such images, one finds oneself in the dark, in a tangle of references, arrested, apprehensive, anxiously grasping, without a thread in a labyrinth of interpretations, casting about for marks of passage. That's what I think. She says, "Let's go further, come on!"

Something happens to us, walking into a forest or field, something quite difficult to describe. Our presence and position change in subtle ways going farther *in.* As the marks and configurations that trace our trajectory fall away, we become *lost*, whether through amnesia, distraction, misrecognition, or inattentive meandering. The skeins that carry the articulate substrates of sense-perception of the forest become increasingly present and immediate: a palimpsest of movements, visible and invisible, animates a sensual field at the edges of cognition. It takes time to notice the wind, branches, stones, water as a familiar habitus slips away, and we find our *self* in the very moment we are lost.

Proximities shift as we move further *into* a forest. A sense of direction and orientation dissolves, dilates, changes, and, in reflection, we feel enclosed or surrounded by something else—a sense of (dis)-placement operating in the depths of our grammar and the extent of our countenance.

In.

From the Proto-Germanic, this word has subsidiary connotations of touch, movement, physical contact, access, all consonant with a register of linguistic descriptors, reflexes, and biases that we carry over into this *place*. But at a certain moment, everything is suspended, and we are just *there*. (Re)-cognition is transformed, as the "outside" diminishes and almost disappears.

HEMLOCK Handmade (2021) emerges out of curiosity, the discomfiture and unexpected epiphany of seeing not merely a forest (nor just trees) but also an entirely different configuration, an unforeseen pattern, unknown—and in that moment, recognizing both the poverty of memory and the artifactuality of technology. It is almost impossible to retain the experience, as the deferrals of an artificial technical memory (the camera) lay claim to another index of loss and withdrawal. These themes are latent in all of Leslie Thornton's work and reappear in her most recent project. She has described this essay as being "written out of the ether," an attempt to trace out, in advance, a work that does not yet fully exist and may be endlessly in progress. Regardless, there is something *there*, an immanent presence in the restless exfoliation of her method.

Arlette Farge, in the first few pages of *Le goût de l'archive* (The Allure of the Archive), speaks of the unsettling gigantism of archives, of their daunting capacity to overwhelm, of the sudden harshness of the unfamiliar as it opens out into an unstable living space. No matter how unfamiliar, archives make certain announcements, create beliefs, and modify the states of things by advancing a particular narrative or commentary—texts are ordered according to systems that are more or less discernible. But there are also documents that are nothing like this, the rough, incomplete traces of lives that never asked to be represented, words recorded and swept away, things that would have remained unspoken, untethered to events and identities. "The archival document is a tear in the fabric of time," she writes, "an unplanned glimpse offered into an unexpected event."[2] What we find in an archive may be the haphazard impress of a moment, captured randomly, chaotically. What Farge loves about these sorts of fragments is that they are material traces, lists, or sketches caught in an interstitial space: they have not yet become narratives, stories, pictures, or evidence.

There is a poverty in the troubling dispositions of the image and in the varied modes of indexing, the tacit archive of (absent) experience, for example, in regarding a forest of fallen trees. What has happened? The material forms of attention, interpretation, identification, inference, and metaphor contribute little to the formation of knowledge. To perceive an event or place (a forest, for example) via its representation as an image, memory, or pictorial souvenir is an inherent part of Thornton's artistic method. In *HEMLOCK Handmade*, however, it is also about the apprehension of surfaces, demarcations of presence and absence, the intuitions of impossible loss. How to write of something that is never quite *there*, that never stops coming (*avenir*), that never ends?

Out.

Thornton's work and research traverse a common ground, which often involves a move to the exterior—*ekstasis* or withdrawal, a step outside, to the edge of a given paradigm or concept—to reveal a common trait in creative reasoning. They render permeable or break the given frame of reference to admit an unexpected perspective, open a new space for thinking, knowledge, or creation, which might otherwise have remained inaccessible. The term "ecstasy" presents a subtle, tacit lens through which one might consider the affinities between aesthetic and scientific practices, much as Thornton does. It is difficult to work in this register (at times violent, destructive), and it throws one off-balance, outside oneself (and one's practice). Artists and research scientists trace similar contours: experimentalists deal with phenomenality in different ways—moving toward the exterior of established media, scientific convention, or artistic configurations to open up other spaces and types of inquiry. It is a withdrawal, an address of the marginal. And so, through other forms of abstraction, an image, experiment, construct, a sense of phenomenon, or an event may be registered and enter differently into a public sphere, admitting an apprehension and engagement otherwise unobtainable. Access to the invisible becomes a possibility. In her deep imbrication in history, both intimate and global, Thornton seeks out, articulates,

1 During 2020 and 2021, Leslie Thornton and I spent much time in rural New Hampshire and Vermont. It was a transformative experience, admitting different forms of withdrawal, engagement, and solitude, and in the end, a reorientation and deepening of ongoing concerns. While Thornton's new works have been inflected by this experience, she has also realized that preceding pieces, such as *Cut from Liquid to Snake* (2018) and *Ground* (2020), are related to and form a suite with her current projects. *HEMLOCK Handmade* not only initiates a new body of exploration but also carries on in directions latent in preceding works.

2 Arlette Farge, *Le goût de l'archive* (Paris: Éditions du Seuil, 1998), 6.

and addresses complex interactions between different practices, confronting the diverse relations between materiality and abstraction that knit together an image of the contemporary world.

HEMLOCK Handmade consists of two primary screens (flatscreen monitors) and a number of secondary or tertiary screens (screens within screens) that form an abyssal structure, a *mise en abyme* of reflexive referentiality and deferral. On the topmost screen, a hypnotic, almost chaotic, vertical movement resembling tree bark appears, melting, animate, fluid (it is an image of waves turned on its side). The intuition of wind slips elegantly between forest and wave—though there is barely an ambient sound of wind; it is a surface. The camera's indexicality is further tampered with when, on closer inspection, what might initially have been considered natural waves has an almost invisible technical overlay, a digital skein, an algorithmic arrestment, and a blurring of the image. This condition occludes any form of naturalization.

On the lower screen, there is a series of indistinct fields—an interwoven, curvilinear patchwork of metallic foil with copper and silver tones, filmed by Thornton in one of the research and fabrication laboratories at Caltech. At times, a hand, or its shadow, appears, touching, pointing, caressing. It is a working hand, gesturing, indexical, as if to explain something. Flesh colors anchor the field, placing it within an artisanal setting outside the reach of the image that broils above it, the monstrous force of uncontainable waves. Archival footage of turbulence studies, similarly artisanal in character, form a faint bridge across incommensurate spaces through strange intuitions of movement. A dynamic scalar disparity overturns whatever idea of place we struggle to preserve. It is an assault, not on the senses but on our earnest, almost touching efforts and capacities to contain and comprehend the forces of nature. Without knowing anything, we are swept up in these anaphoric representations and actually begin to understand the most rudimentary conditions of a narrative—parataxis, a *chronotope*, a spatializing operation involving time and movement and implicating our longing to contain, as if to tame, a universe of forces. It is yet another instance of Thornton's generous embrace of a world—worlding—faced head-on, in what she has taken to calling not her art but her *devices*.

An *intuition*.

Thornton's experience of unease at seeing so many fallen trees is profoundly incommunicable. Like pain, desire, or melancholy, there is no direct, immediate access to the states of others. Her remote positioning, an artifactual abstraction at the very margins, opens up the hidden space of an experiential phenomenology of environment. It is the possibility of an intuition, an abstraction arresting the frame of a mimetic technology, an image/artifact to which other forms of knowledge, information, reference, experience may be tethered. The *Oxford English Dictionary* tells us that to abstract is "to draw away" or "withdraw" and that abstraction is also "a state of being withdrawn." In this sense, all images are abstract—withdrawn from their origins in the world—and the paradoxical movements in Thornton's work reveal this troubled dynamic of appearance and disappearance.

The trees are dying.

Northern Hemlock trees, infested with an invasive insect species (the hemlock wooly adelgid), are, like other aboriginal forests (elm, sycamore), advanced in their decline, hastening the extinction of vast tracts of arboreal species. Sadness and despair trace the contours of an epiphany in the forest, an observation, a salient, mobile apprehension of finitude—death—in the very depths, conducted from the most remote margins, an afterimage, a glimpse into the abyss.

For Leslie

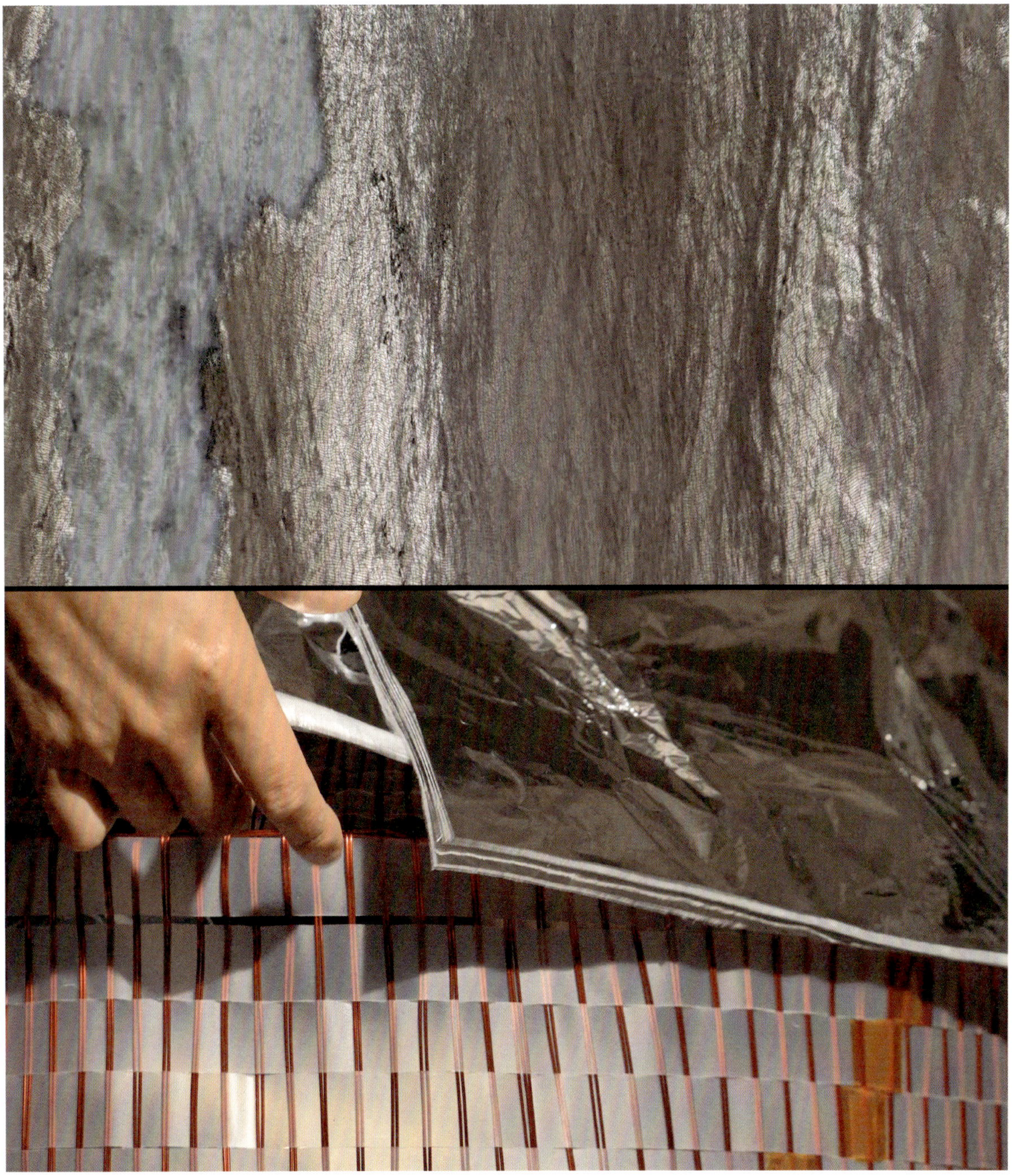

HEMLOCK Handmade, 2021

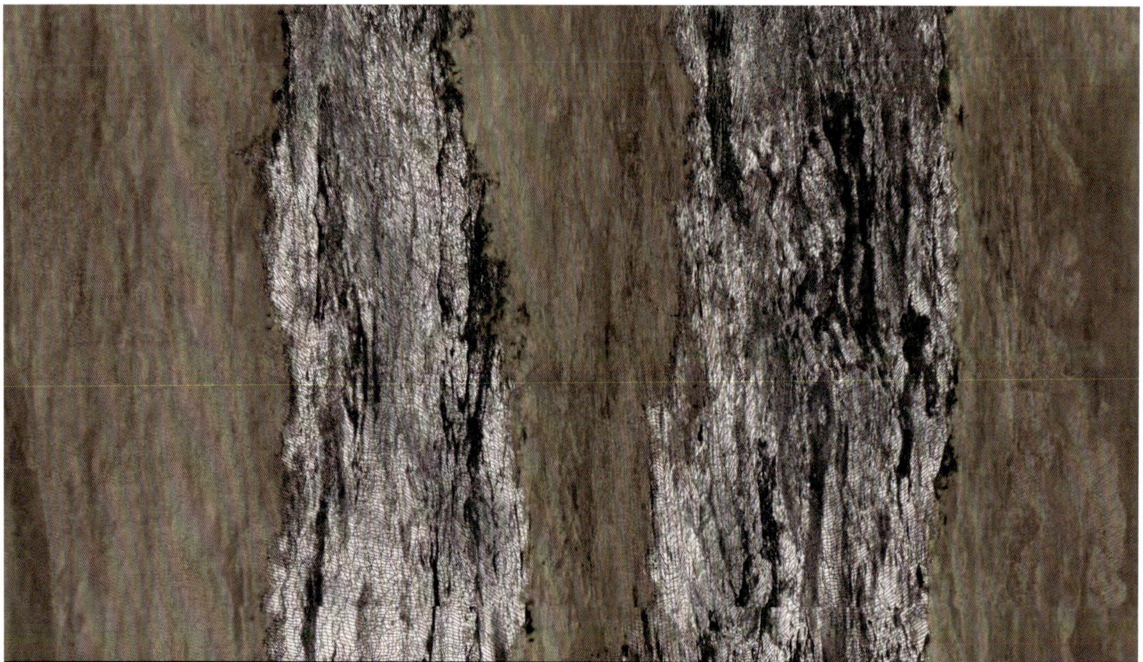

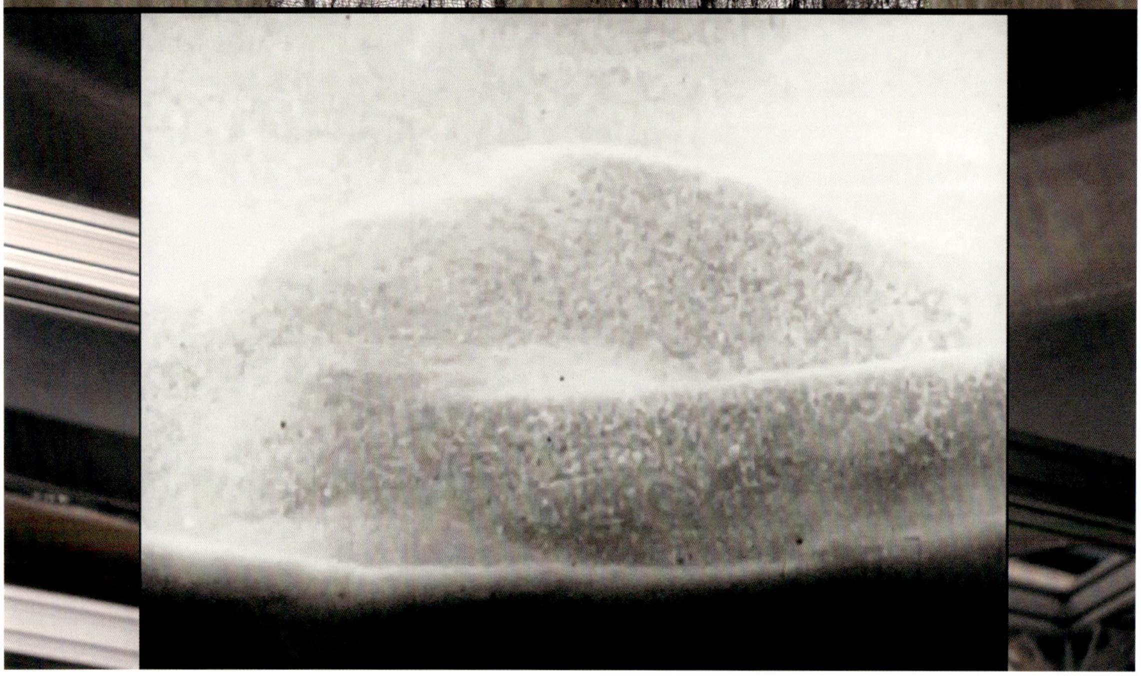

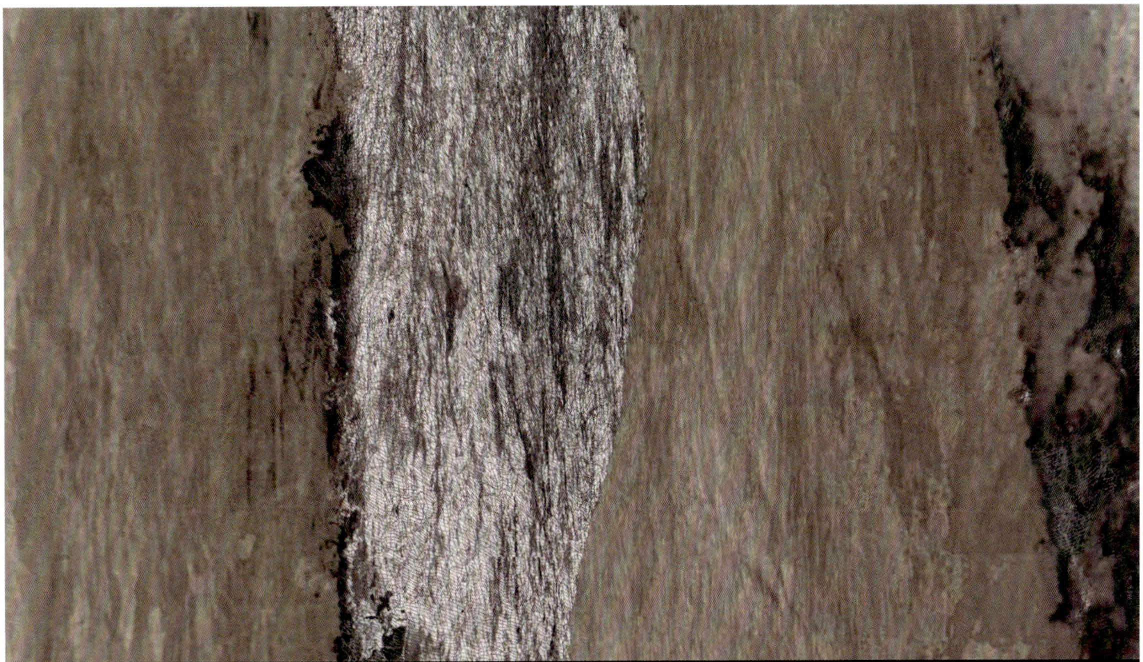

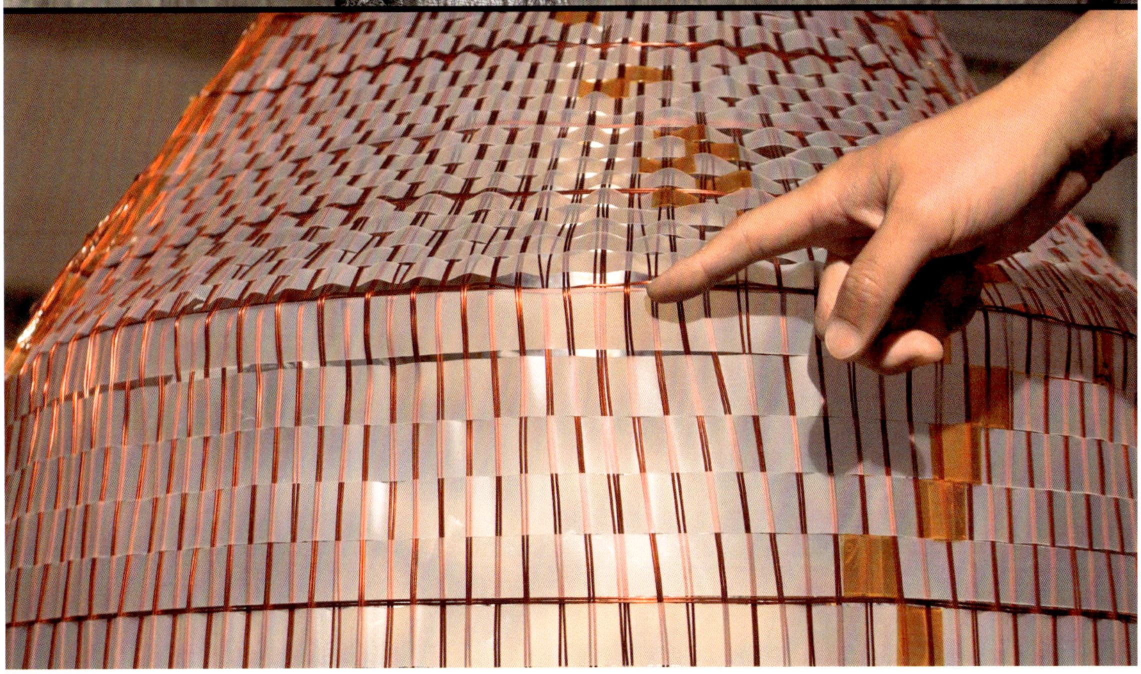

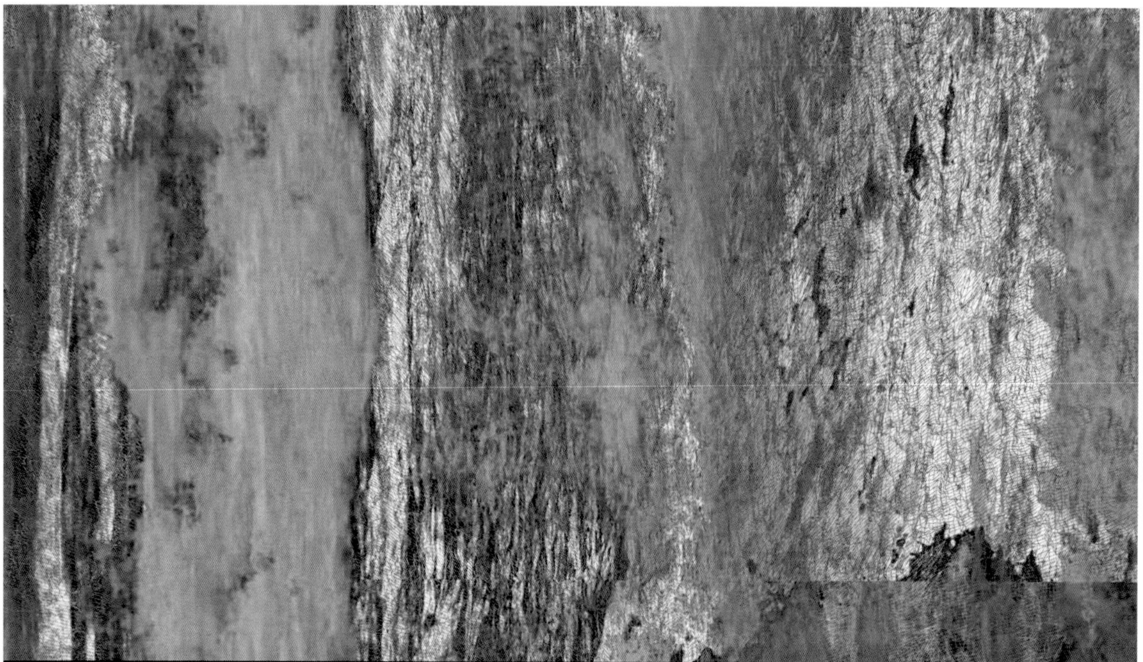

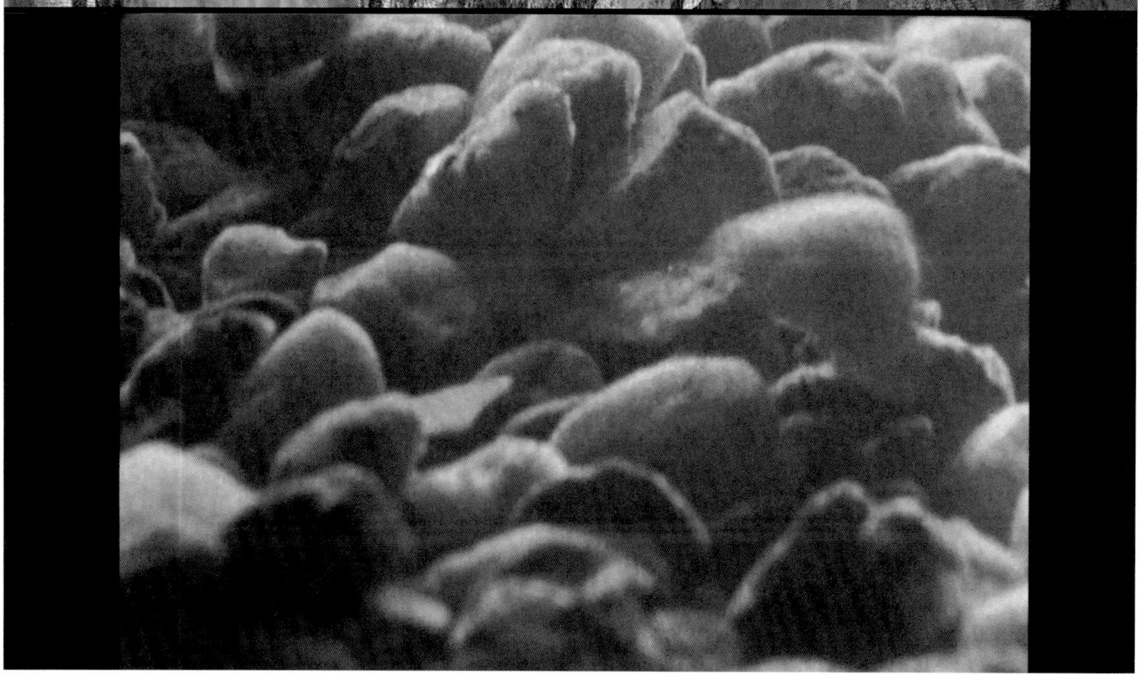

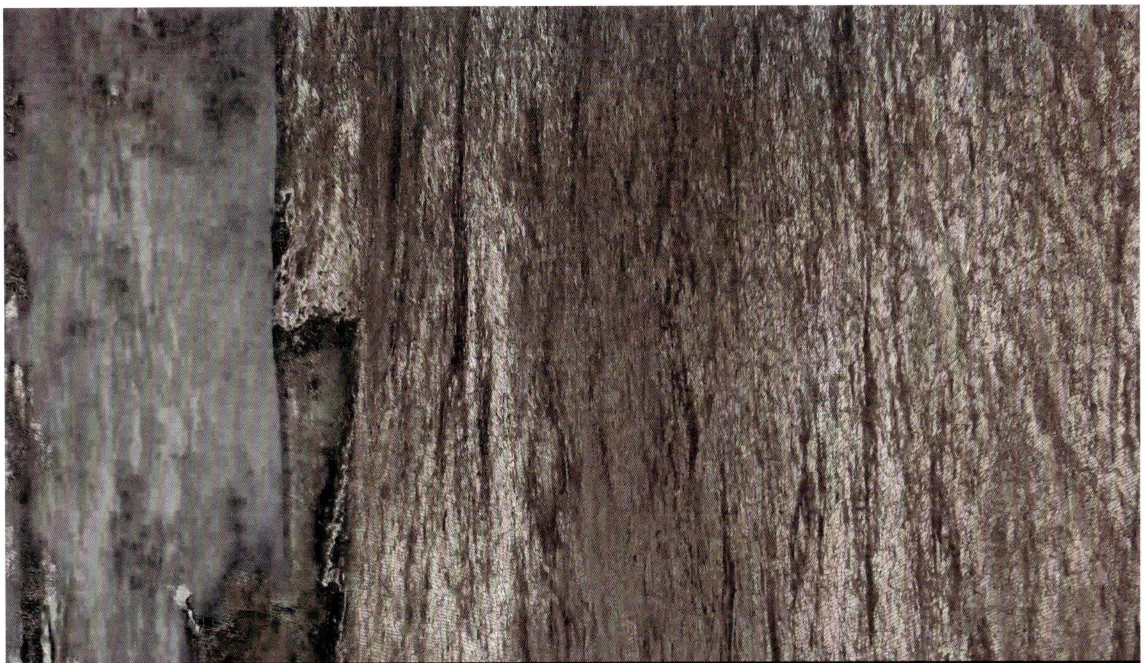

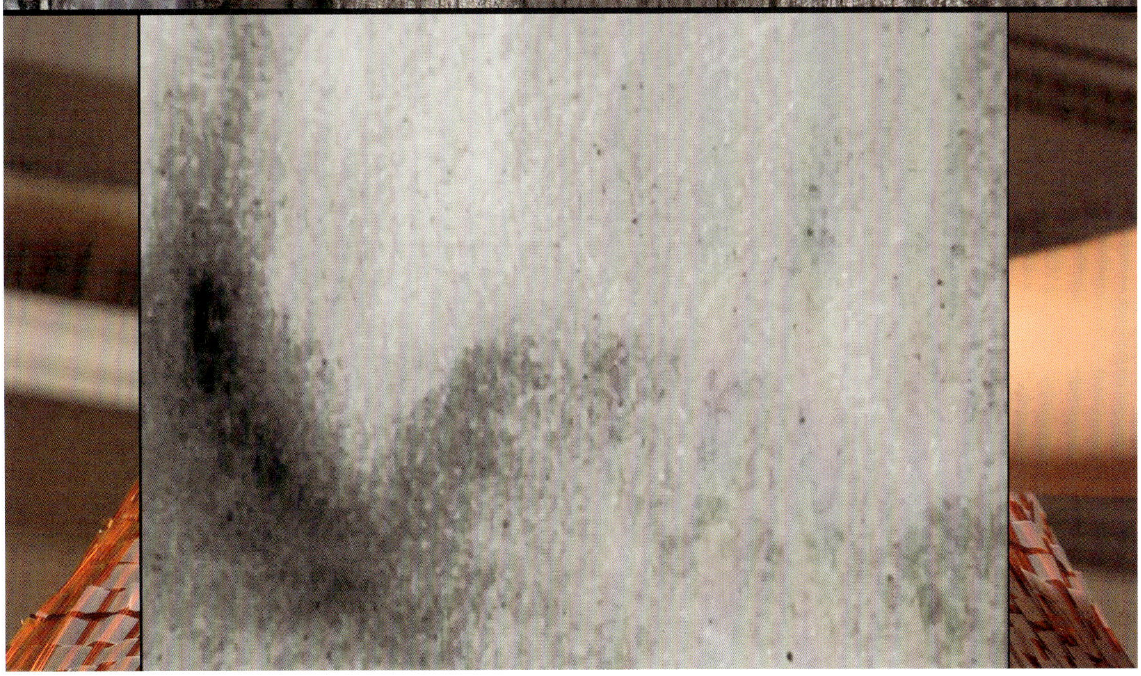

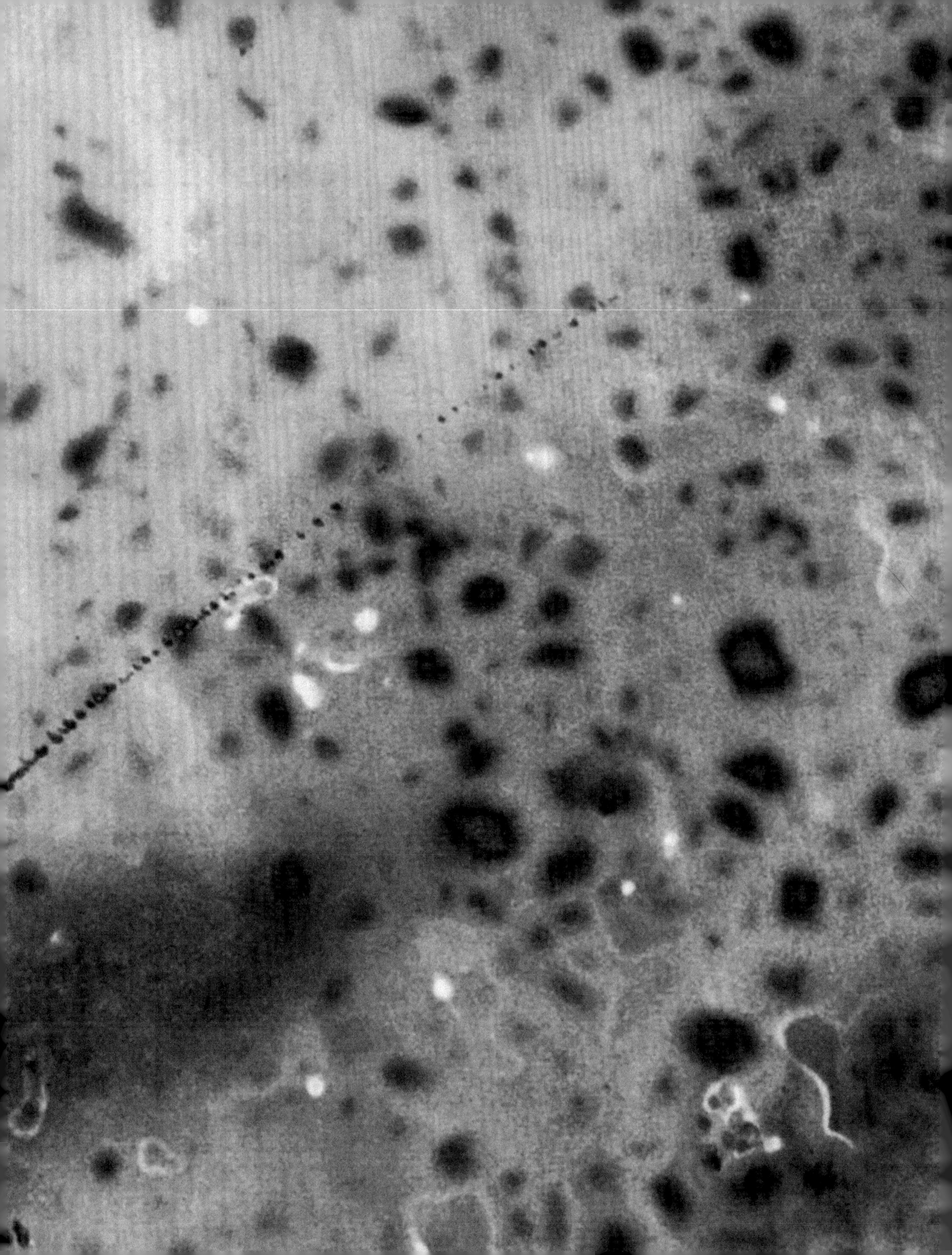

List of Illustrated Works

Leslie Thornton and
Desmond Horsfield
X-TRACTS, 1975
16mm, black and white, sound
9 min.

Leslie Thornton and
Desmond Horsfield
All Right You Guys, 1976
16mm film transferred to
HD video, black and white, sound
16 min.

Leslie Thornton
Jennifer, Where Are You?, 1981
16mm film transferred to HD
video, color, sound
10 min.

Leslie Thornton
Peggy and Fred in Hell: Folding,
1983–2015
16mm film and video transferred
to HD video, black and white,
color, sound
95 min.

Leslie Thornton
Strange Space, 1993
Video transferred to digital,
color, sound
4 min.
Coproduced with Ron Vawter

Leslie Thornton
The Last Time I Saw Ron,
1995
Video transferred to digital,
color, sound
12 min.
Produced by Kaaitheater,
Brussels; Holland
Festival; Hebbeltheater,
Berlin
Coproduced by Felix Meritis,
Amsterdam

Leslie Thornton
Let Me Count the Ways:
Minus 10, Minus 9,
Minus 8, Minus 7,
Minus 6, Minus 5,
2004–ongoing
16mm film and video
transferred to HD video,
color, sound
21 min.

Leslie Thornton
Cut from Liquid to Snake,
2018
HD and 2K video, color,
sound, loop
26 min.
Commissioned by
Künstlerhaus Stuttgart
and Malmö Konsthall

Leslie Thornton
Ground, 2020
HD video, color, sound, loop
13 min.
Commissioned by Kunstverein
Nürnberg with Arts at CERN,
Geneva

Leslie Thornton
HEMLOCK Handmade, 2021
Two-channel digital video, color,
silent, loop
Approx. 7 min.
Commissioned by MIT List
Visual Arts Center

All works courtesy of the artist,
Unit 17, Vancouver, and Rodeo,
London/Piraeus

Artist Biography

Leslie Thornton (b. 1951, Oakridge, TN) lives and works in New York. Her work has been exhibited and widely screened internationally at: documenta 12, Kassel; the Whitney Museum of American Art, MoMA PS1, Brooklyn Academy of Music, and Artists Space in New York; Tate Modern and Raven Row in London; the Walker Art Center, Minneapolis; Centre d'Art Contemporain Genève; and the Rotterdam, Berlin, Buenos Aires, and New York film festivals, among many others. Recent solo and two-person exhibitions have taken place at MIT List Visual Arts Center, Kunstverein Nürnberg, Malmö Konsthall, Secession, Vienna, and Künstlerhaus Stuttgart. She has been an artist-in-residence at CERN in Geneva and the California Institute of Technology, Pasadena.

Thornton is a Hugo Boss Prize nominee and recipient of two Rockefeller Fellowships, a Guggenheim Fellowship, the Maya Deren Award for Lifetime Achievement, and the first Alpert Award in the Arts. She has received numerous grants for her films from the National Endowment for the Arts, New York State Council on the Arts, New York Foundation for the Arts, Jerome Foundation, and Art Matters. Her work *Peggy and Fred in Hell* has been cited in several "Year's Best" lists, including in the *Village Voice* and the *New York Times*, and she was the only female experimental filmmaker noted in *Cahiers du Cinéma*'s *60 Most Important American Directors* publication. Her previous publications include *Peggy and Fred in Hell: The Complete Transcript* (Mono No Aware, 2017) and *Leslie Thornton: EVENT* (Secession/Revolver Publishing, 2018).

Thornton's works are in the collections of: the Museum of Modern Art, New York; Centre Pompidou and Jeu de Paume, Paris; Pacific Film Archive, Berkeley; Walker Art Center, Minneapolis; and Fundación la Caixa and Fundació Antoni Tàpies, Barcelona, among many others. From 1984 to 2018, Thornton was Professor of Modern Culture and Media at Brown University in Providence, RI. She holds a BFA from SUNY Buffalo and an MFA from the Hartford Art School, CT.

Contributors

Erika Balsom is Reader in Film Studies at King's College London. Her research interests include experimental documentary, the intersections of cinema and art, and histories of technological change. She is the author of four books, including *TEN SKIES* (Fireflies Press, 2021) and *After Uniqueness: A History of Film and Video Art in Circulation* (Columbia University Press, 2017). She has contributed essays to numerous exhibition catalogues and writes criticism on art and film that appears regularly in publications such as *Artforum* and *Cinema Scope*. In 2017, Balsom was awarded a Philip Leverhulme Prize.

Natalie Bell is Curator at the MIT List Visual Arts Center, where she organized Thornton's 2021 exhibition "Begin Again, Again." She was previously Associate Curator at the New Museum, New York, where she organized over a dozen solo exhibitions, among them: Lubaina Himid (2019), Marguerite Humeau (2018), Kahlil Joseph (2017), Hiwa K (2018), Lynette Yiadom-Boakye (2017), and Anri Sala (2016). Bell also co-curated several major group exhibitions, including "Trigger: Gender as a Tool and a Weapon" (2017), "The Keeper" (2016), and "Here and Elsewhere" (2014), as well as "The Same River Twice" (2019) and "The Warmth of Other Suns" (2019). She has edited or coedited more than a dozen exhibition publications and has published widely.

Rosalyn Deutsche is an art historian, author, and art critic who teaches modern and contemporary art at Barnard College/Columbia University. She has written extensively on art's relationship to urbanism, the public sphere, civil rights, psychology, and technologies of war, and on feminist theories of subjectivity in visual representation. Her essays have appeared in *Grey Room*, *October*, *Artforum*, *Art in America*, and *Society and Space*, among other journals, in many exhibition catalogues and anthologies, and in numerous translations. Deutsche is the author of *Hiroshima after Iraq: Three Studies in Art and War* (Columbia University Press, 2010) and *Evictions: Art and Spatial Politics* (MIT Press, 1996).

Su Friedrich has directed twenty-three films and videos since 1978, which have been featured in eighteen retrospectives at major museums and film festivals, including one at the Museum of Modern Art, New York, in 2007. The films, widely screened at film festivals, universities, and art centers, have been extensively written about and won numerous awards, including the Grand Prix for *Sink or Swim* (1990) at the Melbourne International Film Festival. Friedrich's DVD collection is distributed by Outcast Films, and she teaches video production at Princeton University.

Chrissie Iles is the Anne and Joel Ehrenkranz Curator at the Whitney Museum of American Art, where she focuses on contemporary art, film and video, and art of the 1960s and seventies. Notable shows at the Whitney include "Dreamlands: Immersive Cinema and Art 1910–2016" (2016), "Into the Light: The Projected Image in American Art 1964–1977" (2001), and solo shows of Cauleen Smith, Madeline Hollander, and Alan Michelson (2020 and 2021). Iles also co-curated the 2004 and 2006 Whitney Biennials. She was awarded an honorary doctorate by the Department of Art History at her alma mater, Bristol University, England.

Dan Kidner is a curator and writer based in London. He is a senior lecturer at Kingston School of Art. He was coeditor of the publication and DVD edition *Nightcleaners* and *'36 to '77*, which focused on the work of the Berwick Street Film Collective and was published by Raven Row, Koenig Books, and LUX in 2018. He was also coeditor of *Working Together: British Film Collectives in the 1970s* (2013) and *A Detour Around Infermental* (2011). He writes regularly for art magazines and journals, and his recent exhibitions include "The Inoperative Community," Raven Row, London (2015) and "The Inoperative Community II," Muzeum Sztuki, Łódź, Poland (2016).

Chris Kraus is the author of four novels, three books of art and cultural criticism, and a biography of the US writer Kathy Acker. Her first novel, *I Love Dick*, has been adapted for television. Kraus is a coeditor of the independent press Semiotexte, alongside Hedi El Kholti and the late Sylvère Lotringer. She is currently researching a book on the Mesabi Trail murder in northern Minnesota. She lives in Los Angeles and teaches writing at ArtCenter, Pasadena, CA.

Mason Leaver-Yap works with artists to produce texts, exhibitions, and events. They have recently been working with Ingrid Pollard, Renée Green and Free Agent Media, Onyeka Igwe, Lin + Lam, Evan Ifekoya, Oreet Ashery, Laura Guy, Sunil Gupta, Sharon Hayes and Mathew Parkin, Lucy McKenzie, Iman Issa, Wendy Jacob, Jimmy Robert, Rachel O'Reilly, Andrea Büttner, Alexis Mitchell and Sharlene Bamboat, Kat Anderson, Jamie Crewe, and Beatrice Gibson. They are based in Glasgow.

James Richards is an artist based in Berlin and London who works in sound and video. Recent exhibitions include "When We Were Monsters" (2021) at Haus Mödrath – Räume für Kunst, Kerpen, Germany, and "Alms for the Birds" (2020) at Castello di Rivoli, Turin. Recent two-person exhibitions with Leslie Thornton have been presented at Secession, Vienna, Künstlerhaus Stuttgart, and Malmö Konsthall, and their collaborative works have screened at the Walker Art Center and Tate Modern, among others. Working as a curator, Richards has presented screenings at LUX and FormContent in London and Light Industry, New York. He was the recipient of the prestigious Derek Jarman Award in 2012 and the Ars Viva Prize in 2014. He was also shortlisted for the 2014 Turner Prize, and in 2017, Richards represented Wales at the 57th Venice Biennale.

Milan Ther is a curator and writer who, since 2018, has served as Director of Kunstverein Nürnberg – Albrecht Dürer Gesellschaft, where he recently organized Thornton's 2020 exhibition "GROUND." Other recent projects at the Kunstverein Nürnberg include exhibitions with Lawrence Abu Hamdan, Veit Laurent Kurz, Hélène Fauquet, Jason Hirata, and Karin Schneider. While at the Kestner Gesellschaft in Hanover, Ther also organized an exhibition of James Richards's work—the catalogue for which, *Requests and Antisongs*, was published with Sternberg Press in 2016.

Thomas Zummer is a scholar, artist, and curator who lectures and publishes on philosophy, aesthetics, and the history of technology. Zummer is part of the faculty in the Philosophy Department at the European Graduate School in Saas-Fee, Switzerland, and Associate Professor and Director of the graduate program in Graphic and Information Design at Central Connecticut State University. His theoretical work tackles the boundaries between the virtual and the real, and his curatorial work investigates the nature of memory in relation to images, cinema, science fiction, and the phantasmagorical in visual biography. Zummer has written texts on Eleanor Antin, Vik Muniz, Heleen Deceuninck, and Harun Farocki, among others. He has also curated several exhibitions in spaces such as CinéClub/ Anthology Film Archives and Thread Waxing Space, New York; the Wexner Center for the Arts, Columbus, OH; Katonah Museum of Art, New York; and the Palais des Beaux-Arts, Brussels.

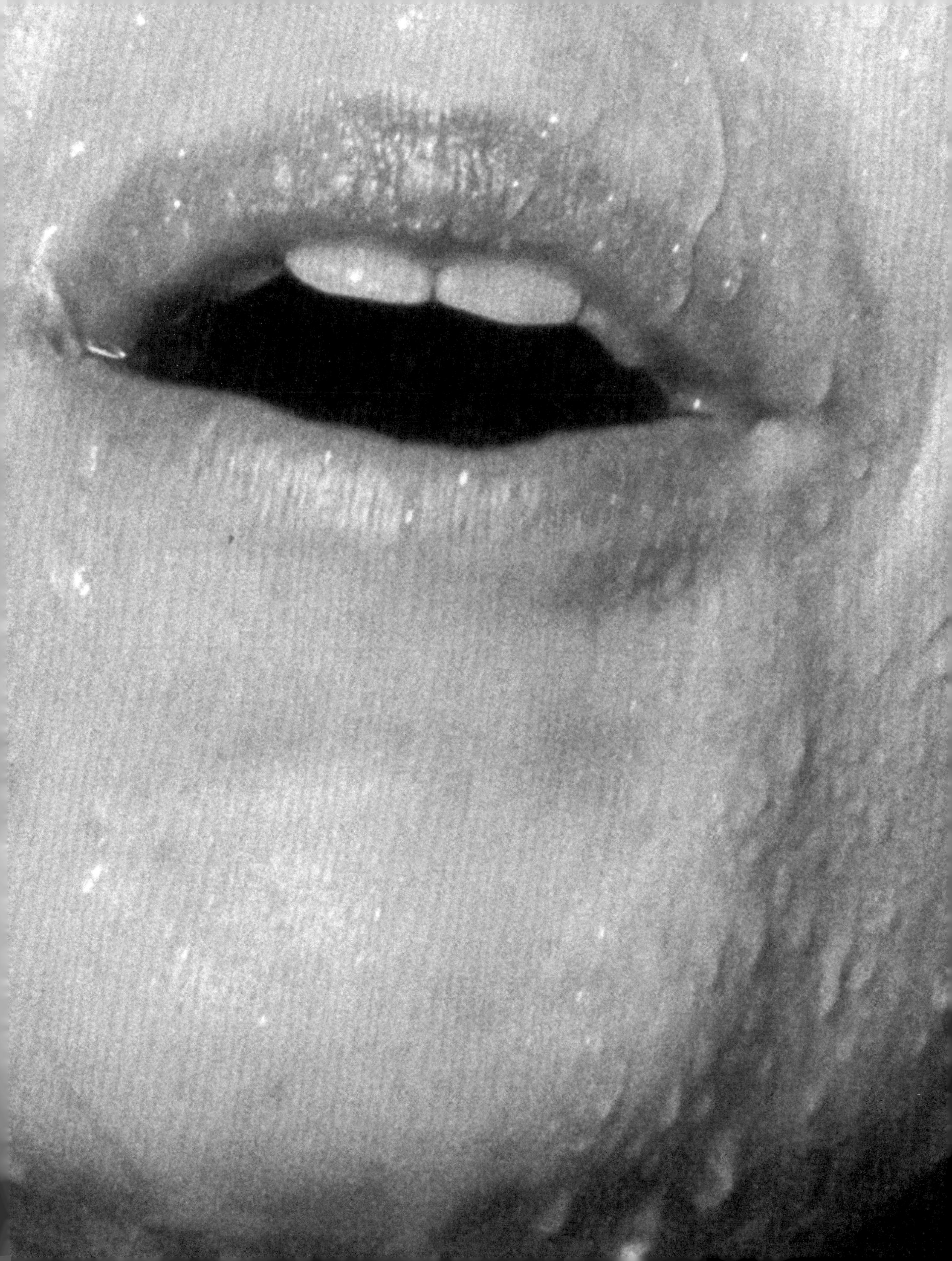

Leslie Thornton

Edited by Natalie Bell, Dan Kidner, and Milan Ther

On the occasion of the exhibitions:
"Leslie Thornton: Begin Again, Again"
October 22, 2021–February 13, 2022
MIT List Visual Arts Center
Curated by Natalie Bell

"Leslie Thornton: GROUND"
February 27–July 26, 2020
Kunstverein Nürnberg
Curated by Milan Ther and Ann-Kathrin Eickhoff

Published by:
Sternberg Press
71–75 Shelton Street
London WC2H 9JQ
United Kingdom
sternberg-press.com

MIT List Visual Arts Center
20 Ames Street
Cambridge, MA 02139
United States
listart.mit.edu

Kunstverein Nürnberg –
Albrecht Dürer Gesellschaft e.V.
Kressengartenstraße 2
D-90402 Nürnberg
Germany
kunstvereinnuernberg.de

Design by Practise
Printing by Wilco Art Books
Lithography by Colour & Books
Typeset in Venus B (Berton Hasebe, 2021) and Venusian Ultra NF (Nick Curtis, 2014)
Copyediting by Sam Korman and Sarah Stephenson

Rosalyn Deutsche's essay is an edited, abridged version of her chapter dedicated to Thornton's *Let Me Count the Ways* in her book *Hiroshima after Iraq: Three Studies in Art and War* (New York: Columbia University Press, 2010).

Mason Leaver-Yap's essay relates to their two other texts on Thornton: "A Nice Record of My Last Few Moments" (Bonner Kunstverein, 2020) and "Comprehensive Horrors and Technological Consequences" (Walker Art Center, 2016).

Milan Ther's essay relates to the press release for Thornton's Kunstverein Nürnberg exhibition. The conversation between Thornton and Ther is drawn from an interview that first appeared on the Kunstverein Nürnberg website in 2020.

 Photo credits: pp. 18–29, Julia Featheringill; pp. 30–33, Rory Witt; pp. 34–35, Marcus J. Leith.

"Leslie Thornton: Begin Again, Again" was made possible through the support of Fotene and Tom Coté, Audrey and James Foster, Idee German Schoenheimer, Joyce Linde, Cynthia and John Reed, and Sara-Ann and Robert Sanders. This exhibition was also supported by generous donors of the 2020 McDermott Award Gala, hosted by the Council for the Arts at MIT.

General operating support for the List Center is provided by the Massachusetts Institute of Technology; the Council for the Arts at MIT; Philip S. Khoury, Associate Provost at MIT; the MIT School of Architecture + Planning; the Mass Cultural Council; and many generous individual donors. In-kind media sponsorship provided by 90.9 WBUR. The Advisory Committee Members of the List Visual Arts Center are gratefully acknowledged.

"Leslie Thornton: GROUND" was made possible by the zumikon Kulturstiftung and Bayerisches Staatsministerium für Wissenschaft und Kunst, with additional support from Rodeo, London/Piraeus, Neutex Home Decoration, Hornberger Raumausstattung, tRÄUME — Ideen Raum geben, The Block, London, and Zerbock Medienwerkstatt.

General operating support for Kunstverein Nürnberg is provided by Stadt Nürnberg – Bürgermeisterin Geschäftsbereich Kultur, Bezirk Mittelfranken, and Beko Grundig Deutschland GmbH.

Special thanks to Sylvia Kouvali and Katy Green from Rodeo, London/Piraeus, Matt Fitts from The Block, and Monique S. Desto, Julia Himmelhuber, Anna Maria Schönrock, Mariko Tsunoka, and Rory Witt.

Special thanks also to the board of the Kunstverein Nürnberg: Peter Naumann, Christiane Böhm, Dr. Christoph Giehl, Ulrike Hammad, Kerstin Hiller, Max Reinhardt, and Elke Antonia Schloter.

ISBN 978-3-95679-598-5

Distributed by The MIT Press, Art Data, and Les presses du réel

Sternberg Press

Kunstverein Nürnberg – Albrecht Dürer Gesellschaft

Leslie Thornton

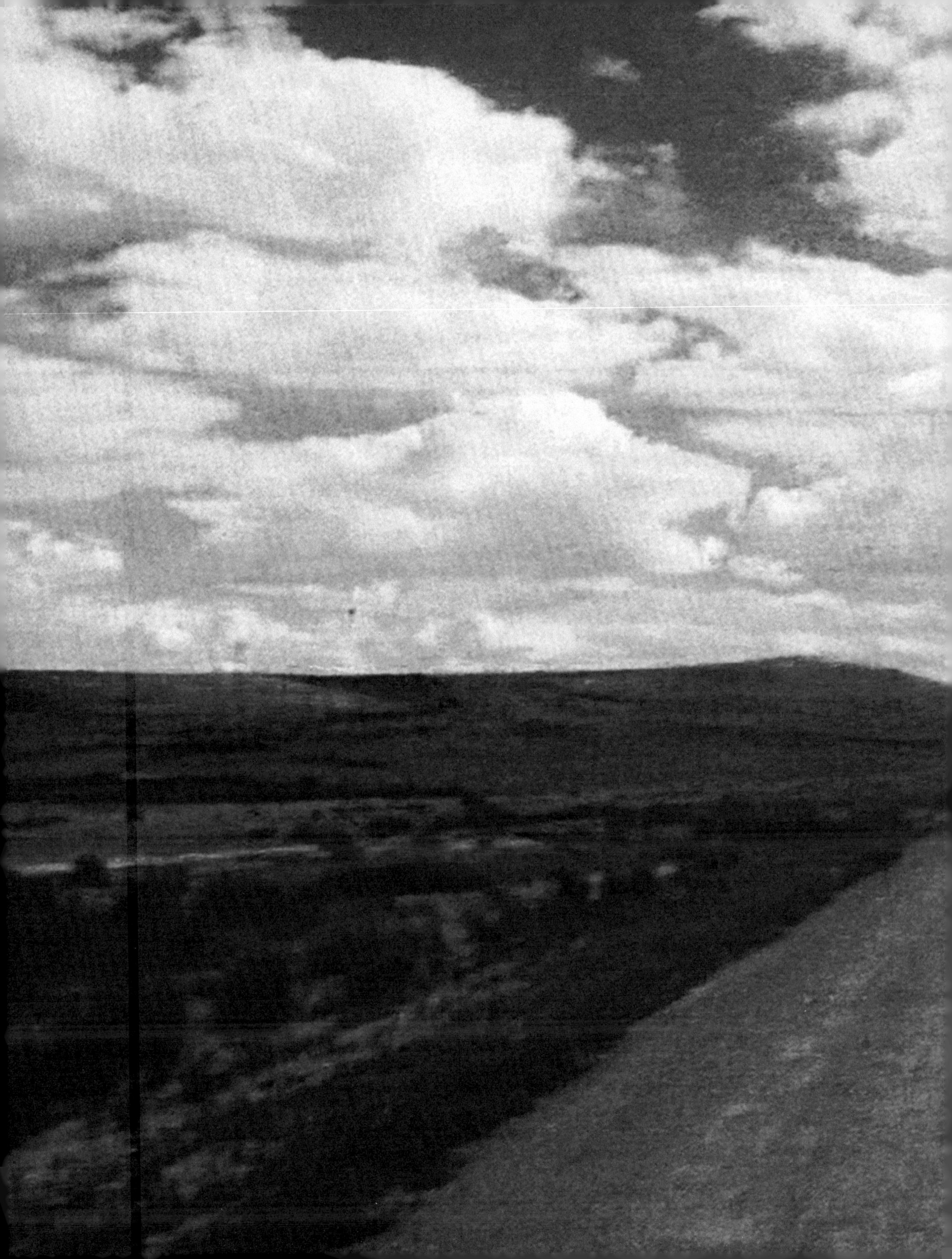